THE BUMPER QUIZ BOOK

THE BUMPER QUIZ BOOK

BOXTREE

First published 2000 by Boxtree
an imprint of Macmillan Publishers Ltd
25 Eccleston Place London SW1W 9NF
Basingstoke and Oxford

Associated companies throughout the world

www.macmillan.com

ISBN 0 7522 7208 X

Produced under licence from Celador Productions Limited

7 9 8 6

A CIP catalogue record for this book is available from the British Library.

Designed by Blackjacks
Printed by Mackays of Chatham plc

CONTENTS

How to play

If you scratched your head and chewed your nails over the teasers in *Who Wants To Be A Millionaire? The Quiz Book* and *The Ultimate Challenge*, then brace yourselves because *The Bumper Quiz Book* is sure to test you to your absolute limits! The question masters have been busy crafting not 1,000 but 2,000 exclusive tantalizers to make this the biggest-ever edition. You can make it personal and challenge yourself, or invite some friends round and see who's got the brawniest brain!

FOR 1 PLAYER

As on *Who Wants To Be A Millionaire?*, the aim of the game is to reach £1,000,000. Before you can even think about the cash, you must first correctly answer a question from the Fastest Finger First section. You have just 30 seconds to put the letters in the correct order. When time's up, follow the page reference at the foot of the page to find out if you can take your place in the hot-seat and begin your climb for the cash!

Once in the hot-seat

Start with a question worth £100 and once you have decided on your final answer (and you are absolutely sure ...) follow the page reference at the foot of the page to find out if you've won that amount. If your answer is correct, you can play to win £200 and so on up the tree. The page where each money level begins is listed in the answer section.

As on the programme you have three lifelines to help you on your way to £1,000,000. These are, of course, optional but each of them can only be used once, so only use them when you really need to.

Fifty-Fifty

This option takes away two incorrect answers leaving the correct answer and one incorrect answer remaining, a page reference at the bottom of each page will direct you to the relevant section.

Phone-A-Friend

If you have a telephone handy (and a willing friend!) ring him/her up to help you out. You have thirty seconds (no cheating, now ...) to read the question to your friend and for them to tell you what they think the answer is. If there's someone else around, ask if they can time it for you.

Ask The Audience

This works in exactly the same way as on *Who Wants To Be A Millionaire?* except we've asked the audience so you don't have to! Simply follow the page reference at the bottom of each page to find out what the audience thought. In the end, however, the final decision is yours.

If you answer incorrectly, you are out of the game. £1,000 and £32,000 are 'safe havens' so if you answer a question incorrectly and you have not reached £1,000 then not only are you out of the game but you won't have won a penny! If you have reached one (or both) of these havens and you answer a question incorrectly, then you are out of the game but you will have won the value of the previous haven you have reached. If at any point during the game you are unsure of an answer and don't want to risk being out of the game if you answer incorrectly, you can 'stick' at the amount you have won so far and that will be your final score. As you play, use the score sheets at the back of the book to keep a running record of the amount you have won and the lifelines you have used.

FOR 2–5 PLAYERS

Players should take it in turns at being 'Chris Tarrant' and posing questions to the other contestant/s. The rules are the same as for a single player (see pages 6–7). If someone reaches £1,000,000, that person is the winner and the game is over. Otherwise, whoever has won the most money when everyone else is out is the winner.

Are you ready to play? Good. With all that money at stake, we're sure we don't need to tell you to think very carefully before you give your final answer. Good luck and be sure to remember at all times the motto of *Who Wants To Be A Millionaire?* – it's only easy if you know the answer!

FASTEST FINGER FIRST

FASTEST FINGER FIRST

1

Starting with the earliest, put these groups in the order in which they first invaded England.

A: Normans
B: Romans
C: Saxons
D: Vikings

2

Put these South American capitals in order from north to south.

A: Bogota
B: Buenos Aires
C: Caracas
D: Lima

3

Starting with the earliest, put these explorers in chronological order of their dates of birth.

A: Erik the Red
B: Ranulph Fiennes
C: Vasco da Gama
D: David Livingstone

4

Put these chemical elements in alphabetical order.

A: Carbon
B: Calcium
C: Cadmium
D: Californium

5

Put the words of the famous Carpenters song in the correct order.

A: Begun
B: Just
C: Only
D: We've

Answers on page 491

6

Starting with the smallest, put these units of area in order.

- A: Acre
- B: Square foot
- C: Square inch
- D: Square yard

7

Beginning with the earliest, put these films in order of their first cinematic release.

- A: Green Card
- B: Black Narcissus
- C: White Mischief
- D: Blue Hawaii

8

Starting with the shortest, put the gestation periods of these animals in order.

- A: Elephant
- B: Horse
- C: Mouse
- D: Pig

9

Starting with the smallest, put these countries in order of area.

- A: Netherlands
- B: Greece
- C: Luxembourg
- D: Spain

10

Starting with the earliest, put these actors in the order in which they died.

- A: Richard Burton
- B: Gary Cooper
- C: Burt Lancaster
- D: John Wayne

Answers on page 491

FASTEST FINGER FIRST

11

Put the name of this fairy tale character in the correct order.

A: Hood
B: Little
C: Red
D: Riding

12

Starting with the most populous, put these countries in order of population.

A: Bangladesh
B: Barbados
C: Brazil
D: Bulgaria

13

Starting with the earliest, put these men in order according to when they first won a Best Director Oscar.

A: Woody Allen
B: Frank Capra
C: Elia Kazan
D: Steven Spielberg

14

Starting with the earliest, put these literary figures in order of birth.

A: T.S. Eliot
B: Ted Hughes
C: Samuel Beckett
D: W.B. Yeats

15

Starting with the nearest, put these places in order according to their distance from London.

A: Bermuda
B: Belfast
C: Bucharest
D: Buenos Aires

Answers on page 491

16

Starting with the oldest, put these inventions in chronological order.

- A: Nylon
- B: Microphone
- C: Lightning conductor
- D: Microprocessor

17

Put these vegetables in reverse alphabetical order.

- A: Chives
- B: Chicory
- C: Chervil
- D: Chard

18

Starting with the earliest, put these politicians in the order they became US president.

- A: Carter
- B: Cleveland
- C: Clinton
- D: Coolidge

19

Starting with the earliest, put these sports personalities in order of birth.

- A: Donald Bradman
- B: Diego Maradona
- C: Jack Nicklaus
- D: Sugar Ray Robinson

20

Starting with the longest, put these units of length in order.

- A: Furlong
- B: Kilometre
- C: Metre
- D: Mile

Answers on page 491

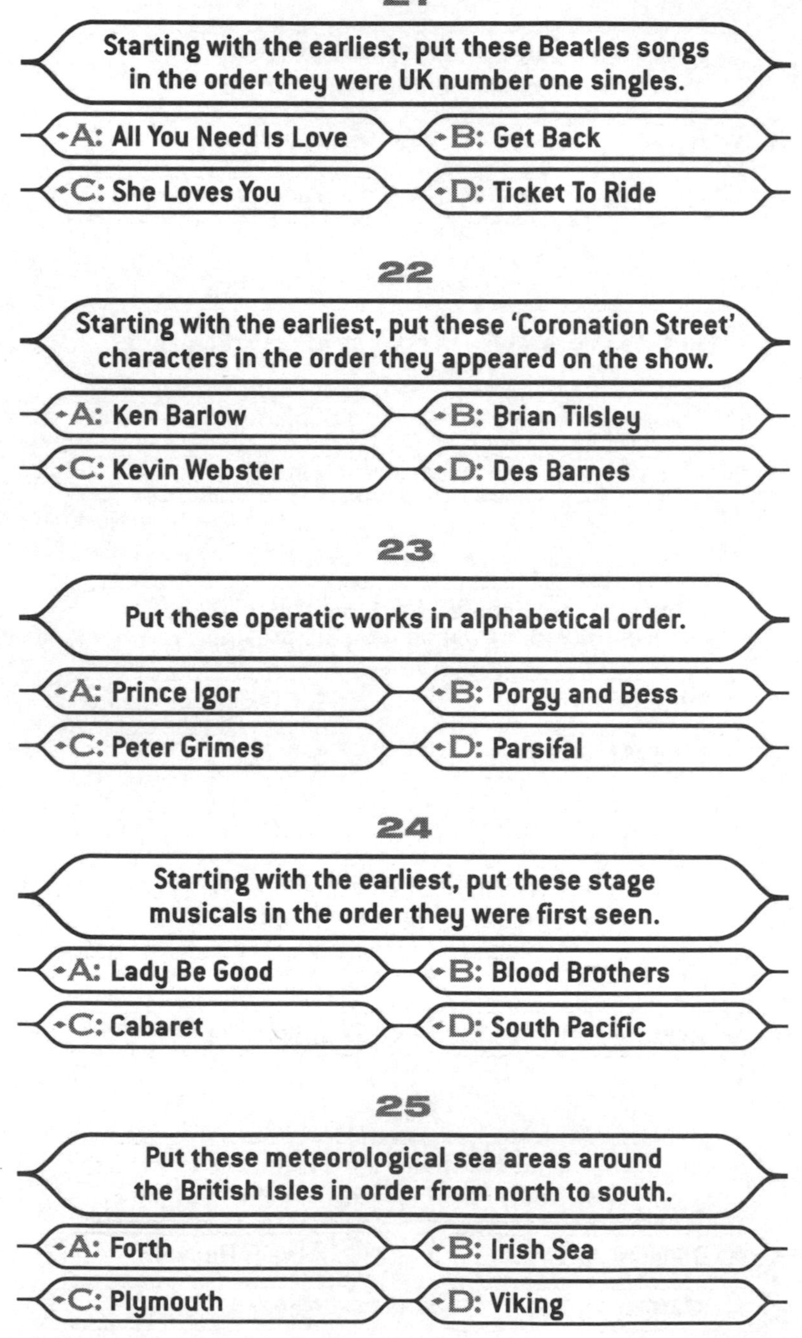

21

Starting with the earliest, put these Beatles songs in the order they were UK number one singles.

- A: All You Need Is Love
- B: Get Back
- C: She Loves You
- D: Ticket To Ride

22

Starting with the earliest, put these 'Coronation Street' characters in the order they appeared on the show.

- A: Ken Barlow
- B: Brian Tilsley
- C: Kevin Webster
- D: Des Barnes

23

Put these operatic works in alphabetical order.

- A: Prince Igor
- B: Porgy and Bess
- C: Peter Grimes
- D: Parsifal

24

Starting with the earliest, put these stage musicals in the order they were first seen.

- A: Lady Be Good
- B: Blood Brothers
- C: Cabaret
- D: South Pacific

25

Put these meteorological sea areas around the British Isles in order from north to south.

- A: Forth
- B: Irish Sea
- C: Plymouth
- D: Viking

Answers on page 491

26

Starting with the least populous, put these US states in order of population.

A: California
B: Michigan
C: New York
D: Vermont

27

Starting with the earliest, put these four Grand National winners in order.

A: Ben Nevis
B: Mr Frisk
C: Last Suspect
D: L'Escargot

28

Starting with the earliest, put these books in the order in which they were written.

A: Little Women
B: Sense and Sensibility
C: The English Patient
D: Brighton Rock

29

Starting with the highest, put these playing card suits in order of their rank in contract bridge.

A: Hearts
B: Clubs
C: Spades
D: Diamonds

30

Starting with the most recent, put these English cricket captains in the order that they first led their country.

A: Douglas Jardine
B: Nasser Hussain
C: Graham Gooch
D: Peter May

Answers on page 491

FASTEST FINGER FIRST

31

Starting with the smallest, put these four mountains in order of height.

- A: Snowdon
- B: Fuji
- C: Matterhorn
- D: Ben Nevis

32

Starting with the most recent, put these films in the order in which they were made.

- A: Citizen Kane
- B: The Matrix
- C: Bonnie and Clyde
- D: Taxi Driver

33

Starting with the earliest, put these conflicts in chronological order.

- A: Crimean War
- B: Hundred Years' War
- C: World War II
- D: Vietnam War

34

Starting with the earliest, put these tennis players in the order they won their first Wimbledon singles title.

- A: Andre Agassi
- B: Bjorn Borg
- C: Lew Hoad
- D: Jimmy Connors

35

Starting with the most recent, place these poets in the order that they became Poet Laureate.

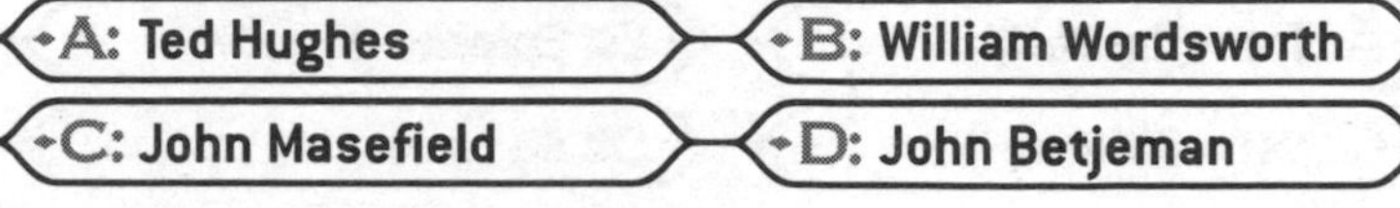

- A: Ted Hughes
- B: William Wordsworth
- C: John Masefield
- D: John Betjeman

Answers on page 491

36

Beginning with the earliest, put these footballers in the order that they became captain of England.

- A: Alan Shearer
- B: Billy Wright
- C: Kevin Keegan
- D: Bobby Moore

37

Starting with the earliest, put these scientists in the order that they were born.

- A: Archimedes
- B: Pasteur
- C: Hawking
- D: Newton

38

Starting with the most recent, put these English monarchs in the order that they ascended to the throne.

- A: William I
- B: Richard III
- C: George III
- D: Henry V

39

Starting with the earliest, place these novels in the order in which they were written.

- A: Catch-22
- B: Wuthering Heights
- C: Bridget Jones's Diary
- D: Of Mice and Men

40

Starting with the earliest, place these religious festivals in the order they occur in a normal calendar year.

- A: Transfiguration
- B: Epiphany
- C: Palm Sunday
- D: All Souls

Answers on page 491

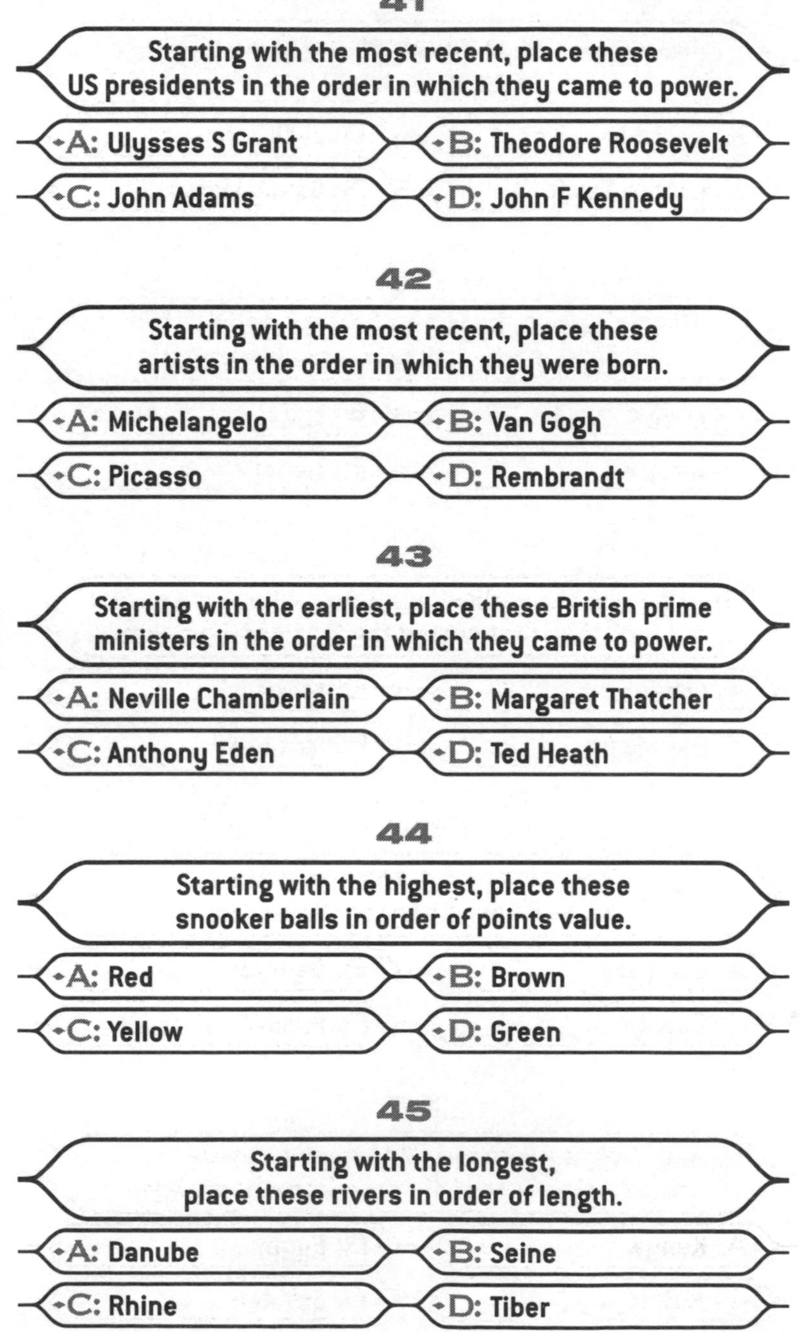

41

Starting with the most recent, place these US presidents in the order in which they came to power.

A: Ulysses S Grant
B: Theodore Roosevelt
C: John Adams
D: John F Kennedy

42

Starting with the most recent, place these artists in the order in which they were born.

A: Michelangelo
B: Van Gogh
C: Picasso
D: Rembrandt

43

Starting with the earliest, place these British prime ministers in the order in which they came to power.

A: Neville Chamberlain
B: Margaret Thatcher
C: Anthony Eden
D: Ted Heath

44

Starting with the highest, place these snooker balls in order of points value.

A: Red
B: Brown
C: Yellow
D: Green

45

Starting with the longest, place these rivers in order of length.

A: Danube
B: Seine
C: Rhine
D: Tiber

Answers on page 491

FASTEST FINGER FIRST

46

Starting with the most recent, put these boxers in the order that they won the world heavyweight title.

- A: Rocky Marciano
- B: Jack Johnson
- C: Lennox Lewis
- D: Sonny Liston

47

Beginning with the earliest, put these TV shows in the order in which they were first broadcast.

- A: Frasier
- B: The Honeymooners
- C: Cheers
- D: Happy Days

48

Starting with the earliest, put these cities in the order in which they first hosted the Summer Olympics.

- A: London
- B: Athens
- C: Barcelona
- D: Moscow

49

Starting with the lowest, place these British army ranks in order.

- A: Colonel
- B: General
- C: Captain
- D: Field Marshal

50

Starting with the closest, place these countries in order of distance from the equator.

- A: Kenya
- B: Egypt
- C: Turkey
- D: Sweden

Answers on page 491

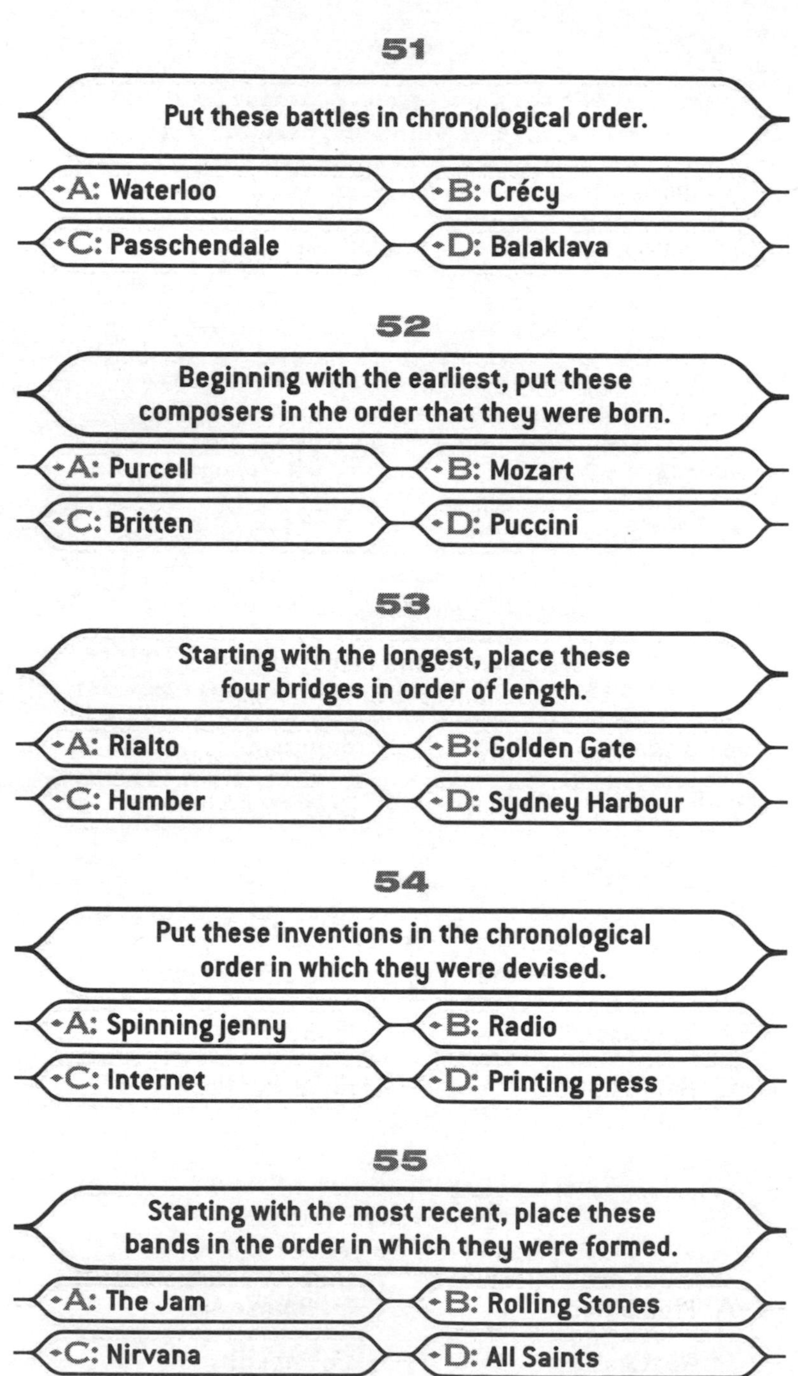

51

Put these battles in chronological order.

- A: Waterloo
- B: Crécy
- C: Passchendale
- D: Balaklava

52

Beginning with the earliest, put these composers in the order that they were born.

- A: Purcell
- B: Mozart
- C: Britten
- D: Puccini

53

Starting with the longest, place these four bridges in order of length.

- A: Rialto
- B: Golden Gate
- C: Humber
- D: Sydney Harbour

54

Put these inventions in the chronological order in which they were devised.

- A: Spinning jenny
- B: Radio
- C: Internet
- D: Printing press

55

Starting with the most recent, place these bands in the order in which they were formed.

- A: The Jam
- B: Rolling Stones
- C: Nirvana
- D: All Saints

Answers on page 491

FASTEST FINGER FIRST

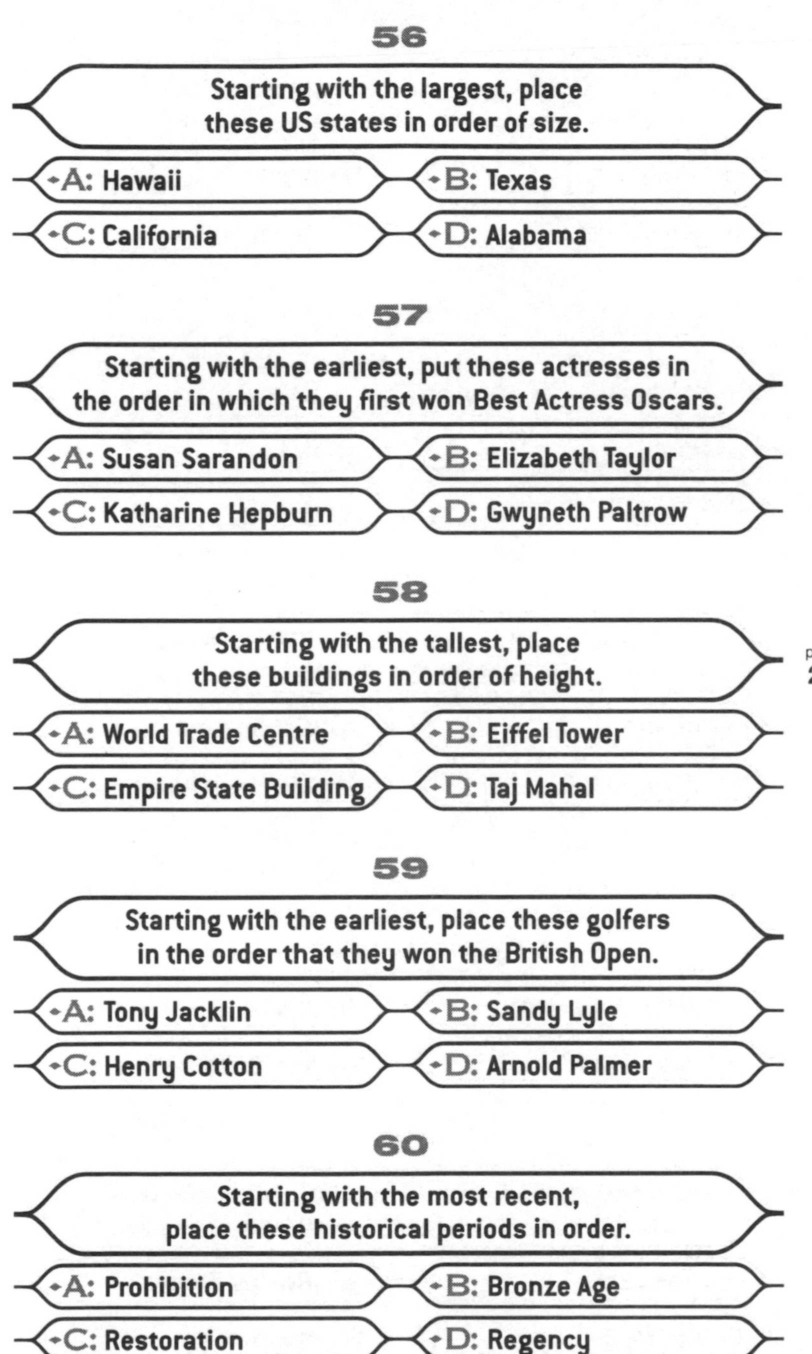

56

Starting with the largest, place these US states in order of size.

- A: Hawaii
- B: Texas
- C: California
- D: Alabama

57

Starting with the earliest, put these actresses in the order in which they first won Best Actress Oscars.

- A: Susan Sarandon
- B: Elizabeth Taylor
- C: Katharine Hepburn
- D: Gwyneth Paltrow

58

Starting with the tallest, place these buildings in order of height.

- A: World Trade Centre
- B: Eiffel Tower
- C: Empire State Building
- D: Taj Mahal

59

Starting with the earliest, place these golfers in the order that they won the British Open.

- A: Tony Jacklin
- B: Sandy Lyle
- C: Henry Cotton
- D: Arnold Palmer

60

Starting with the most recent, place these historical periods in order.

- A: Prohibition
- B: Bronze Age
- C: Restoration
- D: Regency

Answers on page 491

61

Starting with the most recent, place these playwrights in order of birth.

- A: Samuel Beckett
- B: William Shakespeare
- C: Harold Pinter
- D: Oscar Wilde

62

Starting with the earliest, place these four wedding anniversaries in the order that they occur.

- A: Emerald
- B: Cotton
- C: Crystal
- D: Pottery

63

Starting with the most recent, place these revolutions in the order that they occurred.

- A: French Revolution
- B: Russian Revolution
- C: Cultural Revolution
- D: American Revolution

64

Starting with the most recent, place these actors in the order that they played Doctor Who.

- A: William Hartnell
- B: Jon Pertwee
- C: Patrick Troughton
- D: Tom Baker

65

Starting with the most recent, place these Russian leaders in the order in which they came to power.

- A: Putin
- B: Khrushchev
- C: Andropov
- D: Lenin

Answers on page 491

66

Starting with the earliest, place these writers in the order that they won the Nobel Prize for Literature.

A: William Golding
B: Rudyard Kipling
C: Winston Churchill
D: Seamus Heaney

67

Starting with the earliest, place these American TV dramas in the order that they were first transmitted.

A: Dynasty
B: Beverly Hills 90210
C: Peyton Place
D: Dallas

68

Starting with the earliest, place these athletes in the order that they won Olympic gold medals.

A: Mary Peters
B: Harold Abrahams
C: Allan Wells
D: Sally Gunnell

69

Starting with the closest, place these cities in order of distance from the North Pole.

A: Cape Town
B: London
C: Reykjavik
D: Cairo

70

Starting with the earliest, put these men in the order that they became England football manager.

A: Don Revie
B: Graham Taylor
C: Alf Ramsey
D: Terry Venables

Answers on page 491

71

Starting with the earliest, put these TV series in the order that they were first transmitted.

A: The Avengers
B: The Professionals
C: The Paradise Club
D: Bugs

72

Beginning with the most recent, put these Roman emperors in the order in which they came to power.

A: Marcus Aurelius
B: Tiberius
C: Commodus
D: Nero

73

Starting with the most recent, put these buildings in the order of their date of construction.

A: Statue of Liberty
B: Acropolis
C: Sears Tower
D: Taj Mahal

74

Starting with the smallest, place these countries in order of area.

A: Sudan
B: France
C: China
D: Belgium

75

Starting with the most prolific, put these cricketers in order of Test match runs they have scored.

A: Bob Willis
B: Graham Gooch
C: Ian Botham
D: David Gower

Answers on page 491

FASTEST FINGER FIRST

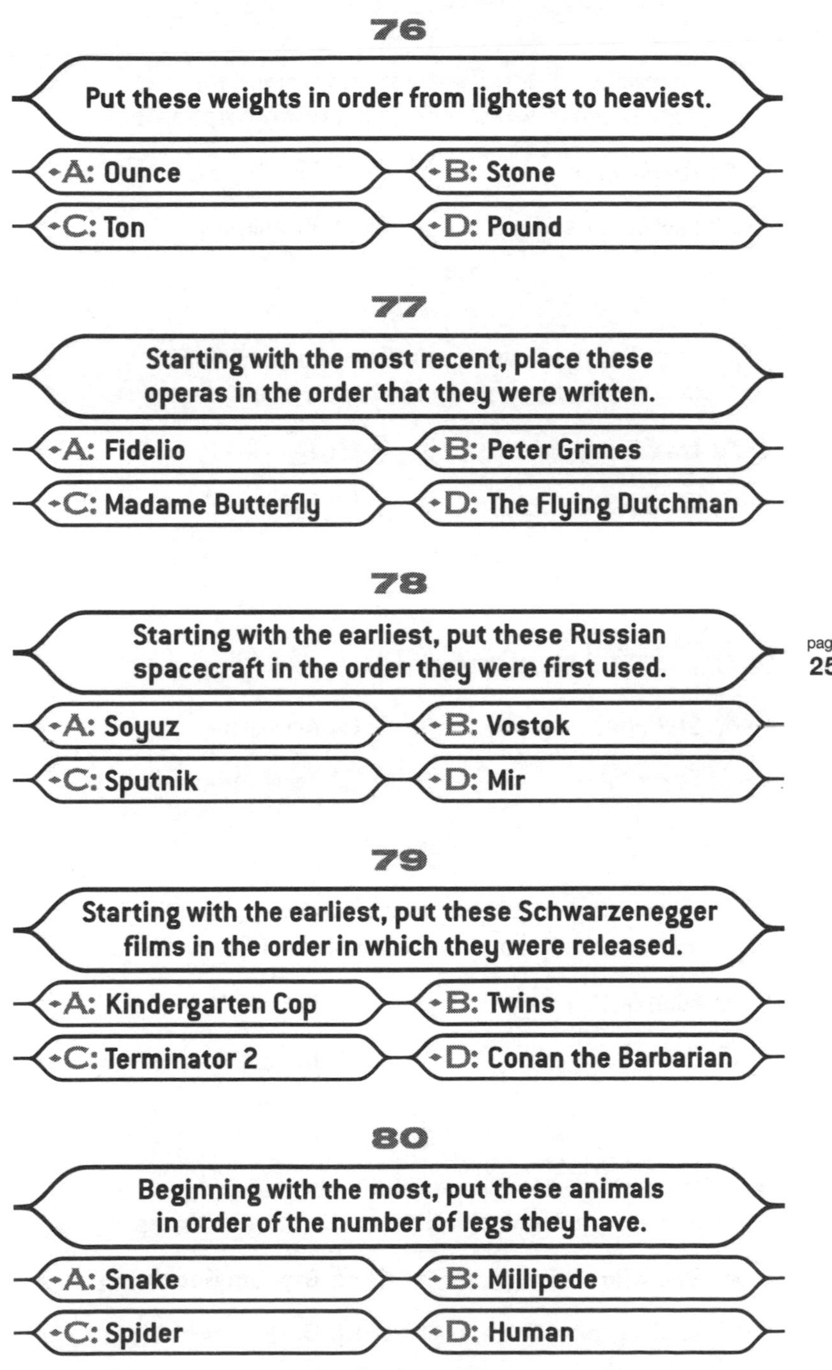

76

Put these weights in order from lightest to heaviest.

- A: Ounce
- B: Stone
- C: Ton
- D: Pound

77

Starting with the most recent, place these operas in the order that they were written.

- A: Fidelio
- B: Peter Grimes
- C: Madame Butterfly
- D: The Flying Dutchman

78

Starting with the earliest, put these Russian spacecraft in the order they were first used.

- A: Soyuz
- B: Vostok
- C: Sputnik
- D: Mir

79

Starting with the earliest, put these Schwarzenegger films in the order in which they were released.

- A: Kindergarten Cop
- B: Twins
- C: Terminator 2
- D: Conan the Barbarian

80

Beginning with the most, put these animals in order of the number of legs they have.

- A: Snake
- B: Millipede
- C: Spider
- D: Human

Answers on page 491

note: dropped 'Arnold' from Q79

81

Starting with the earliest in the year, put the four Scottish quarter days in their correct order.

A: Candelmas
B: Martinmas
C: Lammas
D: Whitsunday

82

Put these words in the order they first appear in the rhyme 'Rock-a-bye-baby'.

A: Cradle
B: Bough
C: Wind
D: Tree

83

Put these Atlantic islands in order from north to south.

A: St. Helena
B: Madeira
C: Tenerife
D: Ascension

84

Starting with the earliest, put these men in the order they became Archbishop of Canterbury.

A: Michael Ramsey
B: George Carey
C: Donald Coggan
D: Robert Runcie

85

Starting with the earliest, put these songs in the order they won the Eurovision Song Contest.

A: Save Your Kisses For Me
B: Puppet On A String
C: Making Your Mind Up
D: Love Shine A Light

Answers on page 491

86

Starting with the highest, put these Roman numerals in order according to the numbers they represent.

- A: DC
- B: CM
- C: MC
- D: CD

87

Starting with the lowest, put these athletics events in order, according to the height of the bar.

- A: Pole vault
- B: Women's 400m hurdles
- C: High jump
- D: Men's 110m hurdles

88

Starting with the lowest, put these German numbers in their correct order.

- A: Zwei
- B: Vier
- C: Eins
- D: Drei

89

Starting with the first, put these words in the order they appear in the rhyme 'The House That Jack Built'.

- A: Cat
- B: Rat
- C: Dog
- D: Malt

90

Starting with the smallest, put these vegetables in order according to their normal mature size.

- A: Pea
- B: Turnip
- C: Pumpkin
- D: Radish

Answers on page 491

91

Put these names in alphabetical order.

- A: United Nations
- B: United Kingdom
- C: United Arab Emirates
- D: United States

92

Starting with the first, put these historic events in chronological order.

- A: Death of Elvis Presley
- B: Attack on Pearl Harbor
- C: First man on Moon
- D: President Kennedy shot

93

Starting with the shortest, put these items in order according to their average size when worn.

- A: Trouser belt
- B: Wristwatch
- C: Neck brace
- D: Wedding ring

94

Starting at Trafalgar Square, put these buildings in their correct sequence along The Mall.

- A: Queen Victoria Monument
- B: Buckingham Palace
- C: Admiralty Arch
- D: Clarence House

95

Starting with the lowest pitched, put these four saxophones in order.

- A: Alto sax
- B: Tenor sax
- C: Soprano sax
- D: Baritone sax

Answers on page 491

FASTEST FINGER FIRST

96

Starting with the lowest, put these films in order, according to the numbers in the titles.

A: Fahrenheit 451
B: Butterfield 8
C: Catch-22
D: Apollo 13

97

Starting with the earliest, put these First Ladies in the order they lived in the White House.

A: Rosalyn Carter
B: Pat Nixon
C: Jackie Kennedy
D: Betty Ford

98

Starting with the lowest, put these amounts in a standard game of draughts in order.

A: Black pieces
B: White squares
C: All squares
D: All pieces

99

Put these British royals in order in the line of succession to the throne.

A: Prince Charles
B: Princess Alexandra
C: Zara Phillips
D: Viscount Linley

100

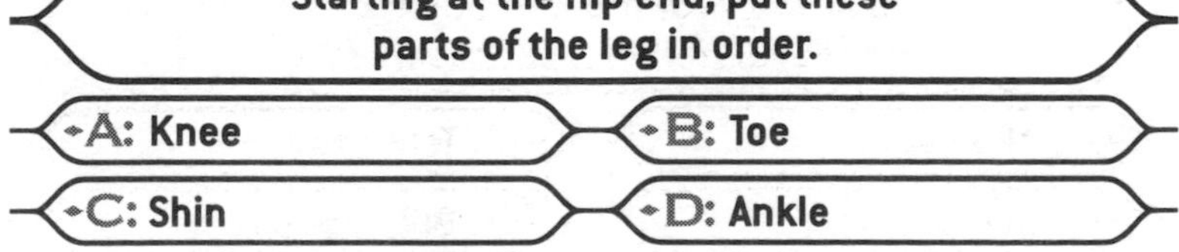

Starting at the hip end, put these parts of the leg in order.

A: Knee
B: Toe
C: Shin
D: Ankle

Answers on page 491

FASTEST FINGER FIRST

101

Starting nearest Birmingham, put these cathedral cities in the order they are situated along the M5.

A: Gloucester
B: Worcester
C: Exeter
D: Bristol

102

Put these Cliff Richard UK number one singles in chronological order.

A: We Don't Talk Anymore
B: Congratulations
C: Mistletoe and Wine
D: Summer Holiday

103

Starting with the earliest, put these Nicholas Lyndhurst sitcoms in order.

A: Going Straight
B: The Piglet Files
C: The Two of Us
D: Butterflies

104

Put these days of the week in alphabetical order.

A: Tuesday
B: Monday
C: Saturday
D: Wednesday

105

Starting in January, put these animals in the order they represent signs of the zodiac.

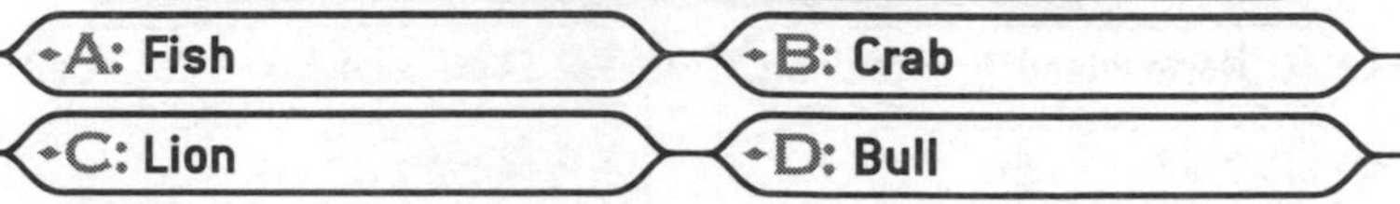

A: Fish
B: Crab
C: Lion
D: Bull

Answers on page 491

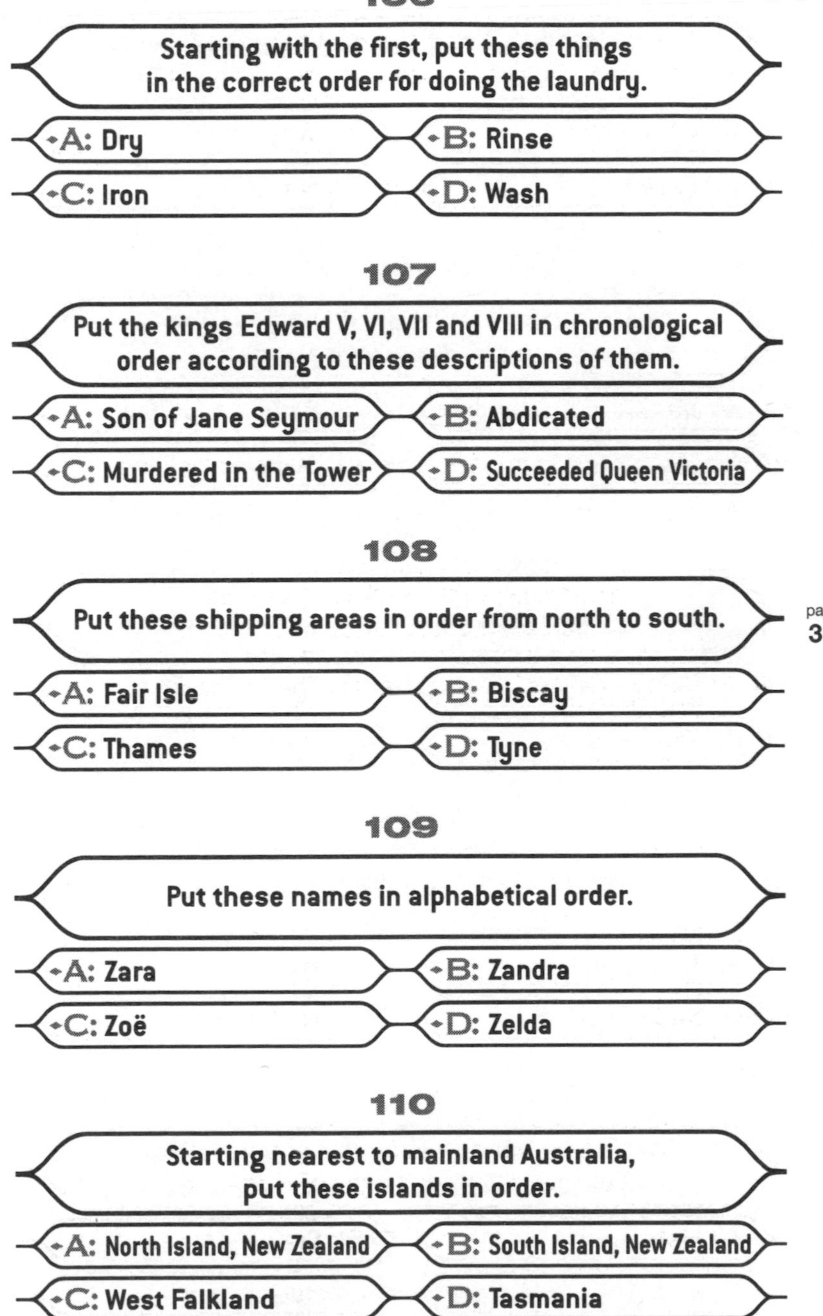

106

Starting with the first, put these things in the correct order for doing the laundry.

A: Dry
B: Rinse
C: Iron
D: Wash

107

Put the kings Edward V, VI, VII and VIII in chronological order according to these descriptions of them.

A: Son of Jane Seymour
B: Abdicated
C: Murdered in the Tower
D: Succeeded Queen Victoria

108

Put these shipping areas in order from north to south.

A: Fair Isle
B: Biscay
C: Thames
D: Tyne

109

Put these names in alphabetical order.

A: Zara
B: Zandra
C: Zoë
D: Zelda

110

Starting nearest to mainland Australia, put these islands in order.

A: North Island, New Zealand
B: South Island, New Zealand
C: West Falkland
D: Tasmania

Answers on page 491

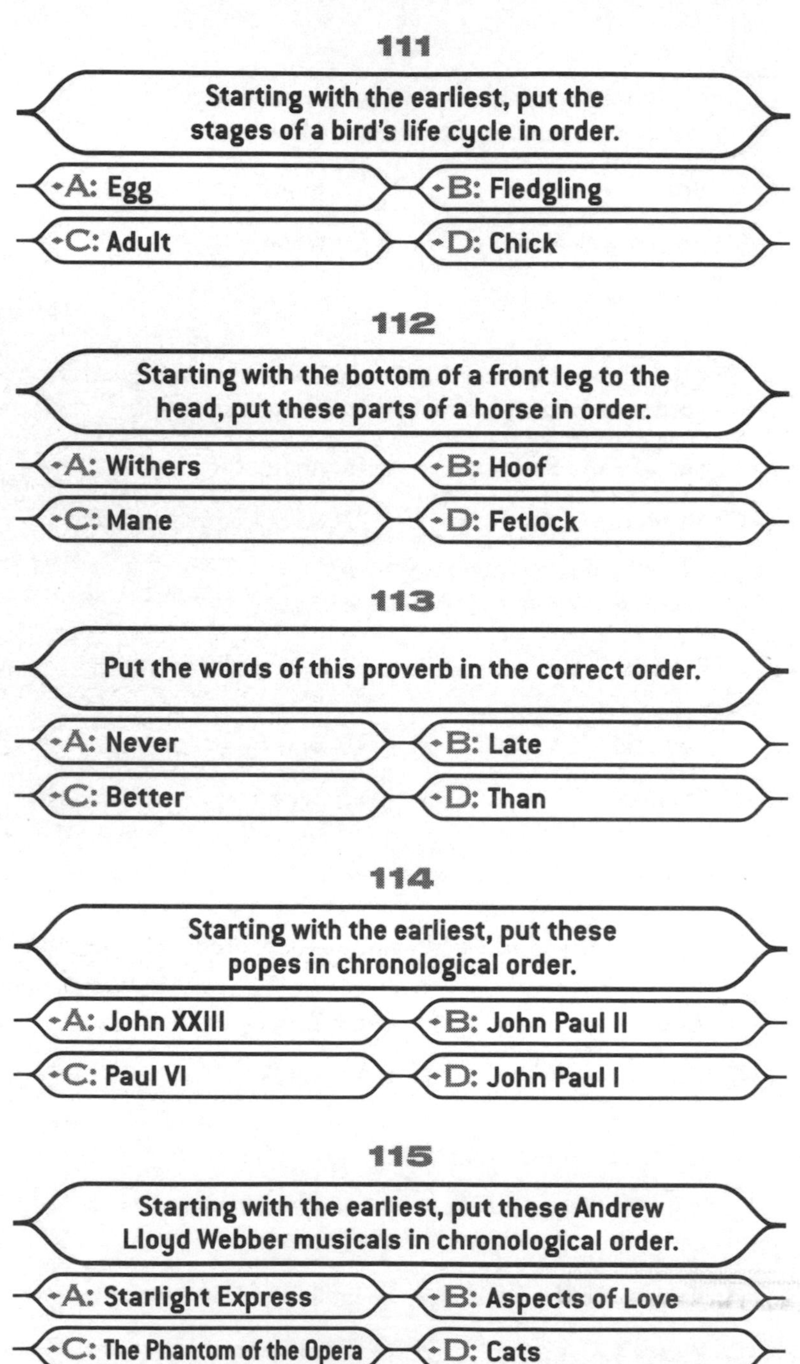

111

Starting with the earliest, put the stages of a bird's life cycle in order.

- A: Egg
- B: Fledgling
- C: Adult
- D: Chick

112

Starting with the bottom of a front leg to the head, put these parts of a horse in order.

- A: Withers
- B: Hoof
- C: Mane
- D: Fetlock

113

Put the words of this proverb in the correct order.

- A: Never
- B: Late
- C: Better
- D: Than

114

Starting with the earliest, put these popes in chronological order.

- A: John XXIII
- B: John Paul II
- C: Paul VI
- D: John Paul I

115

Starting with the earliest, put these Andrew Lloyd Webber musicals in chronological order.

- A: Starlight Express
- B: Aspects of Love
- C: The Phantom of the Opera
- D: Cats

Answers on page 491

116

Starting with the furthest south and working clockwise, put these Scottish firths in order.

- A: Solway Firth
- B: Pentland Firth
- C: Firth of Forth
- D: Firth of Clyde

117

Starting with the earliest, put these four British military figures in the order they were born.

- A: General Gordon
- B: Duke of Wellington
- C: Admiral Nelson
- D: Field Marshal Montgomery

118

Beginning with the earliest, put these children's shows in the order in which they first appeared on television.

- A: Live and Kicking
- B: Saturday Superstore
- C: Going Live
- D: Multi-Coloured Swap Shop

119

Starting with the longest, put these four major African rivers in order of length.

- A: Niger
- B: Nile
- C: Zambezi
- D: Congo

120

Starting with the most general, put these categories in the order in which they classify animals.

- A: Kingdom
- B: Class
- C: Phylum
- D: Order

Answers on page 491

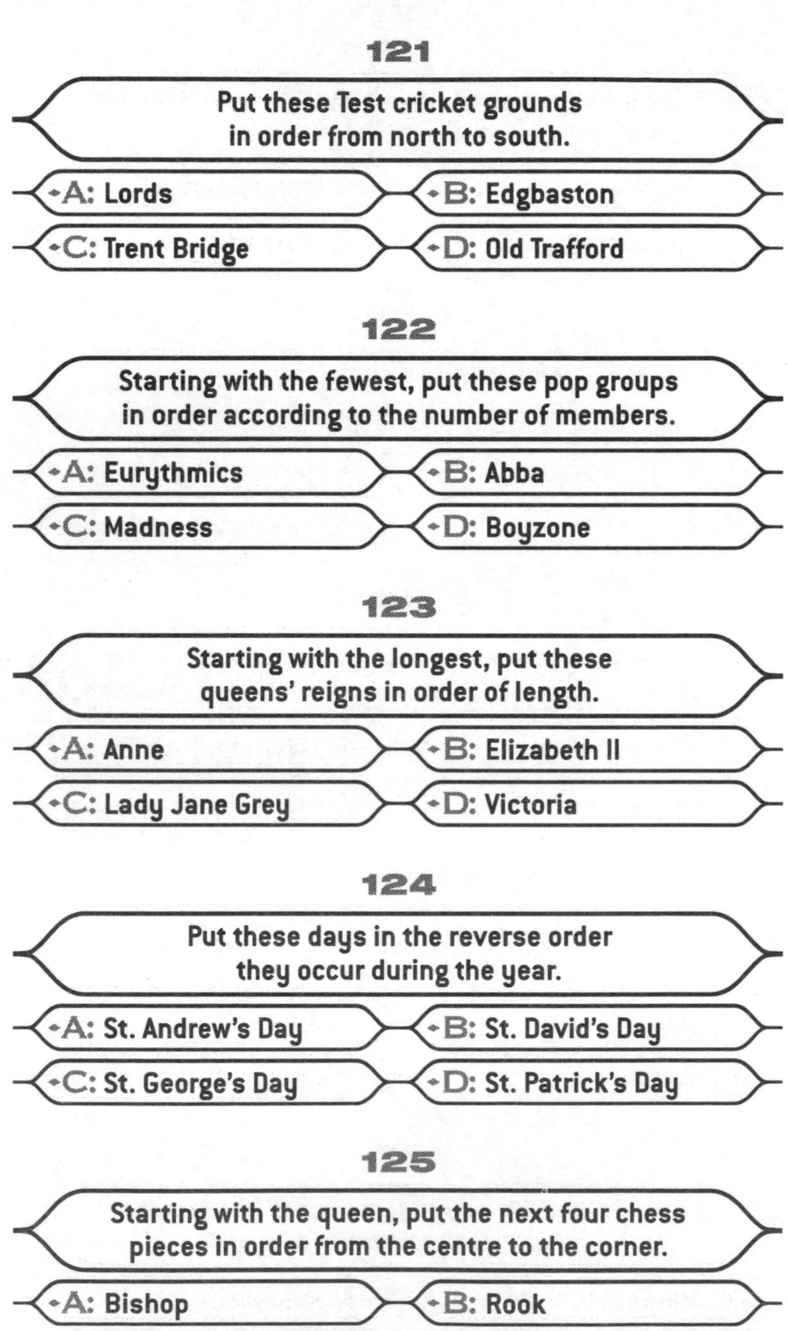

121

Put these Test cricket grounds in order from north to south.

A: Lords
B: Edgbaston
C: Trent Bridge
D: Old Trafford

122

Starting with the fewest, put these pop groups in order according to the number of members.

A: Eurythmics
B: Abba
C: Madness
D: Boyzone

123

Starting with the longest, put these queens' reigns in order of length.

A: Anne
B: Elizabeth II
C: Lady Jane Grey
D: Victoria

124

Put these days in the reverse order they occur during the year.

A: St. Andrew's Day
B: St. David's Day
C: St. George's Day
D: St. Patrick's Day

125

Starting with the queen, put the next four chess pieces in order from the centre to the corner.

A: Bishop
B: Rook
C: King
D: Knight

Answers on page 491

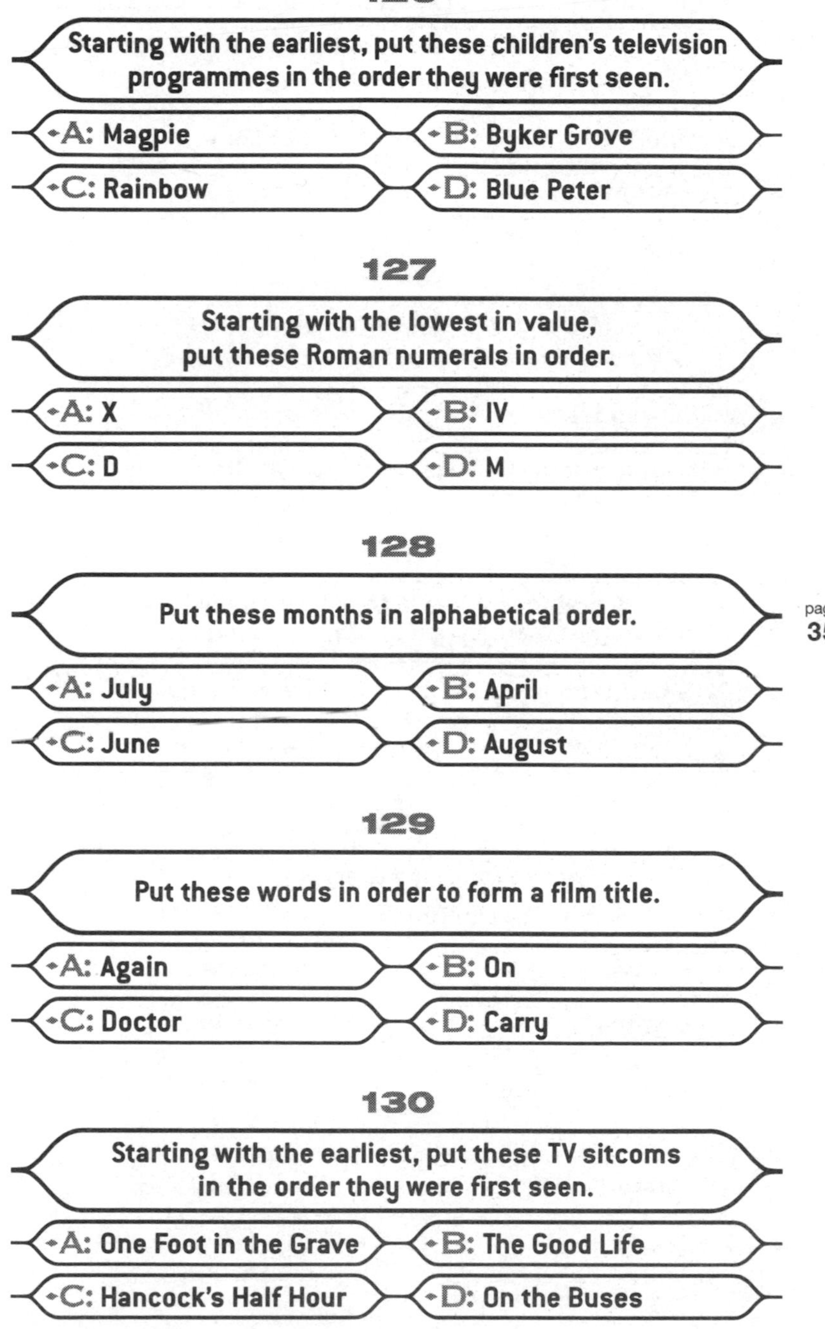

126

Starting with the earliest, put these children's television programmes in the order they were first seen.

A: Magpie
B: Byker Grove
C: Rainbow
D: Blue Peter

127

Starting with the lowest in value, put these Roman numerals in order.

A: X
B: IV
C: D
D: M

128

Put these months in alphabetical order.

A: July
B: April
C: June
D: August

129

Put these words in order to form a film title.

A: Again
B: On
C: Doctor
D: Carry

130

Starting with the earliest, put these TV sitcoms in the order they were first seen.

A: One Foot in the Grave
B: The Good Life
C: Hancock's Half Hour
D: On the Buses

Answers on page 491

131

Starting with the earliest, put these kings in the order they ruled.

A: Henry V
B: William I
C: Edward V
D: Charles I

132

Starting with the earliest, put these composers in the order they were born.

A: Johann Sebastian Bach
B: Edvard Grieg
C: Ludwig van Beethoven
D: Igor Stravinsky

133

Starting with the earliest, put these actors in the order they played Doctor Who on television.

A: Sylvester McCoy
B: Peter Davison
C: Colin Baker
D: Paul McGann

134

Starting with the first, put these books in the order they appear in the Bible.

A: Exodus
B: Numbers
C: Leviticus
D: Deuteronomy

135

Starting with the earliest, put these historical figures in the order they were born.

A: Adolf Hitler
B: Oliver Cromwell
C: Napoleon Bonaparte
D: Ivan the Terrible

Answers on page 491

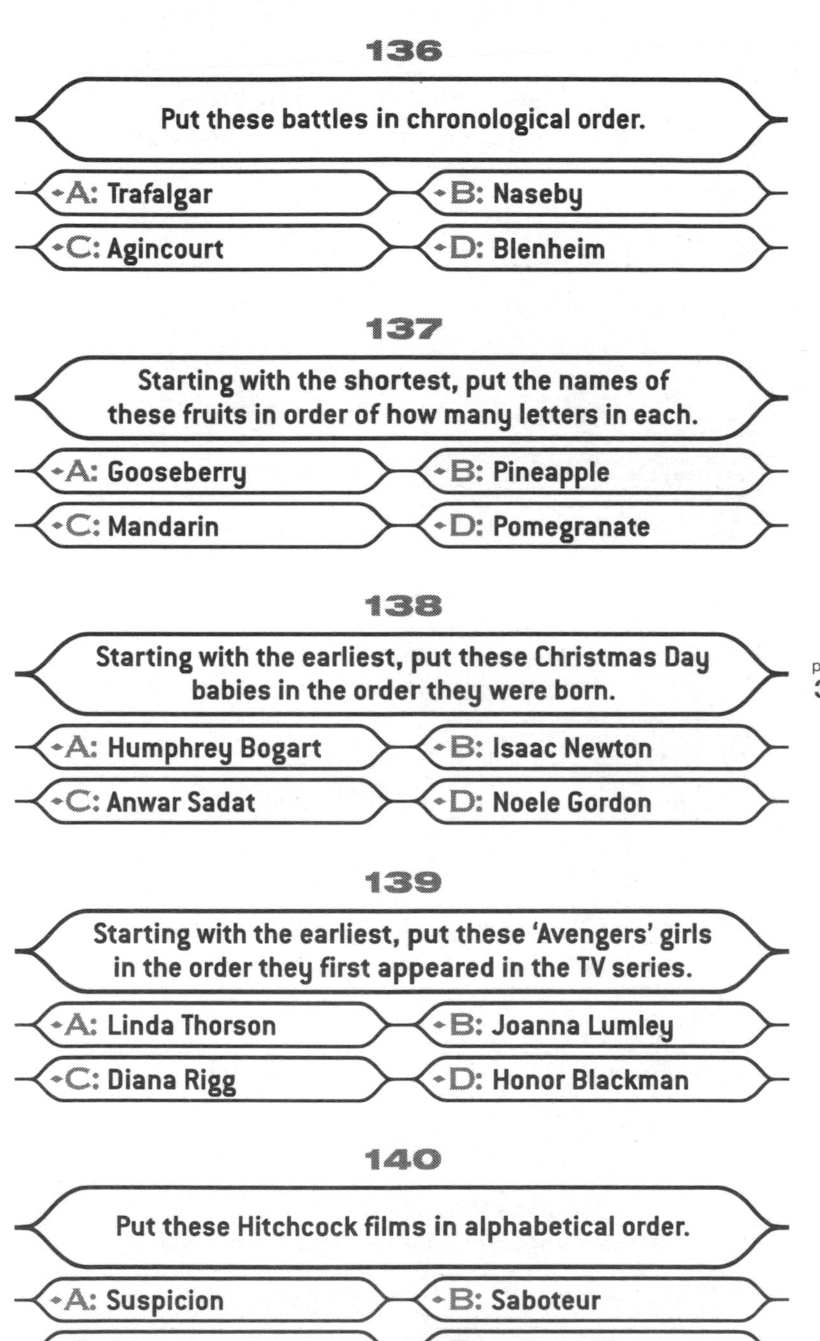

136

Put these battles in chronological order.

- A: Trafalgar
- B: Naseby
- C: Agincourt
- D: Blenheim

137

Starting with the shortest, put the names of these fruits in order of how many letters in each.

- A: Gooseberry
- B: Pineapple
- C: Mandarin
- D: Pomegranate

138

Starting with the earliest, put these Christmas Day babies in the order they were born.

- A: Humphrey Bogart
- B: Isaac Newton
- C: Anwar Sadat
- D: Noele Gordon

139

Starting with the earliest, put these 'Avengers' girls in the order they first appeared in the TV series.

- A: Linda Thorson
- B: Joanna Lumley
- C: Diana Rigg
- D: Honor Blackman

140

Put these Hitchcock films in alphabetical order.

- A: Suspicion
- B: Saboteur
- C: Strangers on a Train
- D: Stage Fright

Answers on page 491

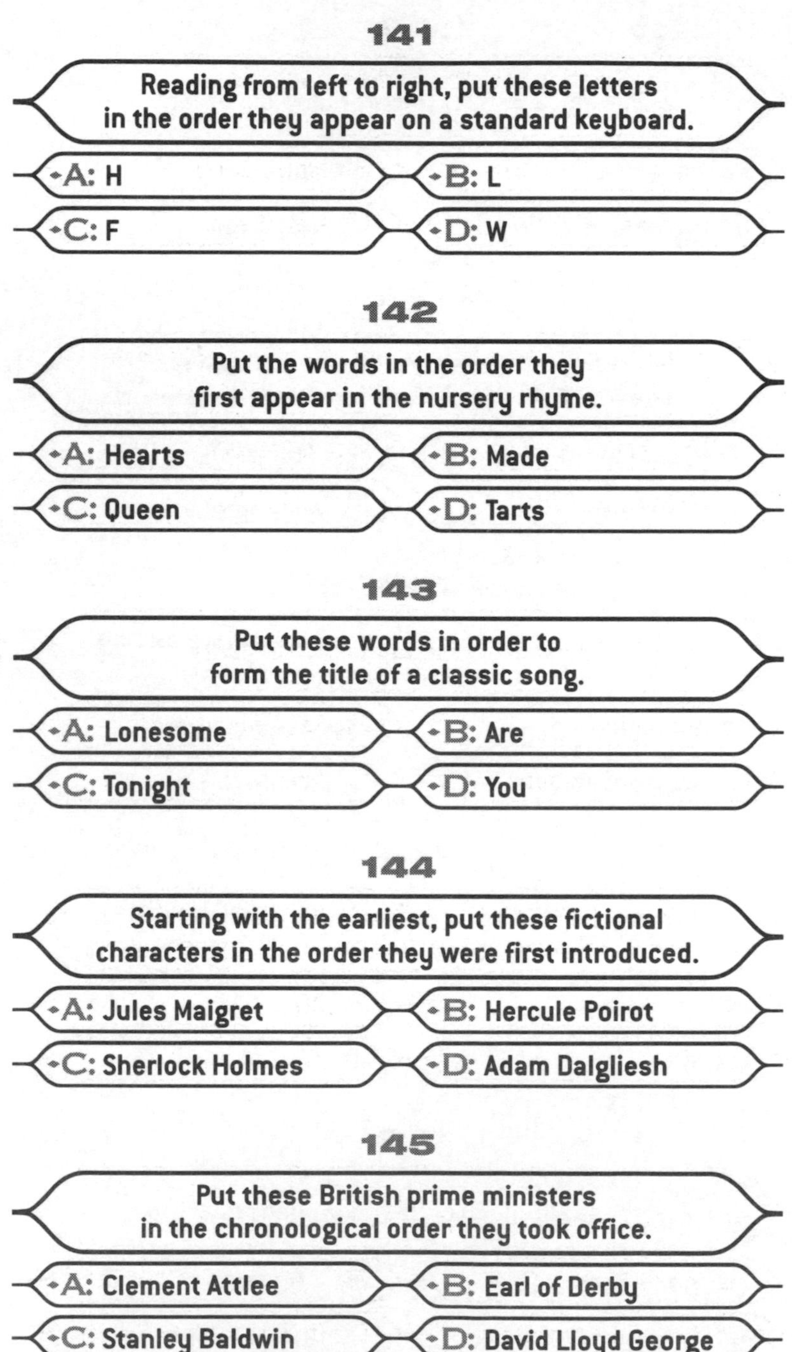

141

Reading from left to right, put these letters in the order they appear on a standard keyboard.

A: H
B: L
C: F
D: W

142

Put the words in the order they first appear in the nursery rhyme.

A: Hearts
B: Made
C: Queen
D: Tarts

143

Put these words in order to form the title of a classic song.

A: Lonesome
B: Are
C: Tonight
D: You

144

Starting with the earliest, put these fictional characters in the order they were first introduced.

A: Jules Maigret
B: Hercule Poirot
C: Sherlock Holmes
D: Adam Dalgliesh

145

Put these British prime ministers in the chronological order they took office.

A: Clement Attlee
B: Earl of Derby
C: Stanley Baldwin
D: David Lloyd George

Answers on page 491

146

Starting with the earliest, put these famous women in the order they were born.

A: Margaret Thatcher
B: Marie Curie
C: Florence Nightingale
D: Nell Gwyn

147

Beginning with the earliest, put these ecclesiastical TV sitcoms in the order they were first seen.

A: Bless Me Father
B: All Gas and Gaiters
C: All in Good Faith
D: Father Ted

148

Put these words in alphabetical order.

A: Accordion
B: Accommodation
C: Accomplishment
D: Accolade

149

Starting with the least, put these numbers in order, according to the number of letters when expressed in words.

A: 13
B: 30
C: 40
D: 17

150

Beginning with the earliest, put these Peter Cushing films in the order they were first released.

A: At the Earth's Core
B: A Chump at Oxford
C: The Hound of the Baskervilles
D: Dr Who and the Daleks

Answers on page 491

50:50

15	£1 MILLION
14	£500,000
13	£250,000
12	£125,000
11	£64,000
10	£32,000
9	£16,000
8	£8,000
7	£4,000
6	£2,000
5	£1,000
4	£500
3	£300
2	£200
1 ◆	£100

1 ◆ £100

1

Which of these is an old-fashioned term for a tomato?

A: Love apple
B: Dream orange
C: Darling cherry
D: Saucy banana

2

A person putting a lot of physical effort into a task is said to be using what?

A: Knuckle oil
B: Elbow grease
C: Knee cream
D: Hip lard

3

In the children's stories, what is the occupation of Mary Poppins?

A: Nanny
B: Prison warder
C: Nun
D: Traffic warden

4

What name is given to a year with 366 days?

A: Stride year
B: Leap year
C: Skip year
D: Vault year

5

Which of these is a Robert De Niro film?

A: Raging Bull
B: Roaring Badger
C: Rampant Hamster
D: Riotous Aardvark

50:50 Go to page 443
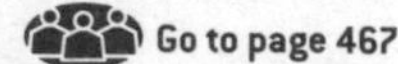
Go to page 467

Answers on page 492

1 ◆ £100

6

Which of these is a famous TV presenter?

- A: Fern Bittern
- B: Anthea Tern
- C: Mary Nightingale
- D: Davina Macaw

7

What kind of powder would be used to make cakes rise?

- A: Baking powder
- B: Talcum powder
- C: Face powder
- D: Gunpowder

8

Complete the title of this famous spaghetti western: 'The Good, the Bad and...'?

- A: The Ugly
- B: The Hairy
- C: The Stupid
- D: The Smelly

9

What is the name of the fried potato dish often eaten for breakfast?

- A: Brownies
- B: Hash browns
- C: Bobby Browns
- D: Charlie Browns

10

What is the name for bubbles of soapy water?

- A: Suds
- B: Duds
- C: Buds
- D: Muds

50:50 Go to page 443

Go to page 467

? Answers on page 492

1 ◆ £100

11

In card games, what name is given to the most important suit?

A: Lumps
B: Bumps
C: Trumps
D: Grumps

12

Which term is applied to a greyish cat with dark stripes?

A: Tabby
B: Flabby
C: Crabby
D: Scabby

13

Ping-pong is another name for which game?

A: Carpet croquet
B: Rooftop rugby
C: Table tennis
D: Bedside baseball

14

What was the name of the charter granted by King John?

A: Magna Carta
B: Chris Carta
C: Howard Carta
D: Jimmy Carta

15

Which of these is an informal term for the clothing industry?

A: Whistle world
B: Rag trade
C: Thread bed
D: Outfit outfit

50:50 Go to page 443 Go to page 467 ? Answers on page 492

1 ◆ £100

16

Complete the name of the musical style originating in the 1950s: 'Rock and...'?

A: Roll | B: Bagel
C: Bun | D: Croissant

17

Proverbially, what is rubbed into the wound to make things worse?

A: Salt | B: Vinegar
C: Chocolate | D: Mayonnaise

18

What name is given to a country's song played on official occasions?

A: National anthem | B: National curriculum
C: National debt | D: National gallery

19

What is the name of Channel 4's popular words and numbers game?

A: Meltdown | B: Countdown
C: Lowdown | D: Eiderdown

20

What do diners in a restaurant use to take away their leftovers?

A: Piggy bag | B: Doggy bag
C: Kitty bag | D: Bunny bag

50:50 Go to page 443 Go to page 467 
Answers on page 492

1 ◆ £100

21

Who would you be most likely to consult if your teeth hurt?

- A: Private detective
- B: Dentist
- C: Butcher
- D: Plasterer

22

The radio time signal is made up of a series of what?

- A: Pips
- B: Peels
- C: Piths
- D: Pulps

23

What is the name for the portable platform which connects a ship to the shore?

- A: Ganglion
- B: Gangway
- C: Gangster
- D: Gangrene

24

What name is given to the control column of an aircraft?

- A: Joystick
- B: Broomstick
- C: Slapstick
- D: Lipstick

25

What is the name of the tough Vietnam veteran played on film by Sylvester Stallone?

- A: Rambo
- B: Bubbles
- C: Twinky
- D: Poppet

50:50 Go to page 443 · Go to page 467 · ? Answers on page 492

1 ◆ £100

26

Which of these is a type of hyena?

A: Chuckling
B: Hooting
C: Laughing
D: Guffawing

27

Which of these are units of heredity?

A: Corduroys
B: Slacks
C: Genes
D: Tracksuit bottoms

28

The world's smallest bird belongs to which family?

A: Hissingbird
B: Hummingbird
C: Tuttingbird
D: Gruntingbird

29

Which of these horror films was released in 1999?

A: The Major Witch Project
B: The Blair Witch Project
C: The Heath Witch Project
D: The Thatcher Witch Project

30

Which of these is a dental instrument?

A: Pickwick
B: Pick 'n' mix
C: Toothpick
D: Pickaxe

50:50 Go to page 443  Go to page 467 ? Answers on page 492

1 ◆ £100

31

In fairy tales, which item is used to transport people through the air?

- A: Magic carpet
- B: Magic mattress
- C: Magic blanket
- D: Magic napkin

32

What is the name of the pastry topping of a pie?

- A: Crust
- B: Rust
- C: Frost
- D: Dust

33

Which of these is a type of insect?

- A: Gorgonbug
- B: Harpymidge
- C: Dragonfly
- D: Minotaurgnat

34

Which of these is a popular type of biscuit?

- A: Digestive
- B: Ingestive
- C: Festive
- D: Suggestive

35

'Jumbo' is a popular name for which animal?

- A: Elephant
- B: Rat
- C: Chimpanzee
- D: Kangaroo

50:50 Go to page 443 Go to page 467 ? Answers on page 492

1 ◆ £100

36

What is worn by a baby to keep its clothes clean while eating?

A: Bib
B: Dib
C: Fib
D: Rib

37

Which of these is a place in Australia?

A: Susie Leaps
B: Alice Springs
C: Mary Jumps
D: Felicity Hops

38

Which kitchen item is used to boil water?

A: Kettle
B: Toaster
C: Fridge
D: Sink

39

Which of these is a type of dance?

A: Cancan
B: Bambam
C: Tintin
D: Dondon

40

Which of these is a world famous natural wonder of Africa?

A: Vanessa Stumbles
B: Victoria Falls
C: Virginia Drops
D: Violet Dives

50:50 Go to page 443  Go to page 467 ? Answers on page 492

1 ◆ £100

41

Which of these means an eccentric person?

A: Crackpot
B: Jackpot
C: Chamberpot
D: Flowerpot

42

A 'goatee' is a small type of what?

A: Fork
B: Goat
C: Cucumber
D: Beard

43

Which town in southwest England shares its name with something found in a bathroom?

A: Bath
B: Plug
C: Sink
D: Bidet

44

What is the popular name for a Yeoman Warder at the Tower of London?

A: Porknibbler
B: Lambscoffer
C: Vealmuncher
D: Beefeater

45

Which of these is a type of nut?

A: Elbownut
B: Stomachnut
C: Chestnut
D: Shouldernut

50:50 Go to page 443  Go to page 467 ? Answers on page 492

1 ◆ £100

46

Which of these was a successful pop star of the 1980s?

A: Adam Ant
B: Billy Bug
C: Chris Cricket
D: Dave Dragonfly

47

What does the 'M' stand for in the road name M25?

A: Madness
B: Motorway
C: Mindless
D: Motorcade

48

One of the most senior judges in Britain is the Master of the...?

A: Rolls
B: Teacakes
C: Muffins
D: Crumpets

49

What type of television programme is 'Coronation Street'?

A: Bleach Pantomime
B: Soap Opera
C: Lard Ballet
D: Starch Theatre

50

What do the initials DIY usually stand for?

A: Do It Yourself
B: Darn It Yourself
C: Dodge It Yourself
D: Dig It Yourself

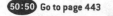

50:50 Go to page 443
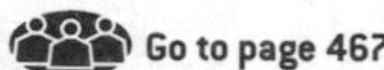
Go to page 467

Answers on page 492

1 ◆ £100

51

Which of these sports originated as a pub game?

A: Alpine skiing
B: Baseball
C: Canoeing
D: Darts

52

The adult Dalmatian is a dog with which type of pattern on its coat?

A: Stripes
B: Spots
C: Paisley
D: Batik

53

Vinnie Jones is most commonly associated with which sport?

A: Yachting
B: Polo
C: Football
D: Rhythmic gymnastics

54

The Eiffel Tower is a feature of which European city?

A: Rome
B: London
C: Paris
D: Madrid

55

Which of these is placed in a field to ward off unwelcome birds?

A: Scarecrow
B: Scarethrush
C: Scarestork
D: Scarepuffin

50:50 Go to page 443 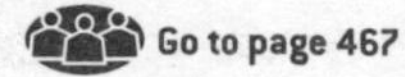 Go to page 467  Answers on page 492

1 ◆ £100

56

Which of these was a type of puzzle popular in the 1980s?

A: Rubik's oval

B: Rubik's rhombus

C: Rubik's prism

D: Rubik's cube

57

What type of food is traditionally eaten on Shrove Tuesday?

A: Oxtail soup

B: Pancakes

C: Lardy cake

D: Cod roe

58

Which kind of animal was the now extinct dodo?

A: Bird

B: Lizard

C: Fish

D: Badger

59

St. George, the patron saint of England, is famous for killing which animal?

A: Lion

B: Dragon

C: Shark

D: Spider

60

What is the defining characteristic of someone described as 'timid'?

A: Strength

B: Anger

C: Fear

D: Confidence

50:50 Go to page 443  Go to page 467 ? Answers on page 492

61

What was the nickname of William I of England?

A: The Lionheart
B: The Unready
C: The Sun King
D: The Conqueror

62

Which of these is a type of card game?

A: Nudger
B: Stroker
C: Poker
D: Slapper

63

'I Just Called To Say I Love You' was a number one hit for which singer in the 1980s?

A: Stevie Marvel
B: Stevie Wonder
C: Stevie Fabulous
D: Stevie Great

64

Which of these is a type of fortified wine?

A: Harbour
B: Quay
C: Port
D: Pier

65

Who was the star of the films 'Ben Hur' and 'The Ten Commandments'?

A: Millwall Heston
B: Watford Heston
C: Arsenal Heston
D: Charlton Heston

50:50 Go to page 443  Go to page 467 ? Answers on page 492

1 ◆ £100

66

The caterpillar is the larval stage of which animal?

A: Butterfly
B: Wasp
C: Dragonfly
D: Daddy-long-legs

67

The statue of which cherubic figure is found in London's Piccadilly Circus?

A: Eros
B: Aphrodite
C: Venus
D: Cilla Black

68

Which pop group were known as the Fab Four?

A: Cokroaches
B: Spyders
C: Antz
D: Beatles

69

What name is traditionally given in the UK to the first weekday after Christmas?

A: Boxing Day
B: Lacrosse Day
C: Rugby Day
D: Ice Hockey Day

70

Which of these is an international code for transmitting messages by wire or radio?

A: Semaphore
B: Braille
C: Shorthand
D: Morse

50:50 Go to page 443
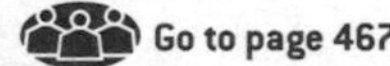
Go to page 467
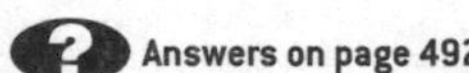
Answers on page 492

1 ◆ £100

71

What is the capital of Wales?

A: Swansea B: Cardiff

C: Pontypool D: Newport

72

Numbered balls and gamecards are a feature of which popular game of chance?

A: Roulette B: Backgammon

C: Blackjack D: Bingo

73

Which of these is another name for the beak of a bird?

A: Bill B: Ben

C: Brian D: Bob

74

Sandringham and Balmoral are residences of which public figure?

A: Prime minister B: Queen

C: US president D: Bobby Davro

75

Which of these birds could also be found on a chess board?

A: Eagle B: Osprey

C: Condor D: Rook

50:50 Go to page 443 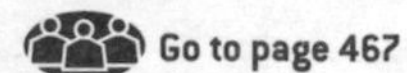 Go to page 467  Answers on page 492

1 ◆ £100

76

Stephenson's Rocket was an early example of which means of transportation?

A: Hovercraft
B: Bicycle
C: Train
D: Hydrofoil

77

Which month heralds the official end of winter and beginning of spring in the UK?

A: January
B: February
C: March
D: April

78

Who did Tony Blair appoint as Home Secretary in 1997?

A: Jack Barley
B: Jack Oats
C: Jack Hay
D: Jack Straw

79

What is the currency of France?

A: Franc
B: Finlay
C: Fred
D: Ferdinand

80

Which of these is a type of ballroom dance?

A: Weaseltrot
B: Foxtrot
C: Rattrot
D: Ferrettrot

50:50 Go to page 443  Go to page 467 ? Answers on page 492

1 ◆ £100

81

The penny-farthing is an early example of which means of transportation?

A: Aeroplane
B: Airship
C: Bicycle
D: Train

82

Rats and mice are examples of which type of animal?

A: Birds
B: Reptiles
C: Rodents
D: Fish

83

Which body of water separates France and Great Britain?

A: English Channel
B: Bering Sea
C: Labrador Sea
D: South China Sea

84

Which type of seafaring craft is known for periscopes and torpedoes?

A: Surfboard
B: Canoe
C: Submarine
D: Pedalo

85

Which of these is the name of a unit of electromotive force?

A: Leap
B: Jump
C: Volt
D: Bound

50:50 Go to page 443 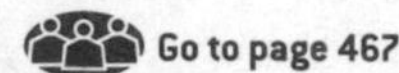 Go to page 467  Answers on page 492

1 ◆ £100

86

The Olympic Games are contested by people in which field?

- A: Science
- B: Sport
- C: Engineering
- D: Music

87

What are dentures?

- A: False legs
- B: False noses
- C: False teeth
- D: False hair

88

Which of these is a name for a male horse?

- A: Silverback
- B: Stallion
- C: Billy
- D: Mallard

89

Como and Coniston Water are examples of which geographical feature?

- A: Mountain
- B: Glacier
- C: Island
- D: Lake

90

Which part of the human body is primarily concerned with breathing?

- A: Liver
- B: Appendix
- C: Lung
- D: Toe

50:50 Go to page 443 Go to page 467 ? Answers on page 492

91

What is the 'Queen' side of a British coin called?

A: Crowns | B: Tops
C: Ma'am | D: Heads

92

Which people regularly slide down a pole to help them get to work very quickly?

A: Policemen | B: Firemen
C: Pawnbrokers | D: Barbers

93

What is a name for a temporary open-air market where second-hand goods are sold?

A: Grub market | B: Flea market
C: Moth market | D: Daddy-long-legs market

94

Which phrase is another way of saying 'covered in bruises'?

A: Black-and-white | B: Black-and-blue
C: Black-and-tan | D: Black-and-decker

95

What is the name for a metal clip that holds a sheaf of paper?

A: Borzoi | B: Beagle
C: Bulldog | D: Bloodhound

50:50 Go to page 443 Go to page 467 ? Answers on page 492

1 ◆ £100

96

Which sportsman is also the name of a breed of dog?

A: Sprinter
B: Boxer
C: Rower
D: Weightlifter

97

Which of these words means a gullible person who is easily taken advantage of?

A: Pullover
B: Pushover
C: Takeover
D: Hangover

98

Which of these is the name of a species of tree growing in the British countryside?

A: Whining willow
B: Wailing willow
C: Weeping willow
D: Whimpering willow

99

What was the chant used by the giant in 'Jack the Giant Killer'?

A: Fe-fi-fo-fum
B: Eeny-meeny-miny-mo
C: Ipp-dipp-dipp
D: Eachy-peachy-peary-plum

100

What is an informal way of saying one is registered unemployed and receiving state benefit?

A: On a roll
B: In a hole
C: On the dole
D: Up the pole

50:50 Go to page 443 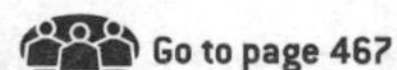 Go to page 467 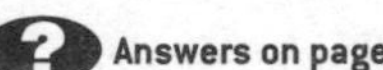 Answers on page 492

1 ◆ £100

101

What is another term for the skill and expertise with which to do a job?

- A: Lie-down
- B: Know-how
- C: How-now
- D: Brown-cow

102

Which animals metaphorically constitute a heavy rainstorm?

- A: Frogs and toads
- B: Sheep and goats
- C: Cats and dogs
- D: Lions and tigers

103

What is put into a novel to indicate the place where you finished reading?

- A: Bookmatthew
- B: Bookmark
- C: Bookluke
- D: Bookjohn

104

What were the names of the two little dickie birds who 'sat upon the wall'?

- A: Stan and Ollie
- B: Eric and Ernie
- C: Peter and Paul
- D: Romulus and Remus

105

What is a handy device for putting on footwear?

- A: Boot pipe
- B: Sandal flute
- C: Shoe horn
- D: Slipper sax

50:50 Go to page 443 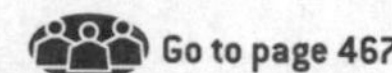 Go to page 467  Answers on page 492

1 ◆ £100

106

What is the early morning call from the hen house?

A: Cock-a-water-loo
B: Cock-a-baker-loo
C: Cock-a-doodle-doo
D: Cock-a-looby-loo

107

Which type of carriageway takes traffic around, instead of through, UK towns and cities?

A: Belt road
B: Ring road
C: Watchstrap road
D: Choker road

108

What is the reverse fold at the bottom of some trouser legs?

A: Turn on
B: Turn up
C: Turn off
D: Turnip

109

Which colourful cat was sought by Inspector Clouseau in the TV cartoon series?

A: Turquoise Tiger
B: Pink Panther
C: Purple Puma
D: Lavender Leopard

110

What is the name for the last-minute news items included in the paper after the printing has started?

A: Stop press
B: Halt printing
C: Hold the front page
D: Spanner in the works

50:50 Go to page 443
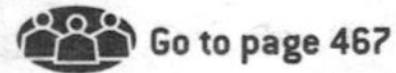

Go to page 467
? Answers on page 492

1 ◆ £100

111

According to the saying, where does charity begin?

A: Over the wall
B: At home
C: On the farm
D: In the bank

112

What do the letters PT stand for when part of a fitness timetable?

A: Physical tasks
B: Physical toil
C: Physical training
D: Physical torture

113

In the rhyme, Simple Simon met a pieman going where?

A: To the market
B: To the fair
C: To the bank
D: To the pub

114

Which of these is a punctuation mark?

A: Semicircle
B: Semiconductor
C: Semicolon
D: Semiconscious

115

Which of these is a famous American Wild West character?

A: Catastrophe Beryl
B: Calamity Jane
C: Devastation Doris
D: Disaster Hilary

50:50 Go to page 443 — Go to page 467 — ? Answers on page 492

1 ◆ £100

116

According to the nursery rhyme, which bush do we go round 'on a cold and frosty morning'?

- A: Burning bush
- B: Gooseberry bush
- C: Mulberry bush
- D: Shepherd's bush

117

Which of these is a type of ballet skirt?

- A: Wonwon
- B: Tutu
- C: Thrithri
- D: Forfor

118

Which of these words means to pamper or overprotect?

- A: Dollywoddle
- B: Mollycoddle
- C: Hollydoddle
- D: Jollytoddle

119

Which of these is a name given to an ideal future husband?

- A: Mr Right
- B: Mr Fine
- C: Mr OK
- D: Mr He'll-Do-I-Suppose

120

Which of these is a union of school teachers?

- A: NUT
- B: FRUIT
- C: CAKE
- D: BREAD

50:50 Go to page 443 Go to page 467

Answers on page 492

1 ◆ £100

121

Which word can refer to a type of carpet and a breed of cat?

A: Flying
B: Persian
C: Fitted
D: Shagpile

122

What is the name for a person with whom you regularly correspond to exchange news?

A: Pencilmate
B: Biropal
C: Ballpointchum
D: Penpal

123

What was the name of Britain's first regular TV breakfast show?

A: Cereal With Selina
B: The Big Bacon
C: Breakfast Time
D: Eamonn and Eggs

124

What does the phrase 'gee up' tell a horse to do?

A: Go faster
B: Stop
C: Go to sleep
D: Eat a sugar lump

125

Which of these is protection against floodwater?

A: Sandbag
B: Windbag
C: Gasbag
D: Handbag

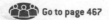

50:50 Go to page 443 Go to page 467  Answers on page 492

1 ◆ £100

126

If information is from a reliable source, it is said to come straight from where?

A: Dog's paw | B: Horse's mouth
C: Rat's tail | D: Pig's ear

127

Which word means the colouring of animal or plant tissue?

A: Pigment | B: Catment
C: Goatment | D: Dogment

128

Which of these are snacks eaten with drinks before a meal?

A: Canastas | B: Canapés
C: Canaries | D: Canadians

129

What does a boxer use to protect his teeth during a match?

A: Gumdrop | B: Gumshield
C: Gumboil | D: Gumboot

130

Which of these words means 'deceive'?

A: Hoodwink | B: Capblink
C: Scarftic | D: Hatsquint

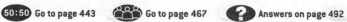

1 ◆ £100

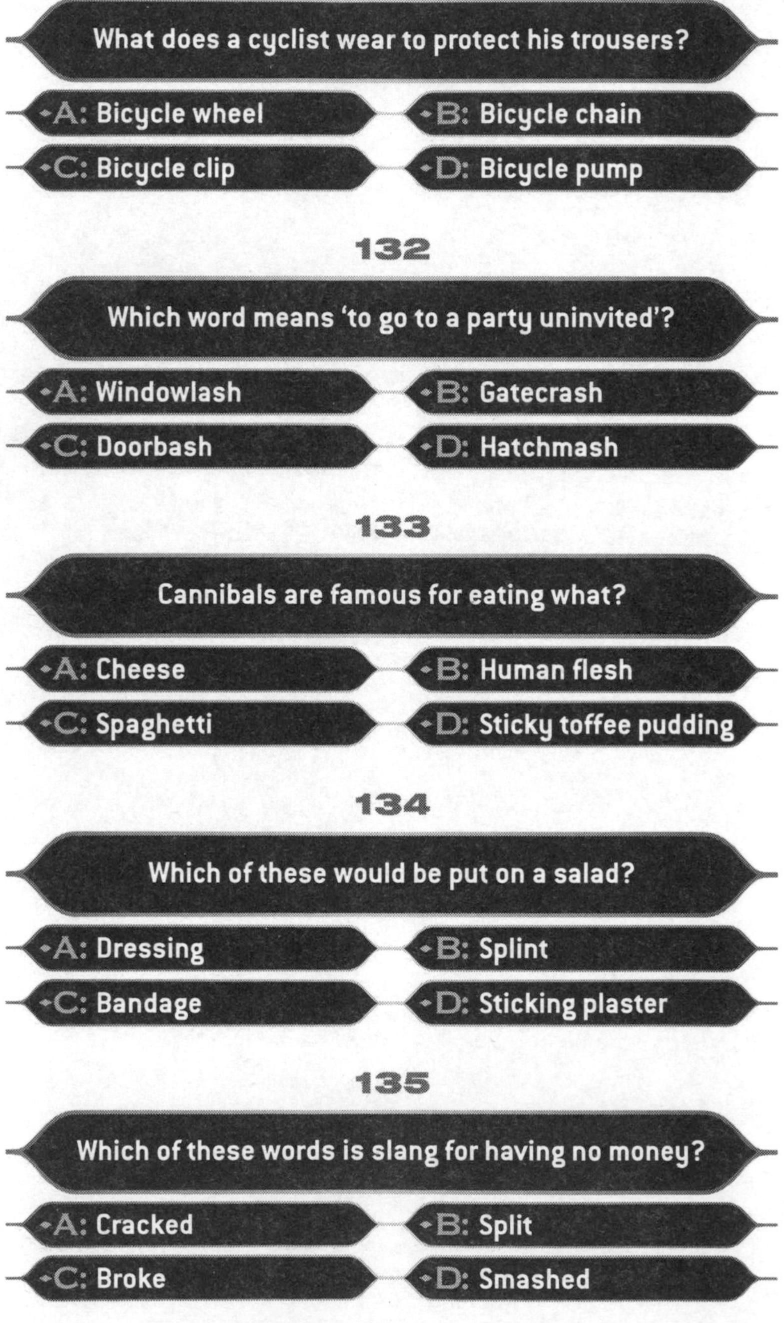

131

What does a cyclist wear to protect his trousers?

A: Bicycle wheel
B: Bicycle chain
C: Bicycle clip
D: Bicycle pump

132

Which word means 'to go to a party uninvited'?

A: Windowlash
B: Gatecrash
C: Doorbash
D: Hatchmash

133

Cannibals are famous for eating what?

A: Cheese
B: Human flesh
C: Spaghetti
D: Sticky toffee pudding

134

Which of these would be put on a salad?

A: Dressing
B: Splint
C: Bandage
D: Sticking plaster

135

Which of these words is slang for having no money?

A: Cracked
B: Split
C: Broke
D: Smashed

50:50 Go to page 443 Go to page 467 ? Answers on page 492

1 ◆ £100

136

Which of these is the surname of a former US president?

A: Hoover
B: Duster
C: Sweeper
D: Cleaner

137

Which of these phrases means 'very inexpensive'?

A: Dirt cheap
B: Filth reasonable
C: Muck cut-price
D: Sludge economical

138

Which of these is a childish name for a bird?

A: Dicky-bird
B: Ricky-bird
C: Nicky-bird
D: Micky-bird

139

Which of these is a famous fictional whale?

A: Carry On Dick
B: Private Dick
C: Moby Dick
D: Spotted Dick

140

Which inflatable building is a popular plaything for children?

A: Bouncy hospital
B: Bouncy castle
C: Bouncy supermarket
D: Bouncy power station

50:50 Go to page 443 Go to page 467

Answers on page 492

1 ◆ £100

141

Which of these might be used to make a path or patio?

A: Crazy paving
B: Mad concrete
C: Dotty flagstone
D: Potty asphalt

142

Which of these is the name of a type of trousers?

A: Flares
B: Flickers
C: Flames
D: Flashes

143

A person at his wit's end is said to be losing what?

A: His draughts
B: His marbles
C: His chessmen
D: His tiddlywinks

144

What is usually sprinkled on top of a cappuccino?

A: Chocolate
B: Cheese
C: Chutney
D: Chives

145

Which of these people presides over a meeting?

A: Chair
B: Bed
C: Sofa
D: Wardrobe

50:50 Go to page 443 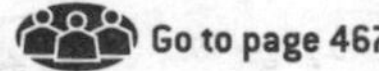 Go to page 467  Answers on page 492

146

Which of these is a type of biscuit?

A: Whiskypop
B: Sherrycrack
C: Brandysnap
D: Martinibang

147

Which of these is a popular TV game show?

A: Supermarket Sweep
B: Grocery Gamble
C: Laundrette Lottery
D: Haberdashery Hazard

148

If someone gets out of a difficult situation, he is said to have saved his what?

A: Ham
B: Bacon
C: Sausage
D: Salami

149

A persuasive or flattering person is said to have the gift of what?

A: The dab
B: The dob
C: The gab
D: The gob

150

Which of these symbolises the election of a new pope?

A: White feathers
B: White smoke
C: White cats
D: White chocolate

50:50 Go to page 443 Go to page 467 ? Answers on page 492

1 ◆ £100

151

What kind of creature was King Kong?

- A: Ape
- B: Rabbit
- C: Fish
- D: Cockroach

152

According to the BBC motto, what shall nation speak unto nation?

- A: Peace
- B: Football
- C: German
- D: Teletubby talk

153

Which of these is most likely to be part of an Internet address?

- A: Dot dash
- B: Dot dot
- C: Dot com
- D: Dot cotton

154

Which of these was a New Romantic singing star?

- A: Boy Alan
- B: Boy George
- C: Boy Kevin
- D: Boy Trevor

155

Which of these is a popular Middle Eastern entertainer?

- A: Belly dancer
- B: Jelly dancer
- C: Telly dancer
- D: Welly dancer

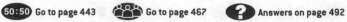

50:50 Go to page 443 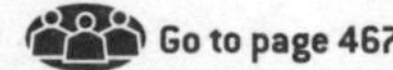 Go to page 467  Answers on page 492

1 ◆ £100

156

Which 'test' was originally used to determine whether something was made of gold?

A: Reflex test
B: Acid test
C: Spelling test
D: Cricket test

157

What is the name of the department store in the sitcom 'Are You Being Served?'?

A: Grace Brothers
B: Righteous Brothers
C: Everly Brothers
D: Beverley Sisters

158

Which of these is a country of North America?

A: USA
B: ABC
C: MFI
D: NUT

159

Which of these is a small portable computer?

A: Tiptop
B: Laptop
C: Softtop
D: Moptop

160

What did Tony and Cherie Blair name their fourth child?

A: Leo
B: Scorpio
C: Sagittarius
D: Capricorn

50:50 Go to page 443 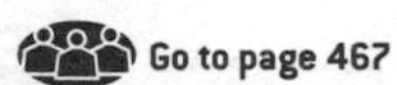 Go to page 467  Answers on page 492

1 ◆ £100

161

What is someone said to run if he risks danger or ridicule?

A: Gauntlet
B: Apron
C: Shinpad
D: Gumboot

162

Which of these capes is on the south coast of South Africa?

A: Good Times
B: Good Hope
C: Good Morning
D: Good Golly

163

In the children's game, who are the traditional enemies of the cowboys?

A: Daddies
B: Nurses
C: Indians
D: Ladders

164

Which of these phrases refers to espionage?

A: Cloak-and-dagger
B: Blazer-and-cudgel
C: Tabard-and-tomahawk
D: Anorak-and-cosh

165

Which word describes something humorous said with a straight face?

A: Milkpan
B: Fryingpan
C: Deadpan
D: Bedpan

50:50 Go to page 443 Go to page 467  Answers on page 492

1 ◆ £100

166

Which of these is a type of open-air sale?

- A: Car boot
- B: Car door
- C: Car engine
- D: Carburettor

167

Which of these phrases describes a pompous person?

- A: Stuffed shirt
- B: Padded dress
- C: Squeezed sock
- D: Crowded trousers

168

Which of these is designed to throw a detective off the scent?

- A: Red herring
- B: Yellow salmon
- C: Blue cod
- D: Green mackerel

169

Which of these is a nickname for a noisy upper-class young man?

- A: Cheerio Charles
- B: Hooray Henry
- C: Jeepers Jeremy
- D: Spiffing Spencer

170

Which of these phrases describes someone who is extremely angry?

- A: Hopping mad
- B: Jumping crazy
- C: Skipping dippy
- D: Leaping loopy

50:50 Go to page 443  Go to page 467 ? Answers on page 492

1 ◆ £100

171

Which of these phrases describes a large, sumptuous meal?

A: Bash-up
B: Slap-up
C: Knock-up
D: Punch-up

172

Which of these is a common childhood illness?

A: Chickenpox
B: Duckpox
C: Goosepox
D: Pheasantpox

173

Which of these phrases refers to a foolish search for something out of reach?

A: Wild goose chase
B: Savage partridge hunt
C: Fierce grouse trail
D: Demented turkey shoot

174

What name is given to a potato cooked and served in its skin?

A: Jacket potato
B: Cardigan potato
C: Blazer potato
D: Tuxedo potato

175

Which of these is a race often held at school sports days?

A: Bacon-and-knife
B: Sausage-and-fork
C: Egg-and-spoon
D: Beans-and-ladle

50:50 Go to page 443 Go to page 467

Answers on page 492

1 ◆ £100

176

Which of these is a name given to a very intelligent person?

A: Egghead | B: Tomatohead
C: Lettucehead | D: Radishhead

177

Complete the title of the Oscar-winning film: 'Shakespeare in...'?

A: Love | B: Trouble
C: Leeds | D: Debt

178

Which of these phrases refers to a snobbish person?

A: Toffee-nosed | B: Pie-eyed
C: Fudge-mouthed | D: Chocolate-eared

179

Which of these is a type of fungus?

A: Toadstool | B: Frogchair
C: Iguanacouch | D: Lizardsofa

180

Which of these is a type of ferry?

A: SeaCat | B: SeaDog
C: SeaBudgie | D: SeaRabbit

50:50 Go to page 443 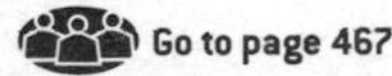 Go to page 467  Answers on page 492

50:50  

15	£1 MILLION
14	£500,000
13	£250,000
12	£125,000
11	£64,000
10	**£32,000**
9	£16,000
8	£8,000
7	£4,000
6	£2,000
5	**£1,000**
4	£500
3	£300
2 ◆	**£200**
1 ◇	£100

2 ◆ £200

1

Complete the proverb: 'Don't put all your eggs in one...'?

A: China cup
B: Basket
C: Bottom drawer
D: Silver box

2

If someone is described as 'poker-faced', how are they looking?

A: Happy
B: Sad
C: Excited
D: Expressionless

3

What is the name for the last line of a joke?

A: Tick line
B: Post line
C: Punch line
D: Flag line

4

Which board game tells its players, 'Do not pass go. Do not collect £200.'?

A: Monopoly
B: Trivial Pursuit
C: Scrabble
D: Risk

5

Complete the title of the novel: 'Dr Jekyll and...'?

A: Mr Peltt
B: Mr Skynne
C: Mr Hyde
D: Mr Coate

50:50 Go to page 445 Go to page 469 ? Answers on page 492

2 ◆ £200

6

What kind of food is sage?

A: Fungus
B: Bean
C: Herb
D: Wine

7

'Plates of meat' is rhyming slang for what?

A: Heat
B: Treat
C: Wheat
D: Feet

8

Which of these structures is intended for religious worship?

A: Windmill
B: Bridge
C: Church
D: Obelisk

9

Which of these is a coin-operated machine which plays songs?

A: Gear box
B: Voice box
C: Juke box
D: Black box

10

Which of these would normally be worn on the feet?

A: Flip-flops
B: Boleros
C: Trilbys
D: Slacks

50:50 Go to page 445 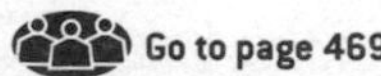 Go to page 469  Answers on page 492

2 ◆ £200

11

Which part of the eye shares its name with a school student?

A: Pupil
B: Iris
C: Cornea
D: Retina

12

Which animal is most associated with a purring sound?

A: Cat
B: Goldfish
C: Rabbit
D: Penguin

13

Which of these words describes a person who carries out menial tasks for others?

A: Doggy bag
B: Dogma
C: Dogsbody
D: Doggerel

14

Which salad ingredient shares its name with a type of firework?

A: Cress
B: Cucumber
C: Rocket
D: Lettuce

15

Where on the body would a bracelet be worn?

A: Neck
B: Wrist
C: Ankle
D: Waist

50:50 Go to page 445 Go to page 469 ? Answers on page 492

2 ◆ £200

16

Which of these is a computer accessory?

- A: Doormat
- B: Beer mat
- C: Mouse mat
- D: Table mat

17

Which of these words is another name for sunglasses?

- A: Dyes
- B: Colours
- C: Tints
- D: Shades

18

What is the name of the basket which holds food for a picnic?

- A: Hinder
- B: Hamper
- C: Harper
- D: Heeder

19

Complete this film title: 'Four Weddings and a...'?

- A: Christening
- B: Birthday
- C: Funeral
- D: Holiday

20

Somebody with more important things to do has other...?

- A: Fish to fry
- B: Potatoes to boil
- C: Tomatoes to grill
- D: Eggs to scramble

50:50 Go to page 445  Go to page 469 ? Answers on page 492

2 ◆ £200

21

Which of these was associated with TV's 'Mastermind'?

A: Purple host
B: Black chair
C: Blue contestants
D: Green questions

22

Which of these are you most likely to eat in a pub?

A: Farmer's breakfast
B: Ploughman's lunch
C: Miller's tea
D: Pigbreeder's dinner

23

Which term is applied to early morning birdsong?

A: Dawn chorus
B: Morning concerto
C: Sunrise sonata
D: First verse

24

A clever person is sometimes given which of these nicknames?

A: Bright Frederick
B: Intelligent Archibald
C: Brainy Bill
D: Smart Alec

25

A new barrister is said to be called to the...?

A: Pub
B: Inn
C: Bar
D: Nightclub

50:50 Go to page 445 Go to page 469  Answers on page 492

2 ◆ £200

26

Which of these is edible?

- A: Knuckle sandwich
- B: Traffic jam
- C: Fairy cake
- D: Easy meat

27

Which of these is an item generally found in the bathroom?

- A: Loom
- B: Loofah
- C: Loophole
- D: Lute

28

People packed tightly together are compared to which fish?

- A: Anchovies
- B: Mackerel
- C: Trout
- D: Sardines

29

An old joke is sometimes referred to as an 'old...'?

- A: Chestnut
- B: Hazelnut
- C: Peanut
- D: Coconut

30

What type of surgery is carried out through a very small incision?

- A: Porthole
- B: Keyhole
- C: Loophole
- D: Cakehole

50:50 Go to page 445

Go to page 469
? Answers on page 492

2 ◆ £200

31

People who boast about themselves are said to be 'blowing their own...' what?

- A: Whistle
- B: Horn
- C: Trumpet
- D: Nose

32

What is another term for French fries?

- A: Baked beans
- B: Chips
- C: Sausages
- D: Fish fingers

33

Which word is used to describe a very thin moustache?

- A: Pencil
- B: Stick
- C: Ruler
- D: Twig

34

Complete the title of the famous TV sitcom: 'Steptoe and...'?

- A: Daughter
- B: Nephew
- C: Son
- D: Niece

35

What is the female equivalent of a husband?

- A: Aunt
- B: Wife
- C: Grandmother
- D: Sister

50:50 Go to page 445 Go to page 469 ? Answers on page 492

2 ◆ £200

36

What is the traditional colour of a bow tie worn with a dinner jacket?

A: Red | B: Purple
C: Black | D: Pink

37

Complete the name of the famous Warwickshire town: Stratford-upon-...?

A: Avon | B: Bann
C: Clyde | D: Dee

38

Which soft rock is used to write and draw with, typically on blackboards?

A: Clay | B: Cobble
C: Coal | D: Chalk

39

What is the name of Britain's public broadcasting service?

A: BBC | B: BCB
C: CBB | D: CBC

40

With which product is the name Cadbury most associated?

A: Crisps | B: Sugar
C: Chocolate | D: Honey

50:50 Go to page 445 Go to page 469 ? Answers on page 492

2 ◆ £200

41

In cricket, which object is used to hit the ball?

A: Racket | B: Stick
C: Cue | D: Bat

42

What colour is the typical daffodil?

A: Red | B: Yellow
C: Pink | D: Blue

43

Which of these is an area of central London?

A: Marchfair | B: Aprilfair
C: Mayfair | D: Junefair

44

One of Britain's favourite dishes is fish and...?

A: Eggs | B: Chips
C: Mash | D: Yorkshire pudding

45

Which of these is the name of a famous film actress?

A: Hemi Moore | B: Demi Moore
C: Semi Moore | D: Remi Moore

50:50 Go to page 445 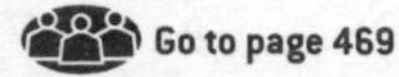 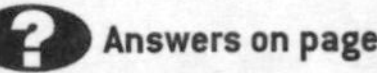 Answers on page 492

2 ◆ £200

46

Which word is used to describe a compulsory outfit for school?

A: Regalia
B: Uniform
C: Habit
D: Garb

47

Which of these sports is played with a racket?

A: Squash
B: Snooker
C: Hockey
D: Table tennis

48

In which of these buildings would one be most likely to see stained glass?

A: Post office
B: Bank
C: Railway station
D: Church

49

What type of drink is vodka?

A: Hot beverage
B: Alcohol
C: Fruit juice
D: Mineral water

50

Which of these is the name of a celebrated jazz singer?

A: Billie Getaway
B: Billie Vacation
C: Billie Holiday
D: Billie Weekend-Break

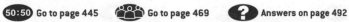

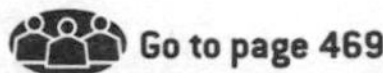

50:50 Go to page 445 Go to page 469 ? Answers on page 492

2 ◆ £200

51

In which sport do participants hit a shuttlecock?

A: Squash
B: Lacrosse
C: Tennis
D: Badminton

52

'The Marseillaise' is the national anthem of which country?

A: France
B: Germany
C: Italy
D: Spain

53

What is the first name of former US president Carter?

A: Johnny
B: Jacky
C: Jerry
D: Jimmy

54

Joan of Arc is a national heroine of which country?

A: Germany
B: France
C: Spain
D: Greece

55

Which of these planets is famous for its rings?

A: Jupiter
B: Mercury
C: Earth
D: Saturn

50:50 Go to page 445 · Go to page 469 · ? Answers on page 492

56

What is the profession of the fictional characters Sam Spade and Philip Marlowe?

A: Professional sportsmen
B: Private detectives
C: Truck drivers
D: TV evangelists

57

What type of person is said to have been born within the sound of Bow Bells?

A: Scouser
B: Geordie
C: Tyke
D: Cockney

58

The polar bear is native to which part of the world?

A: Amazon basin
B: Arctic
C: Himalayas
D: Tierra del Fuego

59

The England cricket team compete against which other nation for the Ashes?

A: New Zealand
B: India
C: West Indies
D: Australia

60

Namib and Sahara are examples of which geographical feature?

A: Lakes
B: Rivers
C: Deserts
D: Mountains

50:50 Go to page 445
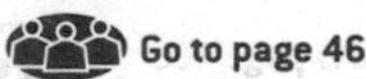
Go to page 469

? Answers on page 492

2 ◆ £200

61

Which of these is the title of a film starring Kate Winslet?

A: Marie Celeste
B: Lusitania
C: Titanic
D: Graf Spee

62

Tenor and soprano are examples of what?

A: Singing voices
B: Banknotes
C: Organised crime syndicates
D: Vegetables

63

Which fictional character was brought up in the jungle by apes?

A: Biggles
B: Dan Dare
C: Tarzan
D: Flash Gordon

64

Which of these events helped spark off the American Revolution?

A: Boston Coffee Morning
B: Boston Tea Party
C: Boston Cordial Drive
D: Boston Wine Tasting

65

Algeria is a country on which continent?

A: South America
B: Europe
C: Africa
D: Asia

50:50 Go to page 445 Go to page 469

Answers on page 492

2 ◆ £200

66

Which of these instruments belongs to the brass section of the orchestra?

A: Snare drum
B: Violin
C: Tambourine
D: French horn

67

Luke Skywalker and Han Solo are characters in which of these films?

A: Star Wars
B: Star Trek
C: Dune
D: Close Encounters of the Third Kind

68

Ayers Rock is a tourist attraction in which country?

A: New Zealand
B: Japan
C: Canada
D: Australia

69

A Boeing 747 is an example of which means of transportation?

A: Automobile
B: Aircraft
C: Yacht
D: Motorcycle

70

Malta is an island in which body of water?

A: South China Sea
B: Arafura Sea
C: Mediterranean Sea
D: North Sea

50:50 Go to page 445

Go to page 469

? Answers on page 492

2 ◆ £200

71

Who or what is a sitar?

A: Spicy curry
B: Religious holiday
C: Sacred river
D: Musical instrument

72

The food sushi is a speciality of which country's cuisine?

A: Italy
B: Mexico
C: Japan
D: Thailand

73

Bobby and Jack Charlton were leading figures in which sport?

A: Rugby
B: Tennis
C: Horse racing
D: Football

74

Which of these is a type of energetic Scottish dance?

A: Gay Gordons
B: Happy Harrys
C: Chuckling Charleses
D: Laughing Larrys

75

What type of sport is the Japanese 'sumo'?

A: Racquet sport
B: Wrestling
C: Ball-kicking
D: Horse riding

50:50 Go to page 445  Go to page 469 ? Answers on page 492

2 ◆ £200

76

What was the first name of the US president Lincoln?

A: Moses
B: Aaron
C: Abraham
D: Isaac

77

The Doctor Martens company is best known for producing what items of clothing?

A: Hats
B: Trousers
C: Cloaks
D: Shoes

78

Which of these is a garden implement with a short handle and curved blade?

A: Bickle
B: Tickle
C: Sickle
D: Fickle

79

The Oscars are awarded for excellence in which field of the arts?

A: Sculpture
B: Cinema
C: Architecture
D: Painting

80

Which of these was a fighter plane used in the Battle of Britain?

A: Hurricane
B: Tsunami
C: Eruption
D: Earthquake

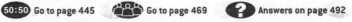

50:50 Go to page 445 Go to page 469

Answers on page 492

2 ◆ £200

81

The name 'dobbin' is usually associated with which animal?

A: Fox
B: Cow
C: Owl
D: Horse

82

'Snares' are part of which musical instruments?

A: Guitars
B: Violins
C: Drums
D: Saxophones

83

What does the P stand for in the abbreviation OAP?

A: Person
B: Pensioner
C: People
D: Purpose

84

From which British city do 'Brummies' come?

A: Newcastle
B: Liverpool
C: Birmingham
D: London

85

Which of these is a type of flat-bottomed barge and a card game?

A: Pontoon
B: Poker
C: Blackjack
D: Cheat

50:50 Go to page 445 Go to page 469 ? Answers on page 492

2 ◆ £200

86

David Gower captained England at which sport?

A: Football
B: Golf
C: Rugby union
D: Cricket

87

What was the first name of the artist Van Gogh?

A: Val
B: Vikram
C: Vincent
D: Vernon

88

What type of vehicles are traditionally kept in a marina?

A: Helicopters
B: Boats
C: Bicycles
D: Scooters

89

According to the proverb, what shouldn't you shut after the horse has bolted?

A: Stage door
B: Barn door
C: Stable door
D: Trap door

90

What do the Americans call Autumn?

A: The Topple
B: The Drop
C: The Tumble
D: The Fall

50:50 Go to page 445

Go to page 469
? Answers on page 492

2 ◆ £200

91

Which of these is a firework?

- A: Sparkler
- B: Sprinkler
- C: Spinnaker
- D: Spanker

92

Which article of woollen clothing is also a type of athlete?

- A: Jumper
- B: Cardigan
- C: Jersey
- D: Muffler

93

Which bird is especially known for its red breast?

- A: Thrush
- B: Heron
- C: Stork
- D: Robin

94

What was the title of the long-running TV comedy series, featuring Mr Barker and Mr Corbett?

- A: The Two Freddies
- B: The Two Dickies
- C: The Two Ronnies
- D: The Two Charlies

95

What is the second half of the proverb that begins 'Nothing ventured'?

- A: Nothing gained
- B: Nothing doing
- C: Nothing for it
- D: Nothing lost

50:50 Go to page 445 Go to page 469 Answers on page 492

2 ◆ £200

96

Where was Francis Drake playing bowls when he heard of the Spanish Armada in 1588?

A: Portsmouth Rake
B: Plymouth Hoe
C: Falmouth Spade
D: Devonport Dibber

97

In the movie world, whose 'Last Crusade' followed his 'Temple of Doom'?

A: Davey Jones
B: Dow Jones
C: Indiana Jones
D: Vinnie Jones

98

What colour is the classic British telephone box?

A: Yellow
B: Green
C: Blue
D: Red

99

What are the dubious facts passed on by word of mouth as traditional beliefs?

A: Great aunts' stories
B: Spinsters' fables
C: Old wives' tales
D: Grandmas' anecdotes

100

What is an affectionate name for a cleaning lady?

A: Mrs Mop
B: Mrs Broom
C: Mrs Hoover
D: Mrs Feather-duster

50:50 Go to page 445

Go to page 469
? Answers on page 492

2 ◆ £200

101

On a standard soccer pitch, what is always taken from a central spot 12 yards from the goal line?

A: Free kick
B: Goal kick
C: Corner kick
D: Penalty kick

102

Which phrase means that everything will turn out all right?

A: Bill's your brother
B: Bob's your uncle
C: Tom's your dad
D: Tim's your cousin

103

What is the name of the man who can turn his hand to all trades but can master none?

A: Jack
B: Jerry
C: Joel
D: Justin

104

Who is the sidekick of the cartoon hero Batman?

A: Merlin
B: Puffin
C: Martin
D: Robin

105

Which parts of the body are said metaphorically to burn when someone is talking about you?

A: Eyes
B: Cheeks
C: Ears
D: Nostrils

50:50 Go to page 445 Go to page 469

Answers on page 492

2 ◆ £200

106

The county of Worcestershire is famous for which type of food?

A: Cheese
B: Soup
C: Sausage
D: Sauce

107

What was the name for the sudden influx of prospectors to California in the 1840s?

A: Silver dash
B: Diamond surge
C: Gold rush
D: Oil fountain

108

What name is given to an MP's first speech to the House of Commons?

A: Maiden speech
B: Maiden name
C: Maiden voyage
D: Maiden over

109

What is a standard bat-and-ball game played over a six inch net?

A: Junior lawn tennis
B: Badminton
C: Table tennis
D: Nursery lacrosse

110

What is the name for the place where passengers wait to board an aircraft at an airport?

A: Duty Free
B: Departure lounge
C: Passport control
D: Check-in desk

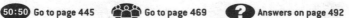

50:50 Go to page 445 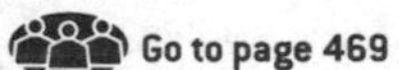 

Go to page 469

Answers on page 492

111

Which phrase refers to Australia and New Zealand?

A: Down over
B: Down below
C: Down under
D: Down and out

112

In France, what is a 'baguette'?

A: Plastic carrier bag
B: Bread
C: Purse
D: Hammock

113

What is the name for the short school break midway between the long holidays?

A: Half term
B: Bank holiday
C: Long weekend
D: Truancy

114

What is the name of the upper chamber of the British Houses of Parliament?

A: House of Earls
B: House of Barons
C: House of Nobles
D: House of Lords

115

Which of these is a type of soup?

A: Scotch bonnet
B: Scotch broth
C: Scotch egg
D: Scotch pancake

50:50 Go to page 445  Go to page 469 ? Answers on page 492

2 ◆ £200

116

In the theatre, the acts of a play are divided into what?

A: Scenes
B: Views
C: Vistas
D: Panoramas

117

Which of these is a British security service?

A: UK5
B: MI5
C: AD5
D: KO5

118

During which geological period was the earth's surface covered in glaciers?

A: Ice Age
B: Stone Age
C: Bronze Age
D: Jurassic Era

119

What is said when a secret must not be revealed?

A: Uncle's the word
B: Auntie's the word
C: Dad's the word
D: Mum's the word

120

What is the name for the small drinks refrigerator in a hotel bedroom?

A: Mini-tavern
B: Mini-pub
C: Mini-bar
D: Mini-inn

50:50 Go to page 445   Go to page 469   Answers on page 492

2 ◆ £200

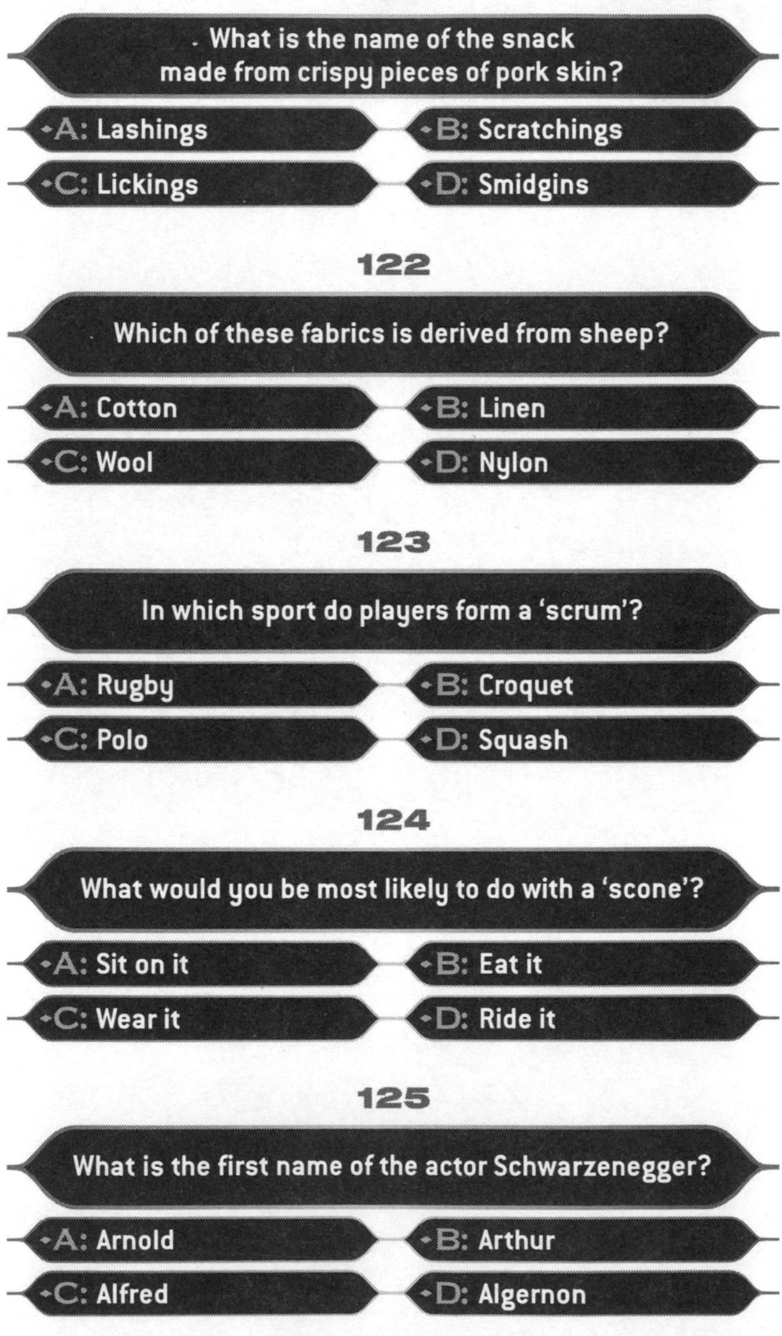

121

What is the name of the snack made from crispy pieces of pork skin?

A: Lashings
B: Scratchings
C: Lickings
D: Smidgins

122

Which of these fabrics is derived from sheep?

A: Cotton
B: Linen
C: Wool
D: Nylon

123

In which sport do players form a 'scrum'?

A: Rugby
B: Croquet
C: Polo
D: Squash

124

What would you be most likely to do with a 'scone'?

A: Sit on it
B: Eat it
C: Wear it
D: Ride it

125

What is the first name of the actor Schwarzenegger?

A: Arnold
B: Arthur
C: Alfred
D: Algernon

50:50 Go to page 445 Go to page 469 ? Answers on page 492

2 ◆ £200

126

Which of these is an Egyptian landmark?

A: Sydney Opera House
B: Sphinx
C: Mount Rushmore
D: Grand Canyon

127

Which of these is a type of glove?

A: Smitten
B: Kitten
C: Mitten
D: Bitten

128

What term refers to a short memorable phrase from a politician?

A: Sound gulp
B: Sound bite
C: Sound munch
D: Sound nibble

129

What is the name of the slow-moving vehicle used for milk delivery?

A: Milk float
B: Milk hover
C: Milk drift
D: Milk flutter

130

What is the name for a ship's record?

A: Twig
B: Tree
C: Branch
D: Log

50:50 Go to page 445 Go to page 469  Answers on page 492

131

What is the first name of the actress whose surname is Streep?

A: Meryl
B: Eryl
C: Beryl
D: Cheryl

132

Complete this proverb: 'Once bitten, twice...'?

A: Forgotten
B: Shy
C: Full
D: Hungry

133

What is the term for a person who doesn't work full time?

A: Part-timer
B: Oven-timer
C: Old-timer
D: Egg-timer

134

Which of these is a nickname for an American?

A: Tug
B: Pull
C: Yank
D: Drag

135

Who shows people to their seats at a wedding?

A: Musher
B: Pusher
C: Rusher
D: Usher

50:50 Go to page 445 | Go to page 469 | ? Answers on page 492

2 ◆ £200

136

According to the proverb, which city was not built in a day?

- A: Rome
- B: Bradford
- C: Bruges
- D: Southampton

137

Which phrase describes farm animals which are allowed to roam freely?

- A: Free-wheeling
- B: Free fall
- C: Free-range
- D: Free hand

138

Which London street is the home of the prime minister?

- A: Regent Street
- B: Sloane Street
- C: Harley Street
- D: Downing Street

139

What does someone do with his head to indicate 'no'?

- A: Nod
- B: Shake
- C: Swivel
- D: Rub

140

Which of these words refers to expensive or top quality goods?

- A: Up-trade
- B: Up-emporia
- C: Up-shop
- D: Up-market

50:50 Go to page 445 Go to page 469 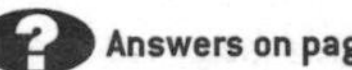 Answers on page 492

141

Which of these is a type of undergarment for men?

A: Cricketer shorts
B: Boxer shorts
C: Footballer shorts
D: Golfer shorts

142

Which of these is a method of photographing bones?

A: Q-rays
B: X-rays
C: Y-rays
D: Z-rays

143

If a person wanted to get fit, what kind of establishment should he visit?

A: Cinema
B: Bakery
C: Gymnasium
D: Library

144

What is the setting for the TV drama 'The Bill'?

A: School
B: Hospital
C: Street market
D: Police station

145

Which stringy item is used to clean between the teeth?

A: Dental moss
B: Dental gloss
C: Dental floss
D: Dental dross

50:50 Go to page 445  Go to page 469 ? Answers on page 492

146

An item that sells quickly is said to sell like hot what?

A: Cakes
B: Chocolate
C: Soup
D: Dogs

147

Which parts of the body make another name for weaponry?

A: Arms
B: Legs
C: Shoulders
D: Ankles

148

Four-poster and water are two types of what?

A: Piano
B: Table
C: Key
D: Bed

149

Which Australian mammal is described as 'duck-billed'?

A: Platypus
B: Wombat
C: Wallaby
D: Koala

150

What is the traditional name for a child's toy bear?

A: Tommy
B: Tony
C: Terry
D: Teddy

50:50 Go to page 445 Go to page 469 ? Answers on page 492

2 ◆ £200

151

Which of these is a name for the aggressive behaviour of a motorist?

- A: Road rage
- B: Avenue anger
- C: Street savagery
- D: Boulevard brutality

152

Which Finn was created by Mark Twain?

- A: Loganberry
- B: Blueberry
- C: Huckleberry
- D: Boysenberry

153

What is usually said to someone who has just sneezed?

- A: Happy birthday
- B: Cheers
- C: Bless you
- D: Merry Christmas

154

Traditionally, what kind of medal is awarded for first place in a sporting event?

- A: Bronze
- B: Gold
- C: Tin
- D: Copper

155

Who was the motor-making partner of Rolls?

- A: Brown
- B: Sullivan
- C: Royce
- D: Hardy

50:50 Go to page 445 · Go to page 469 · ? Answers on page 492

2 ◆ £200

156

Which tree shares its name with a part of the hand?

A: Palm
B: Oak
C: Willow
D: Cedar

157

In sport, which of these phrases means each side has the same number of points or goals?

A: All round
B: All square
C: All oblong
D: All conical

158

Which of these is a national daily newspaper of Britain?

A: The Sun
B: The Moon
C: The Planet
D: The Galaxy

159

In an orchestra, what is the more common name for the timpani?

A: Blenderdrums
B: Kettledrums
C: Ovendrums
D: Spoondrums

160

Which meal is also the name of a drink?

A: Breakfast
B: Lunch
C: Tea
D: Dinner

50:50 Go to page 445  Go to page 469 ? Answers on page 492

2 ◆ £200

161

Which of these is a type of insect?

A: Eyewig | B: Earwig
C: Lipwig | D: Nosewig

162

What is the full name of the national newspaper known by the initials FT?

A: Fiscal Times | B: Fun Times
C: Financial Times | D: Falcon Times

163

Which of these describes a sharp bend in a road?

A: Hairnet | B: Hairpin
C: Hairbrush | D: Hairpiece

164

Complete the title of this song from 'The Wizard of Oz': 'Over the...'?

A: Rainbow | B: Treetops
C: Lagoon | D: Clouds

165

Which colour is traditionally associated with the Conservative Party?

A: Yellow | B: Blue
C: Green | D: Red

50:50 Go to page 445  Go to page 469 ? Answers on page 492

166

What is the name for the facial hair which grows between the upper lip and the nose?

A: Beard
B: Sideburn
C: Moustache
D: Eyebrow

167

Which colour has a shade called 'pillar box'?

A: Blue
B: Green
C: Yellow
D: Red

168

What kind of animal is the puppet Basil Brush?

A: Fox
B: Tiger
C: Rabbit
D: Wolf

169

Which animal is most likely to feed from a nosebag?

A: Dog
B: Sheep
C: Rabbit
D: Horse

170

Rosie Lee is slang for what?

A: Tea
B: Bee
C: Pea
D: Fee

50:50 Go to page 445  Go to page 469 ? Answers on page 492

2 ◆ £200

171

Which of these is an emergency vehicle that takes people to hospital?

A: Tank
B: Moped
C: Ambulance
D: Hovercraft

172

What is the traditional colour of denim?

A: Pink
B: Blue
C: Yellow
D: Beige

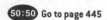

50:50 Go to page 445
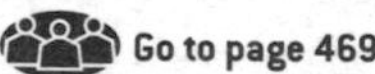
Go to page 469

Answers on page 492

50:50  

15 £1 MILLION
14 £500,000
13 £250,000
12 £125,000
11 £64,000
10 £32,000
9 £16,000
8 £8,000
7 £4,000
6 £2,000
5 £1,000
4 £500
3 ◆ £300
2 ◆ £200
1 ◆ £100

3 ◆ £300

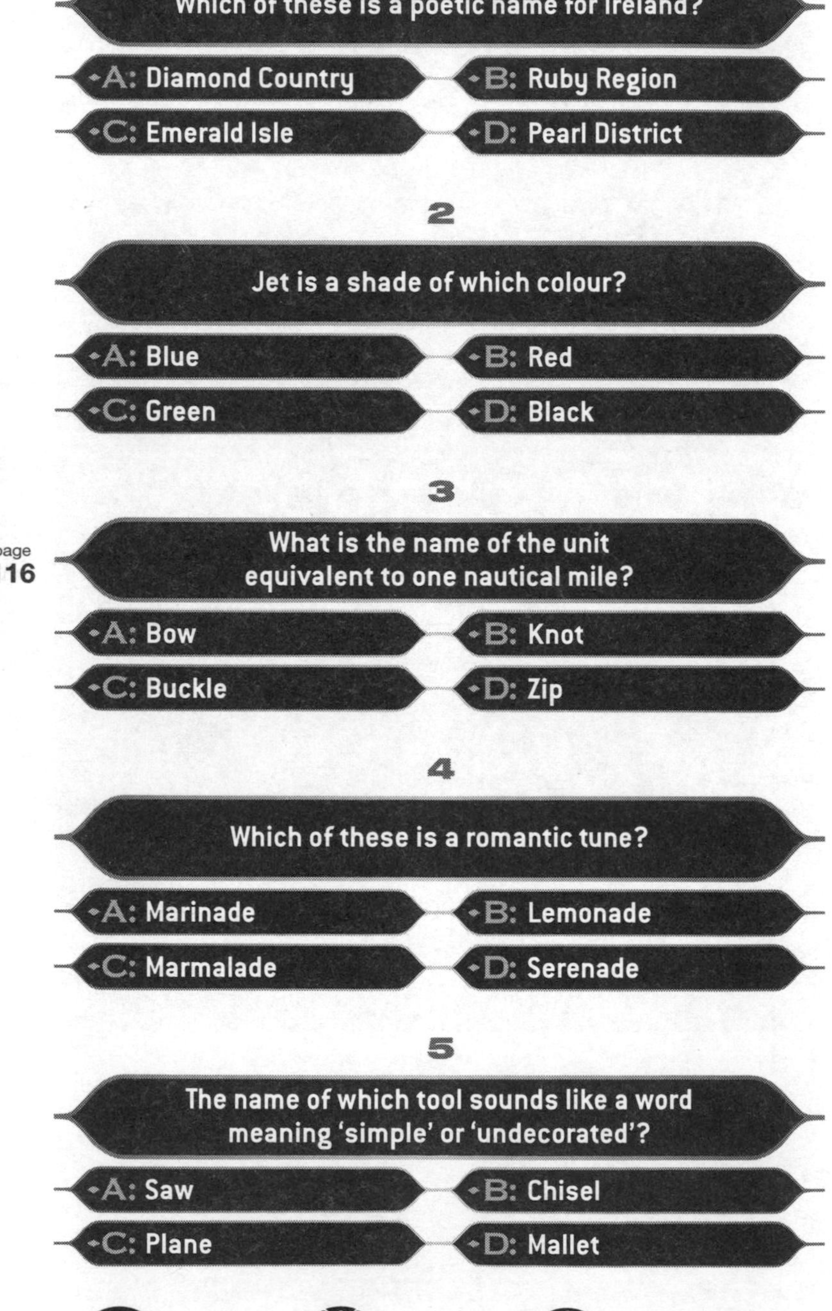

1
Which of these is a poetic name for Ireland?
A: Diamond Country
B: Ruby Region
C: Emerald Isle
D: Pearl District
2
Jet is a shade of which colour?
A: Blue
B: Red
C: Green
D: Black
3
What is the name of the unit equivalent to one nautical mile?
A: Bow
B: Knot
C: Buckle
D: Zip
4
Which of these is a romantic tune?
A: Marinade
B: Lemonade
C: Marmalade
D: Serenade
5
The name of which tool sounds like a word meaning 'simple' or 'undecorated'?
A: Saw
B: Chisel
C: Plane
D: Mallet

50:50 Go to page 447 Go to page 471 ? Answers on page 493

3 ◆ £300

6

Usually, what kind of vehicle is a 'ferry'?

- A: Aeroplane
- B: Car
- C: Bicycle
- D: Ship

7

What is the surname of American chat show hostess Oprah?

- A: Springer
- B: Winfrey
- C: Lake
- D: Letterman

8

Which of these is not an item of crockery?

- A: Cup
- B: Spoon
- C: Plate
- D: Saucer

9

Somebody forced to use their last and poorest resources is said to be scraping the bottom of the...?

- A: Bath
- B: Fridge
- C: Barrel
- D: Kettle

10

Which of these is the name of a famous pop group?

- A: H Heart 4
- B: T Spade 5
- C: P Diamond 6
- D: S Club 7

50:50 Go to page 447  Go to page 471 ? Answers on page 493

3 ◆ £300

11

The region known as Snowdonia is located in which country?

- A: England
- B: Scotland
- C: Wales
- D: Northern Ireland

12

Which of these is a term applied to a useless possession?

- A: Red hippopotamus
- B: Pink rhinoceros
- C: White elephant
- D: Blue giraffe

13

Which of these was a famous highwayman?

- A: Dick Turpin
- B: Dick Van Dyke
- C: Dick Francis
- D: Dick Emery

14

Who would typically wear leg warmers at work?

- A: Architects
- B: Barristers
- C: Cooks
- D: Dancers

15

What is the star sign of people born on the sixth of April?

- A: Aries
- B: Scorpio
- C: Leo
- D: Cancer

50:50 Go to page 447 | Go to page 471 | ? Answers on page 493

16

Donny Osmond had a hit single with which of these?

A: Pony Devotion
B: Puppy Love
C: Kitten Fancy
D: Cub Tenderness

17

Which of these features on a cricket pitch?

A: Fold
B: Crimp
C: Pleat
D: Crease

18

What was the popular name for Indian chief Ta-Sunko-Witko?

A: Mad Badger
B: Barking Dog
C: Crazy Horse
D: Nutty Squirrel

19

Which creatures are kept in an aviary?

A: Bees
B: Birds
C: Butterflies
D: Bears

20

With reference to pencil lead, what do the letters HB stand for?

A: Half board
B: Hard black
C: Hydrogen bomb
D: Head band

50:50 Go to page 447 Go to page 471 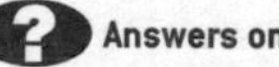 Answers on page 493

3 ◆ £300

21

A person of wealth or high social position may be referred to as a what?

A: Nab
B: Neb
C: Nib
D: Nob

22

The Afghani is the currency of which country?

A: Afghanistan
B: Albania
C: Algeria
D: Andorra

23

Which of these is a name given to a person from the country?

A: Yodel
B: Yokel
C: Yoghurt
D: Yoga

24

What type of organisation is Oxfam?

A: Bank
B: University
C: Bus company
D: Charity

25

Which of these is a well-known type of cheese?

A: Double Gloucester
B: Triple Gloucester
C: Quadruple Gloucester
D: Quintuple Gloucester

50:50 Go to page 447 Go to page 471 ? Answers on page 493

3 ◆ £300

26

What type of publication is 'The Beano'?

A: Newspaper
B: Comic
C: Magazine
D: Pamphlet

27

Which of these is a large forest in Gloucestershire?

A: Forest of Wayne
B: Forest of Carl
C: Forest of Jason
D: Forest of Dean

28

Who was the last King Henry to rule England?

A: Henry VI
B: Henry VII
C: Henry VIII
D: Henry IX

29

Which sea lies between Britain's eastern coast and mainland Europe?

A: North Sea
B: East Sea
C: South Sea
D: West Sea

30

Which part of a house might be 'thatched'?

A: Roof
B: Cellar
C: Door
D: Window

50:50 Go to page 447 Go to page 471 ? Answers on page 493

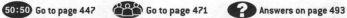

3 ◆ £300

31

With which type of shop is the name Sainsbury's most associated?

A: Department store
B: Travel agency
C: Supermarket
D: Building Society

32

Which of these breeds of dog is often used as sheepdog?

A: Greyhounds
B: Border collies
C: Chihuahuas
D: Dachshunds

33

Which of these alcoholic drinks is also a common girl's name?

A: Sherry
B: Whisky
C: Lager
D: Rum

34

Which colour squirrel is the most common in Britain?

A: Red
B: Yellow
C: White
D: Grey

35

Chequers is the country residence of which public figure?

A: US president
B: British prime minister
C: Russian president
D: Bill Gates

50:50 Go to page 447 Go to page 471 ? Answers on page 493

3 ◆ £300

36

Which ancient civilisation was ruled by the Pharaohs?

- A: Roman
- B: Japanese
- C: Carthaginian
- D: Egyptian

37

Which type of animals featured in the film 'Born Free'?

- A: Whales
- B: Lions
- C: Bears
- D: Llamas

38

The CIA is a law enforcement agency of which country?

- A: Russia
- B: Israel
- C: France
- D: United States

39

Which of these countries lies to the north of Germany?

- A: Denmark
- B: Italy
- C: Spain
- D: Turkey

40

What does the N stand for in the abbreviation NHS?

- A: National
- B: Neurological
- C: Natural
- D: Negative

50:50 Go to page 447 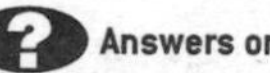 Go to page 471 Answers on page 493

3 ◆ £300

41

Which of these is a tall variety of flower?

A: Bearglove
B: Wolfglove
C: Foxglove
D: Lionglove

42

Cover point and silly mid-off are positions in which sport?

A: Basketball
B: Football
C: Golf
D: Cricket

43

What is the world's largest land mammal?

A: Camel
B: Rhino
C: Hippopotamus
D: Elephant

44

Which of these is a type of ice cream?

A: Cosmopolitan
B: Neapolitan
C: Metropolitan
D: Duopolitan

45

Which rock and roll performer was often referred to as 'The King'?

A: Jerry Lee Lewis
B: Buddy Holly
C: Richie Valens
D: Elvis Presley

50:50 Go to page 447 Go to page 471 ? Answers on page 493

3 ◆ £300

46

Geometry and algebra are part of which academic subject?

A: English literature
B: Sociology
C: Mathematics
D: History

47

The Star of David is a symbol sacred to which religion?

A: Buddhism
B: Judaism
C: Shinto
D: Hinduism

48

Which of these people would be most likely to wear a cassock and maniple?

A: Professional footballer
B: Mountaineer
C: Doctor
D: Clergyman

49

Who played Rick Blaine in the 1942 film 'Casablanca'?

A: Gary Cooper
B: Cary Grant
C: Humphrey Bogart
D: Clark Gable

50

Steve Ovett was a leading figure in which sport during the 1980s?

A: Football
B: Ice dancing
C: Tennis
D: Athletics

50:50 Go to page 447
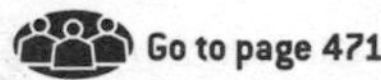
Go to page 471

Answers on page 493

3 ◆ £300

51

Which of these words describes a man who murders his wife?

A: Bluebottle
B: Blueblood
C: Bluebeard
D: Bluenose

52

Bison is another name for which North American animal?

A: Coyote
B: Skunk
C: Racoon
D: Buffalo

53

In the avoirdupois weighting system, what unit of weight is equal to 16 ounces?

A: Stone
B: Pound
C: Ton
D: Hundredweight

54

Kenny Rogers and Dolly Parton are associated with which type of music?

A: Trance
B: Techno
C: Country
D: Garage

55

What is the capital of The Netherlands?

A: Hamburg
B: Amsterdam
C: Vienna
D: Strasbourg

50:50 Go to page 447 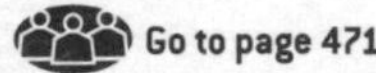  Go to page 471 ? Answers on page 493

3 ◆ £300

56

Which race is run annually at Aintree?

A: Boat Race
B: London Marathon
C: Milk Race
D: Grand National

57

Which work by Shakespeare is set in Scotland?

A: Othello
B: Macbeth
C: Hamlet
D: The Tempest

58

What did Yuri Gagarin do for the first time in 1961?

A: Land on the Moon
B: Orbit Mars
C: Travel in space
D: Orbit Jupiter

59

Rio de Janeiro is a city in which South American country?

A: Brazil
B: Argentina
C: Chile
D: Peru

60

Which Middle Eastern city is also the name of a type of artichoke?

A: Damascus
B: Baghdad
C: Jerusalem
D: Jericho

50:50 Go to page 447 · Go to page 471 · ? Answers on page 493

3 ◆ £300

61

Which English king was married six times?

A: Richard III
B: Henry VIII
C: Edward VI
D: George III

62

Which religious leader lives in the Vatican?

A: Dalai Lama
B: Archbishop of Canterbury
C: Pope
D: Aga Khan

63

The Mediterranean island of Sicily is part of which country?

A: Spain
B: Italy
C: France
D: Greece

64

What type of an animal is a 'tern'?

A: Horse
B: Sheep
C: Fish
D: Bird

65

What job in TV has been held by Peter Sissons and Sandy Gall?

A: Game show host
B: Sports commentator
C: Newsreader
D: Weatherman

50:50 Go to page 447 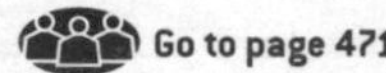 Go to page 471  Answers on page 493

3 ◆ £300

66

Who was the queen of Britain between 1837 and 1901?

A: Mary
B: Anne
C: Elizabeth
D: Victoria

67

The Bronx is an area in which US city?

A: Chicago
B: New York
C: Los Angeles
D: Miami

68

Who was Bob Hope's regular co-star in the popular 'Road to...' series of movies?

A: Jerry Lewis
B: Jimmy Durante
C: Bing Crosby
D: Jack Benny

69

The 'scullery' is usually part of which room in a house?

A: Toilet
B: Kitchen
C: Dining room
D: Bedroom

70

Vesuvius and Fuji are examples of which type of geographical feature?

A: River
B: Salt lake
C: Volcano
D: Forest

50:50 Go to page 447 Go to page 471 ? Answers on page 493

3 ◆ £300

71

What is the name of the white target ball in the game of bowls?

A: John
B: Jamie
C: Jack
D: Jim

72

Which one of these sets of fictional characters is not a group of three?

A: Billy-Goats Gruff
B: Little Pigs
C: Blind Mice
D: Dwarfs

73

Which phrase describes someone who is easily persuaded to lend money?

A: Soft option
B: Soft soap
C: Soft touch
D: Soft spot

74

If you travel by 'Shanks's pony', what is your form of transport?

A: Taxi
B: Bus
C: Carriage and Pair
D: On foot

75

Which phrase is an alternative way of referring to one's native language?

A: Parent parlance
B: Dad dialect
C: Mother tongue
D: Brother brogue

50:50 Go to page 447  Go to page 471 ? Answers on page 493

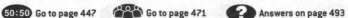

76

What is an alternative way of referring to a former girlfriend or boyfriend?

A: Old flame
B: Old fire
C: Old glow
D: Old ember

77

What is the name of the specific building where new coins are struck?

A: Thyme
B: Mint
C: Sage
D: Dill

78

Which phrase is used to mean 'with great gusto'?

A: Hammer and chisel
B: Hammer and sickle
C: Hammer and nails
D: Hammer and tongs

79

Which town, the largest seaside resort in northern England, is famous for its annual illuminations?

A: Morecambe
B: Blackpool
C: Southport
D: New Brighton

80

Which phrase means 'take all responsibility and accept the blame'?

A: Carry the pot
B: Carry the pan
C: Carry the tin
D: Carry the can

50:50 Go to page 447  Go to page 471 ? Answers on page 493

3 ◆ £300

81

What is the piece of adjustable furniture on which the player of a concert grand sits?

- A: Piano chair
- B: Piano bench
- C: Piano stool
- D: Piano pew

82

Who is the man-cub in 'The Jungle Book' stories?

- A: Kaa
- B: Mowgli
- C: Bagheera
- D: Baloo

83

Which surname is also the slang name for a potato?

- A: Pollitt
- B: Faulkner
- C: Murphy
- D: Gore

84

Which county do you associate with a savoury pudding made from batter?

- A: Yorkshire
- B: Lancashire
- C: Derbyshire
- D: Cheshire

85

What is the name for the celebratory meal after a wedding, whatever the time of day?

- A: Wedding breakfast
- B: Wedding lunch
- C: Wedding tea
- D: Wedding supper

50:50 Go to page 447  Go to page 471 ? Answers on page 493

3 ◆ £300

86

Which adjective is normally used to describe volcanoes that no longer erupt?

- A: Dead
- B: Deceased
- C: Extinct
- D: Quenched

87

What type of creepy-crawly is Incey Wincey of nursery rhyme fame?

- A: Worm
- B: Flea
- C: Spider
- D: Daddy-long-legs

88

What type of 'Old Shop' is the title of a Dickens novel?

- A: Antiquity
- B: Curiosity
- C: Novelty
- D: Mystery

89

What is twenty-to-five in the afternoon on the 24-hour clock?

- A: Fifteen-twenty
- B: Sixteen-forty
- C: Seventeen-twenty
- D: Eighteen-forty

90

In which room are you most likely to find a Welsh dresser?

- A: Bedroom
- B: Bathroom
- C: Sitting room
- D: Kitchen-diner

50:50 Go to page 447 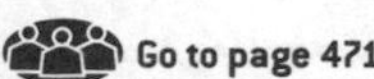 Go to page 471  Answers on page 493

3 ◆ £300

91

Which bird flies the most direct route according to the saying?

A: Crow | B: Raven
C: Jackdaw | D: Rook

92

Which of these fruits has a skin that's usually eaten?

A: Mandarin | B: Satsuma
C: Apple | D: Tangerine

93

Which brown tone is the usual colour of very old photographs?

A: Tan | B: Umber
C: Khaki | D: Sepia

94

Which piece of wood is proverbially a misfit in a round hole?

A: Triangular dowel | B: Square peg
C: Oval plug | D: Split pin

95

What does Alec Stewart use when playing his particular sport?

A: Hockey stick | B: Cricket bat
C: Tennis racquet | D: Baseball bat

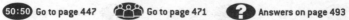

50:50 Go to page 447 Go to page 471

Answers on page 493

3 ◆ £300

96

Which of these is a shade of pink?

A: Shocking | B: Disgusting
C: Appalling | D: Horrifying

97

Cuba is in which sea?

A: South China | B: Mediterranean
C: Caspian | D: Caribbean

98

The name of which bathroom accessory also means vague talk?

A: Flannel | B: Toothbrush
C: Mirror | D: Bubble bath

99

In which country is the city of Dresden?

A: Switzerland | B: Germany
C: France | D: Italy

100

Which comic female character in a pantomime is usually played by a man?

A: Dame | B: Domestic
C: Dowager | D: Duchess

50:50 Go to page 447 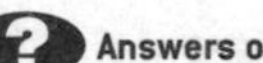 Go to page 471 ? Answers on page 493

3 ◆ £300

101

Which of these is a form of horse-racing?

- A: National Health
- B: National Gallery
- C: National Debt
- D: National Hunt

102

Something difficult to understand is said to be as clear as what?

- A: Glass
- B: Paint
- C: Mud
- D: Water

103

Which of these is a day in Lent?

- A: Mothering Sunday
- B: Fathering Monday
- C: Sistering Tuesday
- D: Brothering Wednesday

104

Someone who does not go to extremes is described as middle-of-the-what?

- A: River
- B: Root
- C: Room
- D: Road

105

Which of these is a popular London landmark?

- A: Drake's Pillar
- B: Raleigh's Post
- C: Nelson's Column
- D: Wellington's Shaft

50:50 Go to page 447 Go to page 471 ? Answers on page 493

3 ◆ £300

106

Which of these is an exaggerated or unbelievable report of an event?

A: Small story
B: High story
C: Low story
D: Tall story

107

Someone with no hair is said to be as bald as which bird?

A: Cormorant
B: Cockerel
C: Coot
D: Cuckoo

108

Which of these words can precede 'pie', 'loaf' and 'cheese' to make types of food?

A: House
B: Cottage
C: Castle
D: Palace

109

What is the name of the piece of metal where a horserider rests his foot?

A: Bit
B: Fetlock
C: Hoof
D: Stirrup

110

What does the 'E' in the everyday abbreviation 'SAE' stand for?

A: Envelope
B: Environment
C: Electricity
D: Engineers

50:50 Go to page 447 Go to page 471  Answers on page 493

111

What is the popular name for the costermongers of the East End of London?

- A: Topazy kings
- B: Emeraldy kings
- C: Pearly kings
- D: Amethysty kings

112

A pedicure is a treatment for which parts of the body?

- A: Hands
- B: Hair
- C: Shoulders
- D: Feet

113

When things go wrong, they are said to go the shape of which fruit?

- A: Pear
- B: Banana
- C: Pineapple
- D: Cherry

114

Which of these is a popular British magazine?

- A: Hello!
- B: Hallo!
- C: Hullo!
- D: Hollo!

115

Which of these is a group of more than two?

- A: Pair
- B: Trio
- C: Brace
- D: Duo

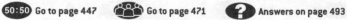

50:50 Go to page 447  Go to page 471 ? Answers on page 493

3 ◆ £300

116

What is the male equivalent of a mermaid?

A: Merlord
B: Merboy
C: Merman
D: Merjohn

117

Which of these is an island in the Pacific?

A: New Farthing
B: New Crown
C: New Groat
D: New Guinea

118

Which of these is a famous children's book by Arthur Ransome?

A: Buntings and Niles
B: Swallows and Amazons
C: Robins and Yangtzes
D: Bluetits and Volgas

119

Which of these words describes someone whose feet turn inwards?

A: Penguin-toed
B: Puffin-toed
C: Peewit-toed
D: Pigeon-toed

120

Eskimos are most associated with which region of the world?

A: Arctic
B: Tropics
C: Polynesia
D: Rainforest

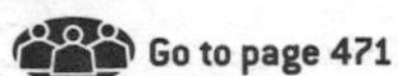 50:50 Go to page 447  Go to page 471 ? Answers on page 493

3 ◆ £300

121

Which of these phrases refers to someone who is no longer popular or successful?

A: Has-done
B: Has-been
C: Has-lost
D: Has-gone

122

Which of these fruits has a core?

A: Cherry
B: Strawberry
C: Apple
D: Melon

123

What were the three traditional divisions of Yorkshire?

A: Boxings
B: Swimmings
C: Runnings
D: Ridings

124

Which political scandal brought down Richard Nixon?

A: Watergate
B: Milkgate
C: Winegate
D: Beergate

125

With which of these countries is vodka most associated?

A: France
B: Netherlands
C: Russia
D: Scotland

50:50 Go to page 447 Go to page 471  Answers on page 493

3 ◆ £300

126

What is the name for the storage section in a car's dashboard?

- A: Glove compartment
- B: Hat department
- C: Sock impartment
- D: Boot apartment

127

Someone from a wealthy family is said to be born with what in their mouth?

- A: Silver sword
- B: Silverside
- C: Silver spoon
- D: Silversmith

128

Which of these was a contagious viral disease?

- A: Smallpox
- B: Fatpox
- C: Largepox
- D: Thinpox

129

Where is the Canary Wharf development?

- A: Isle of Man
- B: Isle of Wight
- C: Isle of Skye
- D: Isle of Dogs

130

A pirate flag depicts a skull and what else?

- A: Cutlasses
- B: Anchors
- C: Bones
- D: Planks

50:50 Go to page 447 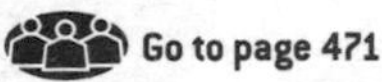 Go to page 471  Answers on page 493

131

Which of these is a type of trousers popular in the 1920s?

A: Oxford bags
B: Cambridge sacks
C: Durham satchels
D: St. Andrews suitcases

132

Terraced and semi-detached are types of what?

A: Piano
B: House
C: Loaf
D: Canoe

133

What kind of tape is associated with excessive bureaucracy?

A: Masking tape
B: Sticky tape
C: Red tape
D: Ticker tape

134

Which word specifically means 'to run away to get married'?

A: Elope
B: Abscond
C: Decamp
D: Vamoose

135

Which of these words does not mean 'miser'?

A: Skinflint
B: Trendsetter
C: Tightwad
D: Cheapskate

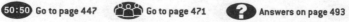

50:50 Go to page 447
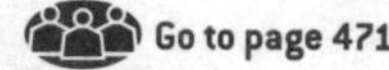
Go to page 471

Answers on page 493

3 ◆ £300

136

Which English king was known as 'the Great'?

A: Harold
B: John
C: Canute
D: Alfred

137

Easter Day always falls in one of which two months?

A: January and February
B: March and April
C: May and June
D: July and August

138

Which organisation was the setting for the best-seller 'Bravo Two Zero'?

A: SAS
B: Salvation Army
C: RSPCA
D: Metropolitan Police

139

'Sassenach' is a Scottish word for what?

A: Porridge
B: Englishman
C: Mountain
D: Pine tree

140

Which TV sitcom features the Walmington-on-Sea branch of the Home Guard?

A: Are You Being Served?
B: Fawlty Towers
C: Dad's Army
D: Only Fools and Horses

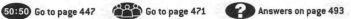

50:50 Go to page 447 Go to page 471

Answers on page 493

3 ◆ £300

141

What is meant by the mathematical sign written as a horizontal line with a dot above and below?

A: Add
B: Subtract
C: Multiply
D: Divide

142

Which of these was a Roman emperor?

A: Hero
B: Nero
C: Vero
D: Zero

143

What is the male equivalent of a nun?

A: Monk
B: Abbey
C: Vesper
D: Compline

144

Complete the title of this song from 'The Sound of Music': 'Climb Every...'?

A: Ladder
B: Mountain
C: Stairway
D: Wall

145

Which pantomime character has a magic lamp?

A: Dick Whittington
B: Mother Goose
C: Aladdin
D: Cinderella

50:50 Go to page 447 Go to page 471 ? Answers on page 493

3 ◆ £300

146

What is the name of the headdress traditionally worn by nuns?

A: Dimple
B: Pimple
C: Simple
D: Wimple

147

Barbara Cartland is best-known for what type of writing?

A: Science fiction
B: Romance
C: Detective
D: Espionage

148

What name is given to the outer markings on a tennis court?

A: Railway lines
B: Tramlines
C: Washing lines
D: Headlines

149

Which of these are Canadian policemen?

A: Mounties
B: Counties
C: Founties
D: Bounties

150

What is done to stop pipes bursting in the winter?

A: Logging
B: Legging
C: Lugging
D: Lagging

50:50 Go to page 447  Go to page 471 ? Answers on page 493

3 ◆ £300

151

What is the name for the writing point of a pen?

A: Rib | B: Bib
C: Nib | D: Fib

152

In which sport is a bunker a frequent hazard?

A: Golf | B: Water polo
C: Ice hockey | D: Curling

153

What name is given to an unauthorised copy of a CD or tape?

A: Dogleg | B: Backleg
C: Pegleg | D: Bootleg

154

Which of these is a dish of minced meat topped with potatoes?

A: Shepherd's pie | B: Ploughman's pasty
C: Swineherd's tartlet | D: Milkmaid's quiche

155

What is the name of the frilly decorative papers put on plates at tea parties?

A: Moilies | B: Doilies
C: Toilies | D: Voilies

50:50 Go to page 447 Go to page 471 ? Answers on page 493

3 ◆ £300

156

Which of these men ruled England?

A: William of Orange
B: James of Pink
C: Charles of Green
D: Edward of Yellow

157

Complete the title of the Marilyn Monroe film: 'The Seven-Year...'?

A: Scratch
B: Itch
C: Rash
D: Scab

158

Which of these is the name of a bird?

A: Paragraph
B: Paragon
C: Paraguay
D: Parakeet

159

What are you said to pull over someone's eyes if you deceive them?

A: The wool
B: The hat
C: The blanket
D: The glasses

160

Traditionally, what does a bride wear round her leg?

A: Veil
B: Wedding ring
C: Garter
D: Bouquet

50:50 Go to page 447  Go to page 471 ? Answers on page 493

161

Which of these is the name of a famous pop group?

A: Shallow Pink | B: Deep Purple
C: Light Green | D: Dark Brown

162

The nickname for a happily married elderly couple is 'Darby and...' who?

A: Julie | B: Jodie
C: Jacqueline | D: Joan

163

Which distance did Roger Bannister run in under four minutes on 6th May 1954?

A: 1500 metres | B: 1 mile
C: 10,000 metres | D: 3,000 metres

164

Which of these is a name for a cheap ornament or trinket?

A: Tick-tack | B: Pick-pack
C: Flick-flack | D: Knick-knack

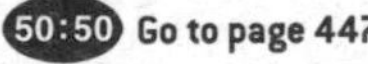 Go to page 447 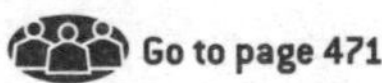 Go to page 471  Answers on page 493

50:50  

15	£1 MILLION
14	£500,000
13	£250,000
12	£125,000
11	£64,000
10	£32,000
9	£16,000
8	£8,000
7	£4,000
6	£2,000
5	£1,000
4 ◆	£500
3 ◆	£300
2 ◆	£200
1 ◆	£100

4 ◆ £500

1

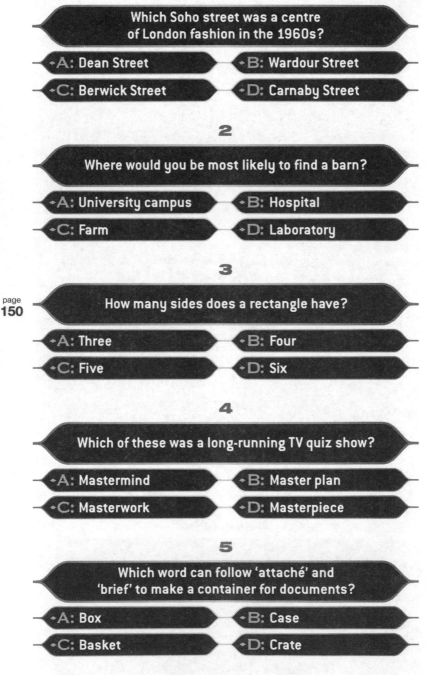

Which Soho street was a centre of London fashion in the 1960s?

A: Dean Street
B: Wardour Street
C: Berwick Street
D: Carnaby Street

2

Where would you be most likely to find a barn?

A: University campus
B: Hospital
C: Farm
D: Laboratory

3

How many sides does a rectangle have?

A: Three
B: Four
C: Five
D: Six

4

Which of these was a long-running TV quiz show?

A: Mastermind
B: Master plan
C: Masterwork
D: Masterpiece

5

Which word can follow 'attaché' and 'brief' to make a container for documents?

A: Box
B: Case
C: Basket
D: Crate

50:50 Go to page 449

Go to page 473
? Answers on page 494

4 ◆ £500

6

Which professional is most likely to be referred to as a 'medic'?

A: Lawyer
B: Policeman
C: Doctor
D: Clergyman

7

According to the Tom Jones song, what colour was the 'Grass of Home'?

A: Green
B: Blue
C: White
D: Red

8

Which of these is a traditional Asian sailing vessel?

A: Garbage
B: Junk
C: Scrap
D: Trash

9

An ingot is an oblong block of what?

A: Cheese
B: Wood
C: Metal
D: Lard

10

Someone lively and cheerful can be said to be 'full of the joys of...' what?

A: Spring
B: Summer
C: Autumn
D: Winter

50:50 Go to page 449 Go to page 473 ? Answers on page 494

4 ◆ £500

11

Which of these words is particularly associated with Sherlock Holmes?

A: Straightforward | B: Elementary

C: Simple | D: Uncomplicated

12

The letters OTT are an informal abbreviation for what?

A: On the town | B: Older than time

C: Off the table | D: Over the top

13

In rhyming slang, who or what is a 'tea leaf'?

A: Wreath | B: Piece of beef

C: Thief | D: Heath

14

Which precious stones 'are forever'?

A: Rubies | B: Emeralds

C: Sapphires | D: Diamonds

15

Which of these scientists had the first name Isaac?

A: Einstein | B: Newton

C: Faraday | D: Pascal

50:50 Go to page 449 Go to page 473

Answers on page 494

4 ◆ £500

16

How many days are there in October?

A: 28 B: 29

C: 30 D: 31

17

Which geographical feature can be dormant or active?

A: Cave B: Volcano

C: Desert D: Lake

18

Which of these names is associated with holiday camps?

A: Boot B: Burton

C: Butlin D: Budgen

19

Which of these football teams is based in London?

A: Arsenal B: Everton

C: Aston Villa D: West Bromwich Albion

20

Which of these rooms is associated with dancing?

A: Kitchen B: Ballroom

C: Lounge D: Bedroom

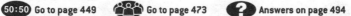

50:50 Go to page 449  Go to page 473 ? Answers on page 494

4 ◆ £500

21

What is the name of the United Kingdom's central bank?

- A: Bank of England
- B: Bank of Ireland
- C: Bank of Scotland
- D: Bank of Wales

22

Which of these are famous Botanic Gardens in London?

- A: Jay Gardens
- B: Exe Gardens
- C: Kew Gardens
- D: Dee Gardens

23

Barristers and solicitors are collectively known as what?

- A: Lawyers
- B: Doctors
- C: Priests
- D: Clerks

24

Pizza is a dish which originated in which country?

- A: Greece
- B: Egypt
- C: Turkey
- D: Italy

25

What type of food is grown in an orchard?

- A: Beef
- B: Fruit
- C: Bread
- D: Rice

50:50 Go to page 449 Go to page 473 ? Answers on page 494

4 ◆ £500

26

The United States of America has a border with which of these countries?

A: Brazil
B: Ecuador
C: Mexico
D: Chile

27

Sweden is considered part of which European peninsula?

A: Balkan
B: Iberian
C: Italian
D: Scandinavian

28

Which fictional detective lived at 221b Baker Street?

A: Miss Marple
B: Hercule Poirot
C: Sherlock Holmes
D: Charlie Chan

29

In English folklore, Robin Hood and his merry men lived in which woodland area?

A: New Forest
B: Forest of Dean
C: Sherwood Forest
D: Forest of Arden

30

In which country is the city of Aberdeen?

A: England
B: Republic of Ireland
C: Scotland
D: Wales

50:50 Go to page 449  Go to page 473 ? Answers on page 494

4 ◆ £500

31

Graham Hill and his son Damon are past world champions in which sport?

A: Boxing
B: Motor racing
C: Sailing
D: Rowing

32

Ned Kelly was a notorious outlaw in which country?

A: England
B: America
C: Australia
D: South Africa

33

What is the capital of Northern Ireland?

A: Derry
B: Belfast
C: Cork
D: Dublin

34

Anfield is the traditional home of which English football club?

A: Manchester United
B: Liverpool
C: Leeds United
D: Arsenal

35

Mohandas K Gandhi played a major role in the fight for independence of which country?

A: India
B: Russia
C: America
D: Mexico

50:50 Go to page 449 · Go to page 473 · ? Answers on page 494

4 ◆ £500

36

Which animals did Hannibal famously lead over the Alps to fight against the Roman empire?

A: Sheep
B: Llamas
C: Gorillas
D: Elephants

37

Who was the celebrated ruler Tutankhamen?

A: Doge of Venice
B: Emperor of Rome
C: King of Spain
D: Pharaoh of Egypt

38

In English folklore, Dick Whittington was aided in his adventures by what type of animal?

A: Pig
B: Sheep
C: Horse
D: Cat

39

In the Bible, which character was created from Adam's rib?

A: Serpent
B: Cain
C: Abel
D: Eve

40

Who played the elderly Jedi Ben Kenobi in the 1977 film 'Star Wars'?

A: Ralph Richardson
B: Laurence Olivier
C: Alec Guinness
D: John Gielgud

50:50 Go to page 449
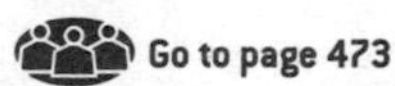
Go to page 473

Answers on page 494

4 ◆ £500

41

Who starred with Deborah Kerr in the 1956 film 'The King and I'?

- A: Yul Brynner
- B: Rex Harrison
- C: Howard Keel
- D: Ernest Borgnine

42

Which of these was a character in TV's 'The Magic Roundabout'?

- A: Dorothy
- B: Pauline
- C: Sylvia
- D: Florence

43

Which of these words describes a cautious and gentle attitude?

- A: So-so
- B: Softly-softly
- C: Bye-bye
- D: There-there

44

What is the British name for what Americans refer to as a 'drugstore'?

- A: Estate agent's
- B: Sweet shop
- C: Transport cafe
- D: Dispensing chemist's

45

What is the collective term for throwing and jumping sports in athletics?

- A: Trackside events
- B: Field events
- C: Off-track events
- D: Grass events

50:50 Go to page 449  Go to page 473 ? Answers on page 494

4 ◆ £500

46

Which phrase means 'split equally between two'?

A: Twenty-twenty
B: Thirty-thirty
C: Forty-forty
D: Fifty-fifty

47

Which animal's name prefixes the words 'dog' and 'terrier' to give the names of two dog breeds?

A: Steer
B: Cow
C: Calf
D: Bull

48

Which French phrase translates as 'new cooking'?

A: A la carte
B: Haute coûture
C: Art nouveau
D: Nouvelle cuisine

49

Which person puts the ball into play in a game of tennis?

A: Bowler
B: Receiver
C: Pitcher
D: Server

50

What type of cream is traditionally served with a Devon cream tea?

A: Single cream
B: Double cream
C: Whipped cream
D: Clotted cream

50:50 Go to page 449 Go to page 473 ? Answers on page 494

4 ◆ £500

51

Lot's wife turned to look back at Sodom and was instantly turned into what?

A: Pillar of stone
B: Pillar of salt
C: Pillar of smoke
D: Pillar of the community

52

Complete the title of the film which starred Robin Williams as a Forces DJ: 'Good Morning...'?

A: Thailand
B: Korea
C: Vietnam
D: Cambodia

53

What type of musical instrument is sometimes called an 'upright'?

A: Harp
B: Double bass
C: Clarinet
D: Piano

54

Which abbreviation often appears after the name of a business to give its full trading title?

A: DLT
B: TLC
C: BLT
D: PLC

55

Complete the title of this film: 'Kind Hearts and...'?

A: Tiaras
B: Coronets
C: Periwigs
D: Bowlers

50:50 Go to page 449 Go to page 473  Answers on page 494

4 ◆ £500

56

In a bird's body, which organ grinds food?

A: Lizard
B: Blizzard
C: Wizard
D: Gizzard

57

What type of 'wizard' did the Who sing about?

A: Bridge
B: Pinball
C: Dominoes
D: Shove ha'penny

58

Which of these is a type of soldier?

A: Debonnaire
B: Legionnaire
C: Questionaire
D: Millionaire

59

Which creatures of folklore are said to be afraid of crucifixes and garlic?

A: Werewolves
B: Changelings
C: Witches
D: Vampires

60

Will Carling captained England in which sport?

A: Rugby league
B: Cricket
C: Rugby union
D: Football

50:50 Go to page 449

Go to page 473

? Answers on page 494

4 ◆ £500

61

Which of these is a term for a sailor?

A: Bar
B: Car
C: Mar
D: Tar

62

Which of these is another name for a bookmaker?

A: Turf accountant
B: Grass banker
C: Lawn ombudsman
D: Straw auditor

63

Who traditionally wear their hair in dreadlocks?

A: Quakers
B: Rastafarians
C: Jehovah's Witnesses
D: Mormons

64

Which of these phrases refers to a deceitful person?

A: Snake-in-the-pond
B: Snake-in-the-sand
C: Snake-in-the-grass
D: Snake-in-the-sink

65

A mangle was once used in which domestic chore?

A: Painting
B: Sweeping
C: Dusting
D: Washing

50:50 Go to page 449 Go to page 473 ? Answers on page 494

4 ◆ £500

66

Proverbially, where do you take coals to?

A: Newcastle
B: Swansea
C: Barnsley
D: Dumbarton

67

Which of these is a name for a collection of writings?

A: Anthropology
B: Anthology
C: Archaeology
D: Apology

68

Which of these is a sparkling wine?

A: Asti
B: Pasta
C: Rosti
D: Paella

69

Complete the title of the John Osborne play: 'Look Back in...'?

A: A Mist
B: Tears
C: Anger
D: Hope

70

What name is given to a hasty wedding, taking place under duress?

A: Hotshot
B: Shotgun
C: Potshot
D: Shotput

50:50 Go to page 449  Go to page 473 ? Answers on page 494

71

By what name is an aircraft's flight recorder also known?

A: Black box
B: Black bag
C: Black board
D: Black bit

72

Which of these is a famous London market?

A: Pinafore Lane
B: Petticoat Lane
C: Pantaloon Lane
D: Pantihose Lane

73

What is the name of the famous spy created by John le Carré?

A: Happy
B: Grumpy
C: Smiley
D: Doc

74

When used with the name of a clergyman, what does the abbreviation 'Rev' mean?

A: Reverend
B: Revealing
C: Revenge
D: Reverse

75

What is the name of the newspaper article written on the death of a notable person?

A: Oblatory
B: Obversity
C: Obscurity
D: Obituary

50:50 Go to page 449 Go to page 473  Answers on page 494

4 ◆ £500

76

Who would be most likely to use greasepaint?

A: Chef
B: Jockey
C: Actor
D: Carpenter

77

How is the English letter 'z' pronounced in North America?

A: Zoo
B: Zad
C: Zee
D: Zay

78

Which word is the full version of the abbreviation 'Mason'?

A: Freemason
B: Oldmason
C: Longmason
D: Roundmason

79

What is the name for bread dipped in beaten egg and then fried?

A: Swedish sandwich
B: Austrian slice
C: French toast
D: Maltese loaf

80

Something socially unacceptable is said to be beyond what?

A: The white
B: The pale
C: The faded
D: The pastel

50:50 Go to page 449 Go to page 473 ? Answers on page 494

4 ◆ £500

81

Which of these is a small hat?

A: Cardboard box
B: Pillar box
C: Brainbox
D: Pillbox

82

Who would facetiously be called a 'luvvie'?

A: Barrister
B: Vet
C: Actor
D: Interior designer

83

Which of these abbreviations refers to an American soldier?

A: GI
B: ID
C: DA
D: AD

84

Which of these refers to the CID of the Metropolitan Police?

A: New England Place
B: New Scotland Yard
C: New Wales Street
D: New Ireland Mews

85

What name is given to a golf course by the sea?

A: Links
B: Chains
C: Loops
D: Knots

50:50 Go to page 449  Go to page 473 ? Answers on page 494

4 ◆ £500

86

In the English language, which vowel usually follows the letter Q?

A: A
B: E
C: O
D: U

87

Which of these is a region of Russia?

A: Anatolia
B: Mesopotamia
C: Siberia
D: Patagonia

88

What is the name given to the dregs of coffee?

A: Grounds
B: Fields
C: Parks
D: Arenas

89

What family name is given to a Mafia boss?

A: Stepfather
B: Godfather
C: Grandfather
D: Father

90

Which paint shares its name with a disease of dogs?

A: Emulsion
B: Gloss
C: Distemper
D: Undercoat

50:50 Go to page 449 Go to page 473 ? Answers on page 494

4 ◆ £500

91

Which word means both 'cut' and 'bargain'?

A: Slip
B: Snip
C: Skip
D: Strip

92

Who go on trial at a court martial?

A: Clergymen
B: Teachers
C: Servicemen
D: Lawyers

93

Which word can mean money and a country's main city?

A: Cash
B: Capital
C: Coinage
D: Currency

94

In a famous musical, who was told to 'Get Your Gun'?

A: Sallie
B: Jillie
C: Annie
D: Millie

95

Which group were known as 'flower people'?

A: Mods
B: Hippies
C: Teddy boys
D: Rockers

50:50 Go to page 449 Go to page 473 ? Answers on page 494

4 ◆ £500

96

In which sport are drop-goals scored?

A: Hockey
B: Basketball
C: Football
D: Rugby

97

Where does a person who plays truant refuse to go?

A: School
B: Church
C: Weddings
D: Dentist

98

Which of these is an international rugby union team?

A: Savages
B: Barbarians
C: Vandals
D: Ruffians

99

Which of these is a famous annual song contest?

A: Eurostar
B: Eurotrash
C: Europium
D: Eurovision

100

What is 'skinny-dipping'?

A: Bobbing for apples
B: Going on a diet
C: Swimming in the nude
D: Reading paperbacks

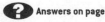

50:50 Go to page 449  Go to page 473 ? Answers on page 494

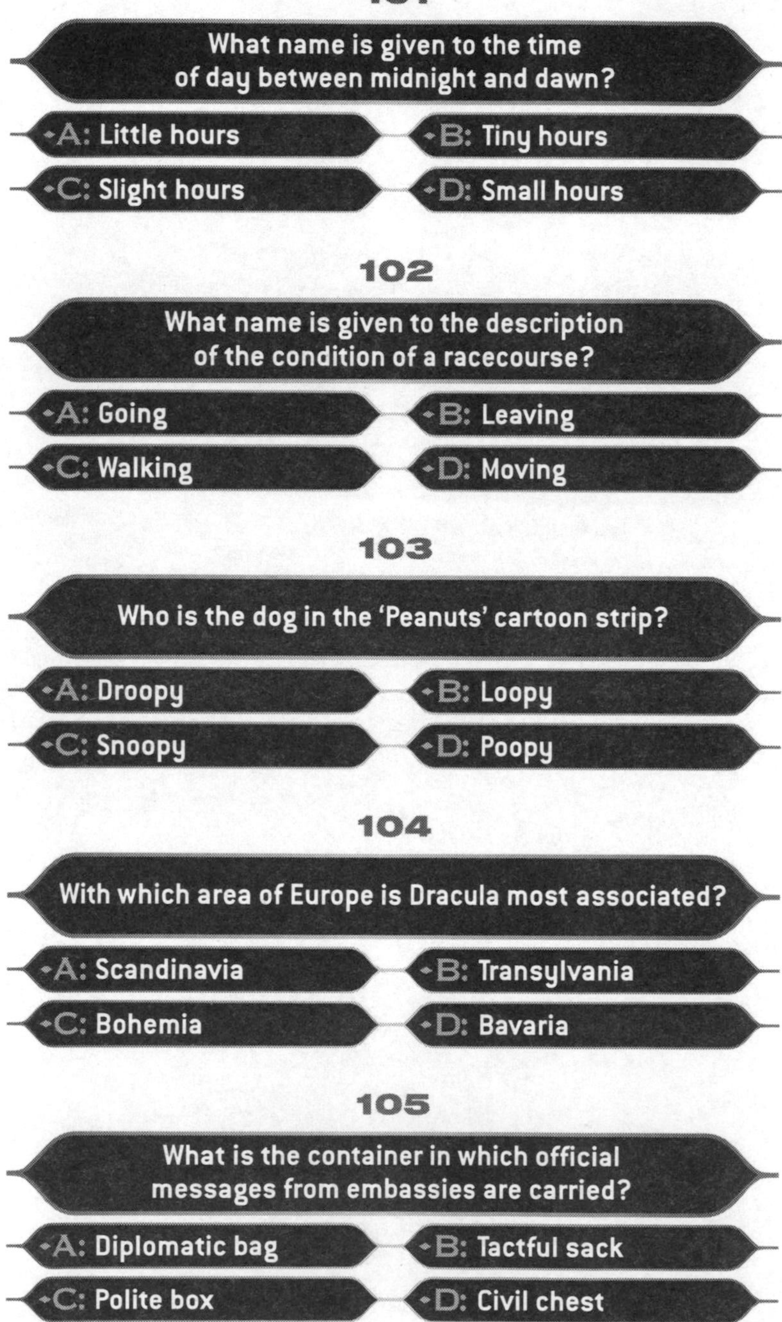

101

What name is given to the time of day between midnight and dawn?

A: Little hours
B: Tiny hours
C: Slight hours
D: Small hours

102

What name is given to the description of the condition of a racecourse?

A: Going
B: Leaving
C: Walking
D: Moving

103

Who is the dog in the 'Peanuts' cartoon strip?

A: Droopy
B: Loopy
C: Snoopy
D: Poopy

104

With which area of Europe is Dracula most associated?

A: Scandinavia
B: Transylvania
C: Bohemia
D: Bavaria

105

What is the container in which official messages from embassies are carried?

A: Diplomatic bag
B: Tactful sack
C: Polite box
D: Civil chest

50:50 Go to page 449 Go to page 473 ? Answers on page 494

4 ◆ £500

106

Which world leader has the first name Fidel?

A: Pinochet
B: Castro
C: Amin
D: Mandela

107

Which of these dishes is associated with Mexico?

A: Chicken chasseur
B: Smörgåsbord
C: Chilli con carne
D: Pizza

108

Traditionally, what is the last word of a Christian prayer?

A: Father
B: Amen
C: Heaven
D: Glory

109

Which of these is a way of describing a small amount of money?

A: Almonds
B: Pistachios
C: Cashews
D: Peanuts

110

Which of these words describes a bank account which is in the red?

A: Overawed
B: Overwrought
C: Overdrawn
D: Overrun

50:50 Go to page 449 Go to page 473 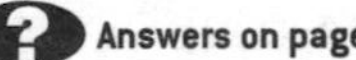 Answers on page 494

4 ◆ £500

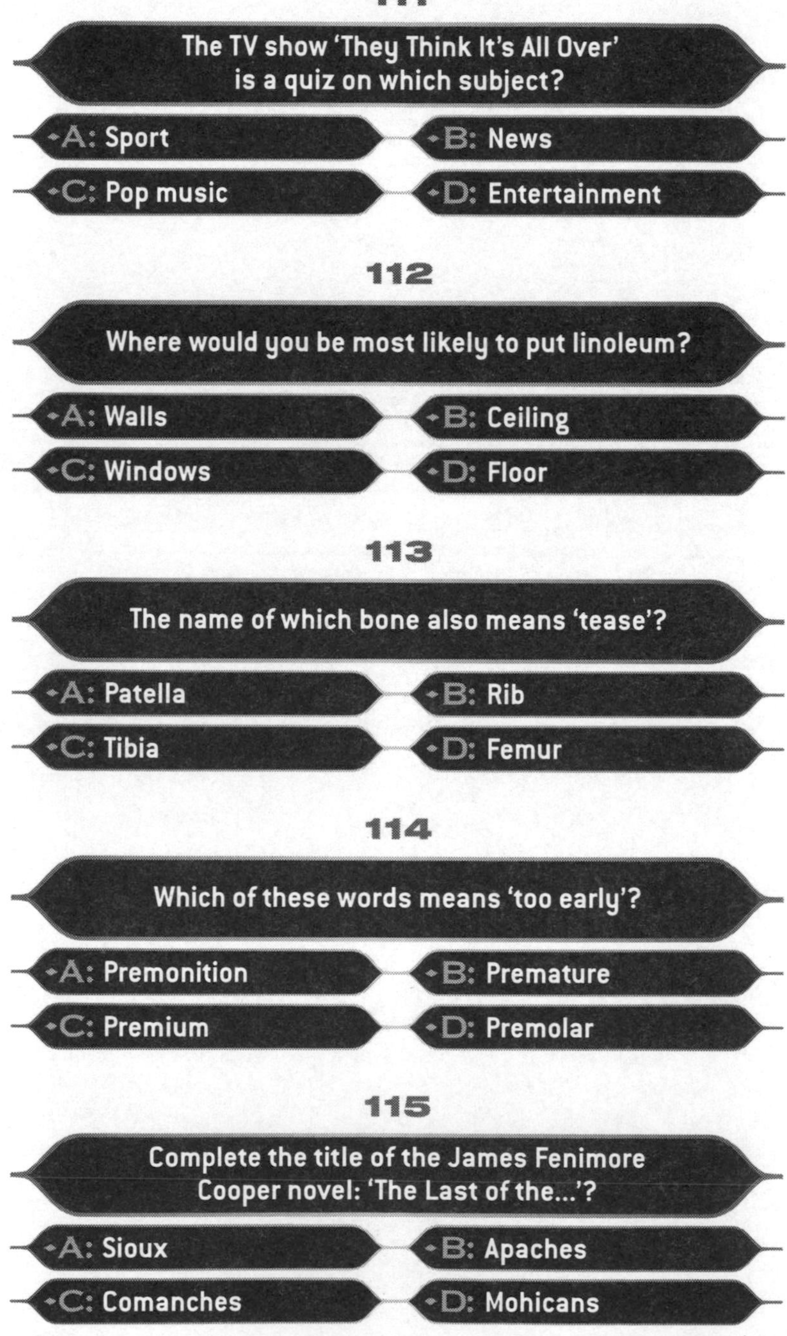

111

The TV show 'They Think It's All Over' is a quiz on which subject?

A: Sport
B: News
C: Pop music
D: Entertainment

112

Where would you be most likely to put linoleum?

A: Walls
B: Ceiling
C: Windows
D: Floor

113

The name of which bone also means 'tease'?

A: Patella
B: Rib
C: Tibia
D: Femur

114

Which of these words means 'too early'?

A: Premonition
B: Premature
C: Premium
D: Premolar

115

Complete the title of the James Fenimore Cooper novel: 'The Last of the...'?

A: Sioux
B: Apaches
C: Comanches
D: Mohicans

50:50 Go to page 449 Go to page 473 ? Answers on page 494

4 ◆ £500

116

Which area of London is famous for its annual spring flower show?

- A: Whitechapel
- B: Chelsea
- C: Tooting
- D: Neasden

117

What is the first name of the former Labour leader Mr Kinnock?

- A: James
- B: Harold
- C: Michael
- D: Neil

118

Where do you sign, when agreeing to a contract?

- A: Dotted line
- B: Blotted line
- C: Slotted line
- D: Potted line

119

If a person has to apologise, what is he said to eat?

- A: Meek bread
- B: Humble pie
- C: Shame tart
- D: Sorry cake

120

What was the first name of the actors Fairbanks Jnr and Fairbanks Snr?

- A: Andrew
- B: Barry
- C: Charles
- D: Douglas

50:50 Go to page 449 Go to page 473 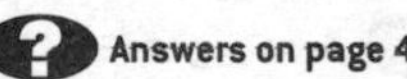 Answers on page 494

4 ◆ £500

121

Earthenware is a type of what?

- A: Pottery
- B: Silk
- C: Glass
- D: Rock

122

On which of these occasions is haggis traditionally eaten?

- A: August Bank Holiday
- B: Burns Night
- C: St. Patrick's Day
- D: Queen's Birthday

123

Which bird has a name which also means 'frolic'?

- A: Wren
- B: Robin
- C: Lark
- D: Plover

124

Which 'virtue' shares its name with a card game?

- A: Charity
- B: Prudence
- C: Hope
- D: Patience

125

What kind of bird is the peregrine?

- A: Owl
- B: Falcon
- C: Penguin
- D: Albatross

50:50 Go to page 449 · Go to page 473 · 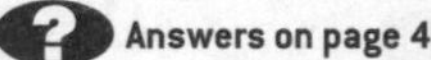Answers on page 494

4 ◆ £500

126

What is the name for the place where a river divides as it meets the sea?

A: Alpha
B: Beta
C: Gamma
D: Delta

127

The name of which type of sausage also means 'nonsense'?

A: Bratwurst
B: Boloney
C: Chorizo
D: Pepperoni

128

What is the name of the seats on the ground floor of a theatre?

A: Booths
B: Shops
C: Counters
D: Stalls

129

Which of these words means 'to answer evasively'?

A: Preview
B: Prevent
C: Prevaricate
D: Prevail

130

Which word can mean a sport and a garden activity?

A: Pruning
B: Fencing
C: Mowing
D: Digging

50:50 Go to page 449 Go to page 473

Answers on page 494

4 ◆ £500

131

In connection with food, what does the M in the abbreviation GM stand for?

- A: Mutilated
- B: Modernised
- C: Modified
- D: Miscellaneous

132

Which of these is a type of high-necked sweater?

- A: Snakeneck
- B: Toadneck
- C: Frogneck
- D: Turtleneck

133

Which word refers to food grown without the use of artificial fertilizers?

- A: Laconic
- B: Dramatic
- C: Organic
- D: Despotic

134

Which liquid is a major part of a hummingbird's diet?

- A: Milk
- B: Nectar
- C: Water
- D: Coffee

135

Which of these is the name of a spiny fish?

- A: Hickleback
- B: Tickleback
- C: Stickleback
- D: Prickleback

50:50 Go to page 449 · Go to page 473 · ? Answers on page 494

4 ◆ £500

136

What would you be trying to buy if someone 'gazumped' you?

- A: Car
- B: Shoes
- C: Washing machine
- D: House

137

What kind of 'arts' are karate and judo?

- A: Fine arts
- B: Culinary arts
- C: Martial arts
- D: Black arts

138

Which of these is the title of a high-ranking academic?

- A: Protector
- B: Professor
- C: Prospector
- D: Prosecutor

139

The traditional opening to the 23rd Psalm is 'The Lord is my...' what?

- A: Guardian
- B: Hope
- C: Shepherd
- D: Father

140

What name is given to someone who is treated in hospital but doesn't stay overnight?

- A: Offpatient
- B: Outpatient
- C: Otherpatient
- D: Omnipatient

50:50 Go to page 449 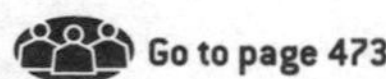 Go to page 473  Answers on page 494

4 ◆ £500

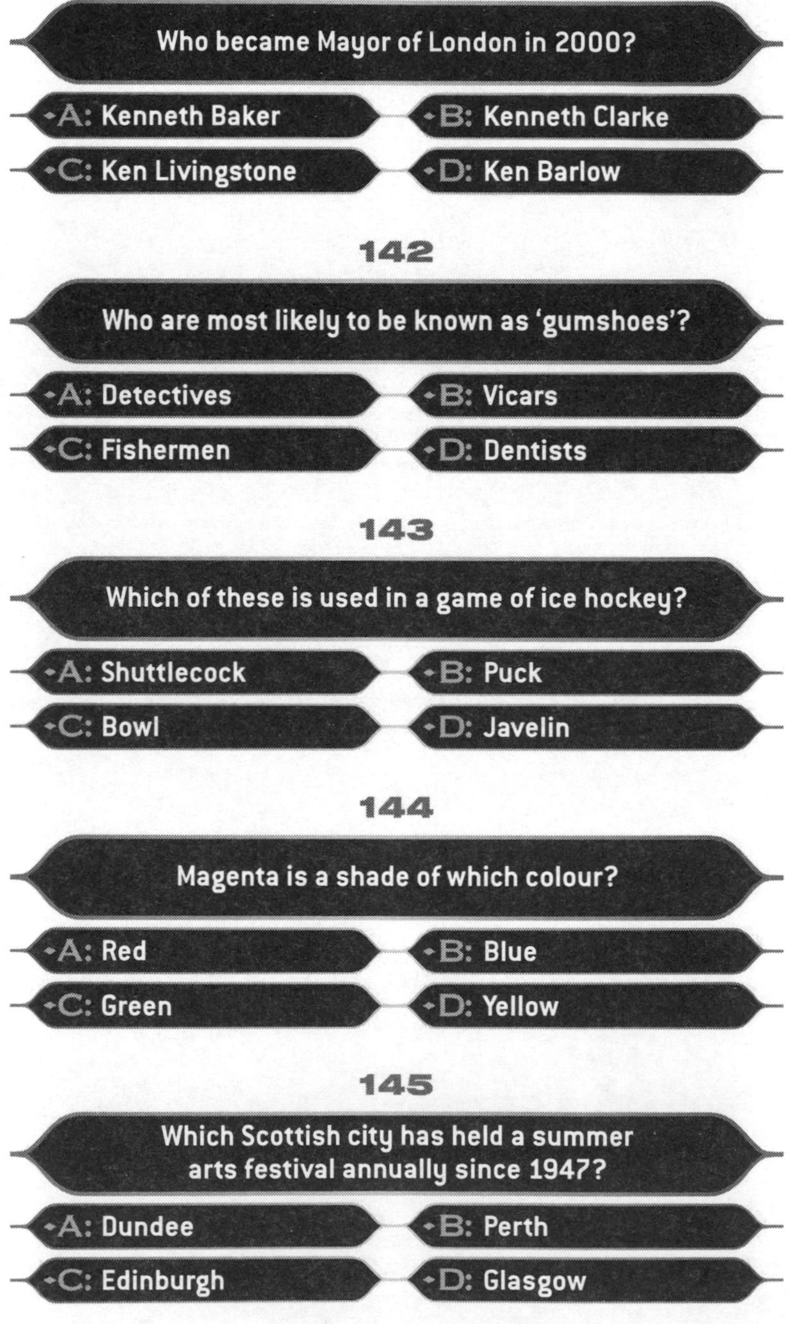

141

Who became Mayor of London in 2000?

A: Kenneth Baker
B: Kenneth Clarke
C: Ken Livingstone
D: Ken Barlow

142

Who are most likely to be known as 'gumshoes'?

A: Detectives
B: Vicars
C: Fishermen
D: Dentists

143

Which of these is used in a game of ice hockey?

A: Shuttlecock
B: Puck
C: Bowl
D: Javelin

144

Magenta is a shade of which colour?

A: Red
B: Blue
C: Green
D: Yellow

145

Which Scottish city has held a summer arts festival annually since 1947?

A: Dundee
B: Perth
C: Edinburgh
D: Glasgow

50:50 Go to page 449 Go to page 473 ? Answers on page 494

4 ◆ £500

146

Cantonese is a language chiefly spoken in which country?

- A: Japan
- B: China
- C: Venezuela
- D: Turkey

147

In the US, what name is given to someone who steals cattle?

- A: Tustler
- B: Bustler
- C: Hustler
- D: Rustler

148

What was the name of the sum of money brought by a woman on her marriage?

- A: Dowager
- B: Dowry
- C: Dowdy
- D: Downpour

149

Which of these is a popular Australian sport?

- A: Australian Rules
- B: Australian Laws
- C: Australian Orders
- D: Australian Regulations

150

What kind of animal are the Bactrian and the dromedary?

- A: Giraffe
- B: Camel
- C: Rat
- D: Goat

50:50 Go to page 449 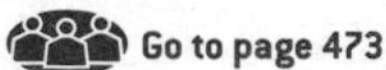 Go to page 473  Answers on page 494

4 ◆ £500

151

The word 'Norse' refers to which region of Europe?

A: French Riviera
B: Balkans
C: Southern Ireland
D: Scandinavia

152

Who would be most likely to use an identikit picture?

A: Doctor
B: Police officer
C: Zookeeper
D: Teacher

153

Which of Doctor Who's enemies frequently said 'Exterminate!'?

A: Daleks
B: Sea Devils
C: Cybermen
D: Ice Warriors

154

In the Bible, what was Gabriel?

A: Demon
B: Angel
C: King
D: Prophet

155

Geese fly in the formation of which letter?

A: S
B: O
C: T
D: V

50:50 Go to page 449 Go to page 473

Answers on page 494

4 ◆ £500

156

Serve and volley are techniques used in which sport?

A: Golf

B: Tennis

C: Cricket

D: Rugby

50:50 Go to page 449

Go to page 473

Answers on page 494

50:50

15 £1 MILLION
14 £500,000
13 £250,000
12 £125,000
11 £64,000
10 £32,000
9 £16,000
8 £8,000
7 £4,000
6 £2,000
5 ◆ £1,000
4 ◇ £500
3 ◇ £300
2 ◇ £200
1 ◇ £100

5 ◆ £1,000

1

A person who refrains from alcohol is said to be on the...?

A: Train
B: Wagon
C: Bus
D: Elephant

2

What is a bream?

A: Wild mushroom
B: Paper quantity
C: Freshwater fish
D: Musical instrument

3

With which city is Spaghetti Junction associated?

A: London
B: Birmingham
C: Manchester
D: Newcastle

4

Where would you be most likely to keep a pet cockatiel?

A: Hutch
B: Kennel
C: Aquarium
D: Cage

5

What kind of chair is made of canvas over a folding frame?

A: Rocking chair
B: Easy chair
C: Deck chair
D: Swivel chair

50:50 Go to page 451 Go to page 475 ? Answers on page 494

5 ◆ £1,000

6

Which of these women was a famous 19th-century cook?

- A: Mrs Mills
- B: Mrs Gaskell
- C: Mrs Beeton
- D: Mrs Siddons

7

Which animal often precedes the words 'derby', 'engine' and 'jacket'?

- A: Horse
- B: Elephant
- C: Cow
- D: Donkey

8

What was the first name of the Victorian prime minister Gladstone?

- A: Walter
- B: William
- C: Wilberforce
- D: Wilkins

9

In which country did the budgerigar originate?

- A: Australia
- B: Belgium
- C: Chad
- D: Denmark

10

Which of these was an open-air venue for chariot racing in ancient Rome?

- A: Velodrome
- B: Aerodrome
- C: Palindrome
- D: Hippodrome

50:50 Go to page 451 Go to page 475

Answers on page 494

5 ◆ £1,000

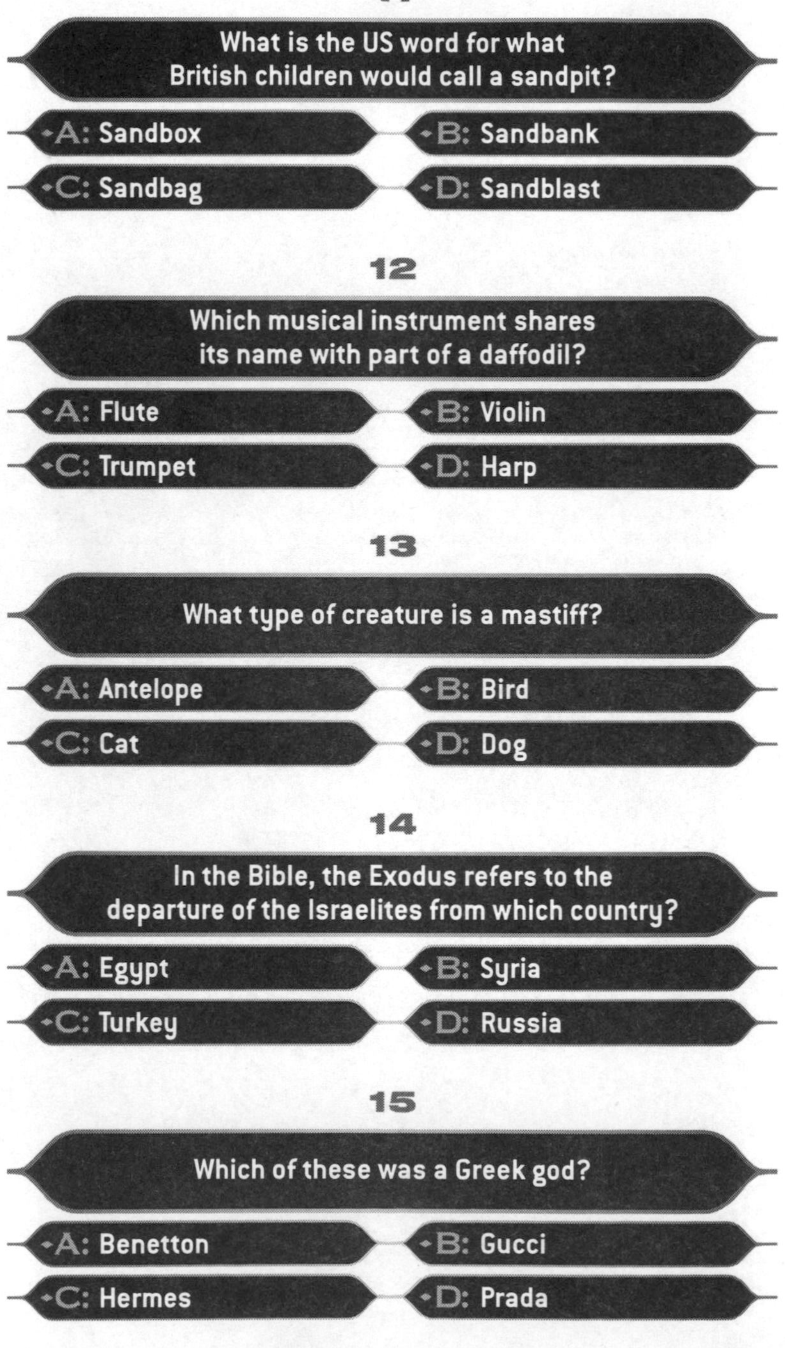

11

What is the US word for what British children would call a sandpit?

A: Sandbox
B: Sandbank
C: Sandbag
D: Sandblast

12

Which musical instrument shares its name with part of a daffodil?

A: Flute
B: Violin
C: Trumpet
D: Harp

13

What type of creature is a mastiff?

A: Antelope
B: Bird
C: Cat
D: Dog

14

In the Bible, the Exodus refers to the departure of the Israelites from which country?

A: Egypt
B: Syria
C: Turkey
D: Russia

15

Which of these was a Greek god?

A: Benetton
B: Gucci
C: Hermes
D: Prada

50:50 Go to page 451 Go to page 475 ? Answers on page 494

5 ◆ £1,000

16

Which London venue for classical music is home to the Proms?

A: Royal Albert Hall
B: Queen Elizabeth Hall
C: Wigmore Hall
D: Barbican Hall

17

What is a cove?

A: Large waterfall
B: Bare hill
C: Small bay
D: Open valley

18

'Hoi polloi' is a derogatory term for whom?

A: The masses
B: Royalty
C: Clergy
D: Soldiers

19

What type of creature is a guillemot?

A: Lizard
B: Bird
C: Whale
D: Beetle

20

Which of these is a famous poem by Tennyson?

A: The Duchess of Unyen
B: The Lord of Gerkin
C: The Duke of Pikkle
D: The Lady of Shalott

50:50 Go to page 451  Go to page 475 ? Answers on page 494

5 ◆ £1,000

21

'Navvies' were best known for building what?

- A: Houses
- B: Ships
- C: Canals
- D: Drains

22

Which British island group lies just off the coast of Normandy?

- A: Shetland Islands
- B: Channel Islands
- C: Orkney Islands
- D: Farne Islands

23

In which London building are the Crown Jewels kept?

- A: Buckingham Palace
- B: Houses of Parliament
- C: Westminster Abbey
- D: Tower of London

24

In which TV comedy drama did Ian McShane play a roguish antiques dealer?

- A: Boon
- B: Lovejoy
- C: Spender
- D: Fish

25

Rik Mayall and Adrian Edmondson starred in which anarchic comedy series in the 1980s?

- A: The Middle-Aged Ones
- B: The Old Ones
- C: The Young Ones
- D: The Ancient Ones

50:50 Go to page 451 | Go to page 475 | ? Answers on page 494

5 ◆ £1,000

26

The British dependency of Gibraltar is joined by land to which other European country?

A: France | B: Germany
C: Italy | D: Spain

27

Often eaten in soup, what are croutons traditionally made of?

A: Bread | B: Beef jerky
C: Boysenberries | D: Broccoli

28

The Royal Mews are part of which London building?

A: St. Paul's Cathedral | B: Lambeth Palace
C: Westminster Abbey | D: Buckingham Palace

29

Which of these ingredients would you traditionally find in a paella?

A: Pasta | B: Potato
C: Rice | D: Couscous

30

The island of Sardinia is part of which European country?

A: Greece | B: France
C: Spain | D: Italy

50:50 Go to page 451 | Go to page 475 | ? Answers on page 494

5 ◆ £1,000

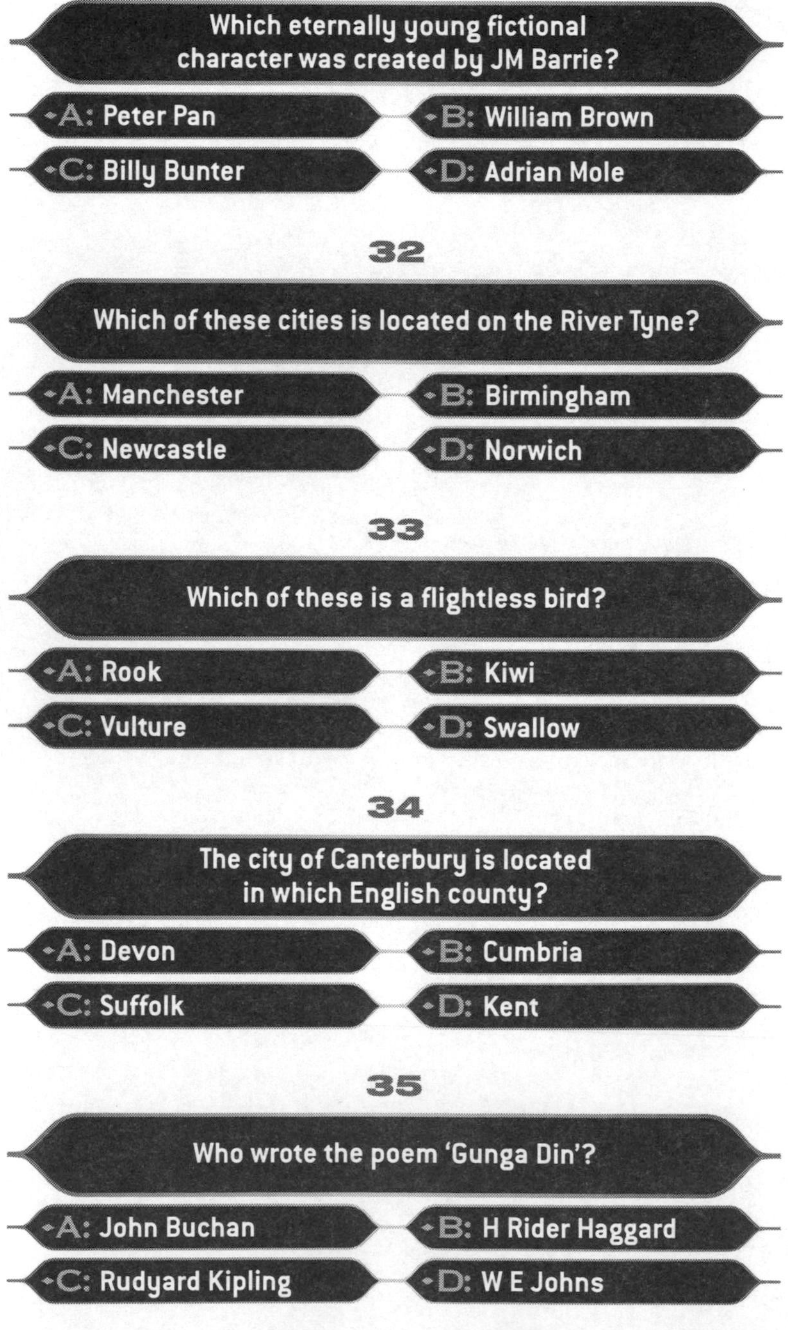

31

Which eternally young fictional character was created by JM Barrie?

A: Peter Pan
B: William Brown
C: Billy Bunter
D: Adrian Mole

32

Which of these cities is located on the River Tyne?

A: Manchester
B: Birmingham
C: Newcastle
D: Norwich

33

Which of these is a flightless bird?

A: Rook
B: Kiwi
C: Vulture
D: Swallow

34

The city of Canterbury is located in which English county?

A: Devon
B: Cumbria
C: Suffolk
D: Kent

35

Who wrote the poem 'Gunga Din'?

A: John Buchan
B: H Rider Haggard
C: Rudyard Kipling
D: W E Johns

50:50 Go to page 451 Go to page 475 ? Answers on page 494

5 ◆ £1,000

36

Which businessman bought both the 'News of the World' and the 'Sun' in the 1960s?

A: Robert Maxwell | B: Rupert Murdoch
C: Richard Branson | D: Alan Sugar

37

The Appalachian mountain range is on which continent?

A: Asia | B: Africa
C: Europe | D: North America

38

Who was known as the 'Demon Barber of Fleet Street'?

A: Dick Turpin | B: Sweeney Todd
C: Ronnie Biggs | D: Kim Philby

39

Which old British coin was typically made of gold?

A: Penny | B: Shilling
C: Farthing | D: Sovereign

40

Which English artist painted 'The Haywain'?

A: John Constable | B: Damien Hirst
C: Francis Bacon | D: Lucien Freud

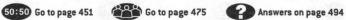

50:50 Go to page 451   Go to page 475

Answers on page 494

5 ◆ £1,000

41

Which mountain range covers much of the western states of the USA?

- A: Urals
- B: Atlas Mountains
- C: Balkans
- D: Rockies

42

Bill Beaumont was a famous name in which sport during the 1970s and 1980s?

- A: Boxing
- B: Rugby union
- C: Football
- D: Cricket

43

Who was the host of 'The Generation Game' on TV between 1971 and 1977?

- A: Larry Grayson
- B: Jim Davidson
- C: Bruce Forsyth
- D: Lenny Bennett

44

Who met his end at the Battle of the Little Bighorn?

- A: George Armstrong Custer
- B: Billy the Kid
- C: Wyatt Earp
- D: Judge Roy Bean

45

Who released the 1973 album 'Goodbye Yellow Brick Road'?

- A: Joe Cocker
- B: Steve Harley
- C: Elton John
- D: David Bowie

50:50 Go to page 451 Go to page 475

Answers on page 494

5 ◆ £1,000

46

What is the name of the national anthem of the United States of America?

A: Star-Spangled Banner
B: Stars and Bars
C: America (My Country 'Tis of Thee)
D: America the Beautiful

47

The world championships of which sport take place at the Crucible Theatre, Sheffield?

A: Bowls
B: Darts
C: Snooker
D: Pool

48

Which phrase connects a burn and an interrogation?

A: Third class
B: Third degree
C: Third estate
D: Third man

49

Which Swedish tennis player won the Wimbledon singles title in 1988 and 1990?

A: Mats Wilander
B: Bjorn Borg
C: Stefan Edberg
D: Anders Jarryd

50

In the British peerage, what is the title of the wife of a Marquess?

A: Marqueterie
B: Marchioness
C: Countess
D: Marquee

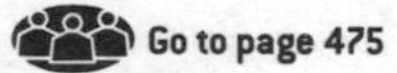
50:50 Go to page 451

Go to page 475
? Answers on page 494

5 ◆ £1,000

51

What is comedienne Dawn French's married surname?

A: Saunders
B: Edwards
C: Henry
D: Fry

52

What was the name of the 'Only Fools and Horses' character named after Roy Rogers' horse?

A: Champion
B: Trigger
C: Lucky
D: Mr Ed

53

Which two articles are traditionally carried by Father Time?

A: Hourglass and scythe
B: Sundial and scissors
C: Clock and sickle
D: Candle and sword

54

How is chef Jamie Oliver described in the title of his TV series?

A: Spicy
B: Tasty
C: Naked
D: Basic

55

Henna is a dye that gives hair a tinge of which colour?

A: Black
B: Blue
C: Blond
D: Red

50:50 Go to page 451 · Go to page 475 · ? Answers on page 494

5 ◆ £1,000

56

Which of these is a species of tree that grows in Britain?

A: Nickel birch | B: Copper beech
C: Bronze maple | D: Silver oak

57

The television soap ‘Brookside’ is set in which road?

A: Brookside Grove | B: Brookside Lane
C: Brookside Close | D: Brookside Avenue

58

How many fish represent the zodiac sign of Pisces?

A: One | B: Two
C: Three | D: Four

59

Which of these are clothes worn by soldiers?

A: Exhaustions | B: Tirednesses
C: Fatigues | D: Wearinesses

60

Who was the Grand Old Man of the Wombles of Wimbledon Common?

A: Great Uncle Romania | B: Great Uncle Estonia
C: Great Uncle Armenia | D: Great Uncle Bulgaria

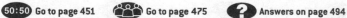

50:50 Go to page 451 · Go to page 475 · 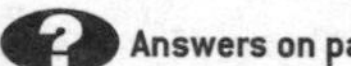Answers on page 494

5 ◆ £1,000

61

What are the names of the bowler-hatted characters in Hergé's Tintin stories?

- A: Thompson and Thomson
- B: Timpson and Timson
- C: Sampson and Samson
- D: Simpson and Simson

62

Which American film star became a European princess when she married in 1956?

- A: Katharine Hepburn
- B: Deborah Kerr
- C: Grace Kelly
- D: Jane Fonda

63

What is the name by which U2's David Evans is better known?

- A: The Rim
- B: The Edge
- C: The Limit
- D: The End

64

What kind of meat is 'scrag-end'?

- A: Mutton
- B: Pork
- C: Turkey
- D: Beef

65

Which is the correct spelling for the word that means 'the reason behind something happening'?

- A: C-O-R-E-S
- B: C-A-W-S
- C: C-A-U-S-E
- D: C-O-U-R-S-E

50:50 Go to page 451
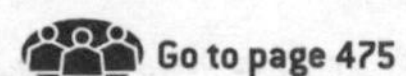
Go to page 475

Answers on page 494

5 ◆ £1,000

66

'Scrivener' is an old name for whom?

A: Vicar
B: Clerk
C: Schoolteacher
D: Pharmacist

67

Who became US president on the resignation of Richard Nixon in 1974?

A: Harry Truman
B: Ronald Reagan
C: Gerald Ford
D: Dwight Eisenhower

68

Which word can mean a barrel and an attack from a goat?

A: Butt
B: Cask
C: Keg
D: Vat

69

What is England's highest mountain?

A: Helvellyn
B: Scafell Pike
C: Snowdon
D: Ben Nevis

70

In which sport does a 'night watchman' play?

A: Baseball
B: Squash
C: Cricket
D: Athletics

50:50 Go to page 451 · Go to page 475 · ? Answers on page 494

5 ◆ £1,000

71

Which of these is a type of sun hat?

A: Pith helmet
B: Rind cap
C: Peel hat
D: Zest scarf

72

What is the main ingredient of piri-piri sauce?

A: Basil
B: Ginseng
C: Chilli
D: Quince

73

Which of these formed a government commission with 'mergers'?

A: Monopolies
B: Scrabbles
C: Cluedos
D: Backgammons

74

Which fictional character was warned away from Mr McGregor's garden?

A: Rupert Bear
B: Babar the Elephant
C: Peter Rabbit
D: Mr Toad

75

The organisation 'Ofsted' monitors standards of what?

A: Education
B: Editing
C: Edibility
D: Edwardiana

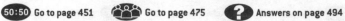

50:50 Go to page 451 Go to page 475  Answers on page 494

76

What is the German word for 'yes'?

A: Si
B: Da
C: Oui
D: Ja

77

Which sauce, eaten with pasta, is made from cream, bacon, cheese and eggs?

A: Carbonara
B: Arabbiata
C: Primavera
D: Americana

78

Lake Victoria is the largest lake of which continent?

A: South America
B: Africa
C: Europe
D: Asia

79

Which of these is flattering talk?

A: Blather
B: Babble
C: Blasphemy
D: Blarney

80

In which US state is Pasadena?

A: Nevada
B: Hawaii
C: California
D: Michigan

50:50 Go to page 451  Go to page 475 ? Answers on page 494

5 ◆ £1,000

81

By what name is Kris Kringle better known?

A: Robin Hood
B: Easter Bunny
C: King Arthur
D: Father Christmas

82

Which of these is a wreath of flowers?

A: Harlow
B: Monroe
C: Garland
D: Bacall

83

What is the more common name for the disease rubella?

A: French chickenpox
B: German measles
C: Italian mumps
D: Spanish whooping-cough

84

Which of these is a type of ball bowled in cricket?

A: Gurgly
B: Giggly
C: Googly
D: Goggly

85

Which process removes calcium and magnesium ions from water?

A: Softening
B: Weakening
C: Smoothing
D: Lessening

50:50 Go to page 451 Go to page 475

Answers on page 494

5 ◆ £1,000

86

Which of these handicrafts involves padding small pieces of fabric?

A: Tatting
B: Batik
C: Quilting
D: Carpentry

87

With which state did Slovakia once make up a country?

A: Czech Republic
B: Bulgaria
C: Croatia
D: Slovenia

88

With which football club is Sir Matt Busby most associated?

A: Arsenal
B: Tottenham Hotspur
C: Liverpool
D: Manchester United

89

What was the nickname of Vera Lynn in World War II?

A: Forces' Sweetheart
B: Navy's Darling
C: RAF's Beloved
D: Army's Sweetie

90

What is the name of the device used to measure spirits in a pub?

A: Optic
B: Aural
C: Nasal
D: Tactile

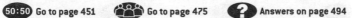

50:50 Go to page 451 Go to page 475
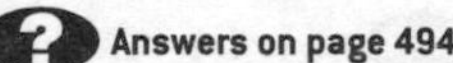
Answers on page 494

5 ◆ £1,000

91

Which film contains the line 'Here's looking at you, kid.'?

A: Casablanca
B: Gone With The Wind
C: Gaslight
D: National Velvet

92

Someone in financial control is said to hold what?

A: Pack lines
B: Bag ropes
C: Sack ties
D: Purse strings

93

Which of these is the name of both a city and a state?

A: New York
B: Las Vegas
C: Philadelphia
D: Richmond

94

What are you said to hit when you go to bed?

A: The road
B: The roof
C: The jackpot
D: The sack

95

What nationality is the jockey Frankie Dettori?

A: Italian
B: Scottish
C: Spanish
D: Irish

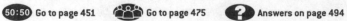

50:50 Go to page 451 Go to page 475

Answers on page 494

5 ◆ £1,000

96

Which spice adds a yellow colour to curries?

A: Turmeric
B: Coriander
C: Paprika
D: Cardamom

97

Which of these is one of the English Classic horseraces?

A: One Thousand Pounds
B: One Thousand Guineas
C: One Thousand Pennies
D: One Thousand Farthings

98

What name is given to the grounds and buildings of a university?

A: Square
B: Plot
C: Field
D: Campus

99

What is a 'jalopy'?

A: Old bed
B: Old car
C: Old horse
D: Old relation

100

The Vatican City State is surrounded by which city?

A: Rome
B: Paris
C: Madrid
D: Lisbon

50:50 Go to page 451  Go to page 475 ? Answers on page 494

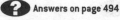

5 ◆ £1,000

101

Followers of which religion worship in a synagogue?

A: Islam
B: Sikhism
C: Judaism
D: Buddhism

102

Who did the original Peeping Tom peep at?

A: Boadicea
B: Lady Godiva
C: Florence Nightingale
D: Lady Hamilton

103

Which vegetable is often shot from small tubes by naughty children?

A: Potato
B: Parsnip
C: Pea
D: Pumpkin

104

What name was given to the Royalist supporters in the English Civil War?

A: Musketeers
B: Cavaliers
C: Cossacks
D: Dragoons

105

A person in an awkward situation is said to be up what kind of tree?

A: Banyan tree
B: Palm tree
C: Fig tree
D: Gum tree

50:50 Go to page 451
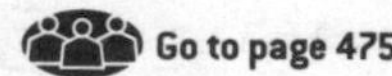
Go to page 475

Answers on page 494

5 ◆ £1,000

106

According to the proverb, what does the hand that rocks the cradle do?

A: Rules the world
B: Makes the tea
C: Sweeps the floor
D: Wakes the baby

107

Which actor said 'You ain't heard nothin' yet' in the film 'The Jazz Singer'?

A: Lionel Barrymore
B: Al Jolson
C: John Gilbert
D: Rudolf Valentino

108

In cookery, what is forcemeat used for?

A: Stuffing
B: Marinating
C: Deep-frying
D: Preserving

109

Which biblical character was swallowed by a great fish?

A: Noah
B: Cain
C: Moses
D: Jonah

110

Which of these might once have been worn on the head?

A: Periwig
B: Periscope
C: Periwinkle
D: Pericles

50:50 Go to page 451 · Go to page 475 ·  Answers on page 494

5 ◆ £1,000

111

Who wrote and sang 'Annie's Song'?

A: John Dallas
B: John Detroit
C: John Denver
D: John Duluth

112

Where are Bantu languages spoken?

A: Canada
B: Africa
C: Tasmania
D: India

113

A maggot is the larva of which insect?

A: Butterfly
B: Beetle
C: Fly
D: Wasp

114

Which of these was not a member of Abba?

A: Agnetha
B: Benny
C: Bjorn
D: Alyce

115

Which of these is an extension to the National Gallery?

A: Sainsbury Wing
B: Asda Wing
C: Waitrose Wing
D: Tesco Wing

50:50 Go to page 451 Go to page 475 ? Answers on page 494

5 ◆ £1,000

116

Who were the 'kamikaze' of World War II?

A: Secret agents
B: Foot soldiers
C: Policemen
D: Pilots

117

Which Mediterranean island gives its name to a type of women's trousers?

A: Gozo
B: Majorca
C: Capri
D: Crete

118

Karl is the first name of which of these fashion designers?

A: Galliano
B: Lacroix
C: Armani
D: Lagerfeld

119

Ibiza is one of which island group?

A: Canaries
B: Azores
C: Balearics
D: Seychelles

120

What is the occupation of Charlotte Bronte's Jane Eyre?

A: Courtesan
B: Governess
C: Actress
D: Poet

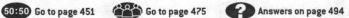

50:50 Go to page 451 Go to page 475  Answers on page 494

5 ◆ £1,000

121

Which London borough shares its name with a horse-drawn carriage?

A: Hillingdon
B: Haringey
C: Hounslow
D: Hackney

122

Which of these words does not mean 'shine'?

A: Glower
B: Glisten
C: Glimmer
D: Gleam

123

What does a campanologist do for a hobby?

A: Arrange flowers
B: Taste wine
C: Climb rocks
D: Ring bells

124

What was the first name of the novelist Defoe?

A: David
B: Daniel
C: Denzil
D: Digby

125

In Lewis Carroll's story, how does Alice get into Wonderland?

A: On a boat
B: Through a wardrobe
C: Down a rabbit hole
D: On a magic carpet

50:50 Go to page 451 Go to page 475 ? Answers on page 494

5 ◆ £1,000

126

Which of these phrases might describe an act of revenge?

A: Bit-for-bat
B: Tit-for-tat
C: Kit-for-kat
D: Spit-for-spat

127

What was the name of the worldwide computer virus released in May 2000?

A: Love Heart
B: Love Apple
C: Love Bug
D: Love Thy Neighbour

128

Wimbledon's All England Lawn Tennis Club is also a centre for which other sport?

A: Polo
B: Rugby league
C: Speedway
D: Croquet

129

In the famous science fiction novel, what are Triffids?

A: Androids
B: Plants
C: Sea monsters
D: Giant birds

130

Members of which pop group star in the film 'Honest'?

A: B*Witched
B: Boyzone
C: All Saints
D: Westlife

50:50 Go to page 451 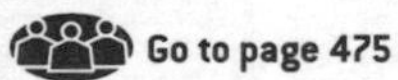 Go to page 475  Answers on page 494

5 ◆ £1,000

131

Which of these is a traditional pattern on porcelain?

A: Sycamore
B: Willow
C: Cedar
D: Pine

132

What name is given to the black mourning clothes worn by a widow?

A: Widow's trees
B: Widow's shrubs
C: Widow's flowers
D: Widow's weeds

133

In which country is the city of Cologne?

A: Netherlands
B: Belgium
C: Luxembourg
D: Germany

134

How many are there in a baker's dozen?

A: 11
B: 12
C: 13
D: 14

135

Which of these is a play by Noel Coward?

A: Influenza
B: Hay Fever
C: Whooping Cough
D: Scarlet Fever

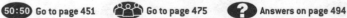

50:50 Go to page 451 Go to page 475 ? Answers on page 494

5 ◆ £1,000

136

Which of these continents is smallest in area?

- A: Asia
- B: Africa
- C: Europe
- D: North America

137

What was the first name of the polar explorer Amundsen?

- A: Roald
- B: Nils
- C: Lars
- D: Henrik

138

In Italy, what kind of food are 'amaretti'?

- A: Sorbets
- B: Biscuits
- C: Sandwiches
- D: Dips

139

Which actor played Ace Ventura on film?

- A: Billy Crystal
- B: Jim Carrey
- C: Bill Murray
- D: Chevy Chase

140

Which sea forms the north coast of Africa?

- A: Caribbean
- B: Red
- C: Mediterranean
- D: Black

50:50 Go to page 451

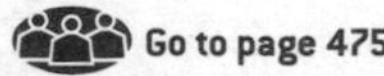

Go to page 475

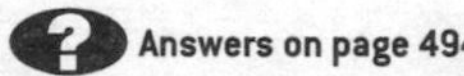

Answers on page 494

5 ◆ £1,000

141

The name of which dance literally means 'double step'?

A: Flamenco
B: Paso doble
C: Tango
D: Samba

142

What flavour is the drink Pernod?

A: Hazelnut
B: Peach
C: Aniseed
D: Coffee

143

The terms 'lot' and 'gavel' are most associated with which occupation?

A: Plumbing
B: Teaching
C: Printing
D: Auctioneering

144

Thor is the god of thunder in which mythology?

A: Roman
B: Greek
C: Norse
D: Egyptian

145

What is the first name of Princess Margaret's former husband, Lord Snowdon?

A: Edward
B: Antony
C: Patrick
D: Hugh

50:50 Go to page 451 Go to page 475 ? Answers on page 494

5 ◆ £1,000

146

Which US state is known as the 'Aloha' state?

- A: Alaska
- B: California
- C: Hawaii
- D: Florida

147

Which meat is traditionally used to make spaghetti bolognese?

- A: Beef
- B: Pork
- C: Lamb
- D: Chicken

148

In which city was President Kennedy assassinated?

- A: New York
- B: Richmond
- C: Dallas
- D: New Orleans

50:50 Go to page 451 Go to page 475 ? Answers on page 494

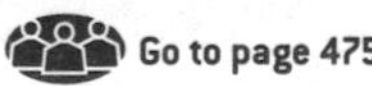

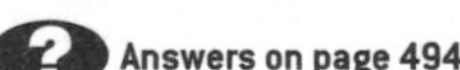

50:50  

15		£1 MILLION
14		£500,000
13		£250,000
12		£125,000
11		£64,000
10		£32,000
9		£16,000
8		£8,000
7		£4,000
6	◆	£2,000
5	◆	£1,000
4	◆	£500
3	◆	£300
2	◆	£200
1	◆	£100

6 ◆ £2,000

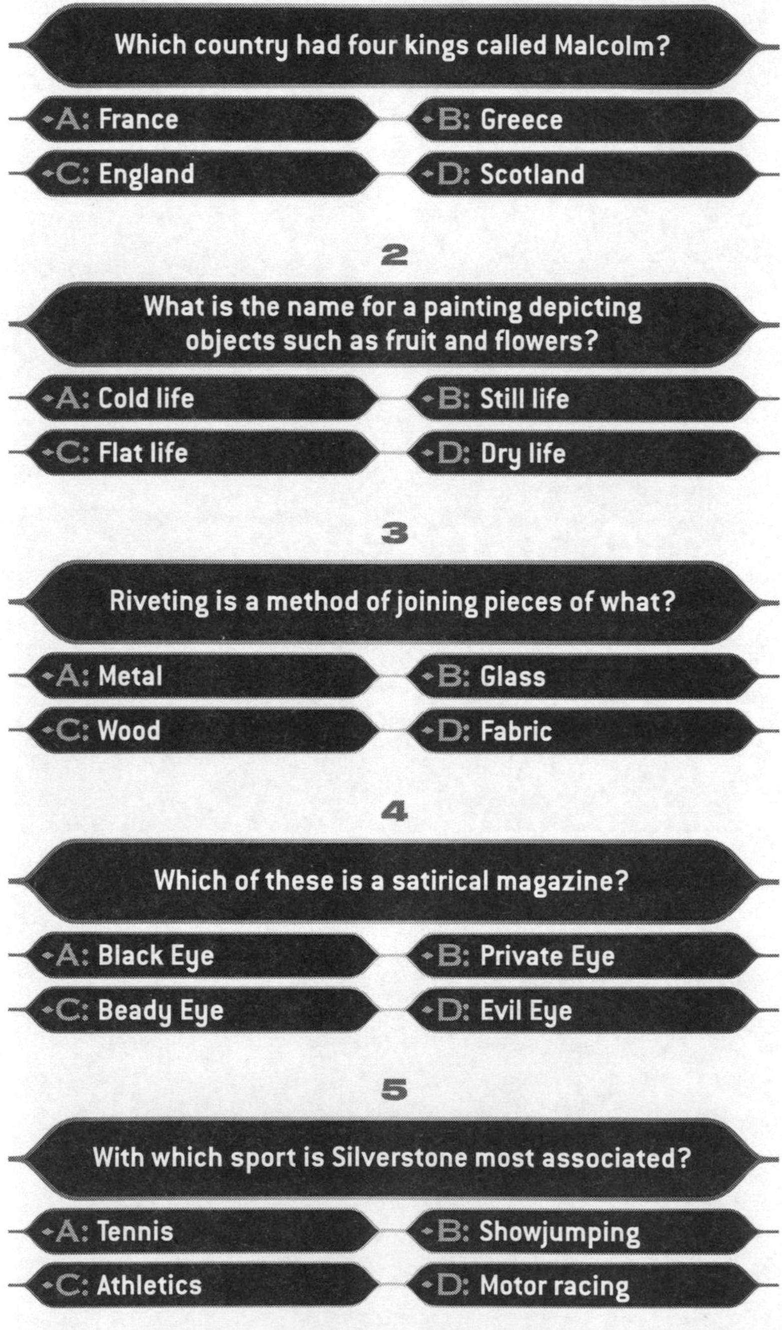

1

Which country had four kings called Malcolm?

A: France
B: Greece
C: England
D: Scotland

2

What is the name for a painting depicting objects such as fruit and flowers?

A: Cold life
B: Still life
C: Flat life
D: Dry life

3

Riveting is a method of joining pieces of what?

A: Metal
B: Glass
C: Wood
D: Fabric

4

Which of these is a satirical magazine?

A: Black Eye
B: Private Eye
C: Beady Eye
D: Evil Eye

5

With which sport is Silverstone most associated?

A: Tennis
B: Showjumping
C: Athletics
D: Motor racing

50:50 Go to page 453 Go to page 477 ? Answers on page 495

6 ◆ £2,000

6

What is the name for the outer part of a citrus fruit?

A: Zip
B: Zing
C: Zest
D: Zap

7

Which of these mountain ranges forms a geographical boundary between Europe and Asia?

A: Andes
B: Himalayas
C: Rockies
D: Urals

8

Little Jimmy Osmond topped the charts with 'Long-Haired Lover from...'?

A: Luton
B: Liverpool
C: Lincoln
D: Lowestoft

9

What does the letter A stand for in the term 'A level'?

A: Advanced
B: Able
C: Achieved
D: Attention

10

What is the North American word for aluminium?

A: Alminium
B: Alumnium
C: Aluminum
D: Aluminim

50:50 Go to page 453  Go to page 477 ? Answers on page 495

6 ◆ £2,000

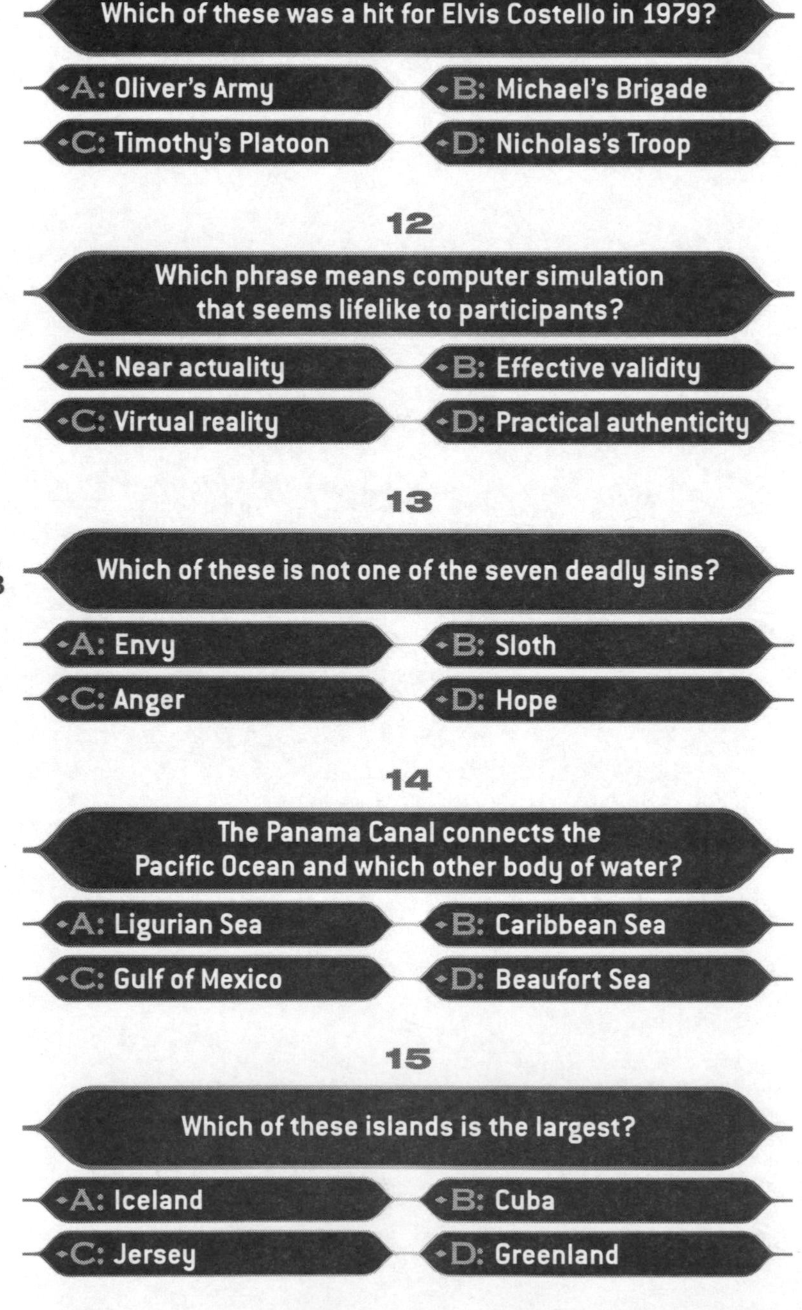

11

Which of these was a hit for Elvis Costello in 1979?

A: Oliver's Army
B: Michael's Brigade
C: Timothy's Platoon
D: Nicholas's Troop

12

Which phrase means computer simulation that seems lifelike to participants?

A: Near actuality
B: Effective validity
C: Virtual reality
D: Practical authenticity

13

Which of these is not one of the seven deadly sins?

A: Envy
B: Sloth
C: Anger
D: Hope

14

The Panama Canal connects the Pacific Ocean and which other body of water?

A: Ligurian Sea
B: Caribbean Sea
C: Gulf of Mexico
D: Beaufort Sea

15

Which of these islands is the largest?

A: Iceland
B: Cuba
C: Jersey
D: Greenland

50:50 Go to page 453 Go to page 477 ? Answers on page 495

6 ◆ £2,000

16

Nostradamus was famous for making what?

A: Cakes
B: Predictions
C: Friends
D: Jokes

17

What name is given to a boxer who leads with his right hand and off his right foot?

A: Northhand
B: Westmitt
C: Southpaw
D: Eastfist

18

Who starred as an alien in the 1970s film 'The Man Who Fell To Earth'?

A: Mick Jagger
B: Willie Nelson
C: Kris Kristofferson
D: David Bowie

19

Which of these is a type of ancient burial mound?

A: Kendal
B: Barrow
C: Storth
D: Coniston

20

What type of food is tortellini?

A: Pizza
B: Bread
C: Pasta
D: Onion soup

50:50 Go to page 453 Go to page 477  Answers on page 495

6 ◆ £2,000

21

Who wrote and directed the 1977 film 'Annie Hall'?

- A: Martin Scorsese
- B: Woody Allen
- C: George Lucas
- D: Peter Bogdanovich

22

What would be the defining characteristic of a narcissistic person?

- A: Wealth
- B: Anxiety
- C: Vanity
- D: Intelligence

23

What is the name for the part of the bone that fits into a socket to form hip and shoulder joints?

- A: Ball
- B: Plug
- C: Knuckle
- D: Pivot

24

What represent the body and blood of Christ in the service of Holy Communion?

- A: Bread and water
- B: Bread and wine
- C: Bread and jam
- D: Bread and butter

25

What is the colour of the maple leaf on the Canadian national flag?

- A: Green
- B: White
- C: Red
- D: Gold

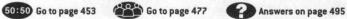

50:50 Go to page 453 Go to page 477

Answers on page 495

6 ◆ £2,000

26

What type of animal was Nana, the nursemaid in the story of 'Peter Pan'?

A: Sheep
B: Badger
C: Horse
D: Dog

27

What is the nickname of the basketball player Earvin Johnson?

A: Wizard
B: Magic
C: Conjuror
D: Warlock

28

Which part of the body does a neuro-surgeon specialise in?

A: Digestive system
B: Respiratory system
C: Nervous system
D: Blood

29

Which book of words has a Latin name that means 'treasure'?

A: Dictionary
B: Thesaurus
C: Encyclopedia
D: Directory

30

What would a gardener do with secateurs?

A: Cover seedlings
B: Mow the lawn
C: Make holes
D: Prune plants

50:50 Go to page 453 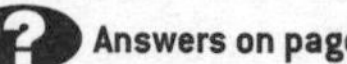 Go to page 477 ? Answers on page 495

6 ◆ £2,000

31

Which of these is a non-commissioned officer in the army?

A: Sergeant
B: Lieutenant colonel
C: General
D: Colonel

32

Where do Grand Prix drivers put their cars at the beginning of the race?

A: Mesh
B: Trellis
C: Net
D: Grid

33

Which sign, used in punctuation, denotes interrogation?

A: Bracket
B: Question mark
C: Inverted comma
D: Exclamation mark

34

Which word refers to the internal diameter of a gun barrel?

A: Merit
B: Worth
C: Calibre
D: Talent

35

Which of these is the name of a room in a pub?

A: Comfy
B: Snug
C: Homely
D: Cosy

50:50 Go to page 453 · Ask the audience: Go to page 477 · ? Answers on page 495

6 ◆ £2,000

36

The company IKEA is best known for selling what?

- A: Furniture
- B: Clothes
- C: Food
- D: Stationery

37

What is the name of the hairstyle in which the head is shaved except for a central strip of hair?

- A: Apache
- B: Sioux
- C: Cherokee
- D: Mohican

38

Which of these deserts is in California?

- A: Atacama
- B: Gibson
- C: Mojave
- D: Simpson

39

What surname links the rock singers Jim and Van?

- A: Brown
- B: Taylor
- C: Diamond
- D: Morrison

40

What was a 'ducat'?

- A: Coin
- B: Shoe
- C: Weapon
- D: Form of punishment

50:50 Go to page 453 | Go to page 477 | ? Answers on page 495

6 ◆ £2,000

41

A dime is equal to how many cents?

- A: Five
- B: Ten
- C: Twenty-five
- D: Fifty

42

What is an 'amulet'?

- A: South African antelope
- B: Three-line poem
- C: Lucky charm
- D: Tree-lined street

43

In which country is the town where Pilsner beer was originally brewed?

- A: Ireland
- B: Great Britain
- C: Australia
- D: Czech Republic

44

What kind of bird is a 'poussin'?

- A: Chicken
- B: Quail
- C: Grouse
- D: Pheasant

45

With what type of reference book is Joseph Whitaker most associated?

- A: Thesaurus
- B: Atlas
- C: Peerage
- D: Almanack

50:50 Go to page 453  Go to page 477 ? Answers on page 495

6 ◆ £2,000

46

The German Opel family was best known for the manufacture of what?

A: Clocks
B: Clothing
C: Cars
D: Carpets

47

Which of these is an attack of nerves suffered by sportsmen, especially golfers?

A: Hips
B: Yips
C: Mips
D: Dips

48

In military slang, which word means to carry heavy equipment on foot over difficult terrain?

A: Lomp
B: Pomp
C: Romp
D: Yomp

49

Which of these is a type of dance?

A: Military two-step
B: Army three-step
C: Services four-step
D: Martial five-step

50

What kind of vegetable is 'calabrese'?

A: Potato
B: Pepper
C: Onion
D: Broccoli

50:50 Go to page 453  Go to page 477 ? Answers on page 495

6 ◆ £2,000

51

Where would you be most likely to see a 'gazebo'?

A: At a zoo
B: On a roof
C: In a garden
D: Under water

52

A shy, retiring person is known as a shrinking what?

A: Rose
B: Violet
C: Buttercup
D: Marigold

53

Which rodents were once thought to commit suicide by jumping off cliffs?

A: Beavers
B: Squirrels
C: Dormice
D: Lemmings

54

What type of scientific equipment was named after the German Bunsen?

A: Microscope
B: Test tube
C: Burner
D: Thermometer

55

Which of these would be most likely to have a watermark?

A: Paper
B: Cheese
C: Violin
D: Gold

50:50 Go to page 453 Go to page 477 ? Answers on page 495

6 ◆ £2,000

56

Louis Pasteur developed a vaccine for which of these conditions?

- A: Polio
- B: German measles
- C: Rabies
- D: Whooping cough

57

What is the main source of vitamin C?

- A: Yeast
- B: Fruit
- C: Liver
- D: Rice

58

In the abbreviation VDU, what does the V stand for?

- A: Visual
- B: Vitreous
- C: Vertical
- D: Varied

59

What is the capital of Malta?

- A: Valladolid
- B: Valletta
- C: Val d'Isere
- D: Valencia

60

What does P stand for in the abbreviation PLO?

- A: Palestine
- B: Peru
- C: Persia
- D: Panama

50:50 Go to page 453  Go to page 477 ? Answers on page 495

6 ◆ £2,000

61

Which of these words means 'assess'?

A: Apply
B: Appoint
C: Appraise
D: Apprehend

62

Lara Croft is a character in which computer game?

A: Crash Bandicoot
B: Doom
C: Half Life
D: Tomb Raider

63

Ireland's River Shannon flows into which ocean?

A: Pacific
B: Indian
C: Atlantic
D: Arctic

64

Which of these is a temporary or part-time policeman?

A: Special constable
B: Extraordinary constable
C: Unusual constable
D: Remarkable constable

65

Someone with firmly fixed opinions
is said to be dyed in what?

A: The cotton
B: The linen
C: The wool
D: The velvet

50:50 Go to page 453 | Go to page 477 | ? Answers on page 495

6 ◆ £2,000

66

What is the name for a match of three games in bridge?

A: Polythene
B: Rubber
C: Nylon
D: Plastic

67

Which of these is an extra in cricket?

A: Wide
B: Broad
C: Large
D: Vast

68

Which of these is a type of drizzle?

A: Welsh fog
B: Scotch mist
C: English smog
D: Irish haze

69

Complete the title of the Umberto Eco book: 'The Name of the...'?

A: Dahlia
B: Lilac
C: Narcissus
D: Rose

70

Which of these is a North American wild cat?

A: Bencat
B: Billcat
C: Bobcat
D: Bertcat

50:50 Go to page 453 Go to page 477 ? Answers on page 495

71

In mythology, Romulus and Remus were brought up by which animal?

A: Wolf
B: Sheep
C: Elephant
D: Monkey

72

Which of these is a high ranking chess player?

A: Grandstander
B: Grandslammer
C: Grandfather
D: Grandmaster

73

What is the name of the square around which 'EastEnders' is based?

A: Albert Square
B: Victoria Square
C: George Square
D: Edward Square

74

Which word describes two lines which are always the same distance apart?

A: Equilateral
B: Parallel
C: Quadratic
D: Tangential

75

'Fax' is short for which word?

A: Facsimile
B: Factual
C: Faculty
D: Factory

50:50 Go to page 453  Go to page 477 ? Answers on page 495

6 ◆ £2,000

76

Who or what would be looked after in a creche?

- A: Dogs
- B: Children
- C: Plants
- D: Documents

77

Jesse Owens is most associated with which sport?

- A: Boxing
- B: Swimming
- C: Athletics
- D: Ice hockey

78

Which of these is not a slang word for prison?

- A: Clink
- B: Can
- C: Jug
- D: Kettle

79

Which of these famous schools is in Scotland?

- A: Harrow
- B: Roedean
- C: Gordonstoun
- D: Rugby

80

Whose tomb was discovered by Howard Carter in 1922?

- A: Alexander the Great
- B: Julius Caesar
- C: Tutankhamen
- D: Genghis Khan

50:50 Go to page 453 Go to page 477

Answers on page 495

6 ◆ £2,000

81

Insulin is commonly used to treat which condition?

- A: Diabetes
- B: Haemophilia
- C: Gout
- D: Asthma

82

By what title was Mohandas K Gandhi known?

- A: Pandit
- B: Guru
- C: Mahatma
- D: Pasha

83

In London, what are Quaglino's and The Ivy?

- A: Restaurants
- B: Night clubs
- C: Department stores
- D: Football grounds

84

Edgbaston is a suburb of which city?

- A: Manchester
- B: Glasgow
- C: Norwich
- D: Birmingham

85

The man known as the 'Red Baron' was famous in which field?

- A: Jazz
- B: Aviation
- C: Economics
- D: Linguistics

50:50 Go to page 453  Go to page 477 ? Answers on page 495

6 ◆ £2,000

86

What kind of poem is Keats's 'To a Nightingale'?

A: Ode
B: Limerick
C: Sonnet
D: Clerihew

87

Eliza Doolittle is a character in which George Bernard Shaw play?

A: Man and Superman
B: Major Barbara
C: Pygmalion
D: Heartbreak House

88

In the acronym 'laser', what does the L stand for?

A: Least
B: Light
C: Length
D: Logic

89

What does a person look like if described as 'wan'?

A: Red-haired
B: Blue-eyed
C: Pale-faced
D: Long-legged

90

Telly Savalas played which TV detective?

A: Kojak
B: Ironside
C: Columbo
D: Magnum

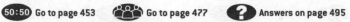

50:50 Go to page 453 Go to page 477

Answers on page 495

6 ◆ £2,000

91

Which fictional land was used to describe John F Kennedy's term as president?

A: Oz
B: Narnia
C: Camelot
D: Wonderland

92

In which city is the Royal Mile?

A: Bristol
B: Edinburgh
C: Nottingham
D: Cardiff

93

The first atom bomb was dropped on which Japanese city?

A: Nagasaki
B: Yokohama
C: Hiroshima
D: Nagoya

94

Complete the title of this radio comedy: 'I'm Sorry I Haven't a...' what?

A: Pencil
B: Microphone
C: Handkerchief
D: Clue

95

Which of these is not a slang name for food?

A: Grub
B: Nosh
C: Hooch
D: Chow

50:50 Go to page 453 Go to page 477 Answers on page 495

6 ◆ £2,000

96

Which of these authors had first names with the initials PG?

A: Lawrence B: Chesterton
C: Cronin D: Wodehouse

97

In sport, what would a person be most likely to do with a 'quoit'?

A: Throw it B: Ride it
C: Wear it D: Kick it

98

Complete the title of this Johnny Cash song: 'A Boy Named...'?

A: Annie B: Sue
C: Helena D: Ruth

99

'Bardolatry' is an excessive admiration for which writer?

A: George Bernard Shaw B: Robert Burns
C: Dylan Thomas D: William Shakespeare

100

Which stand-up comedian stars on TV as Jonathan Creek?

A: Alan Davies B: Eddie Izzard
C: Jack Dee D: Lee Evans

50:50 Go to page 453 Go to page 477 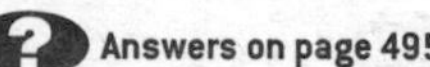 Answers on page 495

6 ◆ £2,000

101

What shape is the head of an Allen key?

A: Triangular
B: Square
C: Pentagonal
D: Hexagonal

102

The Bering Strait divides Russia from which American state?

A: Alaska
B: Arizona
C: Alabama
D: Arkansas

103

Who plays Sergeant Lewis in the TV adaptations of the Inspector Morse novels?

A: Alun Armstrong
B: Jimmy Nail
C: Kevin Whately
D: James Bolam

104

Which bomb, used in the Dambuster raids, was invented by Barnes Wallis?

A: Bending bomb
B: Bounding bomb
C: Breathing bomb
D: Bouncing bomb

105

What is the surname of the England cricketing brothers Ben and Adam?

A: Hollioake
B: Sevenelm
C: Tallash
D: Longpine

50:50 Go to page 453 Go to page 477

Answers on page 495

6 ◆ £2,000

106

Which of these words is a slang name for diamonds?

A: Frost
B: Snow
C: Hail
D: Ice

107

Which poet was a member of the comedy group Scaffold?

A: Roger McGough
B: Ted Hughes
C: Philip Larkin
D: John Betjeman

108

In the Bible, who authorises the Crucifixion?

A: Barabbas
B: Pontius Pilate
C: Caiaphas
D: Joseph of Arimathea

109

The word 'hacienda' comes from which language?

A: French
B: Italian
C: Spanish
D: German

110

Softball is a variation on which game?

A: Baseball
B: Football
C: Netball
D: Handball

50:50 Go to page 453 Go to page 477 ? Answers on page 495

6 ◆ £2,000

111

In which country are 'fajitas' a traditional dish?

A: Lebanon
B: India
C: Thailand
D: Mexico

112

Afrikaans developed from which European language?

A: French
B: Dutch
C: Italian
D: Portuguese

113

Where in Europe is the Barbary ape found in the wild?

A: Gibraltar
B: Corfu
C: Pyrenees
D: Monaco

114

The British Eurostar terminus is at which London station?

A: Liverpool Street
B: Marylebone
C: Victoria
D: Waterloo

115

What nationality was Louis Braille, who devised the reading system for the blind?

A: French
B: German
C: Italian
D: Danish

50:50 Go to page 453 Go to page 477  Answers on page 495

6 ◆ £2,000

116

Sedimentary and igneous are types of what?

- A: Paper
- B: Seaweed
- C: Water
- D: Rock

117

Which of these items would a haberdasher be most likely to sell?

- A: Button
- B: Hammer
- C: Compost
- D: Beer

118

The main square in Venice is named after which saint?

- A: Basil
- B: Paul
- C: Mark
- D: Nicholas

119

In traditional Chinese thought, what is the opposite of 'yin'?

- A: Tao
- B: Yang
- C: Kung
- D: Chi

120

In which country are Mariachi bands traditional?

- A: Greece
- B: Australia
- C: Tunisia
- D: Mexico

50:50 Go to page 453 Go to page 477  Answers on page 495

6 ◆ £2,000

121

Which 'Carry On' actor was the star of the sitcom 'Bless This House'?

A: Sid James
B: Kenneth Williams
C: Charles Hawtrey
D: Bernard Bresslaw

122

What was the name of the character played by Julia Sawalha in 'Absolutely Fabulous'?

A: Cinnamon
B: Ginger
C: Saffron
D: Anise

123

In which sport does a player 'address' the ball?

A: Volleyball
B: Badminton
C: Hockey
D: Golf

124

Which word refers to all the animal life of a specific place or time?

A: Fauna
B: Vista
C: Flora
D: Vespa

125

Which of these instruments would not be in a traditional string quartet?

A: Violin
B: Guitar
C: Viola
D: Cello

50:50 Go to page 453  Go to page 477 ? Answers on page 495

6 ◆ £2,000

126

What nationality is the racing driver Jean Alesi?

A: Brazilian
B: Italian
C: French
D: Canadian

127

What is the main use of tinder?

A: Making bread rise
B: Lighting a fire
C: Cleaning a carpet
D: Riding a horse

128

In the title of a famous book, what kind of creature is Tarka?

A: Otter
B: Mouse
C: Hare
D: Weasel

129

Which of these characters appeared in the TV sitcom 'Are You Being Served'?

A: Miss Brahms
B: Young Mr Beethoven
C: Mrs Liszt
D: Captain Handel

130

Which of these was discovered by accident in 1928?

A: Aspirin
B: Penicillin
C: Ether
D: DNA

50:50 Go to page 453  Go to page 477 ? Answers on page 495

6 ◆ £2,000

131

What is the capital of Iraq?

A: Baghdad
B: Teheran
C: Damascus
D: Beirut

132

William the Conqueror was duke of which French region?

A: Burgundy
B: Aquitaine
C: Normandy
D: Gascony

133

The 'galia' is a variety of which fruit?

A: Banana
B: Melon
C: Orange
D: Strawberry

134

What is the Danish name for Denmark?

A: Danmark
B: Donmark
C: Dinmark
D: Dunmark

135

Which of these animals is a 'pachyderm'?

A: Tiger
B: Elephant
C: Baboon
D: Wolf

50:50 Go to page 453 Go to page 477

Answers on page 495

6 ◆ £2,000

136

The United States Department of Defense is located in which building?

- A: White House
- B: Camp David
- C: House of Representatives
- D: Pentagon

137

Which writer created Jeeves, the ultimate manservant?

- A: Arthur Ransome
- B: P G Wodehouse
- C: Noel Coward
- D: Somerset Maugham

138

Provence is a region in which country?

- A: France
- B: Spain
- C: Portugal
- D: Italy

139

With which singer is the line 'Ground control to Major Tom' associated?

- A: Elvis Costello
- B: David Bowie
- C: Tom Jones
- D: David Essex

140

What was Red Dwarf, in the TV series of the same name?

- A: Alien
- B: Spaceship
- C: Robot
- D: Planet

50:50 Go to page 453  Go to page 477 ? Answers on page 495

50:50  

15 £1 MILLION

14 £500,000

13 £250,000

12 £125,000

11 £64,000

10 £32,000

9 £16,000

8 £8,000

7 ◆ £4,000

6 ◇ £2,000

5 ◇ £1,000

4 ◇ £500

3 ◇ £300

2 ◇ £200

1 ◇ £100

7 ◆ £4,000

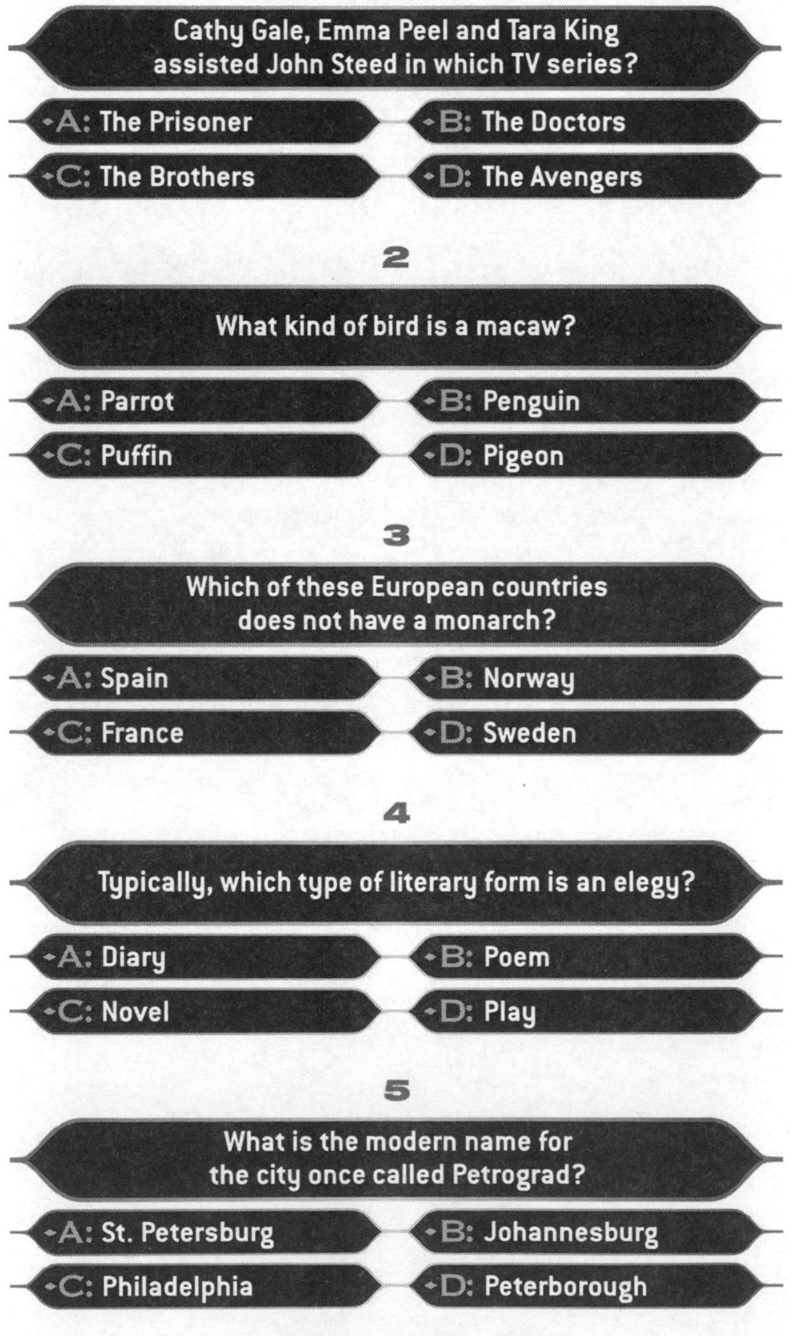

1

Cathy Gale, Emma Peel and Tara King assisted John Steed in which TV series?

A: The Prisoner
B: The Doctors
C: The Brothers
D: The Avengers

2

What kind of bird is a macaw?

A: Parrot
B: Penguin
C: Puffin
D: Pigeon

3

Which of these European countries does not have a monarch?

A: Spain
B: Norway
C: France
D: Sweden

4

Typically, which type of literary form is an elegy?

A: Diary
B: Poem
C: Novel
D: Play

5

What is the modern name for the city once called Petrograd?

A: St. Petersburg
B: Johannesburg
C: Philadelphia
D: Peterborough

50:50 Go to page 455 Go to page 478 Answers on page 495

7 ◆ £4,000

6

What are seraphim and cherubim?

- A: Religious incense
- B: Medieval alchemists
- C: Ranks of angels
- D: Roman emperors

7

What name is given to the salted roe of the sturgeon?

- A: Truffle
- B: Panettone
- C: Scampi
- D: Caviar

8

Which of these is a climbing plant with sweet-smelling flowers, popular in the garden?

- A: Sweet celery
- B: Sweet pea
- C: Sweet cabbage
- D: Sweet bean

9

Who played Granville in the TV sitcom 'Open All Hours'?

- A: David Jason
- B: Nicholas Lyndhurst
- C: Ronnie Barker
- D: Richard Beckinsale

10

On which continent is the Limpopo River?

- A: South America
- B: Asia
- C: Africa
- D: Europe

50:50 Go to page 455 · Go to page 478 · ? Answers on page 495

7 ◆ £4,000

11

What is a 'bantam'?

A: Rug | B: Chicken
C: Grape | D: Pamphlet

12

Where in the world is El Salvador?

A: Central Europe | B: Central Asia
C: Central Africa | D: Central America

13

Complete the title of the Charles Dickens novel: 'Martin...'?

A: Chuzzlewit | B: Bugglehat
C: Gigglewick | D: Fizzlebug

14

Leonardo DiCaprio starred in which of these films?

A: The Cruel Sea | B: The Beach
C: The Swimmer | D: The Sea of Sand

15

What term is applied to the widow of a king?

A: Queen bee | B: Queen consort
C: Queen dowager | D: Queen of puddings

50:50 Go to page 455 Go to page 478 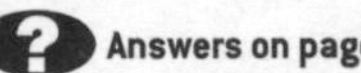 Answers on page 495

7 ◆ £4,000

16

Which car manufacturer produces a model called the 'Laguna'?

A: Renault B: Ford

C: Seat D: Nissan

17

What type of creature is a pollack?

A: Deer B: Fish

C: Chicken D: Beetle

18

What is the county town of Essex?

A: Appleby B: Bedford

C: Chelmsford D: Derby

19

What type of dog is Lady in the cartoon film 'Lady and the Tramp'?

A: Cocker spaniel B: Beagle

C: Chihuahua D: Border collie

20

Which US state has the postal abbreviation 'IN'?

A: Idaho B: Illinois

C: Indiana D: Iowa

50:50 Go to page 455  Go to page 478 ? Answers on page 495

7 ◆ £4,000

21

Which Shakespeare play features the line, 'Something is rotten in the state of Denmark'?

A: Macbeth
B: Hamlet
C: King Lear
D: Othello

22

What is dermatophobia the fear of?

A: Skin
B: Crowds
C: Dentists
D: School

23

In which century was the first skyscraper built?

A: 17th
B: 18th
C: 19th
D: 20th

24

What nationality is the novelist Norman Mailer?

A: American
B: British
C: Cypriot
D: Danish

25

What is the maximum number of consecutive terms that a US president can now serve?

A: One
B: Two
C: Three
D: Four

50:50 Go to page 455 Go to page 478 ? Answers on page 495

7 ◆ £4,000

26

In which county is the town of Newmarket?

A: Lancashire
B: Cornwall
C: Northumberland
D: Suffolk

27

Which of these countries has the highest population?

A: Canada
B: Great Britain
C: Brazil
D: Australia

28

Who played the title role in the 1938 film 'The Adventures of Robin Hood'?

A: Clark Gable
B: Douglas Fairbanks Jnr
C: Tyrone Power
D: Errol Flynn

29

Who played the suave thief, Sir Charles Lytton, in the film 'The Pink Panther'?

A: George Sanders
B: David Niven
C: Michael Redgrave
D: John Mills

30

Which of these artists was born in the United States of America?

A: David Hockney
B: Lucien Freud
C: Jackson Pollock
D: Francis Bacon

50:50 Go to page 455
Go to page 478

Answers on page 495

7 ◆ £4,000

31

Which of these is a region located in the south of Spain?

- A: Provence
- B: Tuscany
- C: Andalusia
- D: Lorraine

32

What is the technical name for the collarbone?

- A: Scapula
- B: Tibia
- C: Humerus
- D: Clavicle

33

The chalky cliffs at Beachy Head look out over which body of water?

- A: North Sea
- B: English Channel
- C: Irish Sea
- D: Bay of Biscay

34

Jupiter is the Roman name for which god of Greek mythology?

- A: Ares
- B: Eros
- C: Apollo
- D: Zeus

35

Which planet in our solar system was discovered most recently?

- A: Saturn
- B: Pluto
- C: Neptune
- D: Jupiter

50:50 Go to page 455 Go to page 478 ? Answers on page 495

7 ◆ £4,000

36

Which musical term means a mass for the dead?

A: Cadenza
B: Libretto
C: Requiem
D: Scherzo

37

The Greek warrior Odysseus played a major role in which war?

A: Punic War
B: Spartan War
C: Minoan War
D: Trojan War

38

What type of creature is a basilisk?

A: Mouse
B: Lizard
C: Bird
D: Monkey

39

In which European country do one hundred groschen equal one schilling?

A: Liechtenstein
B: Hungary
C: Austria
D: Netherlands

40

Which film actor began his climb to stardom in the classic TV cowboy series 'Rawhide'?

A: Steve McQueen
B: Clint Eastwood
C: Robert Redford
D: Jeff Bridges

50:50 Go to page 455 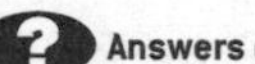 Go to page 478 ? Answers on page 495

7 ◆ £4,000

41

Charcoal is made by heating what?

A: Metal | B: Chalk
C: Wood | D: Coal

42

Instruments made from tea chests and washboards were a feature of which specific type of music?

A: Steel band | B: Skiffle
C: Punk | D: Rock 'n' roll

43

Sephardim are followers of which religion?

A: Islam | B: Hinduism
C: Judaism | D: Methodism

44

Which ballet company is based at the Maryinsky Theatre?

A: Royal Ballet | B: Kirov Ballet
C: American Ballet Theatre | D: English National Ballet

45

In German towns, what is the S-bahn?

A: Motorway | B: University
C: Cathedral | D: Railway

50:50 Go to page 455 · Go to page 478 · ? Answers on page 495

7 ◆ £4,000

46

A 'schipperke' is a breed of which animal?

- A: Cat
- B: Dog
- C: Rabbit
- D: Horse

47

Who is the star of the 2000 film 'The Patriot'?

- A: Russell Crowe
- B: Sylvester Stallone
- C: Kevin Costner
- D: Mel Gibson

48

In yoga, how is the lotus position performed?

- A: Standing upright
- B: Flat on the back
- C: Sitting cross-legged
- D: Upside down

49

What does the word 'maudlin' mean?

- A: Self-important
- B: Self-pitying
- C: Self-sufficient
- D: Self-confident

50

The cap and bells formed the insignia of which group of people?

- A: Travelling minstrels
- B: Crusaders
- C: Jesters
- D: Pilgrims

50:50 Go to page 455 Go to page 478 ? Answers on page 495

7 ◆ £4,000

51

The song 'A Whole New World' comes from which Disney film?

- A: The Lion King
- B: Aladdin
- C: The Little Mermaid
- D: Pocahontas

52

In the abbreviation P & O, what does the O stand for?

- A: Overseas
- B: Orbit
- C: Order
- D: Oriental

53

What is a 'cahier'?

- A: Cookery book
- B: Prayer book
- C: Note book
- D: Library book

54

Which of these is a suet pudding with dried fruit?

- A: Cabinet pudding
- B: Closet pudding
- C: Cupboard pudding
- D: Commode pudding

55

Who wrote the novel 'Valley of the Dolls'?

- A: Anais Nin
- B: Jacqueline Susann
- C: Norman Mailer
- D: Leslie Thomas

50:50 Go to page 455  Go to page 478 ? Answers on page 495

7 ◆ £4,000

56

Which of these is a device to help in remembering things?

A: Paradox
B: Metaphor
C: Anagram
D: Mnemonic

57

Which American footballer won four Super Bowls with the San Francisco 49ers?

A: Joe Montana
B: Dwight Michigan
C: Billy Maine
D: John-Boy Mississippi

58

Which country was once ruled by a Mikado?

A: China
B: Japan
C: India
D: Egypt

59

In literature, who has a servant called Sancho Panza?

A: Don Giovanni
B: Don Juan
C: Don Quixote
D: Don Corleone

60

Which of these books is set in South Africa?

A: Midnight's Children
B: Kidnapped
C: A Town Like Alice
D: Cry the Beloved Country

50:50 Go to page 455 Go to page 478  Answers on page 495

7 ◆ £4,000

61

Who adopted the title 'Il Caudillo'?

A: Gandhi | B: Franco
C: Mussolini | D: Stalin

62

Which of these is an Atlantic island group?

A: Sebastian da Cunha | B: Tarquin da Cunha
C: Tristan da Cunha | D: Quentin da Cunha

63

By what popular name was the Royal Highland regiment known?

A: Black Swan | B: Black Watch
C: Black Smith | D: Black Rod

64

Which of these is the name of a knitting design?

A: Staffa | B: Iona
C: Rhum | D: Fair Isle

65

What is the name of the hammer used by doctors to test a patient's reflexes?

A: Scalpel | B: Forceps
C: Plexor | D: Otoscope

50:50 Go to page 455 · Go to page 478 · ? Answers on page 495

7 ◆ £4,000

66

Who rode the Queen Mother's horse Devon Loch in the 1956 Grand National?

A: Len Deighton
B: Frederick Forsyth
C: Dick Francis
D: Jeffrey Archer

67

Which canal was nationalised in 1956?

A: Manchester Ship
B: Kiel
C: Grand Union
D: Suez

68

What is the name for a line of longitude on a map?

A: Druidian
B: Meridian
C: Oblivion
D: Pavilion

69

Which term connects a type of match and a nickname for the Devil?

A: Beelzebub
B: Satan
C: Lucifer
D: Old Nick

70

Which fish is pickled to make rollmops?

A: Herring
B: Salmon
C: Mackerel
D: Cod

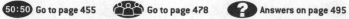

50:50 Go to page 455 Go to page 478

Answers on page 495

7 ◆ £4,000

71

Which of these was a letter of the ancient Germanic alphabet?

A: Dune
B: Tune
C: Lune
D: Rune

72

Which of these is a port on the east of San Francisco Bay?

A: Ashland
B: Elmland
C: Oakland
D: Pineland

73

Which of these refers to the back of a ship?

A: Bow
B: Stern
C: Port
D: Starboard

74

Which acronym refers to someone who does not want anything unpleasant in his locality?

A: NIMBY
B: DIMBY
C: FIMBY
D: WIMBY

75

Which of these names means 'happiness'?

A: Penelope
B: Richard
C: Felicity
D: Paul

50:50 Go to page 455 · Go to page 478 ·  Answers on page 495

7 ◆ £4,000

76

What is a 'shillelagh'?

- A: Musical instrument
- B: Cudgel
- C: Horse
- D: Prayer book

77

Which of these expressions does not mean an excellent person or thing?

- A: Cat's whiskers
- B: Cat's meow
- C: Cat's pyjamas
- D: Cat's cradle

78

Islay is in which island group?

- A: Scillies
- B: Seychelles
- C: Falklands
- D: Hebrides

79

Which dog name is a slang term for a detective?

- A: Alsatian
- B: Bloodhound
- C: Corgi
- D: Dalmatian

80

Who would be described as a 'sophomore'?

- A: Policeman
- B: Poet
- C: Musician
- D: Student

50:50 Go to page 455 Go to page 478  Answers on page 495

7 ◆ £4,000

81

What name is given to young herrings?

A: Whitetails
B: Whitebait
C: Whitefry
D: Whitefins

82

Pitcairn Island was settled by crew members of which ship?

A: Bounty
B: Golden Hind
C: Beagle
D: Mayflower

83

What was the favourite colour of the romantic novelist Barbara Cartland?

A: Cream
B: Navy blue
C: Lavender
D: Pink

84

China has a coastline on which of these seas?

A: Red Sea
B: Yellow Sea
C: Black Sea
D: White Sea

85

What type of drug would be used to treat hay fever?

A: Anti-inflammatory
B: Analgesic
C: Antibiotic
D: Antihistamine

50:50 Go to page 455 Go to page 478  Answers on page 495

7 ◆ £4,000

86

What name is given to an army chaplain?

- A: Deacon
- B: Padre
- C: Beadle
- D: Verger

87

Which of these is a white wine?

- A: Pinot Noir
- B: Cabernet Sauvignon
- C: Merlot
- D: Chardonnay

88

Which company makes the perfume 'Coco'?

- A: Yves Saint Laurent
- B: Christian Dior
- C: Givenchy
- D: Chanel

89

Geographically, what is an eddy?

- A: Whirlpool
- B: Mountain
- C: River mouth
- D: Harbour

90

Paul Newman married which actress?

- A: Anne Bancroft
- B: Faye Dunaway
- C: Natalie Wood
- D: Joanne Woodward

50:50 Go to page 455  Go to page 478 ? Answers on page 495

7 ◆ £4,000

91

Fianna Fail is a political party in which country?

A: Spain
B: Malta
C: Cyprus
D: Ireland

92

What nationality is the singer and actress Björk?

A: Danish
B: Norwegian
C: Icelandic
D: Swedish

93

The Rialto Bridge is most associated with which canal?

A: Kiel Canal
B: Corinth Canal
C: Bridgewater Canal
D: Grand Canal

94

Complete the title of the Travis song: 'Why Does It Always...'?

A: Hail On Me
B: Snow On Me
C: Rain On Me
D: Shine On Me

95

What is the name for the load-line on a ship?

A: Clog line
B: Plimsoll line
C: Brogue line
D: Wader line

50:50 Go to page 455 Go to page 478 ? Answers on page 495

7 ◆ £4,000

96

Grimsby is on which coast of Britain?

A: North
B: South
C: East
D: West

97

Prue Leith is a famous what?

A: Photographer
B: Cookery writer
C: Archaeologist
D: Tennis player

98

What is the smallest independent country in South America?

A: Ecuador
B: Paraguay
C: Surinam
D: Colombia

99

In which county was Gracie Fields born?

A: Cornwall
B: Norfolk
C: Somerset
D: Lancashire

100

Who married the actor Liam Neeson?

A: Sinead Cusack
B: Natasha Richardson
C: Pauline Collins
D: Prunella Scales

50:50 Go to page 455
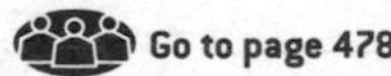

Go to page 478
? Answers on page 495

7 ◆ £4,000

101

The word 'bus' is a shortened form of which other word?

A: Pluribus | B: Erebus
C: Arcquebus | D: Omnibus

102

Which of these is a French order?

A: Purple Heart | B: Order of the Elephant
C: Legion of Honour | D: Order of Merit

103

What was the surname of Isadora, the famous dancer?

A: Gordon | B: Duncan
C: James | D: Gregory

104

Which 20th-century king reigned for less than a year?

A: Edward VII | B: George V
C: Edward VIII | D: George VI

105

Nantucket island is part of which American state?

A: New York | B: Massachusetts
C: South Carolina | D: West Virginia

50:50 Go to page 455 Go to page 478 ? Answers on page 495

7 ◆ £4,000

106

Sepia is obtained from which sea creature?

- A: Cuttlefish
- B: Sea urchin
- C: Starfish
- D: Killer whale

107

Which of these is a style of Japanese theatre?

- A: Jujitsu
- B: Hokkaido
- C: Kabuki
- D: Origami

108

Which of these is a fossil resin?

- A: Peat
- B: Marble
- C: Sand
- D: Amber

109

What was the first name of Baden-Powell, the founder of the Scout movement?

- A: James
- B: Robert
- C: David
- D: Warren

110

Which of these is a feature of South Dakota?

- A: Everglades
- B: Steppes
- C: Badlands
- D: Fjords

50:50 Go to page 455  Go to page 478 ? Answers on page 495

7 ◆ £4,000

111

What is the main ingredient of the Indian dish 'dhal'?

A: Rice
B: Chicken
C: Pulses
D: Potatoes

112

Algy and Ginger are friends of which fictional character?

A: Sherlock Holmes
B: Hornblower
C: Peter Rabbit
D: Biggles

113

Which word describes a male singer singing in a high register?

A: Arpeggio
B: Falsetto
C: Oratorio
D: Rallentando

114

Where does the Iditarod dog sled race take place?

A: Alaska
B: Siberia
C: Tibet
D: Lapland

115

By what name was the American William Cody better known?

A: Wild Bill Hickok
B: Pecos Bill
C: Buffalo Bill
D: Billy the Kid

50:50 Go to page 455 Go to page 478

Answers on page 495

7 ◆ £4,000

116

Which film studio made 'The Lavender Hill Mob'?

- A: Pinewood
- B: Ealing
- C: Elstree
- D: Gainsborough

117

Who directed the 2000 film 'Gladiator'?

- A: John Woo
- B: James Cameron
- C: Ridley Scott
- D: George Lucas

118

What is the technical term for the bones of the fingers and toes?

- A: Phalanges
- B: Clavicles
- C: Vertebrae
- D: Scaphoids

119

Which footballer left Tottenham Hotspur to play for Grampus 8?

- A: Glenn Hoddle
- B: Danny Blanchflower
- C: Martin Peters
- D: Gary Lineker

120

Whose abduction of Helen brought about the Trojan War?

- A: Hector
- B: Achilles
- C: Paris
- D: Ajax

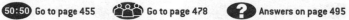

50:50 Go to page 455
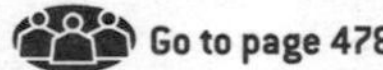
Go to page 478

Answers on page 495

7 ◆ £4,000

121

What was the first name of Captain Bligh, of 'Mutiny on the Bounty' fame?

A: Harold
B: William
C: George
D: Charles

122

Which British scientist invented a safety lamp for miners?

A: Newton
B: Watt
C: Davy
D: Kelvin

123

The popular name for the Royal Military Academy comes from which town?

A: Aldershot
B: Sandhurst
C: Catterick
D: Salisbury

124

The film 'M*A*S*H' was set during which war?

A: World War I
B: World War II
C: Korean War
D: Vietnam War

125

What kind of garment is a 'Sloppy Joe'?

A: Boot
B: Hat
C: Sock
D: Sweater

50:50 Go to page 455 Go to page 478  Answers on page 495

7 ◆ £4,000

126

Which acid is found in yoghurt?

- A: Formic
- B: Lactic
- C: Nitric
- D: Acetic

127

How is a zither played?

- A: Plucked
- B: Hit
- C: Blown
- D: Shaken

128

A person born in which part of Britain is sometimes known as a 'Tyke'?

- A: Cornwall
- B: Merseyside
- C: Scotland
- D: Yorkshire

129

Ferrite is a form of which metal?

- A: Tin
- B: Iron
- C: Aluminium
- D: Copper

130

Where in London is the Albert Memorial?

- A: Hampstead Heath
- B: Regent's Park
- C: Kensington Gardens
- D: Wimbledon Common

50:50 Go to page 455 Go to page 478 ? Answers on page 495

7 ◆ £4,000

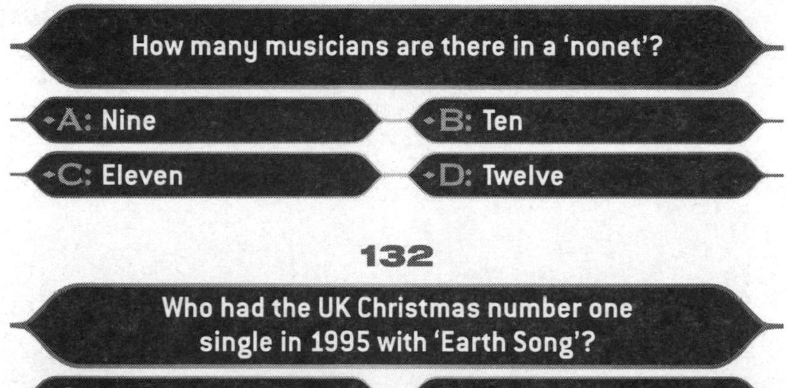

131

How many musicians are there in a ‘nonet’?

A: Nine
B: Ten
C: Eleven
D: Twelve

132

Who had the UK Christmas number one single in 1995 with ‘Earth Song’?

A: Mr Blobby
B: Spice Girls
C: Michael Jackson
D: East 17

50:50 Go to page 455

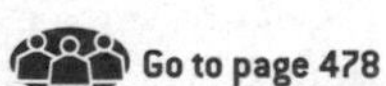

Go to page 478

Answers on page 495

15 £1 MILLION
14 £500,000
13 £250,000
12 £125,000
11 £64,000
10 £32,000
9 £16,000
8 ◆ £8,000
7 ◆ £4,000
6 ◆ £2,000
5 ◆ £1,000
4 ◆ £500
3 ◆ £300
2 ◆ £200
1 ◆ £100

8 ◆ £8,000

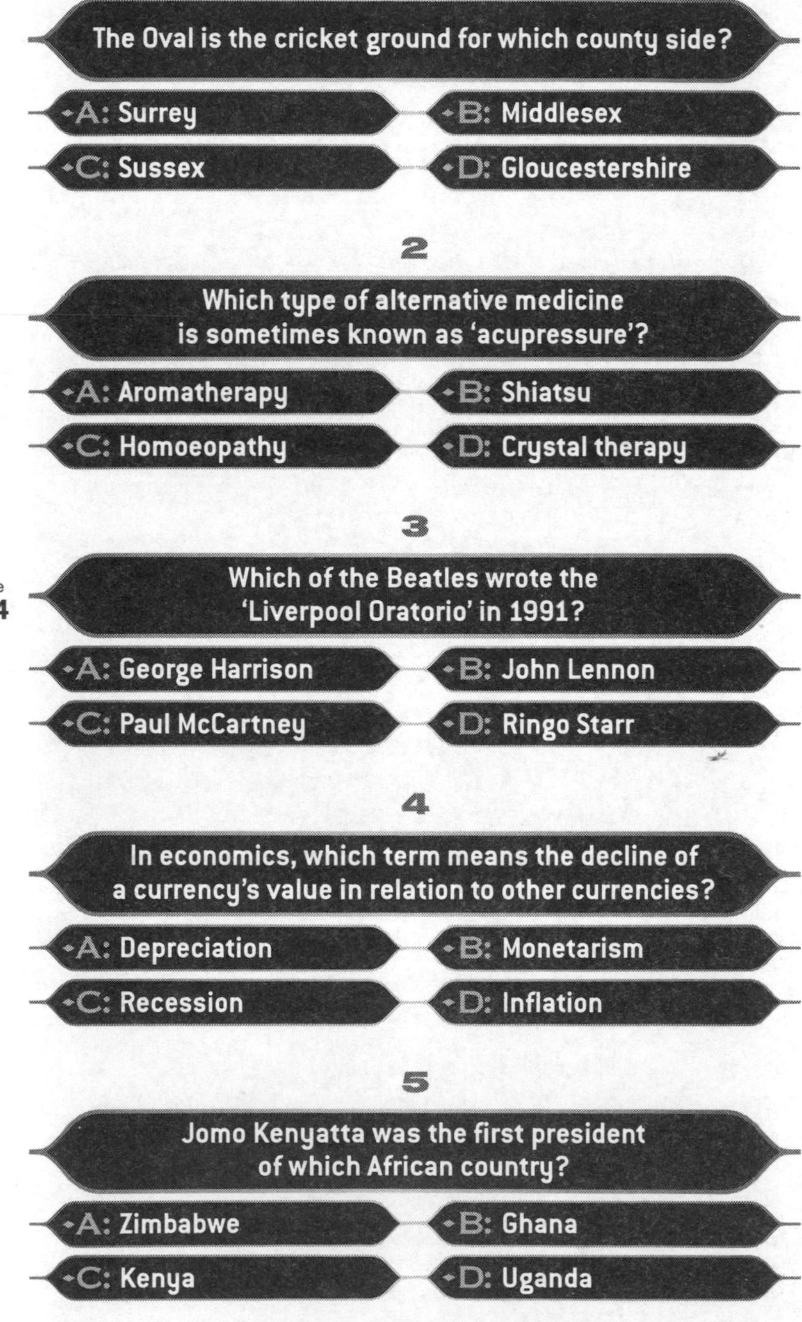

1

The Oval is the cricket ground for which county side?

A: Surrey
B: Middlesex
C: Sussex
D: Gloucestershire

2

Which type of alternative medicine is sometimes known as 'acupressure'?

A: Aromatherapy
B: Shiatsu
C: Homoeopathy
D: Crystal therapy

3

Which of the Beatles wrote the 'Liverpool Oratorio' in 1991?

A: George Harrison
B: John Lennon
C: Paul McCartney
D: Ringo Starr

4

In economics, which term means the decline of a currency's value in relation to other currencies?

A: Depreciation
B: Monetarism
C: Recession
D: Inflation

5

Jomo Kenyatta was the first president of which African country?

A: Zimbabwe
B: Ghana
C: Kenya
D: Uganda

50:50 Go to page 456 · Go to page 480 · ? Answers on page 496

8 ◆ £8,000

6

Which of these diseases is transmitted by the tsetse fly?

- A: Malaria
- B: Lassa fever
- C: Cholera
- D: Sleeping sickness

7

A person who makes a big fuss is said to raise which biblical character?

- A: Adam
- B: Eve
- C: Cain
- D: Abel

8

What sort of weapon is a flintlock?

- A: Sword
- B: Gun
- C: Arrow
- D: Catapult

9

The vegetable okra is also known by what name?

- A: Baby's hair
- B: Children's toes
- C: Gentleman's teeth
- D: Lady's fingers

10

England fought the Hundred Years' War against which country?

- A: Spain
- B: Poland
- C: France
- D: Switzerland

50:50 Go to page 456 Go to page 480  Answers on page 496

8 ◆ £8,000

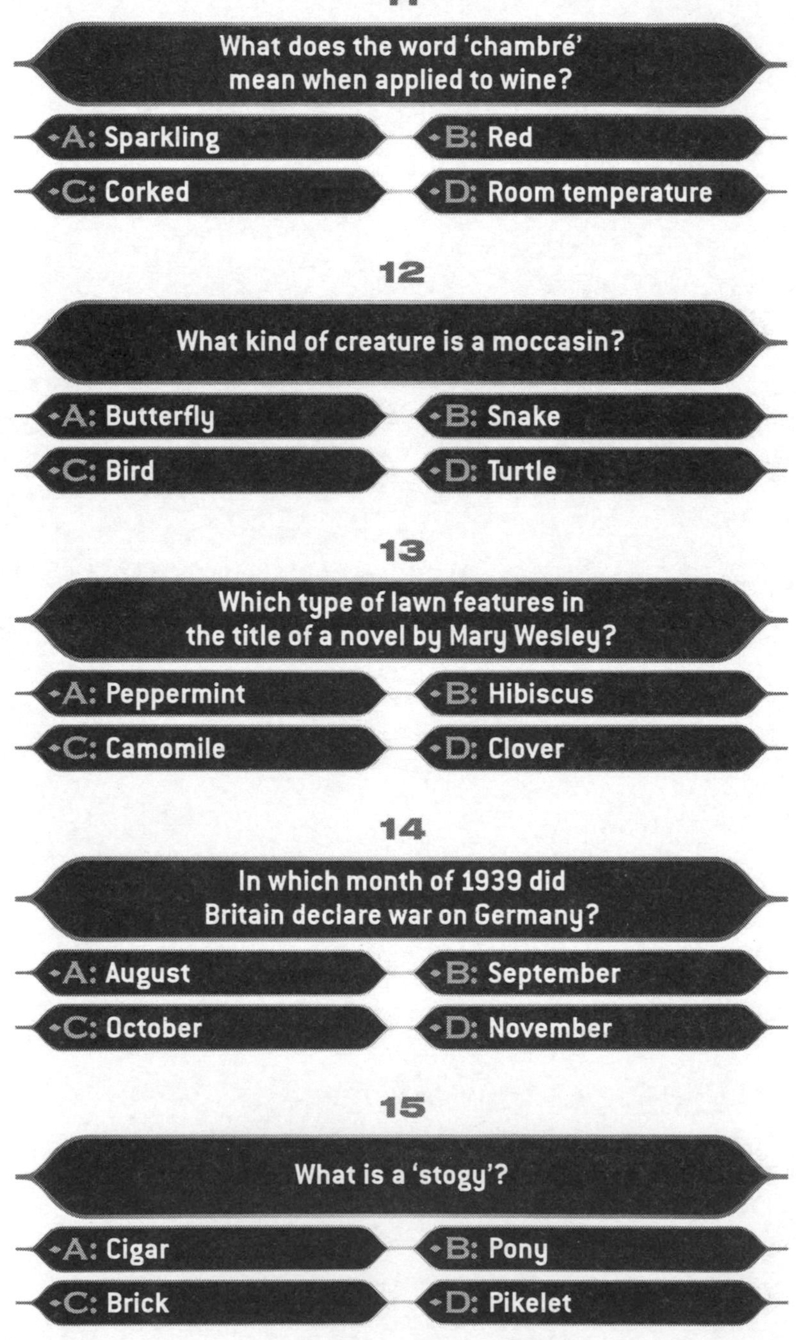

11

What does the word 'chambré' mean when applied to wine?

A: Sparkling
B: Red
C: Corked
D: Room temperature

12

What kind of creature is a moccasin?

A: Butterfly
B: Snake
C: Bird
D: Turtle

13

Which type of lawn features in the title of a novel by Mary Wesley?

A: Peppermint
B: Hibiscus
C: Camomile
D: Clover

14

In which month of 1939 did Britain declare war on Germany?

A: August
B: September
C: October
D: November

15

What is a 'stogy'?

A: Cigar
B: Pony
C: Brick
D: Pikelet

50:50 Go to page 456 Go to page 480 ? Answers on page 496

8 ◆ £8,000

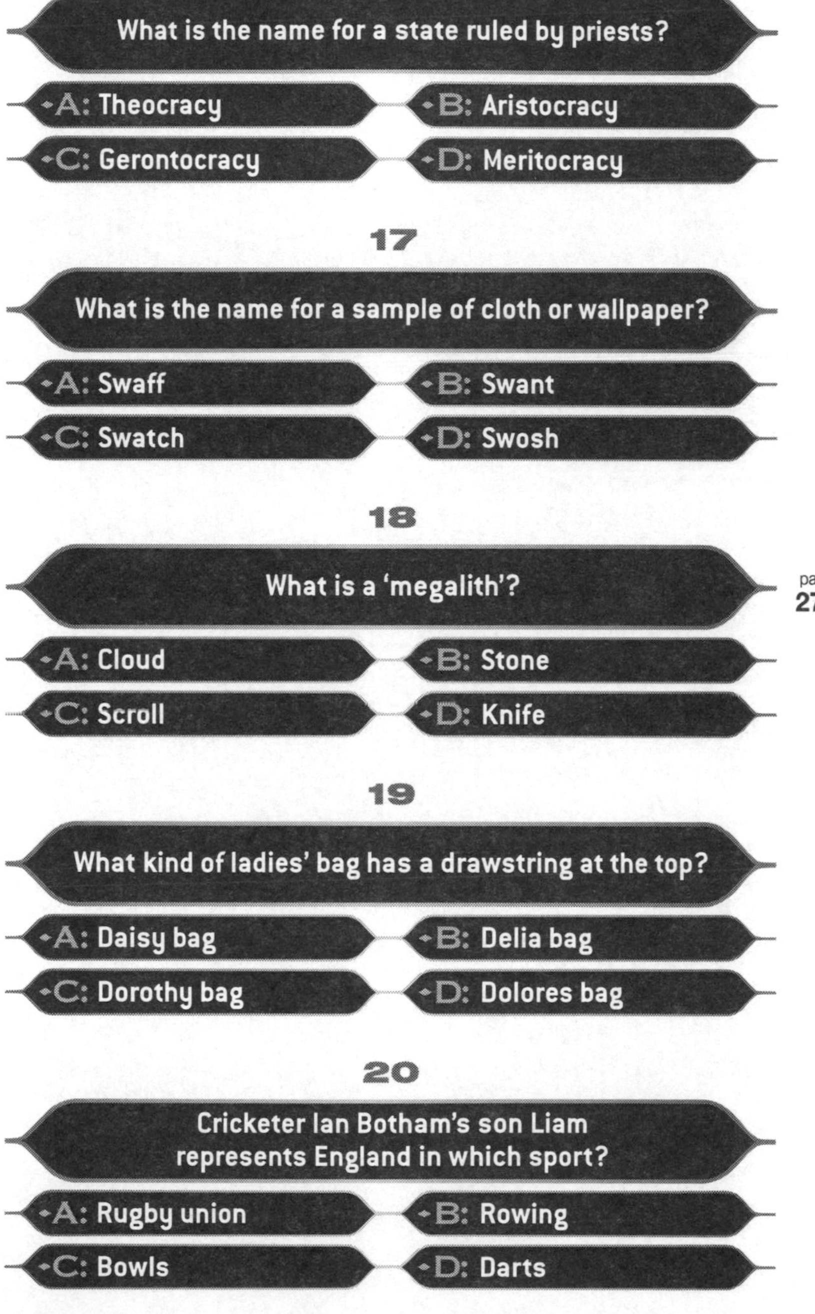

16

What is the name for a state ruled by priests?

A: Theocracy
B: Aristocracy
C: Gerontocracy
D: Meritocracy

17

What is the name for a sample of cloth or wallpaper?

A: Swaff
B: Swant
C: Swatch
D: Swosh

18

What is a 'megalith'?

A: Cloud
B: Stone
C: Scroll
D: Knife

19

What kind of ladies' bag has a drawstring at the top?

A: Daisy bag
B: Delia bag
C: Dorothy bag
D: Dolores bag

20

Cricketer Ian Botham's son Liam represents England in which sport?

A: Rugby union
B: Rowing
C: Bowls
D: Darts

50:50 Go to page 456 Go to page 480 ? Answers on page 496

8 ◆ £8,000

21

Which of these phrases means 'something in its entirety'?

A: Full time
B: Full monty
C: Full board
D: Full sail

22

Which item is put into a can to give beer a head of foam?

A: Grommet
B: Tappet
C: Widget
D: Hatchet

23

In a castle, what was an oubliette?

A: Dungeon
B: Chapel
C: Look-out post
D: Kitchen

24

In mythology, what did Prometheus steal from the gods?

A: Water
B: Music
C: Fire
D: Light

25

What is bladderwrack?

A: Nonsense poetry
B: Seaweed
C: Blasphemy
D: Disease

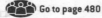

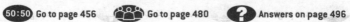

50:50 Go to page 456 Go to page 480

Answers on page 496

8 ◆ £8,000

26

'Garbanzo' is another name for which pulse?

A: Chickpea
B: Lentil
C: Mung bean
D: Kidney bean

27

What is named after the actor F.M. Alexander?

A: Planet
B: Owl species
C: Exercise technique
D: Telescope

28

Valkyries are warrior maidens in which mythology?

A: Norse
B: Greek
C: Slavonic
D: Roman

29

From which animal is the perfume musk obtained?

A: Musquash
B: Muskrat
C: Musk ox
D: Musk deer

30

What makes Rotorua in New Zealand a tourist attraction?

A: Sandy beaches
B: Cathedral
C: Hot springs
D: New Zealand National Gallery

50:50 Go to page 456 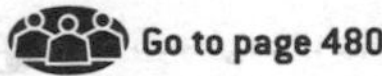 Go to page 480  Answers on page 496

8 ◆ £8,000

31

Which of these words refers to the deliberate sinking of a ship?

A: Skittle
B: Shuttle
C: Settle
D: Scuttle

32

Which of these newsreaders famously danced with Morecambe and Wise?

A: Moira Stuart
B: Angela Rippon
C: Michael Buerk
D: Trevor McDonald

33

What nationality is the opera singer Montserrat Caballé?

A: Spanish
B: Greek
C: American
D: Italian

34

Where did the D-Day landings take place?

A: Germany
B: Netherlands
C: Belgium
D: France

35

In which country is Soweto?

A: South Africa
B: Pakistan
C: Cambodia
D: Zimbabwe

50:50 Go to page 456 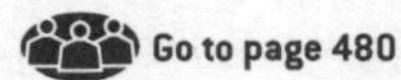 Go to page 480  Answers on page 496

8 ◆ £8,000

36

A quiver is a container for what?

- A: Wine
- B: Sword
- C: Tea
- D: Arrows

37

What is the highest rank in the British Army?

- A: General
- B: Captain
- C: Lieutenant General
- D: Field Marshal

38

Iago is a character in which of Shakespeare's plays?

- A: Othello
- B: Hamlet
- C: Coriolanus
- D: Macbeth

39

Trigonometry is a branch of which science?

- A: Physics
- B: Chemistry
- C: Biology
- D: Mathematics

40

Milan is in which Italian province?

- A: Lombardy
- B: Lazio
- C: Veneto
- D: Tuscany

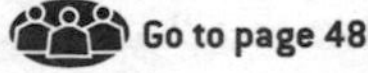
50:50 Go to page 456
Go to page 480

Answers on page 496

8 ◆ £8,000

41

The lychee is native to which country?

- A: India
- B: Australia
- C: Mexico
- D: China

42

In which of these countries might the 'midnight sun' be seen?

- A: Norway
- B: Australia
- C: Sri Lanka
- D: South Africa

43

The Masai are native to which continent?

- A: Asia
- B: Africa
- C: South America
- D: North America

44

Which of these is a type of gemstone?

- A: Cat's-whisker
- B: Cat's-paw
- C: Cat's-tail
- D: Cat's-eye

45

A blouse and a biscuit are named after which soldier?

- A: Wellington
- B: Garibaldi
- C: Napoleon
- D: Schwarzkopf

50:50 Go to page 456 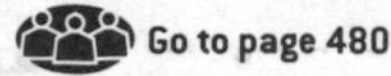 Go to page 480  Answers on page 496

8 ◆ £8,000

46

The liqueur Grand Marnier is based on which spirit?

A: Brandy
B: Rum
C: Whisky
D: Gin

47

Which island was the centre of US immigration?

A: Liberty Island
B: Staten Island
C: Manhattan Island
D: Ellis Island

48

'Jambalaya' is a traditional dish in which of these American states?

A: Alaska
B: Hawaii
C: Louisiana
D: Texas

49

What shape is the pasta 'fettuccini'?

A: Ribbons
B: Butterflies
C: Parcels
D: Shells

50

The ancient town of Luxor stood on which river?

A: Euphrates
B: Orinoco
C: Danube
D: Nile

50:50 Go to page 456  Go to page 480 ? Answers on page 496

8 ◆ £8,000

51

The name of which musical instrument is the Italian word for 'soft'?

A: Piano
B: Piccolo
C: Viola
D: Cello

52

By what name is 'albumen' more commonly known?

A: White of the eye
B: Egg white
C: White hair
D: Whitewash

53

In ancient Rome, what was a denarius?

A: Coin
B: Gladiator
C: Soothsayer
D: Robe

54

What is the name for the bone structure of a person or animal?

A: Musculature
B: Endocrine system
C: Pleura
D: Skeleton

55

What kind of transport were dreadnoughts?

A: Helicopters
B: Ships
C: Aeroplanes
D: Submarines

50:50 Go to page 456 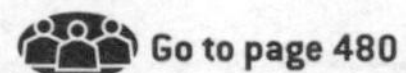 Go to page 480  Answers on page 496

8 ◆ £8,000

56

Which is the name for classical music played by a small group of instruments?

- A: Chamber music
- B: Apartment music
- C: Parlour music
- D: Cubicle music

57

Which civil war was fought in the 1930s?

- A: Spanish
- B: English
- C: American
- D: Russian

58

Which word is the plural of 'magus'?

- A: Maggie
- B: Magi
- C: Mago
- D: Magnum

59

Which food crop has the Latin name 'Saccharum officinarum'?

- A: Rice
- B: Soya bean
- C: Wheat
- D: Sugar cane

60

Which American criminal was known as 'Scarface'?

- A: Al Capone
- B: John Dillinger
- C: Benjamin Siegel
- D: George Moran

50:50 Go to page 456 Go to page 480

Answers on page 496

8 ◆ £8,000

61

Who was the first woman to fly the Atlantic?

- A: Amy Johnson
- B: Amelia Earhart
- C: Beryl Markham
- D: Anne Lindbergh

62

The Topkapi Palace was home to which emperors?

- A: Holy Roman
- B: Russian
- C: Ottoman
- D: Aztec

63

Who wrote 'The Female Eunuch'?

- A: Marilyn French
- B: Betty Friedan
- C: Andrea Dworkin
- D: Germaine Greer

64

In mythology, the labyrinth was built for which monster?

- A: Cyclops
- B: Minotaur
- C: Gorgon
- D: Centaur

65

Sherlock Holmes and Moriarty fought at which famous falls?

- A: Reichenbach
- B: Angel
- C: Yosemite
- D: Niagara

50:50 Go to page 456 Go to page 480  Answers on page 496

8 ◆ £8,000

66

Which of these was not a famous member of the Pankhurst suffragette family?

- A: Sylvia
- B: Christabel
- C: Emmeline
- D: Anastasia

67

Auguste Rodin was famous in which field of the arts?

- A: Sculpture
- B: Acting
- C: Opera
- D: Poetry

68

Who was the last viceroy of India?

- A: Lord Lucan
- B: Lord Elgin
- C: Lord Baden-Powell
- D: Lord Mountbatten

69

'Send in the Clowns' is a song from which Sondheim musical?

- A: Sweeney Todd
- B: A Little Night Music
- C: Company
- D: Into the Woods

70

What is a 'missive'?

- A: Letter
- B: Ship
- C: Monk
- D: Schoolteacher

50:50 Go to page 456
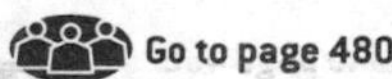
Go to page 480

Answers on page 496

8 ◆ £8,000

71

What name is given to an alloy of mercury and another metal?

- A: Fusion
- B: Amalgam
- C: Blend
- D: Merger

72

What does a barber do with his strop?

- A: Sharpen a razor
- B: Mix a hair colour
- C: Apply cologne
- D: Oil a moustache

73

The Karakoram mountain range is on which continent?

- A: Australia
- B: South America
- C: Africa
- D: Asia

74

What is the main constituent of natural gas?

- A: Nitrogen
- B: Methane
- C: Chlorine
- D: Carbon dioxide

75

What was the name of Michael Jackson's 1995 album?

- A: HIStory
- B: GEOGraphy
- C: CHEmistry
- D: BIOlogy

50:50 Go to page 456 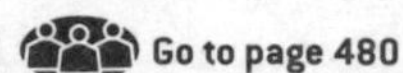 Go to page 480  Answers on page 496

8 ◆ £8,000

76

If something is galvanised, with which metal is it coated?

A: Tin
B: Zinc
C: Copper
D: Steel

77

Which British tennis player was the husband of Chris Evert?

A: Roger Taylor
B: Mark Cox
C: John Lloyd
D: David Lloyd

78

The River Volga flows into which sea?

A: Adriatic Sea
B: Black Sea
C: Aegean Sea
D: Caspian Sea

79

Which Hitchcock film is based on a story by Daphne du Maurier?

A: Psycho
B: The Birds
C: Vertigo
D: Rear Window

80

Which of these is a place in Hertfordshire?

A: Potter's Bar
B: Pitcher's Bar
C: Peeler's Bar
D: Palmer's Bar

50:50 Go to page 456 Go to page 480  Answers on page 496

8 ◆ £8,000

81

Which of these words refers to farm land where no crops have been sown?

A: Callow
B: Fallow
C: Hallow
D: Sallow

82

A Bajan is an inhabitant of which island?

A: Jamaica
B: Cuba
C: Barbados
D: Martinique

83

Where in the body are the adenoids?

A: Throat
B: Eye
C: Ear
D: Lung

84

What name is given to the officials at a race meeting?

A: Wardens
B: Agents
C: Stewards
D: Bailiffs

85

Which building is linked to the Tate Modern by the Millennium Bridge?

A: Tower of London
B: St. Paul's Cathedral
C: Buckingham Palace
D: Canary Wharf Tower

50:50 Go to page 456 · Go to page 480 · ? Answers on page 496

8 ◆ £8,000

86

What is the triangular muscle of the shoulder called?

- A: Triceps
- B: Biceps
- C: Gluteus maximus
- D: Deltoid

87

Which of these comedy characters was created by Johnny Speight?

- A: Basil Fawlty
- B: Reginald Perrin
- C: Alf Garnett
- D: Compo

88

Where is Britain's National Horseracing Museum?

- A: Epsom
- B: Newmarket
- C: Aintree
- D: Cheltenham

89

Where is the 'Laughing Cavalier' on display?

- A: British Museum
- B: Burrell Collection
- C: Victoria and Albert Museum
- D: Wallace Collection

90

Which novel was the subject of a famous 1960 trial?

- A: Ulysses
- B: Doctor Zhivago
- C: Lady Chatterley's Lover
- D: Lucky Jim

50:50 Go to page 456  Go to page 480 ? Answers on page 496

8 ◆ £8,000

91

The football club Galatasaray is based in which country?

A: Greece
B: Turkey
C: Portugal
D: Spain

92

What is the technical name for the voice box?

A: Larynx
B: Epiglottis
C: Coccyx
D: Mandible

93

Nathan Brittles is the hero of which classic Western?

A: High Noon
B: The Magnificent Seven
C: A Fistful of Dollars
D: She Wore a Yellow Ribbon

94

Which of these was a 19th-century artistic group?

A: Pre-Michelangelites
B: Pre-da Vincians
C: Pre-Raphaelites
D: Pre-Botticellians

95

In which sea do eels spawn?

A: Mediterranean
B: Sargasso
C: Caribbean
D: South China

50:50 Go to page 456 Go to page 480 ? Answers on page 496

8 ◆ £8,000

96

What name was given to the period when Charles II regained the throne?

A: Reformation

B: Revolution

C: Regency

D: Restoration

97

Which of these is an island which belongs to Britain?

A: West Florida

B: South Georgia

C: North Tennessee

D: East Louisiana

98

Which newspaper is sometimes known as the 'Thunderer'?

A: Daily Mail

B: The Times

C: The Daily Telegraph

D: The Sun

99

In area, what is the second largest country of South America?

A: Brazil

B: Venezuela

C: Argentina

D: Ecuador

100

Which of these tropical fruits has black seeds in the centre?

A: Papaya

B: Mango

C: Guava

D: Pineapple

50:50 Go to page 456 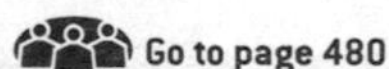 Go to page 480  Answers on page 496

8 ◆ £8,000

101

What was the surname of the rugby player known by the initials JPR?

A: Edwards
B: Williams
C: Evans
D: Davies

102

Which of these London streets is most associated with bespoke tailors?

A: Hatton Garden
B: Fleet Street
C: Savile Row
D: Wardour Street

103

Which country singer wrote the song 'Your Cheatin' Heart'?

A: Tammy Wynette
B: Hank Williams
C: Patsy Cline
D: Jim Reeves

104

Palermo is the capital of which island?

A: Sicily
B: Cyprus
C: Corsica
D: Malta

105

The musician Stephane Grappelli was famous for playing which instrument?

A: Guitar
B: Saxophone
C: Violin
D: Piano

50:50 Go to page 456  Go to page 480 ? Answers on page 496

8 ◆ £8,000

106

What nationality is the snooker player Mark Williams?

A: English
B: Scottish
C: Irish
D: Welsh

107

Of which country was Anwar Sadat the president?

A: Bangladesh
B: Sri Lanka
C: Egypt
D: Libya

108

Which county is sometimes known as the 'Garden of England'?

A: Kent
B: Lincolnshire
C: Cornwall
D: Somerset

109

Ferdinand Marcos was president of which country?

A: Vietnam
B: Malaysia
C: Thailand
D: Philippines

110

The Dead Sea lies on the border of Israel and which other country?

A: Jordan
B: Egypt
C: Turkey
D: Iran

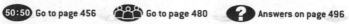

50:50 Go to page 456
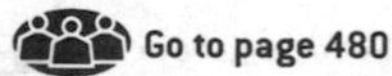

Go to page 480
Answers on page 496

8 ◆ £8,000

111

Which character was played by Roger Moore in 'The Saint'?

- A: Brett Sinclair
- B: Adam Adamant
- C: Simon Templar
- D: George Cowley

112

The Golden Temple at Amritsar is sacred to which religion?

- A: Sikhism
- B: Hinduism
- C: Islam
- D: Buddhism

113

In which field were the Boulting Brothers famous?

- A: Brewing
- B: Cinema
- C: Dance
- D: Equestrianism

114

A yarmulka is a skullcap worn by followers of which religion?

- A: Hinduism
- B: Judaism
- C: Islam
- D: Christianity

115

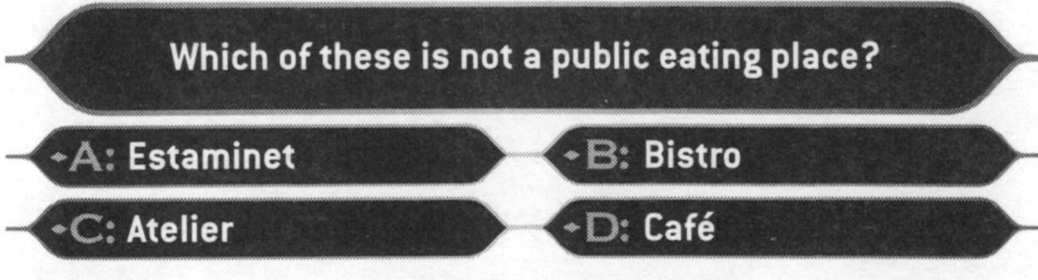

Which of these is not a public eating place?

- A: Estaminet
- B: Bistro
- C: Atelier
- D: Café

50:50 Go to page 456 | Go to page 480 | ? Answers on page 496

8 ◆ £8,000

116

Hugo Drax was the villain of which James Bond book and film?

- A: Goldfinger
- B: From Russia With Love
- C: The Spy Who Loved Me
- D: Moonraker

117

Page 555 on Ceefax gives information about what?

- A: Lottery
- B: Sport
- C: Stocks and shares
- D: Cookery

118

The song 'Evergreen' features in which Barbra Streisand film?

- A: Yentl
- B: Funny Girl
- C: A Star Is Born
- D: The Way We Were

119

The Ural mountains are mainly in which country?

- A: Nepal
- B: Russia
- C: Mongolia
- D: Armenia

120

Bob Ferris and Terry Collier were characters in which classic sitcom?

- A: Dad's Army
- B: The Liver Birds
- C: Citizen Smith
- D: The Likely Lads

50:50 Go to page 456
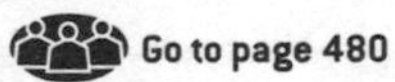
Go to page 480

Answers on page 496

8 ◆ £8,000

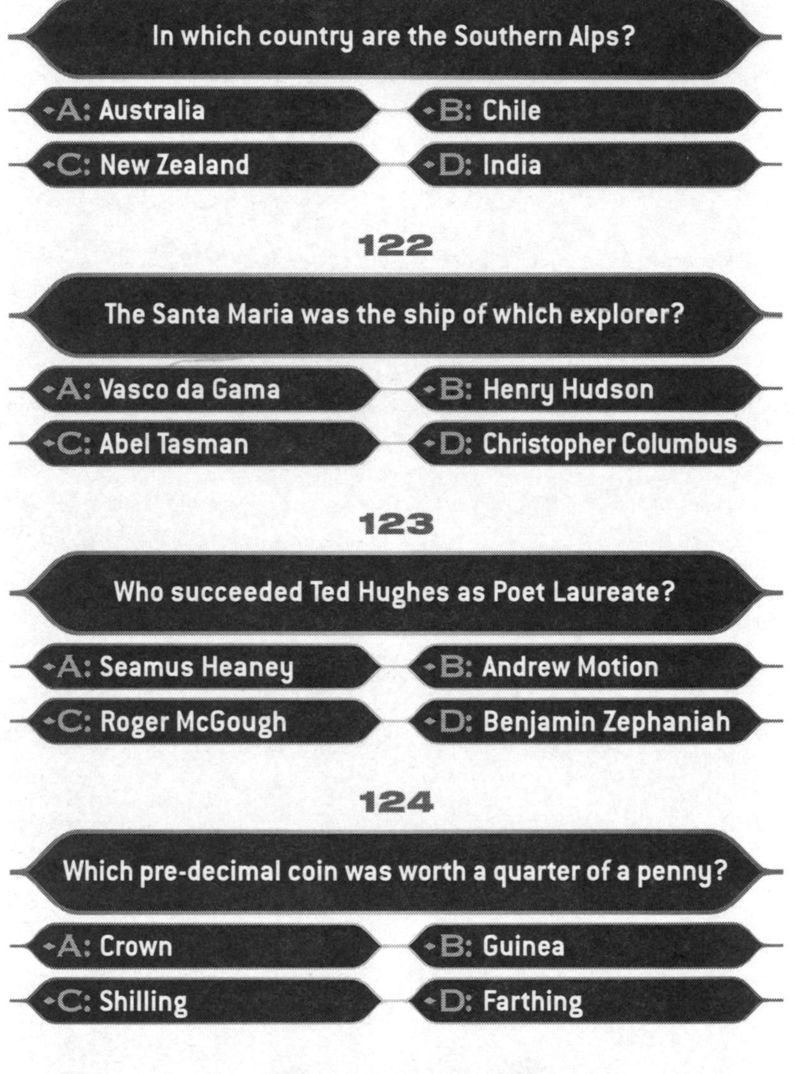

121

In which country are the Southern Alps?

A: Australia
B: Chile
C: New Zealand
D: India

122

The Santa Maria was the ship of which explorer?

A: Vasco da Gama
B: Henry Hudson
C: Abel Tasman
D: Christopher Columbus

123

Who succeeded Ted Hughes as Poet Laureate?

A: Seamus Heaney
B: Andrew Motion
C: Roger McGough
D: Benjamin Zephaniah

124

Which pre-decimal coin was worth a quarter of a penny?

A: Crown
B: Guinea
C: Shilling
D: Farthing

50:50 Go to page 456 Go to page 480 ? Answers on page 496

50:50

15 £1 MILLION

14 £500,000

13 £250,000

12 £125,000

11 £64,000

10 £32,000

9 ◆ £16,000

8 ◆ £8,000

7 ◆ £4,000

6 ◆ £2,000

5 ◆ £1,000

4 ◆ £500

3 ◆ £300

2 ◆ £200

1 ◆ £100

9 ◆ £16,000

1

Which of these cabinet posts was not held by John Major?

A: Home Secretary
B: Foreign Secretary
C: Chancellor of the Exchequer
D: Prime Minister

2

During which war was British Summer Time first introduced?

A: Crimean War
B: Boer War
C: World War I
D: World War II

3

In 1914, Archduke Franz Ferdinand was assassinated in which city?

A: Vienna
B: Sarajevo
C: Prague
D: Berlin

4

Which of these is a name for young fish?

A: Fry
B: Grill
C: Boil
D: Roast

5

Hunter S Thompson wrote about 'Fear and Loathing' in which city?

A: New York
B: Las Vegas
C: Little Rock
D: San Francisco

50:50 Go to page 458 Go to page 482 ? Answers on page 496

9 ◆ £16,000

6

Mount Vesuvius is near which Italian city?

A: Milan | B: Venice

C: Rome | D: Naples

7

Which word means the minimum number who must attend a meeting to make it valid?

A: Quorum | B: Jorum

C: Forum | D: Lorum

8

In computing, which letter of the alphabet represents 1,024 bytes?

A: J | B: K

C: L | D: M

9

Who is the only female tennis player to win the Grand Slam and an Olympic gold medal in the same year?

A: Martina Navratilova | B: Chris Evert

C: Monica Seles | D: Steffi Graf

10

The Stone of Scone is a relic sacred to which country?

A: Wales | B: Ireland

C: Scotland | D: France

50:50 Go to page 458 Go to page 482 ? Answers on page 496

11

Which English river has the same name as a Russian river?

A: Tees | B: Don
C: Thames | D: Severn

12

Geronimo was a leader of which North American Indian people?

A: Apache | B: Blackfoot
C: Cherokee | D: Sioux

13

Mary, Queen of Scots belonged to which royal house?

A: Tudor | B: Stuart
C: York | D: Lancaster

14

Who wrote the best-selling novel 'Fever Pitch'?

A: Nick Hornby | B: Ben Elton
C: Salman Rushdie | D: Colin Dexter

15

What is the nickname of Chicago's hugely successful NBA basketball team?

A: Bears | B: Bulls
C: Hawks | D: Bucks

50:50 Go to page 458 Go to page 482  Answers on page 496

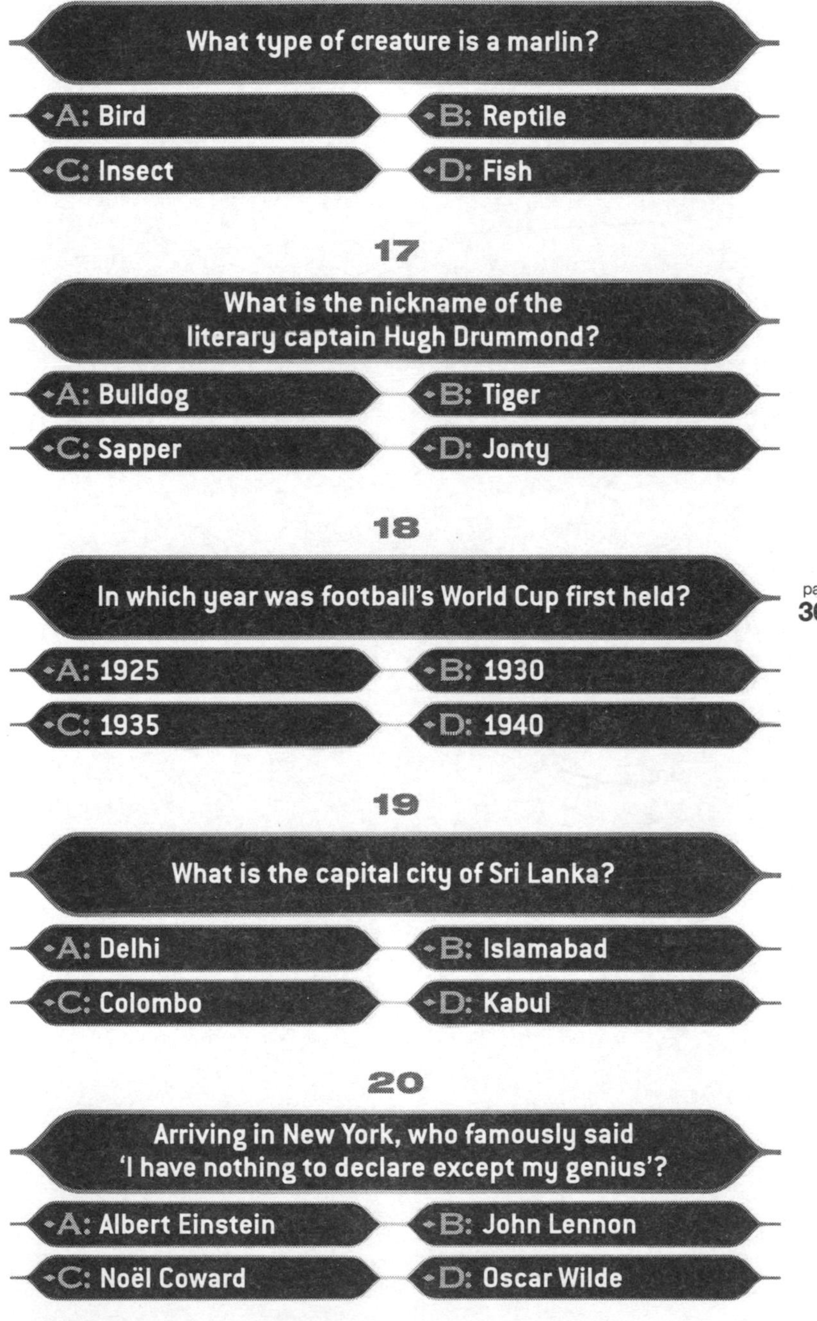

9 ◆ £16,000

16

What type of creature is a marlin?

A: Bird
B: Reptile
C: Insect
D: Fish

17

What is the nickname of the literary captain Hugh Drummond?

A: Bulldog
B: Tiger
C: Sapper
D: Jonty

18

In which year was football's World Cup first held?

A: 1925
B: 1930
C: 1935
D: 1940

19

What is the capital city of Sri Lanka?

A: Delhi
B: Islamabad
C: Colombo
D: Kabul

20

Arriving in New York, who famously said 'I have nothing to declare except my genius'?

A: Albert Einstein
B: John Lennon
C: Noël Coward
D: Oscar Wilde

50:50 Go to page 458 Go to page 482 ? Answers on page 496

9 ◆ £16,000

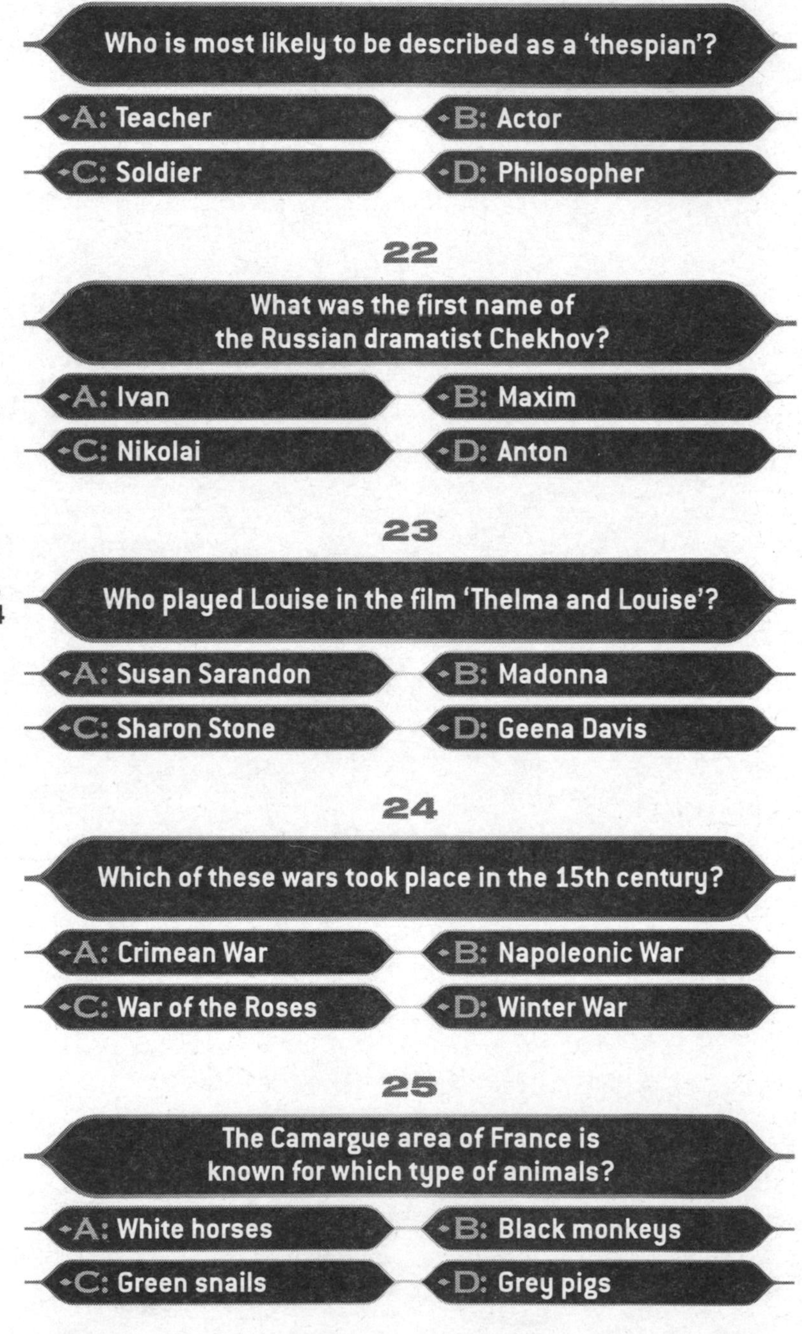

21

Who is most likely to be described as a 'thespian'?

A: Teacher
B: Actor
C: Soldier
D: Philosopher

22

What was the first name of the Russian dramatist Chekhov?

A: Ivan
B: Maxim
C: Nikolai
D: Anton

23

Who played Louise in the film 'Thelma and Louise'?

A: Susan Sarandon
B: Madonna
C: Sharon Stone
D: Geena Davis

24

Which of these wars took place in the 15th century?

A: Crimean War
B: Napoleonic War
C: War of the Roses
D: Winter War

25

The Camargue area of France is known for which type of animals?

A: White horses
B: Black monkeys
C: Green snails
D: Grey pigs

50:50 Go to page 458 Go to page 482 ? Answers on page 496

9 ◆ £16,000

26

In Roman legend, who removed a thorn from a lion's paw?

A: Spartacus
B: Romulus
C: Horatio
D: Androcles

27

Which of these was a court set up in the 15th century for cases affecting the interests of the crown?

A: Moon Chamber
B: Star Chamber
C: Heavenly Chamber
D: Sky Chamber

28

Which chemical element is represented by the symbol S?

A: Sulphur
B: Samarium
C: Silver
D: Selenium

29

Which of these is a dip made from yoghurt, cucumber and mint?

A: Hummus
B: Taramasalata
C: Tzatziki
D: Tarato

30

Which author wrote 'The World According to Garp'?

A: Ken Kesey
B: Kurt Vonnegut Jnr
C: John Updike
D: John Irving

50:50 Go to page 458
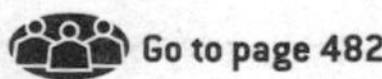
Go to page 482

Answers on page 496

9 ◆ £16,000

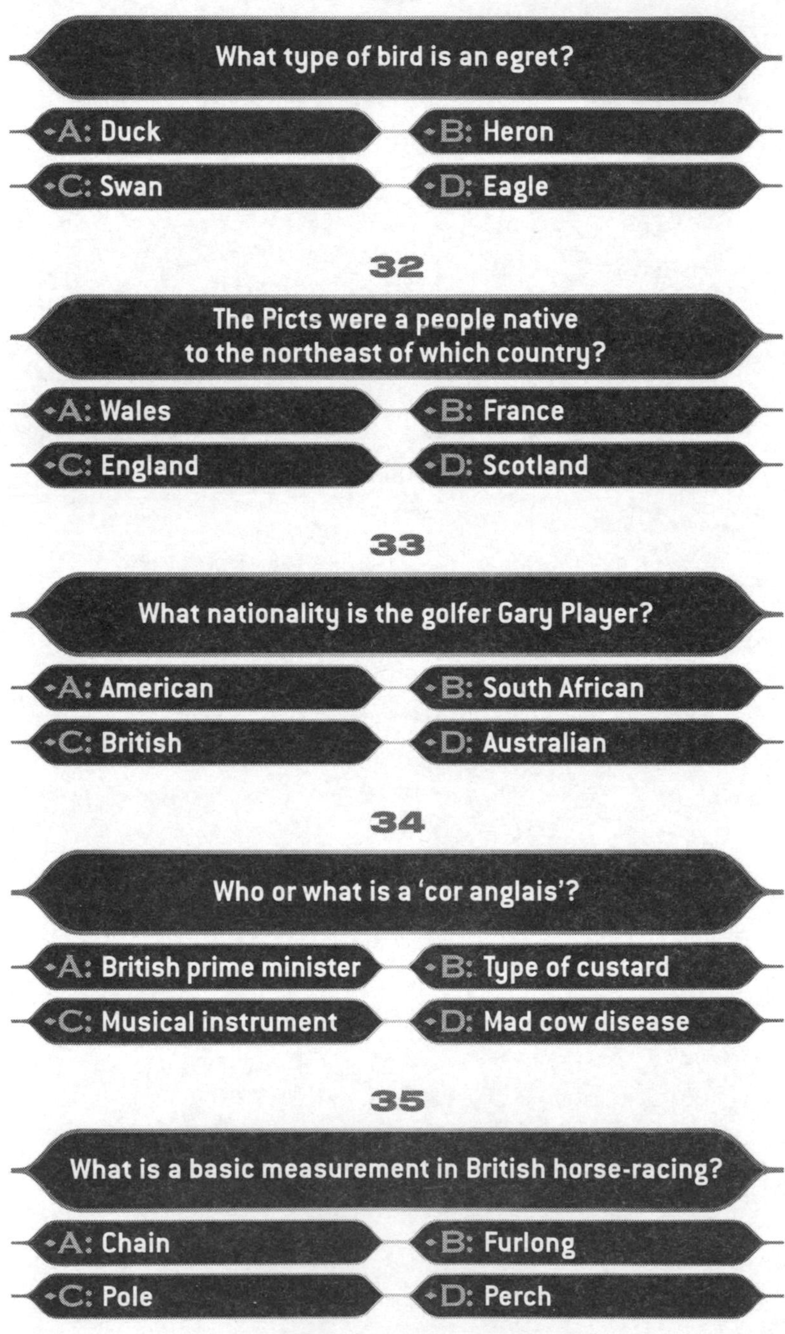

31

What type of bird is an egret?

A: Duck
B: Heron
C: Swan
D: Eagle

32

The Picts were a people native to the northeast of which country?

A: Wales
B: France
C: England
D: Scotland

33

What nationality is the golfer Gary Player?

A: American
B: South African
C: British
D: Australian

34

Who or what is a 'cor anglais'?

A: British prime minister
B: Type of custard
C: Musical instrument
D: Mad cow disease

35

What is a basic measurement in British horse-racing?

A: Chain
B: Furlong
C: Pole
D: Perch

50:50 Go to page 458 Go to page 482 ? Answers on page 496

9 ◆ £16,000

36

Which British monarch was renowned for saying 'We are not amused'?

A: Victoria
B: George I
C: Edward VIII
D: Richard III

37

The Sargasso Sea is part of which ocean?

A: Arctic
B: Atlantic
C: Pacific
D: Indian

38

André Previn made his name as what?

A: Master chef
B: Thriller writer
C: Surrealist painter
D: Orchestral conductor

39

Where in the body are the tendons called 'hamstrings'?

A: In the foot
B: Under the heel
C: On the ankle
D: Behind the knee

40

What is the African Queen in the film starring Humphrey Bogart and Katharine Hepburn?

A: Tribal head
B: Giant butterfly
C: Steamboat
D: Tame lioness

50:50 Go to page 458 | Go to page 482 | ? Answers on page 496

9 ◆ £16,000

41

In British history, which royal houses fought in the Wars of the Roses?

- A: Hanover and Lancaster
- B: Lancaster and York
- C: York and Orange
- D: Tudor and Stuart

42

Winston Smith is the central character in which novel by George Orwell?

- A: The Road to Wigan Pier
- B: Animal Farm
- C: Keep the Aspidistra Flying
- D: Nineteen Eighty-Four

43

Which condition, often involving muscle rigidity or overactivity, is the name of a pop group?

- A: Catatonia
- B: Nirvana
- C: Paradox
- D: Therapy

44

Which of these words relates to the head?

- A: Centric
- B: Ceramic
- C: Celtic
- D: Cephalic

45

With which cartoon strip is Garry Trudeau most associated?

- A: Peanuts
- B: Doonesbury
- C: George and Lynne
- D: Hagar the Horrible

50:50 Go to page 458 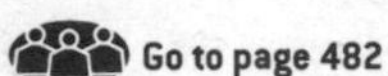 Go to page 482  Answers on page 496

9 ◆ £16,000

46

In Japanese cookery, what is 'nori'?

- A: Bean curd
- B: Raw fish
- C: Rice wine
- D: Seaweed

47

Which athletics event is sometimes known as the Metric Mile?

- A: 400 metres
- B: 800 metres
- C: 1500 metres
- D: 5000 metres

48

Which of these is a science fiction book by John Wyndham?

- A: The Midwich Seagulls
- B: The Midwich Cuckoos
- C: The Midwich Magpies
- D: The Midwich Thrushes

49

Which colour has been potted in snooker if the break goes up from 23 points to 28?

- A: Blue
- B: Pink
- C: Green
- D: Brown

50

The American Robert Oppenheimer is best known for the development of what?

- A: Telephone
- B: Atom bomb
- C: Artificial satellite
- D: Helicopter

50:50 Go to page 458

Go to page 482

Answers on page 496

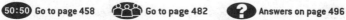

9 ◆ £16,000

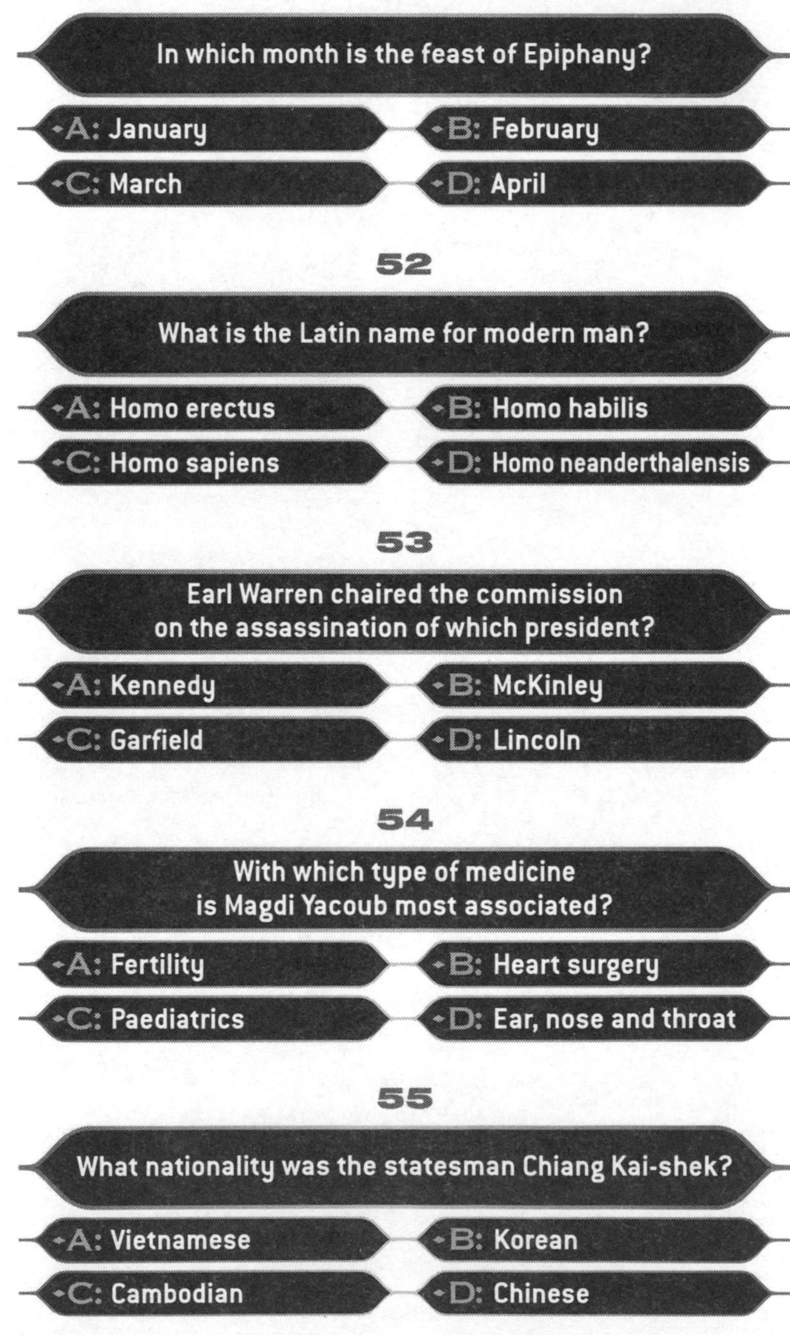

51

In which month is the feast of Epiphany?

A: January
B: February
C: March
D: April

52

What is the Latin name for modern man?

A: Homo erectus
B: Homo habilis
C: Homo sapiens
D: Homo neanderthalensis

53

Earl Warren chaired the commission on the assassination of which president?

A: Kennedy
B: McKinley
C: Garfield
D: Lincoln

54

With which type of medicine is Magdi Yacoub most associated?

A: Fertility
B: Heart surgery
C: Paediatrics
D: Ear, nose and throat

55

What nationality was the statesman Chiang Kai-shek?

A: Vietnamese
B: Korean
C: Cambodian
D: Chinese

50:50 Go to page 458 Go to page 482 ? Answers on page 496

9 ◆ £16,000

56

A 'parsec' is a unit of what?

A: Distance
B: Speed
C: Pressure
D: Height

57

Who wrote the opera 'Porgy and Bess'?

A: Scott Joplin
B: Leonard Bernstein
C: George Gershwin
D: Samuel Barber

58

In which country are the remains of the Mycenaean culture?

A: Egypt
B: Turkey
C: Iraq
D: Greece

59

Which town was the seat of the French government in World War II?

A: Vichy
B: Toulouse
C: Avignon
D: Grenoble

60

Which French phrase means 'required by fashion'?

A: De luxe
B: De nos jours
C: De trop
D: De rigueur

50:50 Go to page 458 · Go to page 482 ·  Answers on page 496

9 ◆ £16,000

61

Which tennis player was known as 'Little Mo'?

A: Maureen Connolly
B: Maria Bueno
C: Martina Navratilova
D: Margaret Court

62

Which animal might be described as 'hircine'?

A: Rabbit
B: Goat
C: Buffalo
D: Pig

63

Which of these creatures is a bird?

A: Cockroach
B: Cockchafer
C: Cock-of-the-rock
D: Cockle

64

Where did the world's first successful human heart transplant take place?

A: Chicago
B: Cape Town
C: Calcutta
D: Copenhagen

65

May was the middle name of which author?

A: Louisa Alcott
B: Susan Coolidge
C: Lucy Montgomery
D: Elinor Brent-Dyer

50:50 Go to page 458 Go to page 482 ? Answers on page 496

9 ◆ £16,000

66

On which river does Middlesbrough stand?

- A: Mersey
- B: Dee
- C: Tees
- D: Trent

67

Which Nobel Prize was won by Henry Kissinger?

- A: Economics
- B: Peace
- C: Literature
- D: Physics

68

The Barents Sea is an arm of which ocean?

- A: Arctic
- B: Atlantic
- C: Indian
- D: Pacific

69

Which gas was named after the Greek word for 'green'?

- A: Argon
- B: Neon
- C: Chlorine
- D: Helium

70

Episodes of which TV comedy are regularly titled 'The One With…'?

- A: South Park
- B: Friends
- C: The Simpsons
- D: Frasier

50:50 Go to page 458

 Go to page 482

? Answers on page 496

9 ◆ £16,000

71

The Ivor Novello Awards are given for achievement in which field?

- A: Architecture
- B: Fashion
- C: Football
- D: Songwriting

72

Henry VIII's wife Catherine of Aragon was born in which country?

- A: Spain
- B: Portugal
- C: France
- D: Italy

73

In a play, what kind of speech reveals a character's innermost thoughts to the audience?

- A: Dialogue
- B: Oration
- C: Soliloquy
- D: Colloquy

74

A Varsovian lives in which city?

- A: Warsaw
- B: Vienna
- C: Vladivostock
- D: Venice

75

In relation to animals, what does the word 'edentate' mean?

- A: No horns
- B: No fur
- C: No teeth
- D: No hooves

50:50 Go to page 458 Go to page 482

Answers on page 496

9 ◆ £16,000

76

With which country did Great Britain sign the Entente Cordiale?

- A: United States
- B: France
- C: Germany
- D: Russia

77

What was the first name of the explorer Shackleton?

- A: Edgar
- B: Ernest
- C: Eldridge
- D: Embury

78

Which children's author wrote the screenplay of 'Chitty Chitty Bang Bang'?

- A: Roald Dahl
- B: Quentin Blake
- C: Raymond Briggs
- D: Michael Bond

79

In which county is Alderley Edge?

- A: Cumbria
- B: Northumberland
- C: Durham
- D: Cheshire

80

The fibre sisal is chiefly used to make what?

- A: Ropes
- B: Hats
- C: Stockings
- D: Sails

50:50 Go to page 458

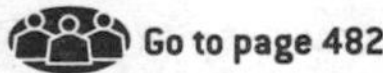

Go to page 482

Answers on page 496

9 ◆ £16,000

81

In which British town is the Lowry Centre?

A: Preston
B: Doncaster
C: Salford
D: Bingley

82

In which year did the Jarrow March take place?

A: 1916
B: 1926
C: 1936
D: 1946

83

Where does the Dalai Lama come from?

A: Tibet
B: Korea
C: Japan
D: Cambodia

84

At which Olympic Games did Olga Korbut win three gymnastics gold medals?

A: Mexico City
B: Munich
C: Montreal
D: Moscow

85

Which instrument was played by the jazz musician Miles Davis?

A: Saxophone
B: Piano
C: Trumpet
D: Guitar

50:50 Go to page 458 · Go to page 482 · ? Answers on page 496

9 ◆ £16,000

86

Robert Clive was known as 'Clive of...' where?

- A: India
- B: China
- C: Australia
- D: Malaysia

87

Which animal was once called the 'camelopard'?

- A: Zebra
- B: Giraffe
- C: Cheetah
- D: Hippopotamus

88

Which prime minister wrote 'A History of the English-Speaking Peoples'?

- A: Disraeli
- B: Baldwin
- C: Salisbury
- D: Churchill

89

Which calendar was introduced into England in 1752?

- A: Gregorian
- B: Julian
- C: Caesarian
- D: Hadriatic

90

On which river is 'Three Men in a Boat' set?

- A: St. Lawrence
- B: Danube
- C: Seine
- D: Thames

50:50 Go to page 458  Go to page 482 ? Answers on page 496

9 ◆ £16,000

91

The most famous work by Edward Gibbon is on the decline and fall of which empire?

A: British | B: Roman

C: Byzantine | D: Turkish

92

Who wrote 'The Ballad of Reading Gaol'?

A: John Masefield | B: Robert Browning

C: Wilfred Owen | D: Oscar Wilde

93

What is the more common name for the condition 'hypermetropia'?

A: Toothache | B: Migraine

C: Long-sightedness | D: Sore throat

94

Where is T S Eliot's play 'Murder in the Cathedral' set?

A: Canterbury Cathedral | B: York Minster

C: St. Paul's Cathedral | D: Salisbury Cathedral

95

What kind of animal is a 'leatherback'?

A: Snake | B: Turtle

C: Shark | D: Toad

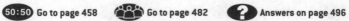

50:50 Go to page 458 Go to page 482  Answers on page 496

9 ◆ £16,000

96

Which football team won the League and FA Cup double in 1961?

A: Tottenham Hotspur
B: Arsenal
C: Chelsea
D: Crystal Palace

97

The famous bridge at Avignon was built over which river?

A: Rhône
B: Seine
C: Marne
D: Loire

98

In the film 'The Conqueror', John Wayne plays which historical character?

A: George Armstrong Custer
B: Davy Crockett
C: Genghis Khan
D: Napoleon Bonaparte

99

'Tinca tinca' is the Latin name for which fish?

A: Roach
B: Rudd
C: Perch
D: Tench

100

In 1995, Michael Schumacher became Formula One world champion for which team?

A: Ferrari
B: Benetton
C: Williams
D: Jordan

50:50 Go to page 458

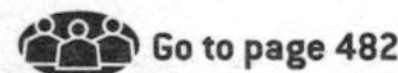

Go to page 482
Answers on page 496

9 ◆ £16,000

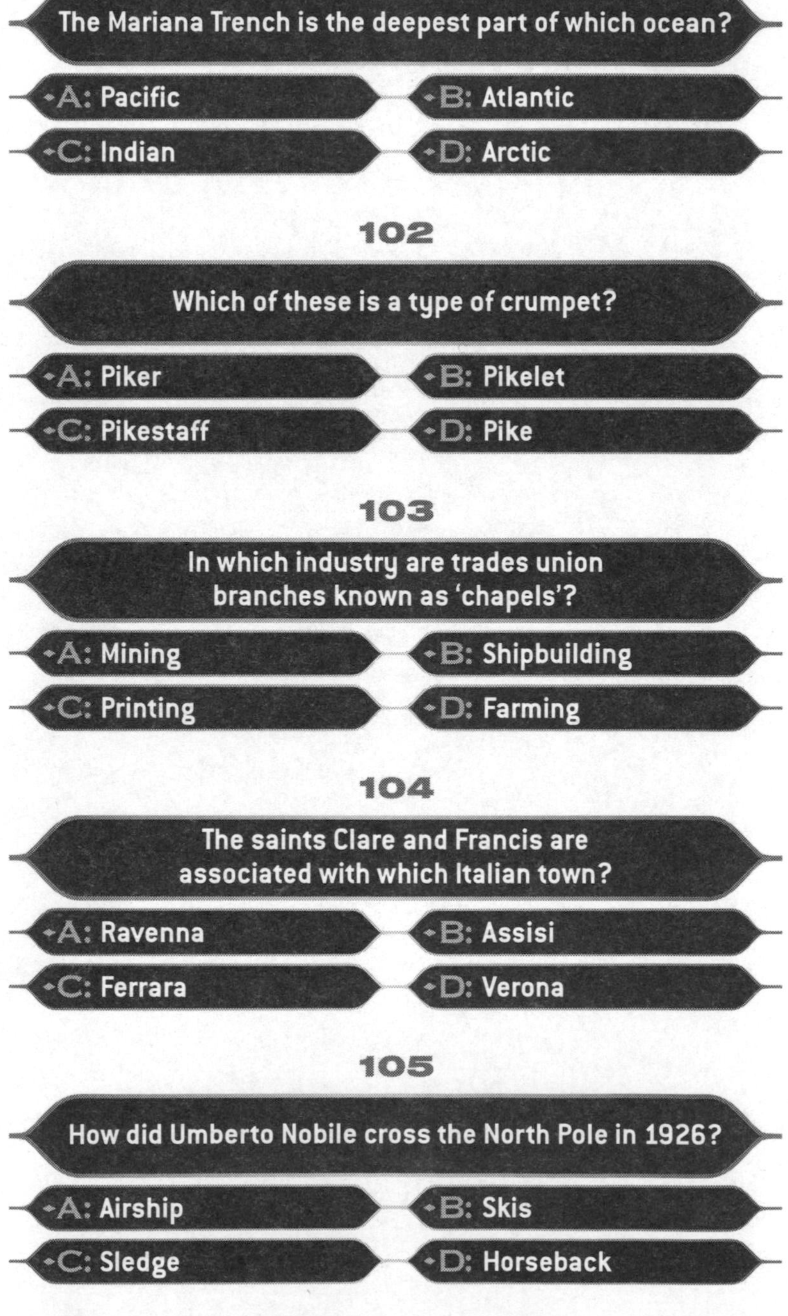

101

The Mariana Trench is the deepest part of which ocean?

A: Pacific
B: Atlantic
C: Indian
D: Arctic

102

Which of these is a type of crumpet?

A: Piker
B: Pikelet
C: Pikestaff
D: Pike

103

In which industry are trades union branches known as 'chapels'?

A: Mining
B: Shipbuilding
C: Printing
D: Farming

104

The saints Clare and Francis are associated with which Italian town?

A: Ravenna
B: Assisi
C: Ferrara
D: Verona

105

How did Umberto Nobile cross the North Pole in 1926?

A: Airship
B: Skis
C: Sledge
D: Horseback

50:50 Go to page 458 Go to page 482 ? Answers on page 496

9 ◆ £16,000

106

What is the top award at the Montreux television festival?

A: Golden Heart
B: Golden Rose
C: Golden Lion
D: Golden Bear

107

Which pastry is traditionally used to make the Greek dish baklava?

A: Choux
B: Suet
C: Puff
D: Filo

108

Which of these countries is not a member of the European Union?

A: Germany
B: Italy
C: Switzerland
D: Belgium

109

The double helix is most associated with the structure of what?

A: BBC
B: DNA
C: ABC
D: KGB

110

The 'sockeye' is a species of which fish?

A: Mackerel
B: Tuna
C: Salmon
D: Eel

50:50 Go to page 458 Go to page 482  Answers on page 496

9 ◆ £16,000

111

With which sport was Brooklands in Surrey most associated?

A: Motor racing
B: Showjumping
C: Shooting
D: Polo

112

What was made by the Bessemer process?

A: Glass
B: Bread
C: Paper
D: Steel

113

Who was the founder of the Salvation Army?

A: William Booth
B: John Wesley
C: Mary Baker Eddy
D: Joseph Smith

114

What is the English name for what Americans call 'confectioner's sugar'?

A: Castor sugar
B: Sugar lumps
C: Icing sugar
D: Demerara sugar

115

In 2000, which author released his novel 'The Plant' on the Internet?

A: Michael Crichton
B: James Herbert
C: John Grisham
D: Stephen King

50:50 Go to page 458 Go to page 482 ? Answers on page 496

9 ◆ £16,000

116

Traditionally, witchetty grubs are eaten by which people?

A: Australian aborigines
B: North American Indians
C: Laplanders
D: Maoris

50:50 Go to page 458 Go to page 482 ? Answers on page 496

50:50

15 £1 MILLION
14 £500,000
13 £250,000
12 £125,000
11 £64,000
10 ◆ £32,000
9 ◆ £16,000
8 ◆ £8,000
7 ◆ £4,000
6 ◆ £2,000
5 ◆ £1,000
4 ◆ £500
3 ◆ £300
2 ◆ £200
1 ◆ £100

10 ◆ £32,000

1

What was the surname of the Scottish outlaw Rob Roy?

A: MacGregor
B: MacTavish
C: MacNab
D: MacDougall

2

The Indonesian capital Jakarta is on which island?

A: Sumatra
B: Bali
C: Borneo
D: Java

3

What is a linnet?

A: Bird
B: Musical instrument
C: Poem
D: Butterfly

4

Which of these is the name of a type of small yellowish-red ant?

A: Mummy
B: Pharaoh
C: Cleopatra
D: Pyramid

5

Aquae Sulis was the Latin name for which English city?

A: Chester
B: Oxford
C: Bath
D: Colchester

50:50 Go to page 459 Go to page 483 
Answers on page 497

10 ◆ £32,000

6

What is the alternative name for a Western film?

A: Horse opera
B: Stagecoach play
C: Sheriff drama
D: Gunfight show

7

What was the nickname of Peter I of Russia?

A: The Terrible
B: The Bold
C: The Great
D: The Vain

8

In the UK version of Cluedo, what is the surname of the murder victim?

A: Black
B: Green
C: White
D: Brown

9

Which pedigree dog breed is the tallest?

A: Afghan hound
B: Irish wolfhound
C: Belgian sheepdog
D: English setter

10

Who was the wife of Henry VI of England?

A: Eleanor of Aachen
B: Isabel of Arles
C: Catherine of Aquitaine
D: Margaret of Anjou

50:50 Go to page 459 · Go to page 483 · ? Answers on page 497

10 ◆ £32,000

11

When English dandy Beau Brummell remarked 'Who's your fat friend?', to whom was he referring?

A: Prince of Wales
B: Queen Victoria
C: Lillie Langtry
D: Prince Albert

12

In which county is the market town of Spalding?

A: Lincolnshire
B: Kent
C: Berkshire
D: Norfolk

13

Which of these is the title of a Hitchcock film?

A: Lead Piping
B: Dagger
C: Rope
D: Candlestick

14

Which eminent Greek philosopher famously tutored Alexander the Great?

A: Aristotle
B: Plato
C: Sophocles
D: Epicurus

15

Which knight of the Round Table was the lover of Queen Guinevere?

A: Gawain
B: Galahad
C: Percival
D: Lancelot

50:50 Go to page 459 Go to page 483 ? Answers on page 497

10 ◆ £32,000

16

Which of these is a method designed to improve posture and movement?

- A: Alfred technique
- B: Allan technique
- C: Alexander technique
- D: Algernon technique

17

Which body of water links the Black Sea and Mediterranean Sea?

- A: Sea of Marmara
- B: Tyrrhenian Sea
- C: Ligurian Sea
- D: Ionian Sea

18

Which English king was known as the 'Hammer of the Scots'?

- A: Richard I
- B: Henry I
- C: William I
- D: Edward I

19

The British island of Lundy is located in which body of water?

- A: North Sea
- B: Bristol Channel
- C: Baltic Sea
- D: English Channel

20

The word 'cataract' refers to what kind of geographical feature?

- A: Mountain
- B: Cave
- C: Lake
- D: Waterfall

50:50 Go to page 459
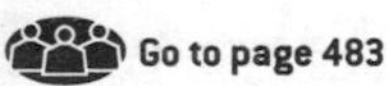
Go to page 483

Answers on page 497

10 ◆ £32,000

21

Which London building stands on the site of Newgate Prison?

A: Old Bailey
B: Westminster Cathedral
C: Battersea Power Station
D: Harrods

22

From what is the traditional English dish of Bath chap made?

A: Horses' hooves
B: Pigs' cheeks
C: Lambs' brains
D: Cows' ears

23

The Molly Maguires was a secret organisation operating in which industry in 19th century America?

A: Coal mining
B: Sheep farming
C: Railroad construction
D: Ship building

24

'The Song of Hiawatha' is a work by which US poet?

A: Walt Whitman
B: Henry Wadsworth Longfellow
C: Allen Ginsberg
D: Robert Lowell

25

Which pop singer sang the theme of the Bond film 'The Man With The Golden Gun'?

A: Sheena Easton
B: Shirley Bassey
C: Lulu
D: Tom Jones

50:50 Go to page 459
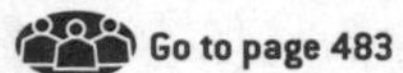
Go to page 483

Answers on page 497

10 ◆ £32,000

26

What is the Southern Cross?

- A: Star constellation
- B: Left-hand boxing punch
- C: Military medal
- D: M4/M25 Junction

27

Mecca is a city in which country?

- A: India
- B: Saudi Arabia
- C: Yemen
- D: Israel

28

The girl's name Erica is also the Latin word for which plant, another girl's name?

- A: Daisy
- B: Lily
- C: Pansy
- D: Heather

29

How does an international air mile compare with a statute mile?

- A: Longer
- B: Shorter
- C: The same
- D: There's no such measure

30

What does a 'canophilist' like?

- A: Music
- B: Dogs
- C: Card games
- D: Eating

50:50 Go to page 459 Go to page 483

Answers on page 497

10 ◆ £32,000

31

Castle Howard is in which county?

A: Cornwall
B: Suffolk
C: Gloucestershire
D: North Yorkshire

32

Selenology is the study of what?

A: Sun
B: Moon
C: Stars
D: Earth

33

Who devised the play 'Abigail's Party'?

A: Mike Leigh
B: Steven Berkoff
C: Arnold Wesker
D: Alan Bennett

34

The calypso originated on which West Indian island?

A: Barbados
B: Antigua
C: Jamaica
D: Trinidad

35

The chador is a robe worn by women of which of these religions?

A: Islam
B: Judaism
C: Buddhism
D: Christianity

50:50 Go to page 459 Go to page 483 ? Answers on page 497

10 ◆ £32,000

36

Which of these composers was born in the 20th century?

A: Edward Elgar
B: Philip Glass
C: Gustav Holst
D: Georges Bizet

37

What type of gas is usually put in canisters of Calor gas?

A: Ethane
B: Methane
C: Butane
D: Pentane

38

In 1969, which politician was involved in a car accident at Chappaquiddick?

A: Pierre Trudeau
B: Gerald Ford
C: Ronald Reagan
D: Edward Kennedy

39

What kind of star sign is Gemini?

A: Earth
B: Air
C: Fire
D: Water

40

In chemistry, what is a 'pipette' used for?

A: Measuring liquids
B: Taking temperatures
C: Timing reactions
D: Separating solids

50:50 Go to page 459 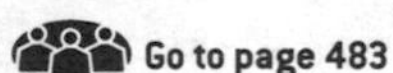 Go to page 483  Answers on page 497

10 ◆ £32,000

41

In which country is the Masai Mara game reserve?

- A: Malawi
- B: Uganda
- C: Tanzania
- D: Kenya

42

In a building, what is a paternoster?

- A: Air vent
- B: Lift
- C: Window
- D: Boiler

43

Which flower, associated with the city of Parma, is used to make perfume?

- A: Rose
- B: Lily-of-the-valley
- C: Violet
- D: Orchid

44

Who gave his name to Parkinson's law?

- A: James Parkinson
- B: C. Northcote Parkinson
- C: Michael Parkinson
- D: Cecil Parkinson

45

In mythology, which creature sprang from the blood of Medusa?

- A: Pegasus
- B: Cerberus
- C: Hydra
- D: Centaur

50:50 Go to page 459

Go to page 483
? Answers on page 497

10 ◆ £32,000

46

Which entertainer said,
'I cried all the way to the bank.'?

A: Liberace
B: Bob Hope
C: Dean Martin
D: Lucille Ball

47

What was the name of President Eisenhower's wife?

A: Maddy
B: Mamie
C: Maisie
D: Milly

48

The Ponte Vecchio, in Florence,
crosses which stretch of water?

A: Arno
B: Tiber
C: Po
D: Grand Canal

49

Which of these elements has a
single letter for its chemical symbol?

A: Astatine
B: Bromine
C: Chlorine
D: Iodine

50

The Rosetta Stone was discovered in which country?

A: Israel
B: Yemen
C: Egypt
D: Ethiopia

50:50 Go to page 459 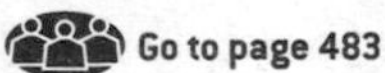 Go to page 483  Answers on page 497

10 ◆ £32,000

51

In printing, what shape is an 'obelus'?

A: Star
B: Diamond
C: Bell
D: Dagger

52

The volcano Mount Pelée is on which island?

A: Saint Lucia
B: Martinique
C: Jamaica
D: Cuba

53

What was the profession of Edward Alleyn, the founder of Dulwich College?

A: Tea importer
B: Bishop
C: Journalist
D: Actor

54

In the body, what would be described as 'adipose'?

A: Hair
B: Skin
C: Fat
D: Bone

55

Utah belongs to which group of states?

A: Rocky Mountain
B: New England
C: Pacific Coast
D: Southern

50:50 Go to page 459
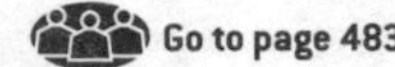
Go to page 483

Answers on page 497

10 ◆ £32,000

56

The Indian god Hanuman is depicted as which animal?

- A: Vulture
- B: Jackal
- C: Elephant
- D: Monkey

57

Which of these is a trellis used to train trees?

- A: Atelier
- B: Chevalier
- C: Espalier
- D: Duvalier

58

The Daiquiri cocktail is named after a place in which country?

- A: Cuba
- B: Venezuela
- C: Mexico
- D: Guyana

59

What kind of food is Bel Paese?

- A: Bread
- B: Cheese
- C: Ham
- D: Pasta

60

In which city is the Prater funfair?

- A: Berlin
- B: Copenhagen
- C: Vienna
- D: Helsinki

50:50 Go to page 459 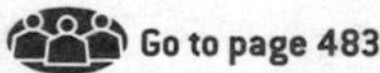 Go to page 483  Answers on page 497

61

Which religious leader is said to have found enlightenment while sitting under a tree?

A: Jesus
B: Moses
C: Buddha
D: Mohammed

62

Who wrote the wartime film 'In Which We Serve'?

A: Ivor Novello
B: Noel Coward
C: J B Priestley
D: Michael Powell

63

Which of these states was affected by the Dust Bowl in America in the 1930s?

A: Connecticut
B: Alaska
C: Washington
D: Oklahoma

64

Which animal is known as the 'prairie wolf'?

A: Hyena
B: Dingo
C: Coyote
D: Arctic fox

65

Which 'Coronation Street' character was played by Jean Alexander?

A: Annie Walker
B: Elsie Tanner
C: Minnie Caldwell
D: Hilda Ogden

50:50 Go to page 459 Go to page 483 ? Answers on page 497

10 ◆ £32,000

66

A 'Habanero' is a native of which city?

- A: Havana
- B: Houston
- C: Helsinki
- D: Honolulu

67

Which of these was invented by Joseph Bramah?

- A: Road surface
- B: Lock
- C: Shorthand system
- D: Pen

68

Which of these is a coast of India?

- A: Malabar
- B: Skeleton
- C: Ivory
- D: Gold

69

In which mythology does the Happy Hunting Ground feature?

- A: Zulu
- B: Maori
- C: Australian Aborigine
- D: North American Indian

70

The chemical ethylene glycol is most commonly used as what?

- A: Bleach
- B: Starch
- C: Nail varnish remover
- D: Antifreeze

50:50 Go to page 459 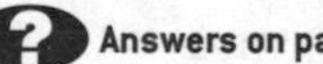 Go to page 483 ? Answers on page 497

10 ◆ £32,000

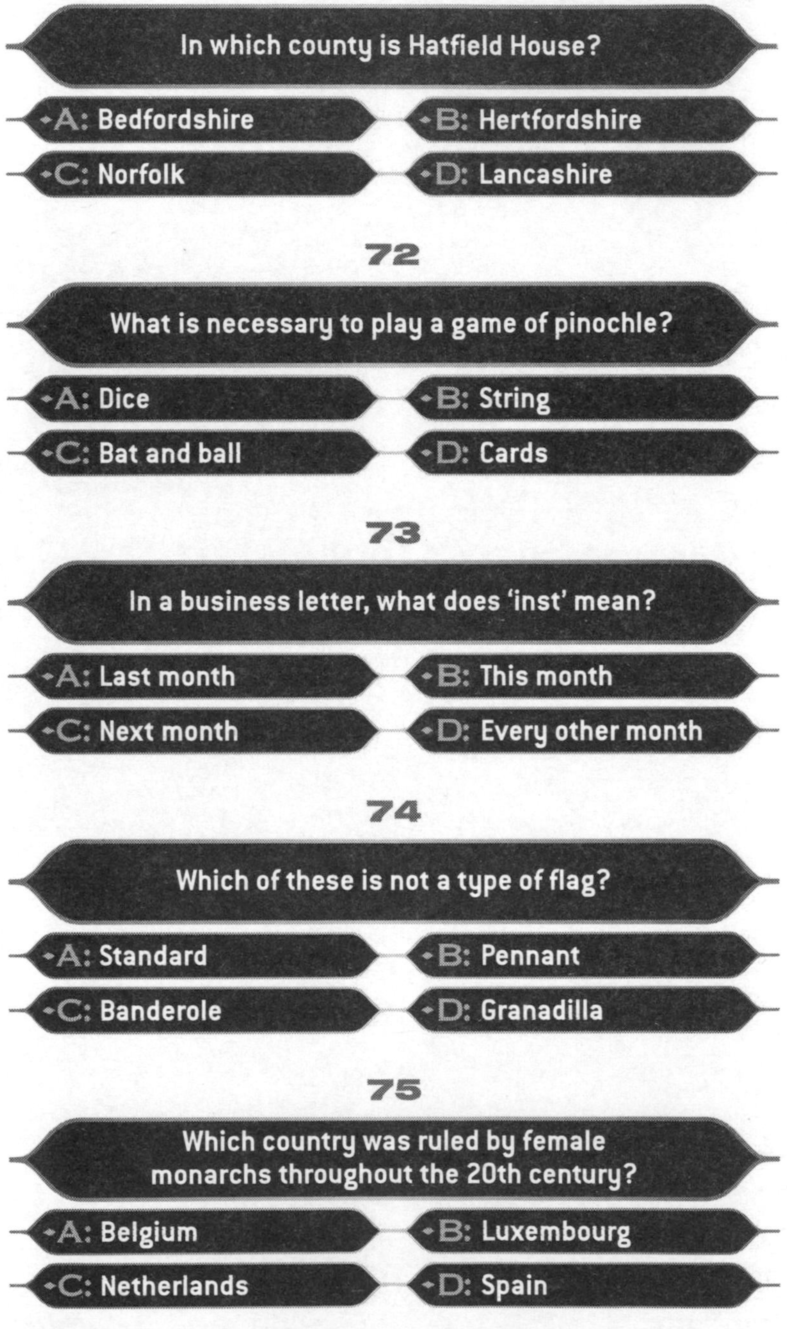

71

In which county is Hatfield House?

A: Bedfordshire
B: Hertfordshire
C: Norfolk
D: Lancashire

72

What is necessary to play a game of pinochle?

A: Dice
B: String
C: Bat and ball
D: Cards

73

In a business letter, what does 'inst' mean?

A: Last month
B: This month
C: Next month
D: Every other month

74

Which of these is not a type of flag?

A: Standard
B: Pennant
C: Banderole
D: Granadilla

75

Which country was ruled by female monarchs throughout the 20th century?

A: Belgium
B: Luxembourg
C: Netherlands
D: Spain

50:50 Go to page 459 Go to page 483 ? Answers on page 497

10 ◆ £32,000

76

Which stretch of water separates Skye from the Outer Hebrides?

- A: Little Inch
- B: Little Minch
- C: Little Pinch
- D: Little Winch

77

What nationality was the athlete Emil Zatopek?

- A: Russian
- B: Finnish
- C: Hungarian
- D: Czechoslovakian

78

Archie Leach was the central character in which British film?

- A: Withnail and I
- B: A Fish Called Wanda
- C: The Full Monty
- D: Brassed Off

79

Westmorland became part of which new county?

- A: Avon
- B: Cumbria
- C: Humberside
- D: Cleveland

80

Doctor Crippen was arrested on board which ship?

- A: Lusitania
- B: Montrose
- C: Forfar
- D: Queen Mary

50:50 Go to page 459 Go to page 483

Answers on page 497

10 ◆ £32,000

81

Who was the first parliamentary leader of the Labour Party?

A: James Ramsay MacDonald
B: Keir Hardie
C: Herbert Morrison
D: Aneurin Bevan

82

Baku is the capital of which country?

A: Algeria
B: Angola
C: Armenia
D: Azerbaijan

83

Which regular solid has faces which are all pentagons?

A: Octahedron
B: Dodecahedron
C: Icosahedron
D: Cube

84

In which country is the pilgrimage centre of Fatima?

A: Ireland
B: Portugal
C: Croatia
D: Italy

85

Sir Anthony Dowell is most associated with which field of the arts?

A: Ballet
B: Opera
C: Poetry
D: Conducting

50:50 Go to page 459 · Go to page 483 · ? Answers on page 497

10 ◆ £32,000

86

Which of these is a type of grass grown for grazing?

A: Michael grass
B: Hilary grass
C: Timothy grass
D: Nicholas grass

87

The two obelisks known as Cleopatra's Needles are in London and which other city?

A: Paris
B: Rome
C: Alexandria
D: New York

88

Which insect is sometimes known as a 'darning needle'?

A: Dragonfly
B: Ladybird
C: Water boatman
D: Wasp

89

Who replaced Charles Dickens on the Bank of England £10 note?

A: Rudyard Kipling
B: Charles Darwin
C: Joshua Reynolds
D: Francis Drake

90

Which Tennessee Williams play features the characters Maggie and Brick?

A: A Streetcar Named Desire
B: The Glass Menagerie
C: Sweet Bird of Youth
D: Cat on a Hot Tin Roof

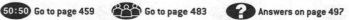

50:50 Go to page 459 Go to page 483  Answers on page 497

10 ◆ £32,000

91

The most northerly point of mainland Africa is in which country?

A: Egypt
B: Tunisia
C: Libya
D: Morocco

92

Who was the mother of King John?

A: Catherine of Aragon
B: Mary of Modena
C: Anne of Cleves
D: Eleanor of Aquitaine

93

Which arteries carry blood to the head and neck?

A: Pulmonary
B: Subclavian
C: Carotid
D: Popliteal

94

Which of these seas is the largest?

A: South China
B: Baltic
C: Irish
D: Red

95

Which of these fictional policemen was created by Georges Simenon?

A: Clouseau
B: Morse
C: Lestrade
D: Maigret

50:50 Go to page 459 Go to page 483 ? Answers on page 497

10 ◆ £32,000

96

What was the name of the area presided over by a bailiff?

- A: Bailie
- B: Bail
- C: Bailiwick
- D: Bailer

97

In the computing acronym BASIC, what does the B stand for?

- A: Beginners
- B: British
- C: Byte
- D: Barium

98

In which adventure novel is Harry Feversham the hero?

- A: Kidnapped
- B: Beau Geste
- C: The Four Feathers
- D: She

99

Which animal appears on the national flag of Sri Lanka?

- A: Tiger
- B: Elephant
- C: Parrot
- D: Lion

100

In France, what kind of building is a 'moulin'?

- A: Castle
- B: Mill
- C: Hospital
- D: Farmhouse

50:50 Go to page 459  Go to page 483 ? Answers on page 497

10 ◆ £32,000

101

Which British queen was excommunicated by the Pope?

A: Anne
B: Mary I
C: Elizabeth I
D: Elizabeth II

102

In which US state is the city of Minneapolis?

A: Nevada
B: Alaska
C: Texas
D: Minnesota

103

What kind of bird is a capercaillie?

A: Grouse
B: Pigeon
C: Goose
D: Penguin

104

Ferdinand and Isabella were joint rulers in which country?

A: France
B: Portugal
C: Netherlands
D: Spain

105

Who played the title role in the US sitcom 'Rhoda'?

A: Julie Kavner
B: Mary Tyler Moore
C: Valerie Harper
D: Rhea Perlman

50:50 Go to page 459 · Go to page 483 · ? Answers on page 497

10 ◆ £32,000

106

Which small republic makes up Yugoslavia with Serbia?

- A: Montenegro
- B: Slovenia
- C: Macedonia
- D: Slovakia

107

In the sitcom 'The Golden Girls', which character was played by Betty White?

- A: Dorothy
- B: Blanche
- C: Sophia
- D: Rose

108

Which sporting event was won five times by Eddy Merckx?

- A: Epsom Derby
- B: US Masters Golf
- C: Tour de France
- D: French Open Tennis

50:50 Go to page 459

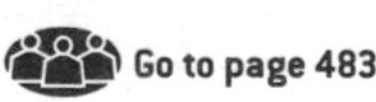
Go to page 483

Answers on page 497

50:50  

15 £1 MILLION

14 £500,000

13 £250,000

12 £125,000

11 ◆ £64,000

10 ◆ £32,000

9 ◆ £16,000

8 ◆ £8,000

7 ◆ £4,000

6 ◆ £2,000

5 ◆ £1,000

4 ◆ £500

3 ◆ £300

2 ◆ £200

1 ◆ £100

11 ◆ £64,000

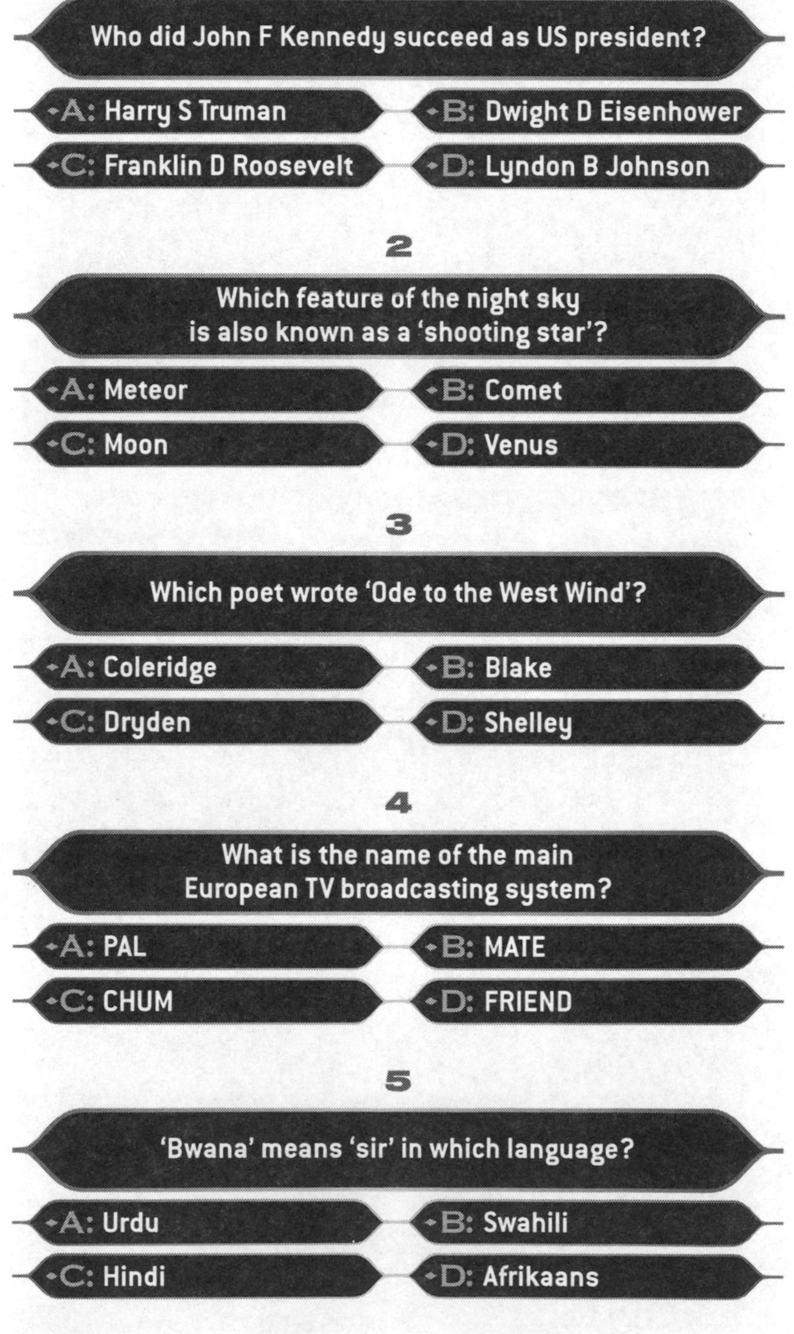

1
Who did John F Kennedy succeed as US president?
A: Harry S Truman
B: Dwight D Eisenhower
C: Franklin D Roosevelt
D: Lyndon B Johnson
2
Which feature of the night sky is also known as a 'shooting star'?
A: Meteor
B: Comet
C: Moon
D: Venus
3
Which poet wrote 'Ode to the West Wind'?
A: Coleridge
B: Blake
C: Dryden
D: Shelley
4
What is the name of the main European TV broadcasting system?
A: PAL
B: MATE
C: CHUM
D: FRIEND
5
'Bwana' means 'sir' in which language?
A: Urdu
B: Swahili
C: Hindi
D: Afrikaans

50:50 Go to page 461 Go to page 484 ? Answers on page 497

11 ◆ £64,000

6

Which institution is known as the 'Fourth Estate'?

- A: House of Commons
- B: House of Lords
- C: Church of England
- D: The Press

7

Who was the first cricketer to score 10,000 Test match runs?

- A: Viv Richards
- B: Sunil Gavaskar
- C: David Gower
- D: Greg Chappell

8

Petrography is concerned with what?

- A: Soil
- B: Fossils
- C: Rocks
- D: Oceans

9

Graham Sutherland's portrait of whom was deliberately destroyed by the subject's widow?

- A: George VI
- B: Winston Churchill
- C: Dylan Thomas
- D: Edward Elgar

10

Which officer commands a platoon?

- A: Major
- B: Lieutenant
- C: Captain
- D: Brigadier

50:50 Go to page 461  Go to page 484 ? Answers on page 497

11 ◆ £64,000

11

In which part of the world is the EC dollar a unit of currency?

- A: Caribbean
- B: Europe
- C: South America
- D: Former Soviet Union

12

Cape Verde is a former colony of which country?

- A: France
- B: Portugal
- C: Spain
- D: Great Britain

13

With which theatrical style is William Congreve most associated?

- A: Restoration comedy
- B: Jacobean tragedy
- C: Kitchen sink drama
- D: Theatre of the Absurd

14

What is the literal meaning of the word 'Pharaoh'?

- A: River of light
- B: Eat well
- C: Great house
- D: Lover of gods

15

Which spirit is the base of a White Lady cocktail?

- A: Tequila
- B: Gin
- C: Rum
- D: Bourbon

50:50 Go to page 461  Go to page 484 ? Answers on page 497

11 ◆ £64,000

16

The name of which dog breed is also the name for an animal's footprint?

A: Pug | B: Spitz
C: Pointer | D: Spaniel

17

What is the name of the point in a planet's orbit when it is nearest to the sun?

A: Aphelion | B: Perihelion
C: Zenith | D: Nadir

18

In which modern country is the site of the Battle of Balaklava?

A: Armenia | B: Turkey
C: Ukraine | D: Georgia

19

Which chemical element takes its name from a German word for a goblin?

A: Chromium | B: Calcium
C: Copper | D: Cobalt

20

Which herb is used to make the garnish 'gremolata'?

A: Basil | B: Parsley
C: Mint | D: Thyme

50:50 Go to page 461 · Go to page 484 ·  Answers on page 497

11 ◆ £64,000

21

Who was made the first Holy Roman Emperor?

A: Augustus | B: Saladin
C: Attila | D: Charlemagne

22

The Korat plateau in Thailand gives its name to what kind of animal?

A: Sheep | B: Wolf
C: Eagle | D: Cat

23

Which of these is a character in Chaucer's 'Canterbury Tales'?

A: Worthy of Barnsley | B: Woman of Birmingham
C: Wife of Bath | D: Witch of Bristol

24

The word 'bandit' comes from which language?

A: Greek | B: Italian
C: Hindi | D: Swahili

25

The Bosman ruling was a legal decision relating to which sport?

A: Football | B: Tennis
C: Athletics | D: Gymnastics

50:50 Go to page 461
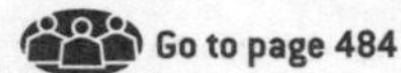

11 ◆ £64,000

26

In science, which term refers to the number of protons in the nucleus of an atom?

- A: Atomic weight
- B: Atomic number
- C: Atomic heat
- D: Atomic clock

27

Which of these writers had a brother called Branwell?

- A: Charlotte Bronte
- B: Virginia Woolf
- C: Jane Austen
- D: Dorothy Parker

28

In which cathedral town was Doctor Johnson born?

- A: Ely
- B: Lichfield
- C: Beverley
- D: Rochester

29

With which industry is Northampton traditionally associated?

- A: Optical instrument-making
- B: Steel-making
- C: Shoe-making
- D: Lace-making

30

What kind of musical work is Strauss's 'Die Fledermaus'?

- A: Oratorio
- B: Symphony
- C: Concerto
- D: Operetta

50:50 Go to page 461  Go to page 484  Answers on page 497

11 ◆ £64,000

31

The Olduvai Gorge, famous for its fossils, is in which country?

A: Uganda
B: Kenya
C: Tanzania
D: Malawi

32

Mount Athos is famous for its many monasteries of which religion?

A: Roman Catholic
B: Greek Orthodox
C: Buddhist
D: Shinto

33

The European title 'Count' is equivalent to which British title?

A: Earl
B: Duke
C: Marquess
D: Baron

34

'Riotous Assembly' was the first novel by which author?

A: Malcolm Bradbury
B: Tom Sharpe
C: John Braine
D: Keith Waterhouse

35

What name was given to the 8th century Muslim invaders of Spain?

A: Moors
B: Vales
C: Wolds
D: Fells

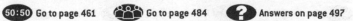

50:50 Go to page 461 Go to page 484

Answers on page 497

11 ◆ £64,000

36

Who was the father of Icarus?

A: Theseus
B: Daedalus
C: Menelaus
D: Paris

37

What is the name of the body part which separates the nostrils?

A: Pentum
B: Hexum
C: Septum
D: Octum

38

For which film did James Cagney win his Oscar?

A: The Public Enemy
B: Yankee Doodle Dandy
C: Angels With Dirty Faces
D: Ragtime

39

Which country is ruled by two Captains Regent?

A: San Marino
B: Monaco
C: Andorra
D: Vatican City

40

The architect Edwin Lutyens is best known for his plans for which capital city?

A: Brasilia
B: Canberra
C: New Delhi
D: Stockholm

50:50 Go to page 461 Go to page 484 ? Answers on page 497

11 ◆ £64,000

41

Which artist painted 'Guernica'?

A: Dali
B: Picasso
C: Cezanne
D: Van Gogh

42

In mediaeval history, who was the lover of Héloïse?

A: Tristan
B: Gawain
C: Abelard
D: Bernard

43

Which of these is a place in Cambridgeshire?

A: Derby
B: Caerphilly
C: Gloucester
D: Stilton

44

During the 20th century, who was the only England bowler to take a hat trick in an Ashes Test?

A: Bob Willis
B: Darren Gough
C: Fred Trueman
D: Ian Botham

45

Who was the Greek equivalent of the Roman god Vulcan?

A: Hephaestus
B: Morpheus
C: Hades
D: Dionysus

50:50 Go to page 461 · Go to page 484 · Answers on page 497

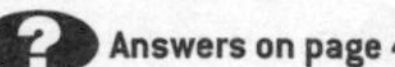

11 ◆ £64,000

46

What is the literal meaning of the word 'cenotaph'?

- A: Single pillar
- B: Old monument
- C: Silent stone
- D: Empty tomb

47

Who was the mother of Princess Alexandra?

- A: Princess Marina
- B: Princess Alice
- C: Princess Sophia
- D: Princess Anne

48

The eohippus was an early form of which animal?

- A: Hippopotamus
- B: Horse
- C: Hare
- D: Hedgehog

49

Where was the first Three Tenors concert held?

- A: Atlanta
- B: Barcelona
- C: Pasadena
- D: Rome

50

What is the many-legged mythological sea creature of Scandinavia?

- A: Kraken
- B: Merman
- C: Hydra
- D: Cerberus

50:50 Go to page 461 Go to page 484  Answers on page 497

11 ◆ £64,000

51

What kind of insect is a 'whirligig'?

A: Aphid | B: Beetle
C: Dragonfly | D: Termite

52

Who would use an 'embouchure' in their work?

A: Jockey | B: Seamstress
C: Pilot | D: Musician

53

Who or what might be given an Apgar rating?

A: Racehorse | B: Baby
C: Earthquake | D: Bridge player

54

The Battle of Inkerman took place during which war?

A: Crimean War | B: Napoleonic Wars
C: Seven Years' War | D: Wars of the Roses

55

In the body, what may be endocrine or exocrine?

A: Bones | B: Muscles
C: Glands | D: Veins

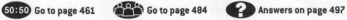

50:50 Go to page 461 Go to page 484

Answers on page 497

11 ◆ £64,000

56

What is the most northerly town in Europe?

- A: Uppsala
- B: Hammerfest
- C: Murmansk
- D: Helsinki

57

Which of these composers was English?

- A: Debussy
- B: Delibes
- C: Delius
- D: Dukas

58

Which Russian word means 'openness'?

- A: Glasnost
- B: Izvestiya
- C: Perestroika
- D: Pravda

59

The Palio, held in Siena, is what kind of race?

- A: Motorcycle
- B: Running
- C: Horse
- D: Vintage car

60

Which modern city was once called Byzantium?

- A: Athens
- B: Istanbul
- C: St. Petersburg
- D: Florence

50:50 Go to page 461 Go to page 484

Answers on page 497

11 ◆ £64,000

61

In mythology, which maiden was saved from a sea monster by Perseus?

A: Atalanta
B: Leda
C: Andromeda
D: Lucretia

62

In which cult novel do gang members known as 'droogs' appear?

A: Catcher in the Rye
B: A Clockwork Orange
C: Trainspotting
D: American Psycho

63

In which city is Napier University based?

A: Edinburgh
B: Glasgow
C: Cardiff
D: Belfast

64

With which industry was the first Lord Beaverbrook most associated?

A: Film
B: Newspaper
C: Brewing
D: Oil

65

Who was assassinated in Mexico in 1940?

A: Lenin
B: Stalin
C: Rasputin
D: Trotsky

50:50 Go to page 461 Go to page 484 ? Answers on page 497

11 ◆ £64,000

66

'Night of the Hunter' was the only film directed by which actor?

A: Leslie Howard
B: Charles Laughton
C: James Mason
D: Boris Karloff

67

In which field was Dame Ellen Terry famous?

A: Astronomy
B: Acting
C: Politics
D: Children's literature

68

The Winter Olympics were first held in which country?

A: Switzerland
B: Austria
C: Finland
D: France

69

Which magazine was founded by the American Dewitt Wallace?

A: Time
B: Reader's Digest
C: Punch
D: National Geographic

70

Which people are known in their own language as 'Saami'?

A: Lapps
B: Maoris
C: Tamils
D: Quechua

50:50 Go to page 461 Go to page 484 ? Answers on page 497

11 ◆ £64,000

71

Which Russian Tsar died at Ekaterinburg in 1918?

- A: Alexander I
- B: Nicholas II
- C: Peter I
- D: Ivan IV

72

The Mabinogion is a collection of legends from which country?

- A: Wales
- B: Ireland
- C: France
- D: Germany

73

The Frenchwoman Jeanne Poisson was better known by what name?

- A: Joan of Arc
- B: Marie Antoinette
- C: Sarah Bernhardt
- D: Madame de Pompadour

74

In which African country is the city of Bulawayo?

- A: Zambia
- B: Zimbabwe
- C: Namibia
- D: South Africa

75

With which natural phenomena are Baily's Beads associated?

- A: Lightning storm
- B: Tidal wave
- C: Solar eclipse
- D: Volcanic eruption

50:50 Go to page 461 · Go to page 484 · ? Answers on page 497

11 ◆ £64,000

76

On which continent are the Iguacu waterfalls?

A: South America
B: Australia
C: Africa
D: North America

77

According to the title of a famous novel, there are how many 'Years of Solitude'?

A: Ten
B: One Hundred
C: One Thousand
D: One Million

78

Whose teachings are collected in the Hadith?

A: Muhammad
B: Confucius
C: Buddah
D: Saint Paul

79

Who won the Booker Prize with the novel 'The Bone People'?

A: James Kelman
B: Keri Hulme
C: Thomas Keneally
D: Pat Barker

80

Which country was the first to elect a woman as head of state?

A: Argentina
B: New Zealand
C: Sri Lanka
D: Iceland

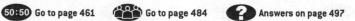

50:50 Go to page 461 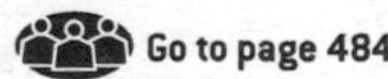 Go to page 484  Answers on page 497

11 ◆ £64,000

81

Which singer starred in the 1968 film 'Girl on a Motorcycle'?

A: Sandie Shaw
B: Helen Shapiro
C: Marianne Faithfull
D: Lulu

82

Which of these people is not a fashion designer?

A: Kenzo
B: Kazuo Ishiguro
C: Issey Miyake
D: Yohji Yamamoto

83

June Whitfield and Jimmy Edwards were members of which radio 'family'?

A: The Archers
B: The Lyons
C: The Glums
D: The Dales

84

Who wrote the classic science fiction novel 'Helliconia Spring'?

A: Isaac Asimov
B: Brian Aldiss
C: Arthur C Clarke
D: Ray Bradbury

85

Ceres was the Roman goddess of what?

A: Storms
B: Agriculture
C: Rainbows
D: Love

50:50 Go to page 461 Go to page 484 ? Answers on page 497

11 ◆ £64,000

86

In the Gasden Purchase, the USA bought territory from which country?

A: Mexico
B: Russia
C: Spain
D: France

87

In Greek mythology, the nymph Callisto was turned into which creature?

A: Swan
B: Bear
C: Spider
D: Peacock

88

Which epic film is based on a novel by Lew Wallace?

A: Gone With The Wind
B: The Agony and the Ecstasy
C: Ben Hur
D: The Robe

89

Which sport is played by the Sheffield Steelers?

A: Ice hockey
B: American football
C: Basketball
D: Cricket

90

Of which country was Salvador Allende president?

A: Venezuela
B: Chile
C: Peru
D: Mexico

50:50 Go to page 461  Go to page 484 ? Answers on page 497

11 ◆ £64,000

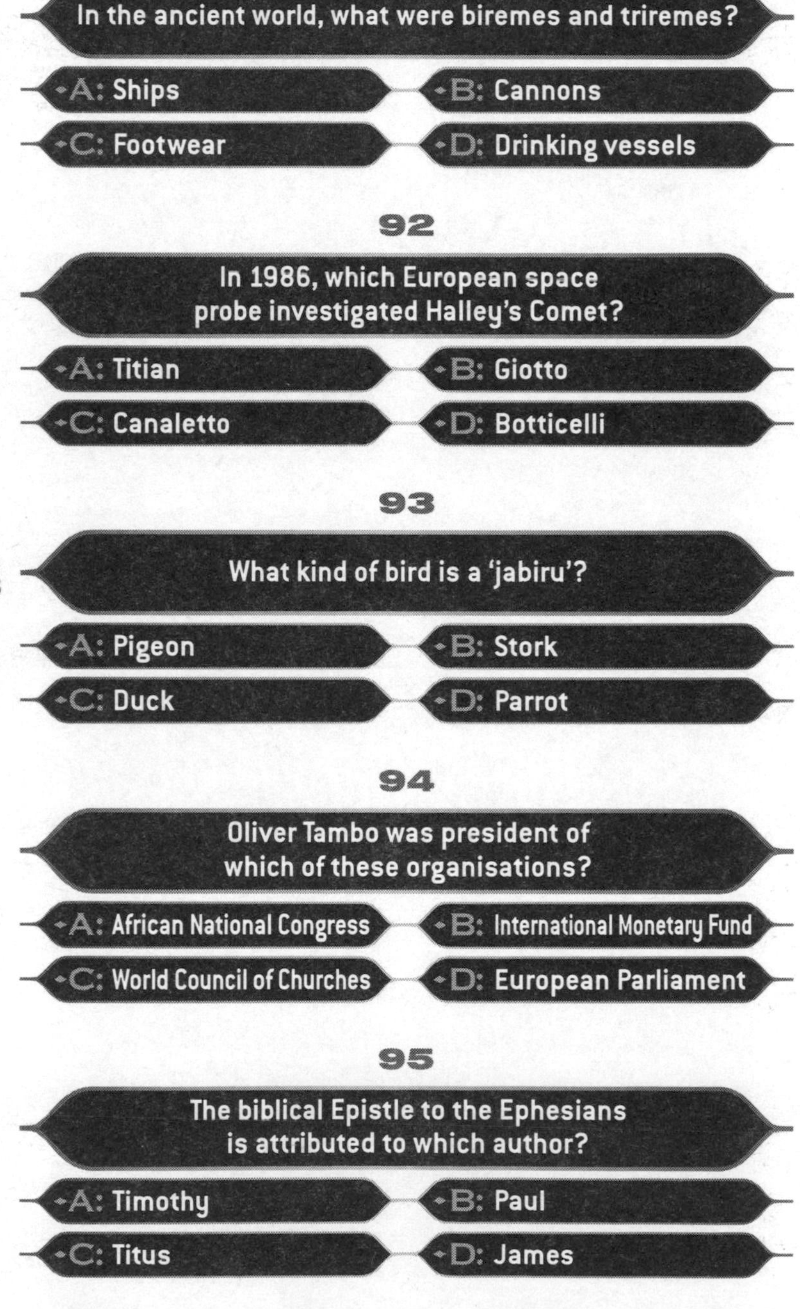

91

In the ancient world, what were biremes and triremes?

A: Ships
B: Cannons
C: Footwear
D: Drinking vessels

92

In 1986, which European space probe investigated Halley's Comet?

A: Titian
B: Giotto
C: Canaletto
D: Botticelli

93

What kind of bird is a 'jabiru'?

A: Pigeon
B: Stork
C: Duck
D: Parrot

94

Oliver Tambo was president of which of these organisations?

A: African National Congress
B: International Monetary Fund
C: World Council of Churches
D: European Parliament

95

The biblical Epistle to the Ephesians is attributed to which author?

A: Timothy
B: Paul
C: Titus
D: James

50:50 Go to page 461 Go to page 484 ? Answers on page 497

11 ◆ £64,000

96

What is the standard boiling point of water on the Fahrenheit scale?

- A: 111
- B: 212
- C: 313
- D: 414

97

Sidon is a town in which Mediterranean country?

- A: Greece
- B: Libya
- C: Israel
- D: Lebanon

98

'Fluff' is the nickname of which disc jockey?

- A: Tony Blackburn
- B: Jimmy Savile
- C: Alan Freeman
- D: Chris Tarrant

99

Who composed the opera 'Boris Godunov'?

- A: Borodin
- B: Mussorgsky
- C: Tchaikovsky
- D: Rimsky-Korsakov

100

Which biblical character is known as 'the second Adam'?

- A: Abraham
- B: David
- C: Jesus
- D: Peter

50:50 Go to page 461  Go to page 484 ? Answers on page 497

15		£1 MILLION
14		£500,000
13		£250,000
12	◆	£125,000
11	◆	£64,000
10	◆	£32,000
9	◆	£16,000
8	◆	£8,000
7	◆	£4,000
6	◆	£2,000
5	◆	£1,000
4	◆	£500
3	◆	£300
2	◆	£200
1	◆	£100

12 ◆ £125,000

1

What was the title of Jung Chang's best-selling memoir of China?

A: Wild Orchids
B: Wild Swans
C: Wild Lotuses
D: Wild Peacocks

2

Which architect designed the Marble Arch in London?

A: Inigo Jones
B: Robert Adam
C: Christopher Wren
D: John Nash

3

Which of these women has a book of the Bible named after her?

A: Naomi
B: Mary
C: Ruth
D: Jezebel

4

Who was the mother of Mary I of England?

A: Catherine of Aragon
B: Jane Seymour
C: Anne of Cleves
D: Catherine Parr

5

By what name is the fictional character Percy Blakeney better known?

A: Hooded Claw
B: Superman
C: Scarlet Pimpernel
D: Tarzan

50:50 Go to page 462 Go to page 486 ? Answers on page 498

12 ◆ £125,000

6

What was pioneered by the Austrian physician Dr Mesmer?

A: Reflexology
B: Aromatherapy
C: Psychoanalysis
D: Hypnotism

7

What kind of creature is a golden oriole?

A: Bird
B: Fish
C: Snake
D: Beetle

8

Which of these is a Japanese form of drama?

A: Yess
B: Noh
C: O-kay
D: May-bee

9

Which of these Rolling Stones is the eldest?

A: Mick Jagger
B: Ronnie Wood
C: Charlie Watts
D: Keith Richards

10

The Disney cartoon 'One Hundred and One Dalmatians' was based on a novel by whom?

A: Nina Bawden
B: Muriel Spark
C: Angela Carter
D: Dodie Smith

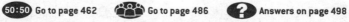

50:50 Go to page 462 Go to page 486  ? Answers on page 498

12 ◆ £125,000

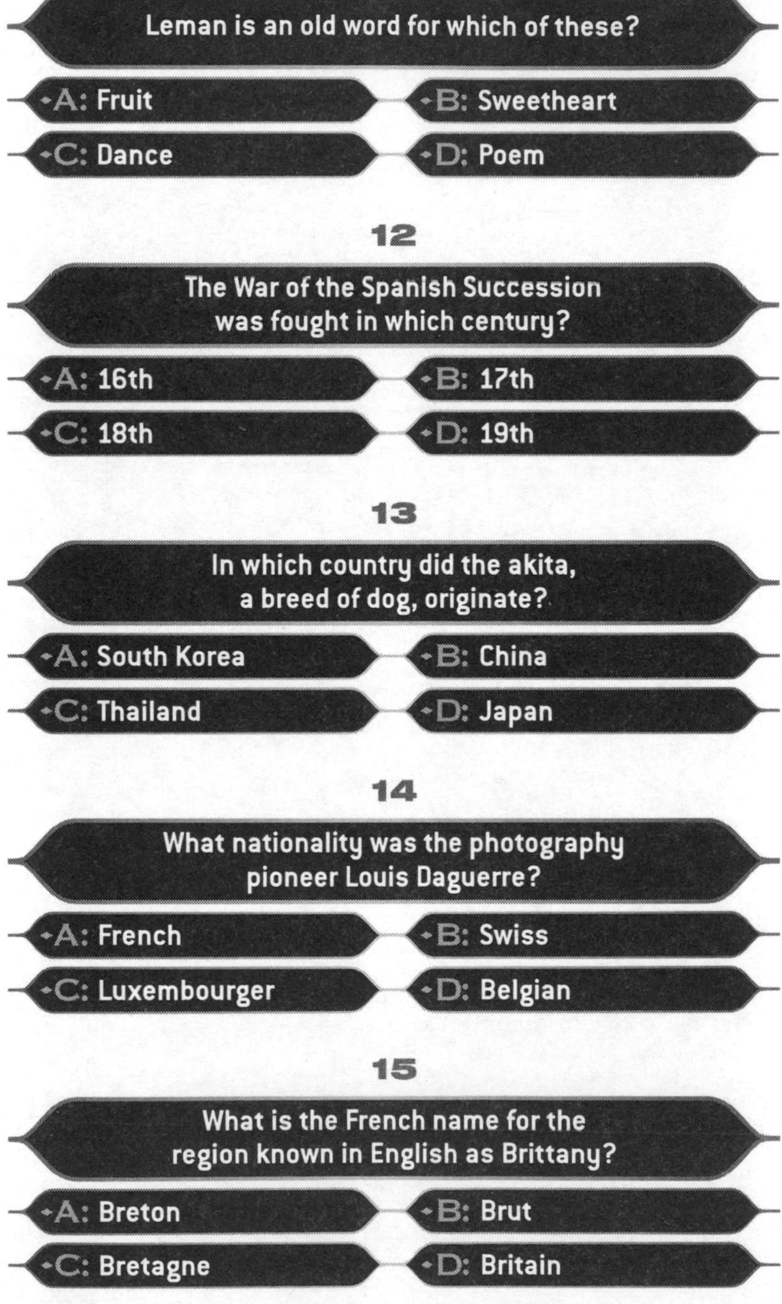

11

Leman is an old word for which of these?

A: Fruit
B: Sweetheart
C: Dance
D: Poem

12

The War of the Spanish Succession was fought in which century?

A: 16th
B: 17th
C: 18th
D: 19th

13

In which country did the akita, a breed of dog, originate?

A: South Korea
B: China
C: Thailand
D: Japan

14

What nationality was the photography pioneer Louis Daguerre?

A: French
B: Swiss
C: Luxembourger
D: Belgian

15

What is the French name for the region known in English as Brittany?

A: Breton
B: Brut
C: Bretagne
D: Britain

50:50 Go to page 462 Go to page 486 ? Answers on page 498

12 ◆ £125,000

16

Much in the news in 1999, who or what was 'Melissa'?

- A: Supermodel
- B: Talk show hostess
- C: Giant panda
- D: Computer virus

17

Which animal is affected by the disease 'strangles'?

- A: Horse
- B: Cow
- C: Pig
- D: Sheep

18

Which river forms much of the boundary between Devon and Cornwall?

- A: Dee
- B: Tamar
- C: Irwell
- D: Ribble

19

Who directed the film 'Casablanca', starring Ingrid Bergman?

- A: Michael Curtiz
- B: John Ford
- C: Frank Capra
- D: John Huston

20

In photography, what does an 'ISO' number indicate about camera film?

- A: Manufacturer
- B: Age
- C: Country of origin
- D: Sensitivity to light

50:50 Go to page 462 Go to page 486  Answers on page 498

12 ◆ £125,000

21

Who played Timothy Hutton's mother in the film 'Ordinary People'?

A: Sally Field
B: Jane Fonda
C: Mary Tyler Moore
D: Sissy Spacek

22

The footballer Stefan Schwarz represents which country at international level?

A: Sweden
B: Germany
C: Denmark
D: Belgium

23

With which sport is the name Kareem Abdul-Jabbar associated?

A: American football
B: Basketball
C: Ice hockey
D: Baseball

24

Who wrote the novel 'Schindler's Ark'?

A: V S Naipaul
B: Kazuo Ishiguro
C: David Storey
D: Thomas Keneally

25

Eric Burdon was the lead singer with which British group of the 1960s?

A: Kinks
B: Animals
C: Herman's Hermits
D: Beatles

50:50 Go to page 462 Go to page 486

Answers on page 498

12 ◆ £125,000

26

Managua is the capital of which country?

- A: Paraguay
- B: Guatemala
- C: Uraguay
- D: Nicaragua

27

What is the national anthem of Australia?

- A: O, Australia!
- B: Australia Forever
- C: Advance Australia Fair
- D: Land of Freedom and Sun

28

Wilt Chamberlain was a leading figure in which sport?

- A: Baseball
- B: Ice hockey
- C: American football
- D: Basketball

29

Which Scottish leader was vanquished at the Battle of Culloden?

- A: William Wallace
- B: Rob Roy
- C: Bonnie Prince Charlie
- D: Robert the Bruce

30

Which fictional detective was created by Dorothy L Sayers?

- A: Inspector Morse
- B: Lord Peter Wimsey
- C: Adam Dalgleish
- D: Jim Bergerac

50:50 Go to page 462 Go to page 486

Answers on page 498

12 ◆ £125,000

31

Who played Sherlock Holmes alongside Nigel Bruce's Watson in a series of films in the 1940s?

A: Claude Rains
B: David Niven
C: Basil Rathbone
D: George Sanders

32

Which notorious pirate was known as Blackbeard?

A: Henry Learn
B: Edward Teach
C: James Mark
D: David Chide

33

What is the meaning of the German word 'blitzkrieg'?

A: Lightning war
B: Thunder bombs
C: Storm of power
D: Hurricane force

34

Who wrote the novel 'Of Human Bondage'?

A: Evelyn Waugh
B: Anthony Burgess
C: Christopher Isherwood
D: Somerset Maugham

35

The Profumo affair helped to bring about the resignation of which British prime minister?

A: Edward Heath
B: Harold Wilson
C: Clement Attlee
D: Harold Macmillan

50:50 Go to page 462 Go to page 486 ? Answers on page 498

12 ◆ £125,000

36

Which of these is the title of a hit record by The Jam?

- A: The Eton Rifles
- B: The Winchester Rifles
- C: The Harrow Rifles
- D: The Gordonstoun Rifles

37

Who wrote the 1964 play 'Entertaining Mr Sloane'?

- A: Harold Pinter
- B: Alan Ayckbourn
- C: David Hare
- D: Joe Orton

38

Speaker's Corner is a feature of which London park?

- A: Regent's Park
- B: Hyde Park
- C: Richmond Park
- D: Green Park

39

Which actor received an Oscar nomination for his role in 'Serpico'?

- A: Robert De Niro
- B: Gene Hackman
- C: Al Pacino
- D: Jack Nicholson

40

What does the F stand for in the name of US president John F Kennedy?

- A: Franklin
- B: Finnegan
- C: Frobisher
- D: Fitzgerald

50:50 Go to page 462 Go to page 486

Answers on page 498

12 ◆ £125,000

41

The stage play 'Shadowlands' is based on the life of which writer?

A: JRR Tolkien
B: CS Lewis
C: Mervyn Peake
D: Lewis Carroll

42

Gangs called the Sharks and the Jets appear in which musical?

A: West Side Story
B: On the Town
C: Kismet
D: Show Boat

43

What is the popular name for the University of Paris, especially its science and literature faculties?

A: Bourse
B: Sorbonne
C: Versailles
D: Louvre

44

Ray Manzarek was the keyboard player with which band?

A: Jefferson Airplane
B: The Beach Boys
C: The Doors
D: The Monkees

45

Which of these countries has never won the football world cup?

A: Holland
B: France
C: Italy
D: Uruguay

50:50 Go to page 462 Go to page 486
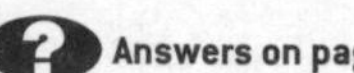
Answers on page 498

12 ◆ £125,000

46

Who wrote the book 'Breakfast at Tiffany's'?

A: Norman Mailer
B: Truman Capote
C: J D Salinger
D: Tom Wolfe

47

With whom did John McEnroe win four Wimbledon doubles titles?

A: Jimmy Connors
B: Bjorn Borg
C: Peter Fleming
D: Boris Becker

48

What is the reference for the Prime Meridian that runs through Greenwich?

A: 0
B: 180 E
C: 180 W
D: 360 E & W

49

What kind of British wildlife is a 'loach'?

A: Burrowing rodent
B: Water bird
C: Sea snail
D: Freshwater fish

50

Where in Britain is the Royal Naval College in which officers train for the Royal Navy?

A: Dartmouth
B: Portsmouth
C: Southampton
D: Plymouth

50:50 Go to page 462
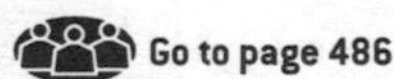
Go to page 486

Answers on page 498

12 ◆ £125,000

51

What colour is the pigment chlorophyll?

A: Brown
B: Violet
C: Green
D: Yellow

52

What does the prefix 'photo' mean?

A: Image
B: Process
C: Monochrome
D: Light

53

Which fruit has a name that literally means 'apple full of seeds'?

A: Pomegranate
B: Melon
C: Grapefruit
D: Tomato

54

How many dots and dashes make up the SOS distress signal in Morse Code?

A: Three
B: Six
C: Nine
D: Twelve

55

Which of Shakespeare's Kings says the words 'Cry "God for Harry! England and St. George"'?

A: Henry IV
B: Henry V
C: Henry VI
D: Henry VIII

50:50 Go to page 462 — Go to page 486 — ? Answers on page 498

12 ◆ £125,000

56

Brett Anderson and Bernard Butler formed which band in 1990?

A: Suede | B: Blur
C: Pulp | D: Verve

57

Greg LeMond has won which famous race three times?

A: Le Mans 24 Hour | B: Indianapolis 500
C: Tour de France | D: Boston Marathon

58

In October 1956, which country of the Eastern Bloc was invaded by the Soviet Union?

A: Czechoslovakia | B: Hungary
C: Yugoslavia | D: Poland

59

Which oil is used in the manufacture of putty?

A: Linseed | B: Sesame
C: Olive | D: Palm

60

The Voortrekkers were settlers in which country?

A: USA | B: New Guinea
C: Mexico | D: South Africa

50:50 Go to page 462 Go to page 486 ? Answers on page 498

12 ◆ £125,000

61

Which amendment to the US constitution says that no-one may be forced to testify against himself in court?

A: First
B: Fourth
C: Fifth
D: Fifteenth

62

Benghazi, a port on the Mediterranean, is the second city of which country?

A: Libya
B: Turkey
C: Tunisia
D: Morocco

63

Which of Queen Victoria's four sons was great-grandfather to Elizabeth II?

A: Alfred
B: Arthur
C: Edward
D: Leopold

64

Which word represents the letter U in the phonetic alphabet?

A: Uncle
B: Uniform
C: Ultra
D: Urgent

65

MIRAS was a government tax relief on what?

A: Mortgage
B: Income
C: Relatives
D: Savings

50:50 Go to page 462 Go to page 486

Answers on page 498

12 ◆ £125,000

66

Malmö is the third largest city in which Scandinavian country?

A: Finland | B: Denmark
C: Sweden | D: Norway

67

In which field of the arts was Antonio Canova famous?

A: Opera | B: Ballet
C: Painting | D: Sculpture

68

Bishop Auckland is the home of which bishop?

A: Durham | B: Lincoln
C: Salisbury | D: Winchester

69

Which of these is a type of pottery made by Wedgwood?

A: Jonathan | B: Julian
C: Joseph | D: Jasper

70

In heraldry, a cockatrice is a monster with the tail of which creature?

A: Eagle | B: Lion
C: Dragon | D: Horse

50:50 Go to page 462 Go to page 486 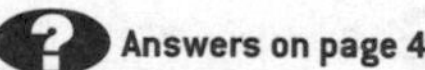 Answers on page 498

12 ◆ £125,000

71

What kind of musical instrument is a 'musette'?

A: Bagpipes
B: Harp
C: Flute
D: Drum

72

What name is given to the study of animal and plant tissues?

A: Conchology
B: Mycology
C: Cryology
D: Histology

73

Hafez al-Assad, who died in 2000, was president of which Middle Eastern country?

A: Lebanon
B: Syria
C: Iraq
D: Iran

74

Originally, the phrase 'back of beyond' referred to which part of the world?

A: Australia
B: Brazil
C: Russia
D: Antarctica

75

Which French ruler was known as the 'Citizen King'?

A: Charles Henri
B: Georges Claude
C: Alexandre Lucas
D: Louis Philippe

50:50 Go to page 462 · Go to page 486 · ? Answers on page 498

12 ◆ £125,000

76

The ruins of Tintern Abbey stand beside which river?

A: Wear
B: Derwent
C: Wye
D: Dove

77

Which of these writers was a governor general of Canada?

A: Rudyard Kipling
B: Joseph Conrad
C: H G Wells
D: John Buchan

78

What is the approximate length of the earth's circumference at the Equator?

A: 25,000 miles
B: 35,000 miles
C: 45,000 miles
D: 55,000 miles

79

Holden Caulfield is the central character of which novel?

A: To Kill a Mockingbird
B: The Naked and the Dead
C: The Catcher In the Rye
D: The Good Earth

80

In which country was the battle of El Alamein fought?

A: Egypt
B: Libya
C: Algeria
D: Morocco

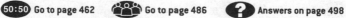

50:50 Go to page 462 · Go to page 486 · ? Answers on page 498

12 ◆ £125,000

81

Which explorer sailed to the New World for Henry VII?

A: Martin Frobisher
B: Francis Drake
C: John Cabot
D: Henry Hudson

82

Douglas Bader was a hero of which war?

A: World War I
B: World War II
C: Boer War
D: Crimean War

83

What nationality was the astronomer Kepler?

A: German
B: Danish
C: Polish
D: Swiss

84

Puck is another name for which of these characters?

A: Robin Redbreast
B: Robin Goodfellow
C: Robin Hood
D: Robinson Crusoe

85

Westminster Abbey is dedicated to which saint?

A: Peter
B: Michael
C: Elizabeth
D: Nicholas

50:50 Go to page 462 Go to page 486 ? Answers on page 498

12 ◆ £125,000

86

Which word, meaning fear or anxiety, is derived from the name of a Greek god?

- A: Alarm
- B: Hysteria
- C: Trepidation
- D: Panic

87

'Experience', published in 2000, is the autobiography of which novelist?

- A: Martin Amis
- B: P.D. James
- C: Peter Carey
- D: Anita Brookner

88

Jane Rossington played which character in 'Crossroads'?

- A: Meg Richardson
- B: Diane Parker
- C: Barbara Hunter
- D: Jill Harvey

89

In which field of the arts is Jessye Norman famous?

- A: Opera
- B: Ballet
- C: Sculpture
- D: Poetry

90

Stewart Island is part of which country?

- A: South Africa
- B: New Zealand
- C: Canada
- D: Australia

50:50 Go to page 462   Go to page 486

Answers on page 498

12 ◆ £125,000

91

What was Rod Stewart's first solo number one hit single in the UK?

A: Do Ya Think I'm Sexy? B: Baby Jane

C: Maggie May D: Sailing

92

Caliban is a character in which Shakespeare play?

A: The Tempest B: Measure For Measure

C: Julius Caesar D: King John

50:50 Go to page 462 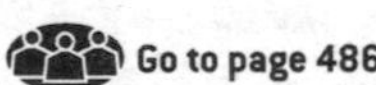 Go to page 486  Answers on page 498

15		£1 MILLION
14		£500,000
13	◆	£250,000
12	◆	£125,000
11	◆	£64,000
10	◆	£32,000
9	◆	£16,000
8	◆	£8,000
7	◆	£4,000
6	◆	£2,000
5	◆	£1,000
4	◆	£500
3	◆	£300
2	◆	£200
1	◆	£100

13 ◆ £250,000

1

What was the occupation of Miss Marple's nephew, Raymond West, in Agatha Christie's novels?

- A: Author
- B: Doctor
- C: Policeman
- D: Lawyer

2

Which European capital city lies on the estuary of the river Tagus?

- A: Madrid
- B: Lisbon
- C: Rome
- D: Athens

3

If you found a footprint fossilised in stone, which professional would you contact?

- A: Hemipterologist
- B: Sindologist
- C: Filicologist
- D: Ichnologist

4

What is a demijohn?

- A: Bottle
- B: Cake
- C: Painting
- D: Cocktail

5

Ludwig von Köchel catalogued the works of which composer?

- A: Bach
- B: Handel
- C: Beethoven
- D: Mozart

50:50 Go to page 463 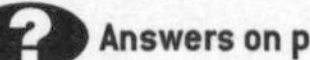 Go to page 487 ? Answers on page 498

13 ◆ £250,000

6

To which group of Mediterranean islands does Rhodes belong?

- A: Cyclades
- B: Ionian
- C: Dodecanese
- D: Aeolian

7

How old was Pitt the Younger when he became prime minister for the first time?

- A: 24
- B: 26
- C: 28
- D: 30

8

In Jonathan Swift's 'Gulliver's Travels', what is Gulliver's first name?

- A: Lionel
- B: Lemuel
- C: Leon
- D: Ludovic

9

How many players are there in a hurling team?

- A: 12
- B: 13
- C: 14
- D: 15

10

Which London landmark is situated at the junction of Oxford Street, Park Lane and Bayswater Road?

- A: Battersea Power Station
- B: Piccadilly Circus
- C: Marble Arch
- D: Leicester Square

50:50 Go to page 463  Go to page 487 ? Answers on page 498

13 ◆ £250,000

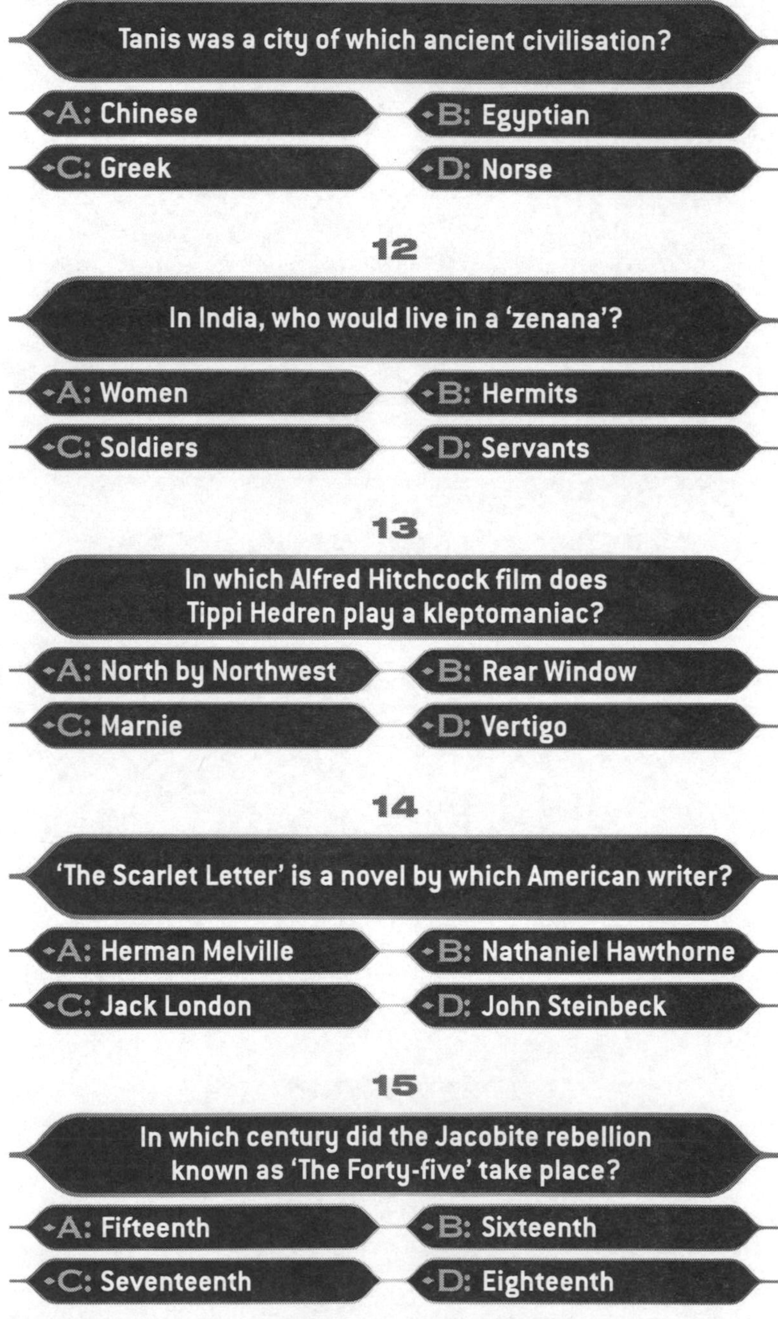

11

Tanis was a city of which ancient civilisation?

- A: Chinese
- B: Egyptian
- C: Greek
- D: Norse

12

In India, who would live in a 'zenana'?

- A: Women
- B: Hermits
- C: Soldiers
- D: Servants

13

In which Alfred Hitchcock film does Tippi Hedren play a kleptomaniac?

- A: North by Northwest
- B: Rear Window
- C: Marnie
- D: Vertigo

14

'The Scarlet Letter' is a novel by which American writer?

- A: Herman Melville
- B: Nathaniel Hawthorne
- C: Jack London
- D: John Steinbeck

15

In which century did the Jacobite rebellion known as 'The Forty-five' take place?

- A: Fifteenth
- B: Sixteenth
- C: Seventeenth
- D: Eighteenth

50:50 Go to page 463 · Go to page 487 · ? Answers on page 498

13 ◆ £250,000

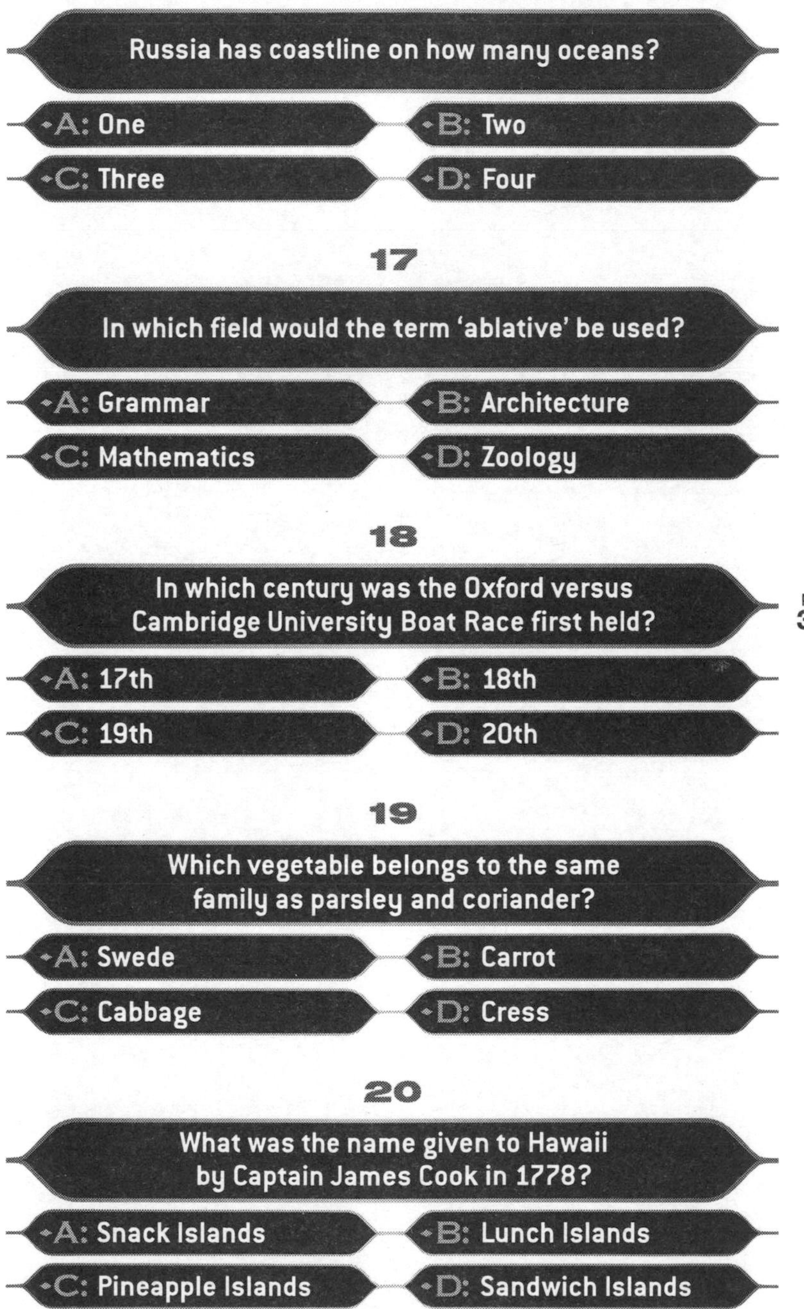

16

Russia has coastline on how many oceans?

A: One
B: Two
C: Three
D: Four

17

In which field would the term 'ablative' be used?

A: Grammar
B: Architecture
C: Mathematics
D: Zoology

18

In which century was the Oxford versus Cambridge University Boat Race first held?

A: 17th
B: 18th
C: 19th
D: 20th

19

Which vegetable belongs to the same family as parsley and coriander?

A: Swede
B: Carrot
C: Cabbage
D: Cress

20

What was the name given to Hawaii by Captain James Cook in 1778?

A: Snack Islands
B: Lunch Islands
C: Pineapple Islands
D: Sandwich Islands

50:50 Go to page 463 Go to page 487 ? Answers on page 498

13 ◆ £250,000

21

Shakespeare's 'Romeo and Juliet' was used as a base for which musical?

A: Aspects of Love
B: Me and My Girl
C: West Side Story
D: Guys and Dolls

22

Which operatic character marries Lieutenant Pinkerton?

A: Madame Butterfly
B: Carmen
C: Aida
D: Lucia di Lammermoor

23

Excluding 1, which is the tenth prime number?

A: 23
B: 29
C: 31
D: 37

24

Which girl's name is also the word that describes the reigns of Charles I and Charles II?

A: Caroline
B: Charmaine
C: Catherine
D: Christine

25

A horse described as 'skewbald' has patches of white and any other colour except what?

A: Grey
B: Brown
C: Black
D: Roan

50:50 Go to page 463 Go to page 487 ? Answers on page 498

13 ◆ £250,000

26

How many sides had a pre-decimal threepenny bit?

- A: Five
- B: Seven
- C: Ten
- D: Twelve

27

What was the first name of the fashion designer Schiaparelli?

- A: Lisa
- B: Maria
- C: Elsa
- D: Bianca

28

Which author wrote about the Five Towns?

- A: Wilkie Collins
- B: Arnold Bennett
- C: Anthony Trollope
- D: George Eliot

29

Who composed the entertainment 'Facade'?

- A: Gustav Holst
- B: Benjamin Britten
- C: William Walton
- D: Michael Tippett

30

In 2000, the Rover car company was sold for how much?

- A: £1
- B: £10
- C: £100
- D: £1000

50:50 Go to page 463  Go to page 487 ? Answers on page 498

13 ◆ £250,000

31

What kind of condition is ‘protanopia’?

- A: Colour blindness
- B: Itchiness
- C: Hair loss
- D: Earache

32

When Agatha Christie went missing in the 1920s, where did she reappear?

- A: Cheltenham
- B: Buxton
- C: Malvern
- D: Harrogate

33

What were the first names of T E Lawrence, known as ‘Lawrence of Arabia’?

- A: Thomas Edward
- B: Terence Ernest
- C: Tobias Edgar
- D: Timothy Eric

34

Which of these sporting events first took place in 1903?

- A: Monte Carlo Rally
- B: One Thousand Guineas
- C: Tour de France
- D: US Masters Golf

35

Dapsang is another name for which major mountain?

- A: Everest
- B: K2
- C: Annapurna
- D: Kanchenjunga

50:50 Go to page 463

Go to page 487

Answers on page 498

13 ◆ £250,000

36

Madame Tussaud, the waxworks founder, was born in which city?

A: Paris
B: Geneva
C: Strasbourg
D: Cologne

37

Which planet has a year lasting approximately 88 Earth days?

A: Pluto
B: Mercury
C: Venus
D: Jupiter

38

Alan Ayckbourn's plays are often premiered at the Stephen Joseph Theatre in which town?

A: Scarborough
B: Whitby
C: Blackpool
D: Skegness

39

Owen Glendower led an uprising against which king?

A: Henry I
B: Henry II
C: Henry III
D: Henry IV

40

Which Cumbrian town was the birthplace of the poet William Wordsworth?

A: Kendal
B: Keswick
C: Cockermouth
D: Carlisle

50:50 Go to page 463 Go to page 487 ? Answers on page 498

13 ◆ £250,000

41

Which religious order was founded by Saint Bruno?

A: Dominican
B: Carthusian
C: Franciscan
D: Cistercian

42

Which British prime minister was born in Canada?

A: David Lloyd-George
B: Clement Attlee
C: Ramsay MacDonald
D: Andrew Bonar Law

43

In Edward Lear's poem, who married the Owl and the Pussy-cat?

A: Pig
B: Fowl
C: Turkey
D: The man-in the-moon

44

Kappelhoff is the real surname of which actress?

A: Jane Russell
B: Doris Day
C: Lana Turner
D: Jane Wyman

45

What is the title of Harold Brighouse's most famous play?

A: Hobson's Choice
B: Trelawney of the Wells
C: The Government Inspector
D: Charley's Aunt

50:50 Go to page 463 | Go to page 487 | ? Answers on page 498

13 ◆ £250,000

46

The ancient monument at Silbury Hill is in which county?

A: Suffolk
B: Wiltshire
C: Dorset
D: Cornwall

47

If someone from Australia is Australian, what is someone from New Zealand?

A: New Zealandish
B: New Zealer
C: New Zealandian
D: New Zealand

48

Which female novelist drowned in the River Ouse?

A: George Eliot
B: Emily Brontë
C: Virginia Woolf
D: Jane Austen

49

Lake Eyre, Australia's lowest point, is in which state?

A: Western Australia
B: South Australia
C: New South Wales
D: Victoria

50

Which saint translated the Vulgate Bible?

A: Justinian
B: James
C: Jerome
D: John

50:50 Go to page 463  Go to page 487 ? Answers on page 498

13 ◆ £250,000

51

Who painted the 'Rokeby Venus'?

A: Rubens
B: Titian
C: Vermeer
D: Velazquez

52

What was the name of the English riots of 1780?

A: Godfrey Riots
B: Gordon Riots
C: Graham Riots
D: Gilbert Riots

53

Which of these buildings was designed by John Vanbrugh?

A: Balmoral Castle
B: Chatsworth House
C: Castle Howard
D: Westminster Abbey

54

In which state is Yale University?

A: New York
B: Connecticut
C: Massachusetts
D: Virginia

55

James Abbott McNeill were the first names of which artist?

A: Turner
B: Frith
C: Whistler
D: Sisley

50:50 Go to page 463 · Go to page 487 · ? Answers on page 498

13 ◆ £250,000

56

In which language was the poem 'Beowulf' written?

A: Latin
B: Old English
C: Welsh
D: Icelandic

57

Which of these kings was not a member of the House of York?

A: Richard II
B: Richard III
C: Edward IV
D: Edward V

58

Florizel and Perdita are characters in which Shakespeare play?

A: The Tempest
B: The Winter's Tale
C: The Taming of the Shrew
D: The Two Gentlemen of Verona

59

The Parthenon in Athens is built in which architectural style?

A: Doric
B: Ionic
C: Corinthian
D: Tuscan

60

Which of these is a newly-coined word?

A: Neophyte
B: Neorealism
C: Neovitalism
D: Neologism

50:50 Go to page 463

Go to page 487
? Answers on page 498

13 ◆ £250,000

61

The thickness of what is given an 'swg' rating?

- A: Glass
- B: Leather
- C: Wire
- D: Paper

62

In which US state is the Lowell Observatory?

- A: Arizona
- B: Alaska
- C: Arkansas
- D: Alabama

63

Of what is agrostology the study?

- A: Moss
- B: Fungi
- C: Grasses
- D: Shells

64

'I sing of arms and the man' is the first line of which famous work?

- A: The Aeneid
- B: The Odyssey
- C: The Divine Comedy
- D: Paradise Lost

65

In India, what is 'pachisi'?

- A: High-ranking caste
- B: Lentil dish
- C: Board game
- D: Gold fabric

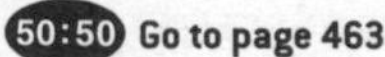 Go to page 463  Go to page 487 ? Answers on page 498

13 ◆ £250,000

66

In which country was the Pahlavi family a ruling dynasty?

A: Iran | B: Saudi Arabia

C: Kuwait | D: Morocco

67

Benthos are plants and animals living where?

A: Snow | B: Water

C: Soil | D: Tree bark

68

At which racecourse is the Eclipse Stakes run?

A: Ascot | B: Newmarket

C: Doncaster | D: Sandown

69

In the 1960s, who played shopkeeper Leonard Swindley in 'Coronation Street'?

A: Max Wall | B: Arthur Lowe

C: Gordon Kaye | D: Paul Shane

70

Lake Nyasa forms most of which country's eastern border?

A: Malawi | B: Zambia

C: Kenya | D: Angola

50:50 Go to page 463 · Go to page 487 ·  Answers on page 498

13 ◆ £250,000

71

Which British order is limited to 65 members?

A: Order of Merit
B: Companion of Honour
C: Order of the Garter
D: George Cross

72

In which city does Rocky live, in the film of the same name?

A: Detroit
B: Pittsburgh
C: Baltimore
D: Philadelphia

73

In which year was Diana, Princess of Wales born?

A: 1960
B: 1961
C: 1962
D: 1963

74

Which city is located at the confluence of the Rivers Caldew and Eden?

A: Aberdeen
B: Blackburn
C: Carlisle
D: Durham

75

Whose last words are said to have been 'Let not poor Nelly starve'?

A: James I
B: Charles I
C: James II
D: Charles II

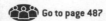

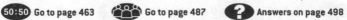

50:50 Go to page 463 Go to page 487

Answers on page 498

13 ◆ £250,000

76

As what did Colly Cibber achieve fame?

A: Poet Laureate | B: Composer
C: Philosopher | D: Astronomer Royal

77

Which of these artistic terms was named after a French finance minister?

A: Caricature | B: Portraiture
C: Aquarelle | D: Silhouette

78

In mythology, the fountain Aganippe was sacred to whom?

A: Muses | B: Fates
C: Oracle | D: Gorgons

79

The ELO system is used to rate leading players of which board game?

A: Scrabble | B: Chess
C: Monopoly | D: Draughts

80

Which part of the body is most affected by the disease diphtheria?

A: Heart | B: Liver
C: Throat | D: Skin

50:50 Go to page 463 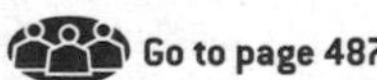 Go to page 487 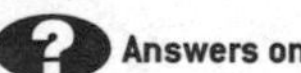 Answers on page 498

13 ◆ £250,000

81

What is the capital city of Lithuania?

A: Riga
B: Tallinn
C: Minsk
D: Vilnius

82

Richard I was the son of which English monarch?

A: William I
B: Henry II
C: George III
D: Edward IV

83

Which of these is a landlocked country?

A: Nepal
B: Myanmar
C: Pakistan
D: Oman

84

In Greek mythology, who was the husband of Helen of Troy?

A: Achilles
B: Menelaus
C: Orpheus
D: Hector

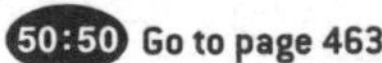

Go to page 463
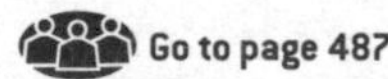
Go to page 487

Answers on page 498

15 £1 MILLION
14 ◆ £500,000
13 ◆ £250,000
12 ◆ £125,000
11 ◆ £64,000
10 ◆ £32,000
9 ◆ £16,000
8 ◆ £8,000
7 ◆ £4,000
6 ◆ £2,000
5 ◆ £1,000
4 ◆ £500
3 ◆ £300
2 ◆ £200
1 ◆ £100

14 ◆ £500,000

1

Who includes among his titles Earl of Merioneth and Baron Greenwich?

- A: Duke of Edinburgh
- B: Prince of Wales
- C: Duke of York
- D: Prince William

2

Augustine Aloysius were the middle names of which author?

- A: Wilfred Owen
- B: John Keats
- C: Aldous Huxley
- D: James Joyce

3

Whose album 'Pearl' was released posthumously?

- A: Jimi Hendrix
- B: Billie Holiday
- C: Elvis Presley
- D: Janis Joplin

4

Which year of the Chinese calendar began in the year 2000?

- A: Rabbit
- B: Dragon
- C: Snake
- D: Horse

5

In 1942, which comedian became the first castaway on 'Desert Island Discs'?

- A: Robb Wilton
- B: Arthur Askey
- C: Sandy Powell
- D: Vic Oliver

50:50 Go to page 464 · Go to page 488 · ? Answers on page 499

14 ◆ £500,000

6

Who was the first-ever winner of the Booker Prize for Fiction?

A: A S Byatt
B: V S Naipaul
C: P H Newby
D: J M Coetzee

7

Hokusai and Hiroshige were famous Japanese what?

A: Sumo wrestlers
B: Chefs
C: Artists
D: Shinto priests

8

In which country was Graham Greene's novel 'A Burnt-Out Case' set?

A: Paraguay
B: Haiti
C: Belgian Congo
D: Liberia

9

Who was prime minister in the year Queen Victoria married?

A: Robert Peel
B: Viscount Melbourne
C: Earl Grey
D: Lord Grenville

10

Port Louis is the capital of which island state in the Indian Ocean?

A: Mauritius
B: Seychelles
C: Maldives
D: Madagascar

50:50 Go to page 464 · Go to page 488 · ? Answers on page 499

14 ◆ £500,000

11

T S Eliot wrote 'Old Possum's Book of Practical Cats', but who nicknamed him 'Old Possum'?

- A: Virginia Woolf
- B: John Masefield
- C: Henry Wadsworth Longfellow
- D: Ezra Pound

12

Which horse won the Grand National in 1998?

- A: Rough Quest
- B: Lord Gyllene
- C: Earth Summit
- D: Bobbyjo

13

What is the middle name of Spice Girl Melanie C?

- A: Lee
- B: Janine
- C: Caroline
- D: Jayne

14

Which of the United States is nicknamed the Equality State?

- A: Wyoming
- B: Washington
- C: Wisconsin
- D: West Virginia

15

Which of these tennis players has won the most grand slam singles titles?

- A: Ivan Lendl
- B: John McEnroe
- C: Boris Becker
- D: Jim Courier

50:50 Go to page 464 Go to page 488

Answers on page 499

14 ◆ £500,000

16

Sable is the heraldic name for which colour?

A: Blue
B: Red
C: Yellow
D: Black

17

What does the musical term 'pesante' mean?

A: Heavy
B: Lively
C: Jaunty
D: Discordant

18

Which football club won the European Cup the first five years in which it was held?

A: Barcelona
B: Juventus
C: Liverpool
D: Real Madrid

19

Which English king was the first of the Plantagenets?

A: Henry II
B: Henry III
C: Henry IV
D: Henry V

20

Which part of the tree produces the aromatic 'bitter' of Angostura bitters?

A: Root
B: Leaf
C: Bark
D: Seed

50:50 Go to page 464 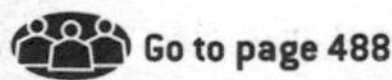 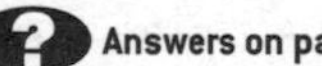 Answers on page 499

14 ◆ £500,000

21

Which garden bird is sometimes called a 'merle' in Scotland?

A: Starling
B: Thrush
C: Sparrow
D: Blackbird

22

Which American author wrote 'Moby Dick'?

A: Mark Twain
B: James Fenimore Cooper
C: Washington Irving
D: Herman Melville

23

The State Duma is the lower house of assembly in the parliament of which country?

A: Russia
B: Hungary
C: Japan
D: Pakistan

24

What is the meaning of the word 'Dodecanese'?

A: Ten islands
B: Eleven islands
C: Twelve islands
D: Thirteen islands

25

Which of these novels was written by Emily Brontë?

A: The Tenant of Wildfell Hall
B: Jane Eyre
C: Wuthering Heights
D: Villette

50:50 Go to page 464 · Go to page 488 · ? Answers on page 499

14 ◆ £500,000

26

What was the title of Oliver Cromwell when he was head of the Commonwealth?

A: Lord President
B: Lord Privy Seal
C: Lord Protector
D: Lord Chancellor

27

Ebenezer Howard is most associated with the foundation of what?

A: Sunday schools
B: Garden cities
C: Vegetarianism
D: Workhouses

28

What relation was Louis XV of France to Louis XIV?

A: Son
B: Nephew
C: Grandson
D: Great-grandson

29

What kind of animal is named after the botanist Peter Pallas?

A: Deer
B: Monkey
C: Cat
D: Goat

30

Who wrote the opera 'The Thieving Magpie'?

A: Rossini
B: Donizetti
C: Verdi
D: Puccini

50:50 Go to page 464  Go to page 488 ? Answers on page 499

14 ◆ £500,000

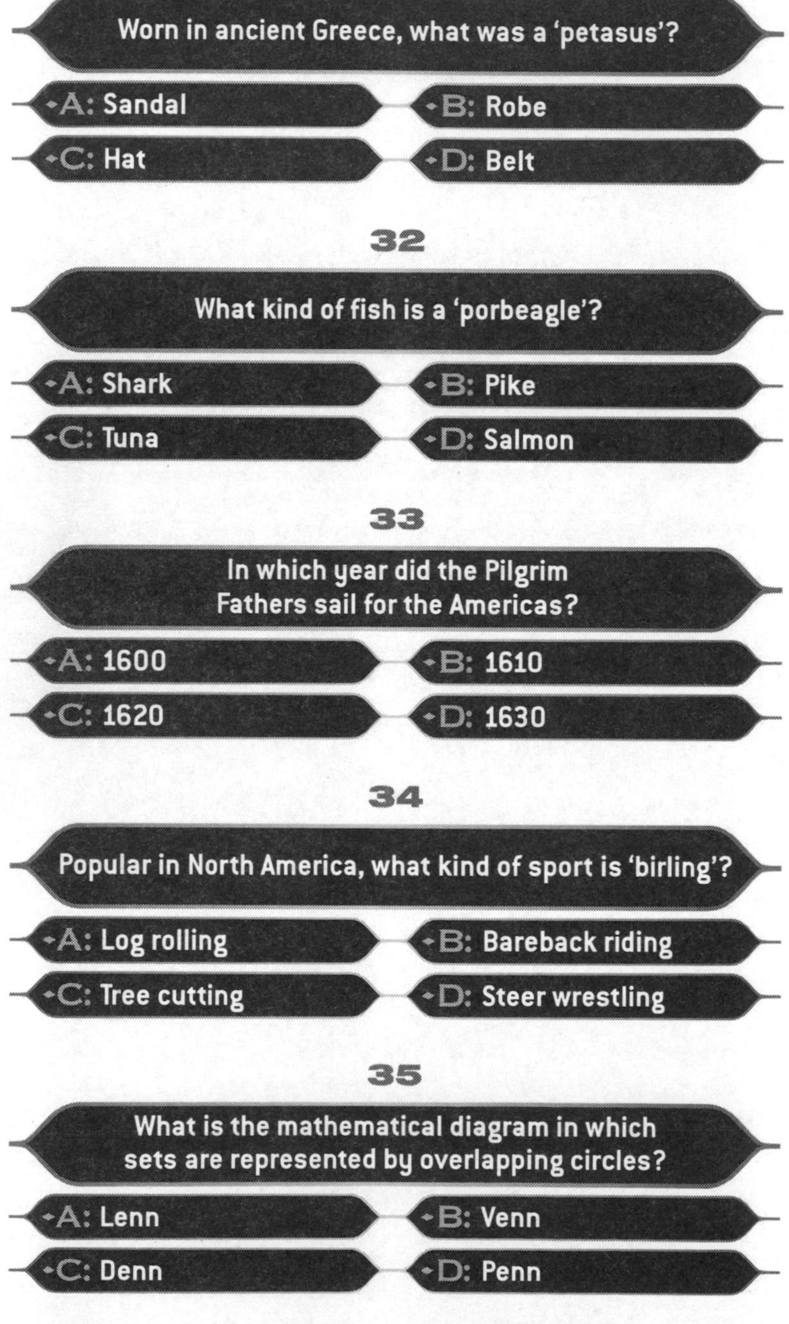

31

Worn in ancient Greece, what was a 'petasus'?

- A: Sandal
- B: Robe
- C: Hat
- D: Belt

32

What kind of fish is a 'porbeagle'?

- A: Shark
- B: Pike
- C: Tuna
- D: Salmon

33

In which year did the Pilgrim Fathers sail for the Americas?

- A: 1600
- B: 1610
- C: 1620
- D: 1630

34

Popular in North America, what kind of sport is 'birling'?

- A: Log rolling
- B: Bareback riding
- C: Tree cutting
- D: Steer wrestling

35

What is the mathematical diagram in which sets are represented by overlapping circles?

- A: Lenn
- B: Venn
- C: Denn
- D: Penn

50:50 Go to page 464 · Go to page 488 · ? Answers on page 499

14 ◆ £500,000

36

Who directed the films 'La Strada' and 'La Dolce Vita'?

A: Visconti
B: Pasolini
C: Bertolucci
D: Fellini

37

Zen is the form of Buddhism in which country?

A: Japan
B: Thailand
C: India
D: Sri Lanka

38

'Zephyr' is the poetic name for what?

A: North wind
B: South wind
C: East wind
D: West wind

39

Which of these is a keyboard designed for minimum finger movement?

A: DVORAK
B: HANDEL
C: BARTOK
D: BRAHMS

40

'Erse' is another name for which language?

A: Flemish
B: Welsh
C: Cornish
D: Gaelic

50:50 Go to page 464 — Go to page 488 — ? Answers on page 499

14 ◆ £500,000

41

Which part of the body is affected by the condition 'blepharism'?

- A: Eyelid
- B: Fingernail
- C: Shoulderblade
- D: Kneecap

42

Who wrote the poem 'Hudibras'?

- A: Samuel Pepys
- B: Samuel Johnson
- C: Samuel Richardson
- D: Samuel Butler

43

Malcolm Cooper is an Olympic gold medal winner in which sport?

- A: Rowing
- B: Swimming
- C: Shooting
- D: Skiing

44

Which island is called Kalaallit Nunaat in its own language?

- A: Easter Island
- B: Tasmania
- C: Greenland
- D: Iceland

45

King Ludwig of Bavaria was patron of which composer?

- A: Beethoven
- B: Haydn
- C: Chopin
- D: Wagner

50:50 Go to page 464 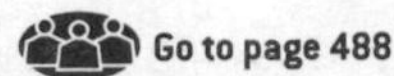 Go to page 488  Answers on page 499

14 ◆ £500,000

46

Which Pacific republic was formerly known as the New Hebrides?

A: Kiribati B: Nauru

C: Tuvalu D: Vanuatu

47

Which musical instrument has a mouthpiece called a 'fipple'?

A: Recorder B: Piccolo

C: Oboe D: Trombone

48

Which palace was built by Henry VIII on the site of a leper hospital?

A: Whitehall B: Saint James's

C: Greenwich D: Buckingham

49

Which of these Spanish towns is farthest north?

A: San Sebastian B: Madrid

C: Saragossa D: Barcelona

50

Gordon Richards won his only Derby riding which horse?

A: Dante B: Pinza

C: Grundy D: Relko

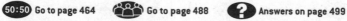

50:50 Go to page 464  Go to page 488 ? Answers on page 499

14 ◆ £500,000

51

What is the birthstone of someone born on Christmas Day?

A: Ruby | B: Topaz
C: Emerald | D: Turquoise

52

The extinct elephant bird was native to which island?

A: Mauritius | B: Tasmania
C: Madagascar | D: Greenland

53

The coelacanth, once thought to be extinct, is what kind of creature?

A: Reptile | B: Bird
C: Amphibian | D: Fish

54

In mythology, who continued to weep after she had been turned to stone?

A: Electra | B: Chloe
C: Niobe | D: Antigone

55

In the Bible, who was the mother of Ishmael?

A: Hagar | B: Miriam
C: Sarah | D: Rebecca

50:50 Go to page 464 Go to page 488
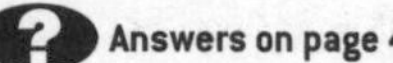
Answers on page 499

14 ◆ £500,000

56

Who wrote the novel 'King Solomon's Mines'?

- A: R M Ballantine
- B: H Rider Haggard
- C: Robert Louis Stevenson
- D: Erskine Childers

57

In India, who or what is a 'dacoit'?

- A: Priest
- B: Farmer
- C: Robber
- D: Shoemaker

58

What kind of creatures are 'ratites'?

- A: Mammals
- B: Fish
- C: Insects
- D: Birds

59

What nationality was the artist Hieronymus Bosch?

- A: German
- B: Norwegian
- C: Dutch
- D: Swiss

60

Which prime minister was created first Earl of Oxford?

- A: Baldwin
- B: Salisbury
- C: Asquith
- D: Eden

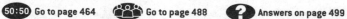

50:50 Go to page 464 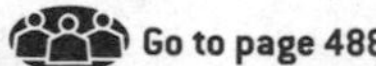 Go to page 488 ? Answers on page 499

14 ◆ £500,000

61

Bodrum in Turkey is on the site of which ancient city?

A: Ephesus
B: Troy
C: Carthage
D: Halicarnassus

62

A 'dybbuk' is an evil spirit in which folklore?

A: Jewish
B: Irish
C: West African
D: Central American

63

The Admiralty Islands are part of which country?

A: Australia
B: Indonesia
C: Papua New Guinea
D: Philippines

64

The Cassini Division is associated with which planet?

A: Jupiter
B: Mercury
C: Saturn
D: Mars

65

Which playwright received the Order of Merit in May 2000?

A: Harold Pinter
B: Alan Ayckbourn
C: David Hare
D: Tom Stoppard

50:50 Go to page 464 Go to page 488

Answers on page 499

14 ◆ £500,000

66

What was the real first name of the playwright Tennessee Williams?

- A: Teddy
- B: Thomas
- C: Terence
- D: Timothy

67

Burke and Wills are most associated with the exploration of which continent?

- A: Africa
- B: North America
- C: South America
- D: Australia

68

Nephrite is a variety of which substance?

- A: Jet
- B: Ivory
- C: Jade
- D: Mother-of-pearl

69

The conqueror Temujin was better known by what name?

- A: Attila the Hun
- B: Tamerlaine
- C: Genghis Khan
- D: Alexander the Great

70

In which country is the city of Samarkand?

- A: Tajikistan
- B: Turkmenistan
- C: Kyrgyzstan
- D: Uzbekistan

50:50 Go to page 464 Go to page 488

Answers on page 499

14 ◆ £500,000

71

Which of these Cambridge colleges was founded for women?

- A: King's
- B: Trinity
- C: Girton
- D: Fitzwilliam

72

What kind of animal is a margay?

- A: Cat
- B: Dog
- C: Bear
- D: Horse

73

A marigraph is a device which records what?

- A: Earthquake intensity
- B: Tide level
- C: Acid strength
- D: Wind direction

74

What kind of creature is a 'hoatzin'?

- A: Bird
- B: Fish
- C: Insect
- D: Marsupial

75

What does the constellation Vulpecula represent?

- A: Fox
- B: Wolf
- C: Horse
- D: Unicorn

50:50 Go to page 464 Go to page 488

Answers on page 499

14 ◆ £500,000

76

What nationality was the playwright August Strindberg?

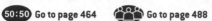

A: Norwegian

B: Finnish

C: Danish

D: Swedish

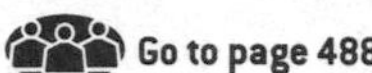

50:50 Go to page 464 Go to page 488 Answers on page 499

15 ◆ £1 MILLION

14 ◆ £500,000

13 ◆ £250,000

12 ◆ £125,000

11 ◆ £64,000

10 ◆ £32,000

9 ◆ £16,000

8 ◆ £8,000

7 ◆ £4,000

6 ◆ £2,000

5 ◆ £1,000

4 ◆ £500

3 ◆ £300

2 ◆ £200

1 ◆ £100

15 ◆ £1,000,000

1

Which New Mexico town adopted the name of a radio quiz show?

A: 64,000 Dollar Question
B: Truth or Consequences
C: Twenty-One
D: Jeopardy

2

Which of these comedians did not appear in a 'Doctor Who' story?

A: Ken Dodd
B: Alexei Sayle
C: John Cleese
D: Harry Enfield

3

Which of these monarchs was born in Buckingham Palace?

A: Victoria
B: Edward VII
C: George V
D: Edward VIII

4

In which year was the sculptor and painter Alberto Giacommetti born?

A: 1900
B: 1901
C: 1902
D: 1903

5

Bougainville is part of which island group?

A: Virgin Islands
B: Marshall Islands
C: Solomon Islands
D: Windward Islands

50:50 Go to page 465 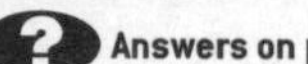 Go to page 489 ? Answers on page 499

15 ◆ £1,000,000

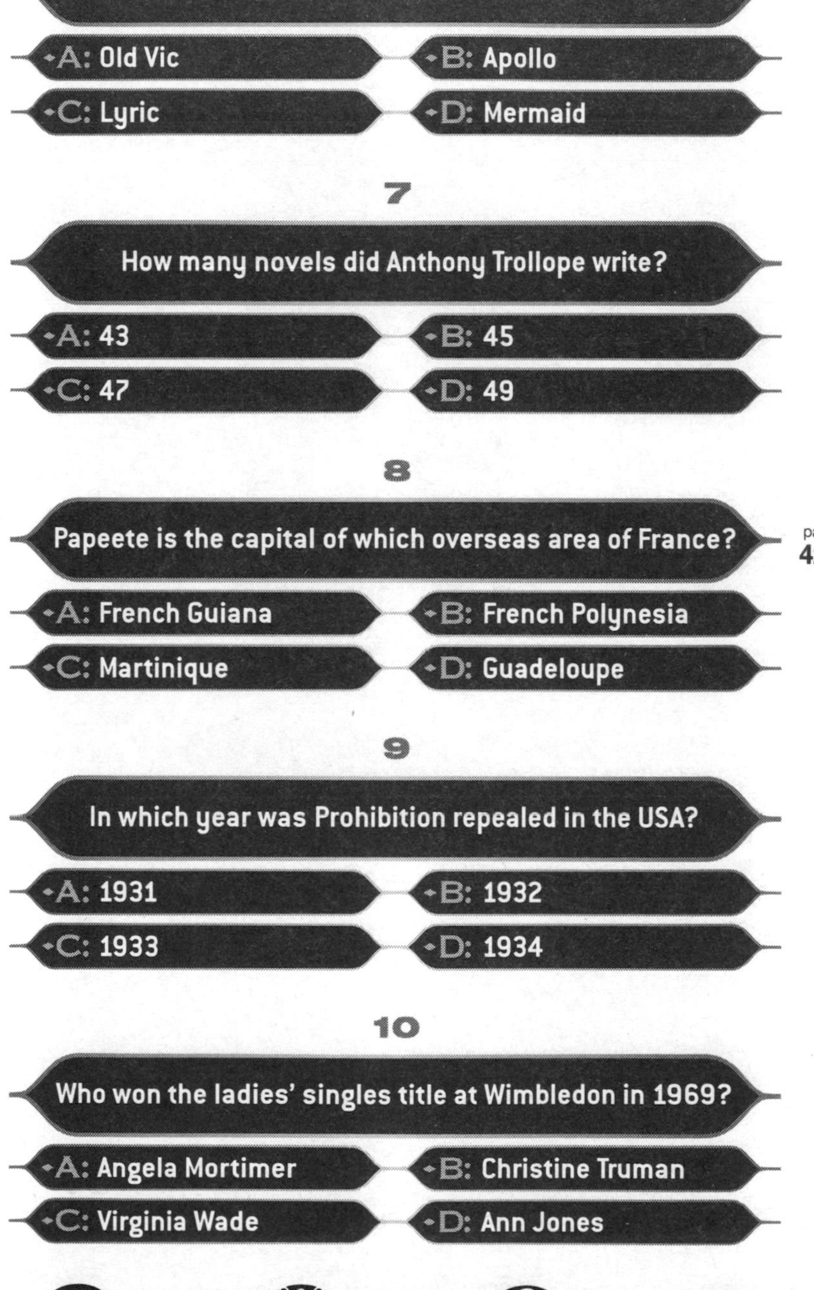

6

Which London theatre did Bernard Miles found in 1951?

- A: Old Vic
- B: Apollo
- C: Lyric
- D: Mermaid

7

How many novels did Anthony Trollope write?

- A: 43
- B: 45
- C: 47
- D: 49

8

Papeete is the capital of which overseas area of France?

- A: French Guiana
- B: French Polynesia
- C: Martinique
- D: Guadeloupe

9

In which year was Prohibition repealed in the USA?

- A: 1931
- B: 1932
- C: 1933
- D: 1934

10

Who won the ladies' singles title at Wimbledon in 1969?

- A: Angela Mortimer
- B: Christine Truman
- C: Virginia Wade
- D: Ann Jones

50:50 Go to page 465 Go to page 489 ? Answers on page 499

15 ◆ £1,000,000

11

Peter Sellers had a top ten hit single in 1960 with which other film star?

- A: Sophia Loren
- B: Ursula Andress
- C: Britt Ekland
- D: Claudia Cardinale

12

Which Oscar-winning actress married media mogul Ted Turner in 1991?

- A: Liz Taylor
- B: Jane Fonda
- C: Susan Sarandon
- D: Meryl Streep

13

Who won the 1980 Pulitzer Prize for literature for 'The Executioner's Song'?

- A: Philip Roth
- B: Gore Vidal
- C: Truman Capote
- D: Norman Mailer

14

Jazz musician Bud Powell was best-known for his prowess on which instrument?

- A: Saxophone
- B: Piano
- C: Drums
- D: Trumpet

15

A Victoria Cross is struck from the gunmetal of Russian cannons captured at which battle?

- A: Balaclava
- B: Salamanca
- C: Sebastopol
- D: Inkerman

50:50 Go to page 465 · Go to page 489 · ? Answers on page 499

15 ◆ £1,000,000

16

What is an 'ocarina'?

A: Italian dance
B: South American bird
C: Wind instrument
D: Old Italian coin

17

Which British politician was President of the European Community from 1977 to 1981?

A: Roy Jenkins
B: Norman St. John Stevas
C: Edward Heath
D: David Owen

18

What is the title of the representative of the Crown in each English county?

A: Chief Constable
B: Lord Lieutenant
C: Governor General
D: District Commissioner

19

What is the largest species of toad?

A: Midwife toad
B: Cane toad
C: Natterjack toad
D: Common toad

20

Albert Einstein worked at which American university?

A: Harvard
B: Cornell
C: Yale
D: Princeton

50:50 Go to page 465 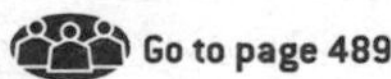 Go to page 489 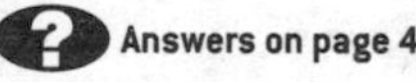 Answers on page 499

15 ◆ £1,000,000

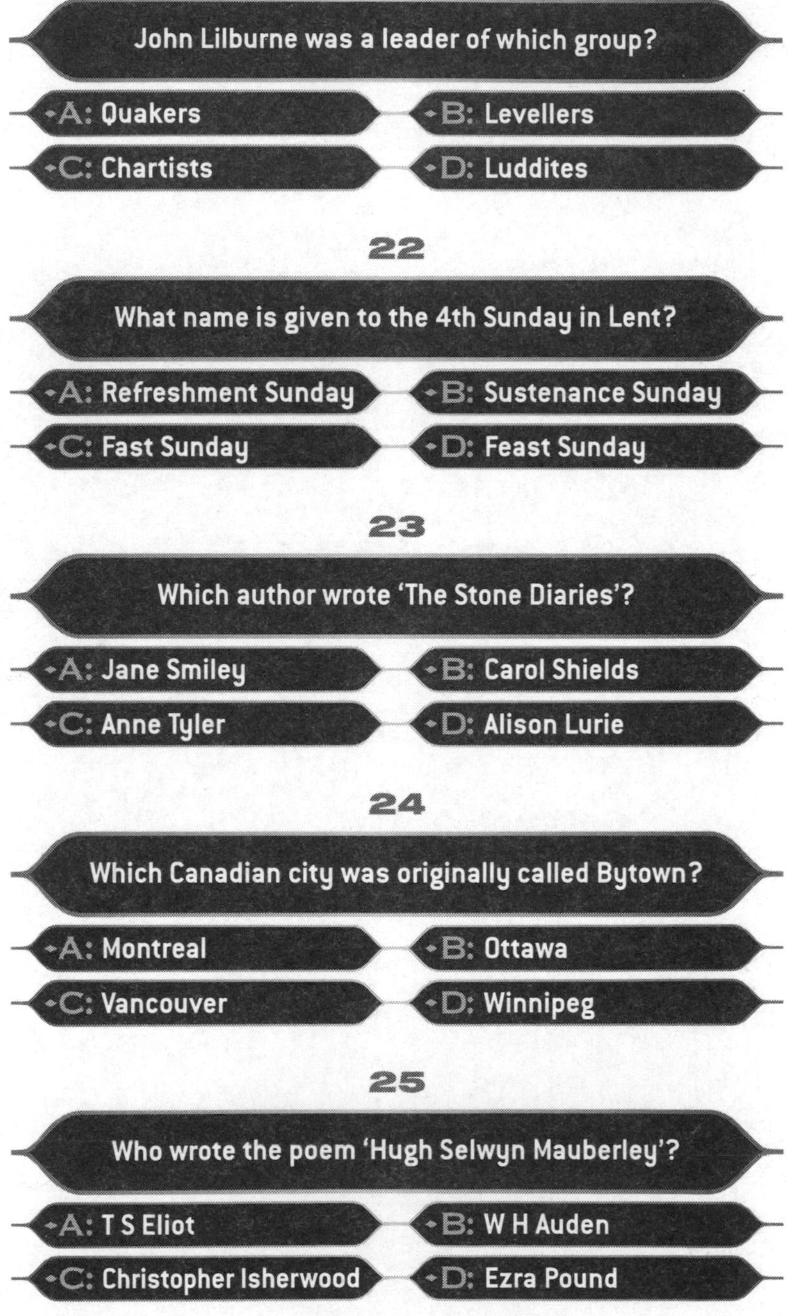

21
John Lilburne was a leader of which group?
A: Quakers
B: Levellers
C: Chartists
D: Luddites
22
What name is given to the 4th Sunday in Lent?
A: Refreshment Sunday
B: Sustenance Sunday
C: Fast Sunday
D: Feast Sunday
23
Which author wrote 'The Stone Diaries'?
A: Jane Smiley
B: Carol Shields
C: Anne Tyler
D: Alison Lurie
24
Which Canadian city was originally called Bytown?
A: Montreal
B: Ottawa
C: Vancouver
D: Winnipeg
25
Who wrote the poem 'Hugh Selwyn Mauberley'?
A: T S Eliot
B: W H Auden
C: Christopher Isherwood
D: Ezra Pound

50:50 Go to page 465 Go to page 489 ? Answers on page 499

15 ◆ £1,000,000

26

In which century was the Ming Dynasty founded in China?

A: Thirteenth
B: Fourteenth
C: Fifteenth
D: Sixteenth

27

Mount Dashan is in which African country?

A: Morocco
B: Nigeria
C: Ethiopia
D: Angola

28

The Welsh monk Asser is best known for his biography of which monarch?

A: Edward the Confessor
B: King Alfred
C: Boudicca
D: William the Conqueror

29

A 'gam' is a collection of which creatures?

A: Whales
B: Wolves
C: Worms
D: Woodpeckers

30

Tirich Mir is the highest point in which mountain range?

A: Sierra Madre
B: Hindu Kush
C: Mountains of Mourne
D: Ghats

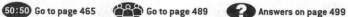

50:50 Go to page 465 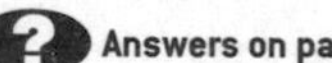 Go to page 489 ? Answers on page 499

15 ◆ £1,000,000

31

'Gowk' is a dialect word for which bird?

- A: Magpie
- B: Cuckoo
- C: Tawny owl
- D: Nightingale

32

Which leader was defeated at the Battle of Salamis?

- A: Xerxes
- B: Alexander
- C: Darius
- D: Julius Caesar

33

What was the former name of Burkina Faso in Africa?

- A: Dahomey
- B: Upper Volta
- C: Gold Coast
- D: Ivory Coast

34

The word 'batrachian' describes which animals?

- A: Monkeys and apes
- B: Rats and mice
- C: Frogs and toads
- D: Hares and rabbits

35

Which Latin American author wrote 'The War of the End of the World'?

- A: Pablo Neruda
- B: Mario Vargas Llosa
- C: Isabel Allende
- D: Gabriel Garcia Marquez

50:50 Go to page 465 Go to page 489 ? Answers on page 499

15 ◆ £1,000,000

36

Which animal has the Latin name 'Bos grunniens'?

- A: Gnu
- B: Springbok
- C: Yak
- D: Water buffalo

37

The author Jules Verne was born in which city?

- A: Nantes
- B: Bordeaux
- C: Arles
- D: Nancy

38

What does an 'oologist' study?

- A: Leaks in pipelines
- B: Birds' eggs
- C: Dust
- D: Sedimentary rocks

39

What is the largest lake in Central America?

- A: Lake Honduras
- B: Lake Guatemala
- C: Lake Costa Rica
- D: Lake Nicaragua

40

What is the largest wholly Indonesian island?

- A: Java
- B: Bali
- C: Sumatra
- D: Sulawesi

50:50 Go to page 465  Go to page 489 ? Answers on page 499

15 ◆ £1,000,000

41

Which French author wrote 'The Outsider'?

A: Simone de Beauvoir
B: Albert Camus
C: Marguerite Duras
D: Jean-Paul Sartre

42

What is the highest mountain in Canada?

A: Mount Hogan
B: Mount Wogan
C: Mount Cogan
D: Mount Logan

43

What instrument was played by jazz musician Chet Baker?

A: Guitar
B: Trumpet
C: Saxophone
D: Piano

44

Lifford is the county town of which Irish county?

A: Mayo
B: Roscommon
C: Donegal
D: Westmeath

45

The Egyptian goddess Bastet was depicted with the head of which creature?

A: Antelope
B: Jackal
C: Falcon
D: Cat

50:50 Go to page 465 Go to page 489 ? Answers on page 499

15 ◆ £1,000,000

46

The balboa is the unit of currency in which country?

A: Bolivia | B: Belize
C: Paraguay | D: Panama

47

Which town was the capital of the British king Cymbeline?

A: Chester | B: Colchester
C: Coventry | D: Cambridge

48

In a church, what is a 'galilee'?

A: Altar | B: Bell
C: Porch | D: Prayer book

49

Who painted the famous picture of Marat assassinated in his bath?

A: Géricault | B: David
C: Ingres | D: Fragonard

50

Calamine, used as an ointment, contains a carbonate of which element?

A: Calcium | B: Sodium
C: Magnesium | D: Zinc

50:50 Go to page 465 Go to page 489 ? Answers on page 499

15 ◆ £1,000,000

51

In mathematics, which prefix refers to 10 to the power of minus 9?

A: Pico
B: Femto
C: Atto
D: Nano

52

In Greek mythology, who was the mother of Uranus?

A: Erato
B: Thetis
C: Gaia
D: Hecate

53

Gustavus Vasa was the king of which Scandinavian country?

A: Sweden
B: Norway
C: Denmark
D: Finland

54

The name of which plant comes from the Greek meaning 'earth-apple'?

A: Peppermint
B: Camomile
C: Fennel
D: Nettle

55

Which of these scientists was a co-discoverer of nuclear fission?

A: Ernest Rutherford
B: James Chadwick
C: Robert Goddard
D: Otto Hahn

50:50 Go to page 465 · Go to page 489 · ? Answers on page 499

15 ◆ £1,000,000

56

In which constellation is the star cluster Pleiades?

A: Taurus
B: Orion
C: Pegasus
D: Leo

57

Which author married the critic John Middleton Murry?

A: Virginia Woolf
B: Edith Sitwell
C: Katherine Mansfield
D: Rebecca West

58

Epaminondas was a general of which ancient state?

A: Thebes
B: Sparta
C: Athens
D: Macedon

59

Titus Oates was the instigator of which historical plot?

A: Gunpowder
B: Babington
C: Popish
D: Rye House

60

Which shipping forecast area lies between Bailey and Shannon?

A: Faeroes
B: Dogger
C: Sole
D: Rockall

50:50 Go to page 465   Go to page 489    Answers on page 499

15 ◆ £1,000,000

61

With which instrument was the musician Dennis Brain associated?

A: Viola
B: French horn
C: Bassoon
D: Harp

62

The Black Prince was the first holder of which royal title?

A: Duke of Edinburgh
B: Duke of Clarence
C: Duke of Gloucester
D: Duke of Cornwall

63

In which county is the stately home Kedleston Hall?

A: Derbyshire
B: Lincolnshire
C: Nottinghamshire
D: Cheshire

64

N'Djamena is the capital of which African country?

A: Senegal
B: Guinea-Bissau
C: Chad
D: Mali

65

Which book of the Bible tells of the death of Moses?

A: Numbers
B: Exodus
C: Leviticus
D: Deuteronomy

50:50 Go to page 465 · Go to page 489 · ? Answers on page 499

15 ◆ £1,000,000

66

In Greek mythology, who was the father of Iphigenia and Electra?

- A: Agamemnon
- B: Oedipus
- C: Achilles
- D: Odysseus

67

Irian Jaya is the name for the western part of which island?

- A: Madagascar
- B: Java
- C: New Guinea
- D: Borneo

68

The Roman philosopher Seneca was tutor to which emperor?

- A: Trajan
- B: Constantine
- C: Hadrian
- D: Nero

Go to page 465  Go to page 489 

Answers on page 499

50:50

£100

1 Options remaining are A and B
2 Options remaining are A and B
3 Options remaining are A and C
4 Options remaining are A and B
5 Options remaining are A and B
6 Options remaining are B and C
7 Options remaining are A and C
8 Options remaining are A and C
9 Options remaining are B and D
10 Options remaining are A and C
11 Options remaining are B and C
12 Options remaining are A and C
13 Options remaining are A and C
14 Options remaining are A and B
15 Options remaining are B and D
16 Options remaining are A and C
17 Options remaining are A and B
18 Options remaining are A and D
19 Options remaining are B and C
20 Options remaining are B and C
21 Options remaining are B and C
22 Options remaining are A and C
23 Options remaining are A and B
24 Options remaining are A and B
25 Options remaining are A and B
26 Options remaining are A and C
27 Options remaining are B and C
28 Options remaining are A and B
29 Options remaining are B and C
30 Options remaining are C and D
31 Options remaining are A and D
32 Options remaining are A and C
33 Options remaining are B and C
34 Options remaining are A and B
35 Options remaining are A and C
36 Options remaining are A and B
37 Options remaining are A and B
38 Options remaining are A and B
39 Options remaining are A and C
40 Options remaining are B and D
41 Options remaining are A and B
42 Options remaining are B and D
43 Options remaining are A and D
44 Options remaining are A and D
45 Options remaining are A and C
46 Options remaining are A and B
47 Options remaining are B and D
48 Options remaining are A and C
49 Options remaining are B and C
50 Options remaining are A and D
51 Options remaining are A and D
52 Options remaining are A and B
53 Options remaining are B and C
54 Options remaining are C and D
55 Options remaining are A and B
56 Options remaining are B and D
57 Options remaining are B and D
58 Options remaining are A and D
59 Options remaining are A and B
60 Options remaining are A and C
61 Options remaining are B and D
62 Options remaining are A and C
63 Options remaining are B and D
64 Options remaining are B and C
65 Options remaining are A and D
66 Options remaining are A and C
67 Options remaining are A and D
68 Options remaining are A and D
69 Options remaining are A and C
70 Options remaining are B and D
71 Options remaining are B and D
72 Options remaining are A and D
73 Options remaining are A and D
74 Options remaining are B and D

75 Options remaining are A and D
76 Options remaining are A and C
77 Options remaining are A and C
78 Options remaining are A and D
79 Options remaining are A and C
80 Options remaining are B and D
81 Options remaining are A and C
82 Options remaining are A and C
83 Options remaining are A and D
84 Options remaining are A and C
85 Options remaining are A and C
86 Options remaining are A and B
87 Options remaining are A and C
88 Options remaining are B and D
89 Options remaining are A and D
90 Options remaining are A and C
91 Options remaining are A and D
92 Options remaining are A and B
93 Options remaining are A and B
94 Options remaining are B and D
95 Options remaining are A and C
96 Options remaining are A and B
97 Options remaining are A and B
98 Options remaining are C and D
99 Options remaining are A and B
100 Options remaining are C and B
101 Options remaining are A and B
102 Options remaining are C and D
103 Options remaining are B and C
104 Options remaining are A and C
105 Options remaining are A and C
106 Options remaining are C and D
107 Options remaining are B and D
108 Options remaining are A and B
109 Options remaining are B and C
110 Options remaining are A and B
111 Options remaining are B and D
112 Options remaining are A and C
113 Options remaining are A and B
114 Options remaining are A and C
115 Options remaining are B and D
116 Options remaining are A and C
117 Options remaining are A and B
118 Options remaining are B and C
119 Options remaining are A and B
120 Options remaining are A and C
121 Options remaining are A and B
122 Options remaining are A and D
123 Options remaining are B and C
124 Options remaining are A and C
125 Options remaining are A and C
126 Options remaining are A and B
127 Options remaining are A and D
128 Options remaining are B and D
129 Options remaining are B and D
130 Options remaining are A and D
131 Options remaining are B and C
132 Options remaining are B and C
133 Options remaining are B and C
134 Options remaining are A and D
135 Options remaining are C and D
136 Options remaining are A and C
137 Options remaining are A and B
138 Options remaining are A and D
139 Options remaining are B and C
140 Options remaining are B and D
141 Options remaining are A and C
142 Options remaining are A and C
143 Options remaining are B and D
144 Options remaining are A and D
145 Options remaining are A and B
146 Options remaining are A and C
147 Options remaining are A and B
148 Options remaining are B and C
149 Options remaining are C and D
150 Options remaining are A and B
151 Options remaining are A and B
152 Options remaining are A and B
153 Options remaining are B and C
154 Options remaining are A and B
155 Options remaining are A and B
156 Options remaining are A and B
157 Options remaining are A and B
158 Options remaining are A and B
159 Options remaining are B and C
160 Options remaining are A and B

50:50

161 Options remaining are A and B
162 Options remaining are B and C
163 Options remaining are C and D
164 Options remaining are A and B
165 Options remaining are A and C
166 Options remaining are A and B
167 Options remaining are A and D
168 Options remaining are A and B
169 Options remaining are A and B
170 Options remaining are A and B
171 Options remaining are A and B
172 Options remaining are A and C
173 Options remaining are A and B
174 Options remaining are A and B
175 Options remaining are B and C
176 Options remaining are A and C
177 Options remaining are A and D
178 Options remaining are A and C
179 Options remaining are A and B
180 Options remaining are A and B

£200

1 Options remaining are A and B
2 Options remaining are B and D
3 Options remaining are B and C
4 Options remaining are A and B
5 Options remaining are C and D
6 Options remaining are A and C
7 Options remaining are A and D
8 Options remaining are A and C
9 Options remaining are B and C
10 Options remaining are A and D
11 Options remaining are A and C
12 Options remaining are A and C
13 Options remaining are A and C
14 Options remaining are A and C
15 Options remaining are B and C
16 Options remaining are A and C
17 Options remaining are C and D
18 Options remaining are B and C
19 Options remaining are A and C
20 Options remaining are A and D
21 Options remaining are B and D
22 Options remaining are B and C
23 Options remaining are A and C
24 Options remaining are B and D
25 Options remaining are B and C
26 Options remaining are A and C
27 Options remaining are A and B
28 Options remaining are A and D
29 Options remaining are A and D
30 Options remaining are B and C
31 Options remaining are B and C
32 Options remaining are B and D
33 Options remaining are A and B
34 Options remaining are A and C
35 Options remaining are A and B
36 Options remaining are A and C
37 Options remaining are A and C
38 Options remaining are B and D
39 Options rema ining are A and C
40 Options remaining are C and D
41 Options remaining are A and D
42 Options remaining are B and C
43 Options remaining are A and C
44 Options remaining are A and B
45 Options remaining are B and D
46 Options remaining are B and C
47 Options remaining are A and C
48 Options remaining are C and D
49 Options remaining are B and D
50 Options remaining are A and C
51 Options remaining are A and D
52 Options remaining are A and D
53 Options remaining are A and D
54 Options remaining are B and D
55 Options remaining are C and D
56 Options remaining are B and D

50:50

57 Options remaining are A and D
58 Options remaining are B and C
59 Options remaining are A and D
60 Options remaining are A and C
61 Options remaining are A and C
62 Options remaining are A and D
63 Options remaining are A and C
64 Options remaining are B and D
65 Options remaining are A and C
66 Options remaining are A and D
67 Options remaining are A and D
68 Options remaining are A and D
69 Options remaining are B and D
70 Options remaining are A and C
71 Options remaining are A and D
72 Options remaining are A and C
73 Options remaining are A and D
74 Options remaining are A and D
75 Options remaining are B and D
76 Options remaining are A and C
77 Options remaining are B and D
78 Options remaining are A and C
79 Options remaining are A and B
80 Options remaining are A and D
81 Options remaining are A and D
82 Options remaining are A and C
83 Options remaining are B and D
84 Options remaining are A and C
85 Options remaining are A and D
86 Options remaining are A and D
87 Options remaining are A and C
88 Options remaining are B and D
89 Options remaining are B and C
90 Options remaining are B and D
91 Options remaining are A and C
92 Options remaining are A and D
93 Options remaining are A and D
94 Options remaining are C and D
95 Options remaining are A and B
96 Options remaining are A and B
97 Options remaining are C and D
98 Options remaining are A and D
99 Options remaining are A and C
100 Options remaining are A and B
101 Options remaining are B and D
102 Options remaining are A and B
103 Options remaining are A and B
104 Options remaining are B and D
105 Options remaining are B and C
106 Options remaining are A and D
107 Options remaining are A and C
108 Options remaining are A and D
109.Options remaining are B and C
110 Options remaining are A and B
111 Options remaining are C and D
112 Options remaining are B and D
113 Options remaining are A and B
114 Options remaining are C and D
115 Options remaining are A and B
116 Options remaining are A and B
117 Options remaining are B and D
118 Options remaining are A and D
119 Options remaining are C and D
120 Options remaining are B and C
121 Options remaining are B and D
122 Options remaining are B and C
123 Options remaining are A and C
124 Options remaining are B and C
125 Options remaining are A and B
126 Options remaining are B and C
127 Options remaining are B and C
128 Options remaining are B and D
129 Options remaining are A and B
130 Options remaining are A and D
131 Options remaining are A and C
132 Options remaining are A and B
133 Options remaining are A and D
134 Options remaining are A and C
135 Options remaining are C and D
136 Options remaining are A and C
137 Options remaining are A and C
138 Options remaining are C and D
139 Options remaining are A and B
140 Options remaining are C and D
141 Options remaining are B and D
142 Options remaining are A and B

143 Options remaining are C and D
144 Options remaining are C and D
145 Options remaining are B and C
146 Options remaining are A and B
147 Options remaining are A and B
148 Options remaining are A and D
149 Options remaining are A and D
150 Options remaining are A and D
151 Options remaining are A and B
152 Options remaining are A and C
153 Options remaining are B and C
154 Options remaining are A and B
155 Options remaining are A and C
156 Options remaining are A and D
157 Options remaining are A and B
158 Options remaining are A and C
159 Options remaining are A and B
160 Options remaining are C and D
161 Options remaining are A and B
162 Options remaining are A and C
163 Options remaining are B and D
164 Options remaining are A and B
165 Options remaining are B and C
166 Options remaining are B and C
167 Options remaining are C and D
168 Options remaining are A and D
169 Options remaining are B and D
170 Options remaining are A and C
171 Options remaining are B and C
172 Options remaining are B and C

£300

1 Options remaining are A and C
2 Options remaining are C and D
3 Options remaining are A and B
4 Options remaining are A and D
5 Options remaining are A and C
6 Options remaining are A and D
7 Options remaining are B and C
8 Options remaining are B and D
9 Options remaining are B and C
10 Options remaining are B and D
11 Options remaining are C and D
12 Options remaining are C and D
13 Options remaining are A and C
14 Options remaining are C and D
15 Options remaining are A and C
16 Options remaining are B and C
17 Options remaining are A and D
18 Options remaining are B and C
19 Options remaining are A and B
20 Options remaining are B and D
21 Options remaining are C and D
22 Options remaining are A and B
23 Options remaining are A and B
24 Options remaining are B and D
25 Options remaining are A and B
26 Options remaining are B and D
27 Options remaining are B and D
28 Options remaining are C and D
29 Options remaining are A and C
30 Options remaining are A and B
31 Options remaining are B and C
32 Options remaining are A and B
33 Options remaining are A and D
34 Options remaining are A and D
35 Options remaining are B and C
36 Options remaining are A and D
37 Options remaining are B and D
38 Options remaining are A and D
39 Options remaining are A and B
40 Options remaining are A and D
41 Options remaining are A and C
42 Options remaining are B and D
43 Options remaining are B and D
44 Options remaining are A and B
45 Options remaining are B and D
46 Options remaining are B and C

47 Options remaining are A and B
48 Options remaining are A and D
49 Options remaining are A and C
50 Options remaining are A and D
51 Options remaining are A and C
52 Options remaining are A and D
53 Options remaining are B and D
54 Options remaining are A and C
55 Options remaining are A and B
56 Options remaining are A and D
57 Options remaining are B and D
58 Options remaining are A and C
59 Options remaining are A and B
60 Options remaining are C and D
61 Options remaining are B and D
62 Options remaining are A and C
63 Options remaining are A and B
64 Options remaining are A and D
65 Options remaining are A and C
66 Options remaining are B and D
67 Options remaining are B and D
68 Options remaining are A and C
69 Options remaining are B and D
70 Options remaining are B and C
71 Options remaining are A and C
72 Options remaining are A and D
73 Options remaining are B and C
74 Options remaining are C and D
75 Options remaining are A and C
76 Options remaining are A and B
77 Options remaining are B and D
78 Options remaining are A and D
79 Options remaining are A and B
80 Options remaining are B and D
81 Options remaining are A and C
82 Options remaining are B and C
83 Options remaining are C and D
84 Options remaining are A and B
85 Options remaining are A and D
86 Options remaining are B and C
87 Options remaining are B and C
88 Options remaining are B and C
89 Options remaining are B and C
90 Options remaining are A and D
91 Options remaining are A and D
92 Options remaining are A and C
93 Options remaining are B and D
94 Options remaining are B and C
95 Options remaining are B and C
96 Options remaining are A and B
97 Options remaining are A and D
98 Options remaining are A and D
99 Options remaining are A and B
100 Options remaining are A and C
101 Options remaining are C and D
102 Options remaining are B and C
103 Options remaining are A and C
104 Options remaining are A and D
105 Options remaining are A and C
106 Options remaining are B and D
107 Options remaining are A and C
108 Options remaining are A and B
109 Options remaining are A and D
110 Options remaining are A and D
111 Options remaining are A and C
112 Options remaining are A and D
113 Options remaining are A and C
114 Options remaining are A and B
115 Options remaining are B and C
116 Options remaining are A and C
117 Options remaining are A and D
118 Options remaining are A and B
119 Options remaining are A and D
120 Options remaining are A and C
121 Options remaining are B and D
122 Options remaining are C and D
123 Options remaining are A and D
124 Options remaining are A and C
125 Options remaining are B and C
126 Options remaining are A and B
127 Options remaining are A and C
128 Options remaining are A and B
129 Options remaining are A and D
130 Options remaining are A and C
131 Options remaining are A and B
132 Options remaining are A and B

133 Options remaining are B and C
134 Options remaining are A and D
135 Options remaining are A and B
136 Options remaining are A and D
137 Options remaining are B and C
138 Options remaining are A and D
139 Options remaining are B and C
140 Options remaining are A and C
141 Options remaining are B and D
142 Options remaining are B and C
143 Options remaining are A and B
144 Options remaining are A and B
145 Options remaining are B and C
146 Options remaining are C and D
147 Options remaining are B and C
148 Options remaining are B and D
149 Options remaining are A and D
150 Options remaining are B and D
151 Options remaining are B and C
152 Options remaining are A and D
153 Options remaining are B and D
154 Options remaining are A and C
155 Options remaining are A and B
156 Options remaining are A and D
157 Options remaining are B and C
158 Options remaining are B and D
159 Options remaining are A and C
160 Options remaining are A and C
161 Options remaining are B and D
162 Options remaining are C and D
163 Options remaining are B and D
164 Options remaining are C and D

£500

1 Options remaining are B and D
2 Options remaining are A and C
3 Options remaining are A and B
4 Options remaining are A and C
5 Options remaining are A and B
6 Options remaining are C and D
7 Options remaining are A and B
8 Options remaining are A and B
9 Options remaining are B and C
10 Options remaining are A and B
11 Options remaining are B and C
12 Options remaining are A and D
13 Options remaining are B and C
14 Options remaining are A and D
15 Options remaining are B and C
16 Options remaining are C and D
17 Options remaining are B and C
18 Options remaining are C and D
19 Options remaining are A and D
20 Options remaining are B and D
21 Options remaining are A and C
22 Options remaining are A and C
23 Options remaining are A and D
24 Options remaining are A and D
25 Options remaining are B and D
26 Options remaining are C and D
27 Options remaining are A and D
28 Options remaining are A and C
29 Options remaining are A and C
30 Options remaining are B and D
31 Options remaining are B and D
32 Options remaining are A and C
33 Options remaining are B and D
34 Options remaining are B and D
35 Options remaining are A and D
36 Options remaining are C and D
37 Options remaining are B and D
38 Options remaining are B and D
39 Options remaining are A and D
40 Options remaining are C and D
41 Options remaining are A and B
42 Options remaining are A and D
43 Options remaining are B and D
44 Options remaining are B and D

45 Options remaining are B and C
46 Options remaining are A and D
47 Options remaining are A and D
48 Options remaining are C and D
49 Options remaining are A and D
50 Options remaining are C and D
51 Options remaining are A and B
52 Options remaining are B and C
53 Options remaining are A and D
54 Options remaining are B and D
55 Options remaining are A and B
56 Options remaining are C and D
57 Options remaining are B and C
58 Options remaining are A and B
59 Options remaining are A and D
60 Options remaining are A and C
61 Options remaining are A and D
62 Options remaining are A and B
63 Options remaining are B and C
64 Options remaining are A and C
65 Options remaining are B and D
66 Options remaining are A and C
67 Options remaining are A and B
68 Options remaining are A and C
69 Options remaining are C and D
70 Options remaining are B and C
71 Options remaining are A and B
72 Options remaining are A and B
73 Options remaining are B and C
74 Options remaining are A and D
75 Options remaining are B and D
76 Options remaining are C and D
77 Options remaining are C and D
78 Options remaining are A and B
79 Options remaining are C and D
80 Options remaining are A and B
81 Options remaining are B and D
82 Options remaining are C and D
83 Options remaining are A and C
84 Options remaining are A and B
85 Options remaining are A and C
86 Options remaining are C and D
87 Options remaining are B and C
88 Options remaining are A and B
89 Options remaining are A and B
90 Options remaining are A and C
91 Options remaining are B and C
92 Options remaining are A and C
93 Options remaining are B and D
94 Options remaining are A and C
95 Options remaining are A and B
96 Options remaining are B and D
97 Options remaining are A and D
98 Options remaining are B and C
99 Options remaining are A and D
100 Options remaining are B and C
101 Options remaining are C and D
102 Options remaining are A and D
103 Options remaining are A and C
104 Options remaining are B and C
105 Options remaining are A and C
106 Options remaining are A and B
107 Options remaining are C and D
108 Options remaining are A and B
109 Options remaining are C and D
110 Options remaining are C and D
111 Options remaining are A and B
112 Options remaining are C and D
113 Options remaining are B and D
114 Options remaining are B and C
115 Options remaining are C and D
116 Options remaining are A and B
117 Options remaining are C and D
118 Options remaining are A and B
119 Options remaining are B and D
120 Options remaining are C and D
121 Options remaining are A and D
122 Options remaining are B and C
123 Options remaining are C and D
124 Options remaining are B and D
125 Options remaining are A and B
126 Options remaining are C and D
127 Options remaining are B and C
128 Options remaining are A and D
129 Options remaining are C and D
130 Options remaining are B and D

131 Options remaining are B and C
132 Options remaining are A and D
133 Options remaining are A and C
134 Options remaining are A and B
135 Options remaining are C and D
136 Options remaining are A and D
137 Options remaining are C and D
138 Options remaining are B and C
139 Options remaining are B and C
140 Options remaining are A and B
141 Options remaining are B and C
142 Options remaining are A and C
143 Options remaining are B and C
144 Options remaining are A and C
145 Options remaining are C and D
146 Options remaining are A and B
147 Options remaining are C and D
148 Options remaining are A and B
149 Options remaining are A and B
150 Options remaining are B and D
151 Options remaining are B and D
152 Options remaining are A and B
153 Options remaining are A and D
154 Options remaining are B and C
155 Options remaining are C and D
156 Options remaining are B and C

£1,000

1 Options remaining are B and C
2 Options remaining are A and C
3 Options remaining are B and D
4 Options remaining are A and D
5 Options remaining are B and C
6 Options remaining are B and C
7 Options remaining are A and D
8 Options remaining are A and B
9 Options remaining are A and C
10 Options remaining are A and D
11 Options remaining are A and B
12 Options remaining are A and C
13 Options remaining are A and D
14 Options remaining are A and B
15 Options remaining are C and D
16 Options remaining are A and B
17 Options remaining are B and C
18 Options remaining are A and D
19 Options remaining are A and B
20 Options remaining are B and D
21 Options remaining are B and C
22 Options remaining are B and D
23 Options remaining are A and D
24 Options remaining are B and D
25 Options remaining are A and C
26 Options remaining are A and D
27 Options remaining are A and D
28 Options remaining are B and D
29 Options remaining are A and C
30 Options remaining are B and D
31 Options remaining are A and D
32 Options remaining are A and C
33 Options remaining are B and D
34 Options remaining are A and D
35 Options remaining are B and C
36 Options remaining are A and B
37 Options remaining are A and D
38 Options remaining are B and D
39 Options remaining are C and D
40 Options remaining are A and D
41 Options remaining are A and D
42 Options remaining are B and D
43 Options remaining are A and C
44 Options remaining are A and C
45 Options remaining are C and D
46 Options remaining are A and D
47 Options remaining are A and C
48 Options remaining are A and B
49 Options remaining are A and C
50 Options remaining are A and B

51 Options remaining are B and C
52 Options remaining are B and C
53 Options remaining are A and C
54 Options remaining are A and C
55 Options remaining are C and D
56 Options remaining are B and C
57 Options remaining are B and C
58 Options remaining are A and B
59 Options remaining are B and C
60 Options remaining are A and D
61 Options remaining are A and C
62 Options remaining are B and C
63 Options remaining are B and C
64 Options remaining are A and C
65 Options remaining are C and D
66 Options remaining are B and C
67 Options remaining are B and C
68 Options remaining are A and C
69 Options remaining are A and B
70 Options remaining are A and C
71 Options remaining are A and C
72 Options remaining are A and C
73 Options remaining are A and B
74 Options remaining are C and D
75 Options remaining are A and B
76 Options remaining are B and D
77 Options remaining are A and B
78 Options remaining are B and D
79 Options remaining are B and D
80 Options remaining are C and B
81 Options remaining are B and D
82 Options remaining are B and C
83 Options remaining are B and C
84 Options remaining are C and D
85 Options remaining are A and C
86 Options remaining are B and C
87 Options remaining are A and B
88 Options remaining are C and D
89 Options remaining are A and B
90 Options remaining are A and D
91 Options remaining are A and D
92 Options remaining are C and D
93 Options remaining are A and C
94 Options remaining are A and D
95 Options remaining are A and C
96 Options remaining are A and D
97 Options remaining are A and B
98 Options remaining are C and D
99 Options remaining are B and C
100 Options remaining are A and B
101 Options remaining are A and C
102 Options remaining are A and B
103 Options remaining are C and D
104 Options remaining are A and B
105 Options remaining are A and D
106 Options remaining are A and C
107 Options remaining are B and C
108 Options remaining are A and B
109 Options remaining are B and D
110 Options remaining are A and C
111 Options remaining are C and D
112 Options remaining are A and B
113 Options remaining are B and C
114 Options remaining are A and D
115 Options remaining are A and C
116 Options remaining are C and D
117 Options remaining are C and D
118 Options remaining are A and D
119 Options remaining are A and C
120 Options remaining are B and C
121 Options remaining are B and D
122 Options remaining are A and D
123 Options remaining are A and D
124 Options remaining are B and C
125 Options remaining are B and C
126 Options remaining are A and B
127 Options remaining are B and C
128 Options remaining are A and D
129 Options remaining are A and B
130 Options remaining are A and C
131 Options remaining are B and C
132 Options remaining are A and D
133 Options remaining are A and D
134 Options remaining are A and C
135 Options remaining are B and D
136 Options remaining are A and C

137 Options remaining are A and B
138 Options remaining are A and B
139 Options remaining are B and C
140 Options remaining are C and D
141 Options remaining are A and B
142 Options remaining are A and C
143 Options remaining are C and D
144 Options remaining are A and C
145 Options remaining are B and C
146 Options remaining are A and C
147 Options remaining are A and B
148 Options remaining are C and D

£2,000

1 Options remaining are A and D
2 Options remaining are B and C
3 Options remaining are A and C
4 Options remaining are B and C
5 Options remaining are B and D
6 Options remaining are B and C
7 Options remaining are A and D
8 Options remaining are B and D
9 Options remaining are A and C
10 Options remaining are C and D
11 Options remaining are A and C
12 Options remaining are A and C
13 Options remaining are A and D
14 Options remaining are B and C
15 Options remaining are B and D
16 Options remaining are B and D
17 Options remaining are A and C
18 Options remaining are A and D
19 Options remaining are B and C
20 Options remaining are B and C
21 Options remaining are B and D
22 Options remaining are C and D
23 Options remaining are A and D
24 Options remaining are A and B
25 Options remaining are C and D
26 Options remaining are C and D
27 Options remaining are B and D
28 Options remaining are B and C
29 Options remaining are B and C
30 Options remaining are B and D
31 Options remaining are A and D
32 Options remaining are A and D
33 Options remaining are B and D
34 Options remaining are B and C
35 Options remaining are B and D
36 Options remaining are A and B
37 Options remaining are C and D
38 Options remaining are C and D
39 Options remaining are B and D
40 Options remaining are A and B
41 Options remaining are A and B
42 Options remaining are A and C
43 Options remaining are A and D
44 Options remaining are A and D
45 Options remaining are A and D
46 Options remaining are C and D
47 Options remaining are B and D
48 Options remaining are B and D
49 Options remaining are A and D
50 Options remaining are B and D
51 Options remaining are A and C
52 Options remaining are B and D
53 Options remaining are A and D
54 Options remaining are A and C
55 Options remaining are A and D
56 Options remaining are A and C
57 Options remaining are B and C
58 Options remaining are A and C
59 Options remaining are B and D
60 Options remaining are A and C
61 Options remaining are C and D
62 Options remaining are B and D
63 Options remaining are C and D
64 Options remaining are A and B

65 Options remaining are C and D
66 Options remaining are B and D
67 Options remaining are A and B
68 Options remaining are B and D
69 Options remaining are C and D
70 Options remaining are A and C
71 Options remaining are A and B
72 Options remaining are B and D
73 Options remaining are A and B
74 Options remaining are A and B
75 Options remaining are A and C
76 Options remaining are B and D
77 Options remaining are A and C
78 Options remaining are B and D
79 Options remaining are B and C
80 Options remaining are C and D
81 Options remaining are A and B
82 Options remaining are A and C
83 Options remaining are A and C
84 Options remaining are B and D
85 Options remaining are A and B
86 Options remaining are A and C
87 Options remaining are A and C
88 Options remaining are B and D
89 Options remaining are B and C
90 Options remaining are A and B
91 Options remaining are A and C
92 Options remaining are B and D
93 Options remaining are A and C
94 Options remaining are B and D
95 Options remaining are C and D
96 Options remaining are C and D
97 Options remaining are A and D
98 Options remaining are B and C
99 Options remaining are B and D
100 Options remaining are A and C
101 Options remaining are C and D
102 Options remaining are A and D
103 Options remaining are C and D
104 Options remaining are B and D
105 Options remaining are A and C
106 Options remaining are A and D
107 Options remaining are A and C
108 Options remaining are B and C
109 Options remaining are B and C
110 Options remaining are A and D
111 Options remaining are C and D
112 Options remaining are B and D
113 Options remaining are A and C
114 Options remaining are C and D
115 Options remaining are A and B
116 Options remaining are A and D
117 Options remaining are A and B
118 Options remaining are B and C
119 Options remaining are A and B
120 Options remaining are C and D
121 Options remaining are A and D
122 Options remaining are C and D
123 Options remaining are B and D
124 Options remaining are A and C
125 Options remaining are B and C
126 Options remaining are B and C
127 Options remaining are B and D
128 Options remaining are A and C
129 Options remaining are A and D
130 Options remaining are B and D
131 Options remaining are A and C
132 Options remaining are B and C
133 Options remaining are B and C
134 Options remaining are A and B
135 Options remaining are A and B
136 Options remaining are B and D
137 Options remaining are B and C
138 Options remaining are A and B
139 Options remaining are B and D
140 Options remaining are B and D

£4,000

1 Options remaining are C and D
2 Options remaining are A and D
3 Options remaining are A and C
4 Options remaining are B and C
5 Options remaining are A and D
6 Options remaining are A and C
7 Options remaining are C and D
8 Options remaining are A and B
9 Options remaining are A and C
10 Options remaining are A and C
11 Options remaining are A and B
12 Options remaining are A and D
13 Options remaining are A and D
14 Options remaining are B and C
15 Options remaining are B and C
16 Options remaining are A and C
17 Options remaining are B and D
18 Options remaining are A and C
19 Options remaining are A and B
20 Options remaining are B and C
21 Options remaining are B and D
22 Options remaining are A and B
23 Options remaining are C and D
24 Options remaining are A and B
25 Options remaining are A and B
26 Options remaining are C and D
27 Options remaining are B and C
28 Options remaining are A and D
29 Options remaining are B and D
30 Options remaining are B and C
31 Options remaining are A and C
32 Options remaining are A and D
33 Options remaining are B and C
34 Options remaining are A and D
35 Options remaining are B and C
36 Options remaining are B and C
37 Options remaining are A and D
38 Options remaining are B and D
39 Options remaining are A and C
40 Options remaining are B and C
41 Options remaining are C and D
42 Options remaining are B and C
43 Options remaining are A and C
44 Options remaining are B and D
45 Options remaining are A and D
46 Options remaining are A and B
47 Options remaining are A and D
48 Options remaining are B and C
49 Options remaining are B and C
50 Options remaining are A and C
51 Options remaining are A and B
52 Options remaining are A and D
53 Options remaining are B and C
54 Options remaining are A and C
55 Options remaining are A and B
56 Options remaining are C and D
57 Options remaining are A and B
58 Options remaining are A and B
59 Options remaining are A and C
60 Options remaining are C and D
61 Options remaining are B and C
62 Options remaining are C and D
63 Options remaining are B and D
64 Options remaining are B and D
65 Options remaining are B and C
66 Options remaining are A and C
67 Options remaining are C and D
68 Options remaining are B and D
69 Options remaining are A and C
70 Options remaining are A and C
71 Options remaining are C and D
72 Options remaining are C and D
73 Options remaining are A and B
74 Options remaining are A and D
75 Options remaining are A and C
76 Options remaining are A and B
77 Options remaining are B and D
78 Options remaining are C and D
79 Options remaining are A and B
80 Options remaining are A and D
81 Options remaining are B and C
82 Options remaining are A and D
83 Options remaining are C and D
84 Options remaining are B and D

50:50

85 Options remaining are A and D
86 Options remaining are B and C
87 Options remaining are A and D
88 Options remaining are C and D
89 Options remaining are A and D
90 Options remaining are C and D
91 Options remaining are A and D
92 Options remaining are B and C
93 Options remaining are B and D
94 Options remaining are C and D
95 Options remaining are B and D
96 Options remaining are A and C
97 Options remaining are A and B
98 Options remaining are A and C
99 Options remaining are B and D
100 Options remaining are A and B
101 Options remaining are A and D
102 Options remaining are C and D
103 Options remaining are A and B
104 Options remaining are A and C
105 Options remaining are A and B
106 Options remaining are A and B
107 Options remaining are B and C
108 Options remaining are A and D
109 Options remaining are B and D
110 Options remaining are A and C
111 Options remaining are A and C
112 Options remaining are B and D
113 Options remaining are A and B
114 Options remaining are A and B
115 Options remaining are A and C
116 Options remaining are A and B
117 Options remaining are B and C
118 Options remaining are A and D
119 Options remaining are A and D
120 Options remaining are B and C
121 Options remaining are B and C
122 Options remaining are B and C
123 Options remaining are B and B
124 Options remaining are C and D
125 Options remaining are B and D
126 Options remaining are A and B
127 Options remaining are A and C
128 Options remaining are B and D
129 Options remaining are A and B
130 Options remaining are B and C
131 Options remaining are A and D
132 Options remaining are B and C

£8,000

1 Options remaining are A and B
2 Options remaining are A and B
3 Options remaining are A and C
4 Options remaining are A and C
5 Options remaining are B and C
6 Options remaining are C and D
7 Options remaining are A and C
8 Options remaining are B and D
9 Options remaining are C and D
10 Options remaining are A and C
11 Options remaining are A and D
12 Options remaining are B and D
13 Options remaining are A and C
14 Options remaining are A and B
15 Options remaining are A and D
16 Options remaining are A and C
17 Options remaining are A and C
18 Options remaining are A and B
19 Options remaining are C and D
20 Options remaining are A and B
21 Options remaining are B and D
22 Options remaining are B and C
23 Options remaining are A and B
24 Options remaining are C and D
25 Options remaining are B and D
26 Options remaining are A and C
27 Options remaining are B and C
28 Options remaining are A and C

50:50

29 Options remaining are C and D
30 Options remaining are A and C
31 Options remaining are C and D
32 Options remaining are A and B
33 Options remaining are A and D
34 Options remaining are C and D
35 Options remaining are A and D
36 Options remaining are C and D
37 Options remaining are A and D
38 Options remaining are A and C
39 Options remaining are A and D
40 Options remaining are A and D
41 Options remaining are C and D
42 Options remaining are A and C
43 Options remaining are A and B
44 Options remaining are B and D
45 Options remaining are B and C
46 Options remaining are A and C
47 Options remaining are A and D
48 Options remaining are B and C
49 Options remaining are A and C
50 Options remaining are A and D
51 Options remaining are A and B
52 Options remaining are A and B
53 Options remaining are A and B
54 Options remaining are B and D
55 Options remaining are B and D
56 Options remaining are A and C
57 Options remaining are A and D
58 Options remaining are B and C
59 Options remaining are C and D
60 Options remaining are A and B
61 Options remaining are A and B
62 Options remaining are A and C
63 Options remaining are A and D
64 Options remaining are B and C
65 Options remaining are A and B
66 Options remaining are B and D
67 Options remaining are A and D
68 Options remaining are B and D
69 Options remaining are B and C
70 Options remaining are A and C
71 Options remaining are A and B
72 Options remaining are A and D
73 Options remaining are B and D
74 Options remaining are B and D
75 Options remaining are A and B
76 Options remaining are A and B
77 Options remaining are C and D
78 Options remaining are B and D
79 Options remaining are B and D
80 Options remaining are A and C
81 Options remaining are B and D
82 Options remaining are A and C
83 Options remaining are A and C
84 Options remaining are A and C
85 Options remaining are A and B
86 Options remaining are A and D
87 Options remaining are B and C
88 Options remaining are B and C
89 Options remaining are B and D
90 Options remaining are A and C
91 Options remaining are A and B
92 Options remaining are A and B
93 Options remaining are A and D
94 Options remaining are A and C
95 Options remaining are A and B
96 Options remaining are A and D
97 Options remaining are A and B
98 Options remaining are B and C
99 Options remaining are B and C
100 Options remaining are A and C
101 Options remaining are A and B
102 Options remaining are A and C
103 Options remaining are B and C
104 Options remaining are A and C
105 Options remaining are A and C
106 Options remaining are B and D
107 Options remaining are A and C
108 Options remaining are A and D
109 Options remaining are B and D
110 Options remaining are A and B
111 Options remaining are A and C
112 Options remaining are A and B
113 Options remaining are A and B
114 Options remaining are B and C

115 Options remaining are A and C
116 Options remaining are B and D
117 Options remaining are A and B
118 Options remaining are A and C
119 Options remaining are B and D
120 Options remaining are B and D
121 Options remaining are A and C
122 Options remaining are A and D
123 Options remaining ar e A and B
124 Options remaining are B and D

£16,000

1 Options remaining are A and B
2 Options remaining are C and D
3 Options remaining are B and D
4 Options remaining are A and D
5 Options remaining are B and D
6 Options remaining are C and D
7 Options remaining are A and C
8 Options remaining are B and D
9 Options remaining are B and D
10 Options remaining are A and C
11 Options remaining are A and B
12 Options remaining are A and D
13 Options remaining are A and B
14 Options remaining are A and B
15 Options remaining are A and B
16 Options remaining are A and D
17 Options remaining are A and B
18 Options remaining are B and C
19 Options remaining are C and D
20 Options remaining are C and D
21 Options remaining are B and D
22 Options remaining are B and D
23 Options remaining are A and D
24 Options remaining are A and C
25 Options remaining are A and D
26 Options remaining are B and D
27 Options remaining are B and D
28 Options remaining are A and C
29 Options remaining are A and C
30 Options remaining are B and D
31 Options remaining are A and B
32 Options remaining are A and D
33 Options remaining are A and B
34 Options remaining are B and C
35 Options remaining are A and B
36 Options remaining are A and C
37 Options remaining are B and D
38 Options remaining are B and D
39 Options remaining are C and D
40 Options remaining are B and C
41 Options remaining are B and C
42 Options remaining are C and D
43 Options remaining are A and B
44 Options remaining are A and D
45 Options remaining are B and C
46 Options remaining are A and D
47 Options remaining are B and C
48 Options remaining are B and C
49 Options remaining are A and B
50 Options remaining are B and C
51 Options remaining are A and C
52 Options remaining are A and C
53 Options remaining are A and C
54 Options remaining are B and C
55 Options remaining are A and D
56 Options remaining are A and B
57 Options remaining are A and C
58 Options remaining are B and D
59 Options remaining are A and C
60 Options remaining are A and D
61 Options remaining are A and B
62 Options remaining are B and D
63 Options remaining are B and C
64 Options remaining are A and B
65 Options remaining are A and B
66 Options remaining are B and C

67 Options remaining are B and C
68 Options remaining are A and B
69 Options remaining are A and C
70 Options remaining are B and C
71 Options remaining are B and D
72 Options remaining are A and B
73 Options remaining are C and D
74 Options remaining are A and B
75 Options remaining are A and C
76 Options remaining are B and D
77 Options remaining are A and B
78 Options remaining are A and C
79 Options remaining are A and D
80 Options remaining are A and B
81 Options remaining are A and C
82 Options remaining are B and C
83 Options remaining are A and B
84 Options remaining are B and D
85 Options remaining are A and C
86 Options remaining are A and B
87 Options remaining are A and B
88 Options remaining are A and D
89 Options remaining are A and B
90 Options remaining are A and D
91 Options remaining are A and B
92 Options remaining are A and D
93 Options remaining are B and C
94 Options remaining are A and D
95 Options remaining are B and D
96 Options remaining are A and B
97 Options remaining are A and D
98 Options remaining are A and C
99 Options remaining are C and D
100 Options remaining are B and C
101 Options remaining are A and B
102 Options remaining are A and B
103 Options remaining are B and C
104 Options remaining are B and C
105 Options remaining are A and C
106 Options remaining are A and B
107 Options remaining are C and D
108 Options remaining are C and D
109 Options remaining are A and B
110 Options remaining are B and C
111 Options remaining are A and B
112 Options remaining are A and D
113 Options remaining are A and B
114 Options remaining are A and C
115 Options remaining are C and D
116 Options remaining are A and B

£32,000

1 Options remaining are A and D
2 Options remaining are A and D
3 Options remaining are A and C
4 Options remaining are B and D
5 Options remaining are A and C
6 Options remaining are A and D
7 Options remaining are A and C
8 Options remaining are A and D
9 Options remaining are A and B
10 Options remaining are B and D
11 Options remaining are A and B
12 Options remaining are A and D
13 Options remaining are B and C
14 Options remaining are A and D
15 Options remaining are B and D
16 Options remaining are A and C
17 Options remaining are A and C
18 Options remaining are A and D
19 Options remaining are B and D
20 Options remaining are A and D
21 Options remaining are A and B
22 Options remaining are B and D
23 Options remaining are A and D
24 Options remaining are A and B
25 Options remaining are A and C
26 Options remaining are A and C

27 Options remaining are B and C
28 Options remaining are A and D
29 Options remaining are A and D
30 Options remaining are A and B
31 Options remaining are C and D
32 Options remaining are A and B
33 Options remaining are A and B
34 Options remaining are A and D
35 Options remaining are A and B
36 Options remaining are B and D
37 Options remaining are C and D
38 Options remaining are A and D
39 Options remaining are A and B
40 Options remaining are A and D
41 Options remaining are C and D
42 Options remaining are B and C
43 Options remaining are A and C
44 Options remaining are A and B
45 Options remaining are A and B
46 Options remaining are A and C
47 Options remaining are A and B
48 Options remaining are A and B
49 Options remaining are A and D
50 Options remaining are C and D
51 Options remaining are A and D
52 Options remaining are A and B
53 Options remaining are A and D
54 Options remaining are B and C
55 Options remaining are A and C
56 Options remaining are B and D
57 Options remaining are A and C
58 Options remaining are A and B
59 Options remaining are B and C
60 Options remaining are A and C
61 Options remaining are B and C
62 Options remaining are B and C
63 Options remaining are A and D
64 Options remaining are B and C
65 Options remaining are B and D
66 Options remaining are A and D
67 Options remaining are A and B
68 Options remaining are A and B
69 Options remaining are C and D
70 Options remaining are A and D
71 Options remaining are A and B
72 Options remaining are A and D
73 Options remaining are A and B
74 Options remaining are C and D
75 Options remaining are B and C
76 Options remaining are A and B
77 Options remaining are C and D
78 Options remaining are B and C
79 Options remaining are A and B
80 Options remaining are B and C
81 Options remaining are A and B
82 Options remaining are C and D
83 Options remaining are B and C
84 Options remaining are B and C
85 Options remaining are A and C
86 Options remaining are B and C
87 Options remaining are A and D
88 Options remaining are A and D
89 Options remaining are B and C
90 Options remaining are B and D
91 Options remaining are A and B
92 Options remaining are B and D
93 Options remaining are C and D
94 Options remaining are A and D
95 Options remaining are A and D
96 Options remaining are A and C
97 Options remaining are A and B
98 Options remaining are B and C
99 Options remaining are B and D
100 Options remaining are B and D
101 Options remaining are A and C
102 Options remaining are B and D
103 Options remaining are A and C
104 Options remaining are A and D
105 Options remaining are A and C
106 Options remaining are A and C
107 Options remaining are C and D
108 Options remaining are C and D

£64,000

1 Options remaining are B and D
2 Options remaining are A and B
3 Options remaining are A and D
4 Options remaining are A and B
5 Options remaining are B and C
6 Options remaining are C and D
7 Options remaining are A and B
8 Options remaining are A and C
9 Options remaining are B and C
10 Options remaining are B and C
11 Options remaining are A and B
12 Options remaining are B and C
13 Options remaining are A and B
14 Options remaining are A and C
15 Options remaining are B and C
16 Options remaining are A and C
17 Options remaining are A and B
18 Options remaining are B and C
19 Options remaining are C and D
20 Options remaining are A and B
21 Options remaining are A and D
22 Options remaining are A and D
23 Options remaini ng are C and D
24 Options remaining are B and C
25 Options remaining are A and C
26 Options remaining are A and B
27 Options remaining are A and D
28 Options remaining are B and C
29 Options remaining are C and D
30 Options remaining are B and D
31 Options remaining are B and C
32 Options remaining are A and B
33 Options remaining are A and C
34 Options remaining are A and B
35 Options remaining are A and D
36 Options remaining are B and C
37 Options remaining are A and C
38 Options remaining are A and B
39 Options remaining are A and C
40 Options remaining are B and C
41 Options remaining are B and D
42 Options remaining are C and D
43 Options remaining are B and D
44 Options remaining are B and D
45 Options remaining are A and D
46 Options remaining are C and D
47 Options remaining are A and B
48 Options remaining are A and B
49 Options remaining are C and D
50 Options remaining are A and C
51 Options remaining are B and D
52 Options remaining are A and D
53 Options remaining are A and B
54 Options remaining are A and B
55 Options remaining are C and D
56 Options remaining are B and C
57 Options remaining are B and C
58 Options remaining are A and C
59 Options remaining are C and D
60 Options remaining are A and B
61 Options remaining are A and C
62 Options remaining are B and D
63 Options remaining are A and B
64 Options remaining are A and B
65 Options remaining are A and D
66 Options remaining are B and C
67 Options remaining are B and C
68 Options remaining are A and D
69 Options remaining are B and D
70 Options remaining are A and B
71 Options remaining are A and B
72 Options remaining are A and B
73 Options remaining are A and D
74 Options remaining are A and B
75 Options remaining are A and C
76 Options remaining are A and B
77 Options remaining are B and C
78 Options remaining are A and C
79 Options remaining are B and D
80 Options remaining are A and D
81 Options remaining are A and C
82 Options remaining are B and D
83 Options remaining are B and C
84 Options remaining are B and D

85 Options remaining are A and B
86 Options remaining are A and C
87 Options remaining are B and C
88 Options remaining are C and D
89 Options remaining are A and C
90 Options remaining are A and B
91 Options remaining are A and C
92 Options remaining are A and B
93 Options remaining are B and C
94 Options remaining are A and C
95 Options remaining are B and D
96 Options remaining are B and C
97 Options remaining are B and D
98 Options remaining are C and D
99 Options remaining are B and D
100 Options remaining are B and C

£125,000

1 Options remaining are A and B
2 Options remaining are C and D
3 Options remaining are A and C
4 Options remaining are A and D
5 Options remaining are C and D
6 Options remaining are B and D
7 Options remaining are A and B
8 Options remaining are B and C
9 Options remaining are C and D
10 Options remaining are A and D
11 Options remaining are B and D
12 Options remaining are B and C
13 Options remaining are A and D
14 Options remaining are A and C
15 Options remaining are A and C
16 Options remaining are B and D
17 Options remaining are A and B
18 Options remaining are B and C
19 Options remaining are A and D
20 Options remaining are B and D
21 Options remaining are A and C
22 Options remaining are A and B
23 Options remaining are A and B
24 Options remaining are C and D
25 Options remaining are A and B
26 Options remaining are A and D
27 Options remaining are A and C
28 Options remaining are A and D
29 Options remaining are A and C
30 Options remaining are A and B
31 Options remaining are A and C
32 Options remaining are A and B
33 Options remaining are A and D
34 Options remaining are A and D
35 Options remaining are A and D
36 Options remaining are A and B
37 Options remaining are A and D
38 Options remaining are A and B
39 Options remaining are A and C
40 Options remaining are A and D
41 Options remaining are A and B
42 Options remaining are A and D
43 Options remaining are A and B
44 Options remaining are A and C
45 Options remaining are A and D
46 Options remaining are A and B
47 Options remaining are A and C
48 Options remaining are A and D
49 Options remaining are B and D
50 Options remaining are A and B
51 Options remaining are A and C
52 Options remaining are A and D
53 Options remaining are A and C
54 Options remaining are B and C
55 Options remaining are A and B
56 Options remaining are A and D
57 Options remaining are A and C
58 Options remaining are A and B
59 Options remaining are A and D
60 Options remaining are B and D

61 Options remaining are A and C
62 Options remaining are A and C
63 Options remaining are B and C
64 Options remaining are A and B
65 Options remaining are A and D
66 Options remaining are A and C
67 Options remaining are C and D
68 Options remaining are A and C
69 Options remaining are B and D
70 Options remaining are A and C
71 Options remaining are A and D
72 Options remaining are B and D
73 Options remaining are A and B
74 Options remaining are A and C
75 Options remaining are A and D
76 Options remaining are B and C
77 Options remaining are C and D
78 Options remaining are A and B
79 Options remaining are A and C
80 Options remaining are A and B
81 Options remaining are A and C
82 Options remaining are A and B
83 Options remaining are A and C
84 Options remaining are A and B
85 Options remaining are A and B
86 Options remaining are B and D
87 Options remaining are A and C
88 Options remaining are C and D
89 Options remaining are A and B
90 Options remaining are A and B
91 Options remaining are A and C
92 Options remaining are A and B

£250,000

1 Options remaining are A and C
2 Options remaining are B and D
3 Options remaining are B and D
4 Options remaining are A and B
5 Options remaining are A and D
6 Options remaining are A and C
7 Options remaining are A and C
8 Options remaining are B and D
9 Options remaining are A and D
10 Options remaining are A and C
11 Options remaining are B and D
12 Options remaining are A and B
13 Options remaining are C and D
14 Options remaining are A and B
15 Options remaining are C and D
16 Options remaining are B and C
17 Options remaining are A and C
18 Options remaining are A and C
19 Options remaining are A and B
20 Options remaining are C and D
21 Options remaining are B and C
22 Options remaining are A and C
23 Options remaining are B and C
24 Options remaining are A and B
25 Options remaining are B and C
26 Options remaining are C and D
27 Options remaining are B and C
28 Options remaining are B and D
29 Options remaining are B and C
30 Options remaining are B and C
31 Options remaining are A and C
32 Options remaining are B and D
33 Options remaining are A and C
34 Options remaining are A and C
35 Options remaining are B and C
36 Options remaining are A and C
37 Options remaining are B and C
38 Options remaining are A and B
39 Options remaining are C and D
40 Options remaining are A and C
41 Options remaining are B and D
42 Options remaining are C and D
43 Options remaining are C and D
44 Options remaining are B and C

50:50

45 Options remaining are A and B
46 Options remaining are B and C
47 Options remaining are A and D
48 Options remaining are A and C
49 Options remaining are A and B
50 Options remaining are A and C
51 Options remaining are A and D
52 Options remaining are B and D
53 Options remaining are B and C
54 Options remaining are B and C
55 Options remaining are A and C
56 Options remaining are B and C
57 Options remaining are A and C
58 Options remaining are B and D
59 Options remaining are A and B
60 Options remaining are B and D
61 Options remaining are A and C
62 Options remaining are A and B
63 Options remaining are A and C
64 Options remaining are A and B
65 Options remaining are A and C
66 Options remaining are A and C
67 Options remaining are B and C
68 Options remaining are A and D
69 Options remaining are B and D
70 Options remaining are A and B
71 Options remaining are A and B
72 Options remaining are B and D
73 Options remaining are B and C
74 Options remaining are B and C
75 Options remaining are B and D
76 Options remaining are A and D
77 Options remaining are A and D
78 Options remaining are A and C
79 Options remaining are A and B
80 Options remaining are A and C
81 Options remaining are B and D
82 Options remaining are A and B
83 Options remaining are A and D
84 Options remaining are B and D

£500,000

1 Options remaining are A and B
2 Options remaining are C and D
3 Options remaining are B and D
4 Options remaining are B and C
5 Options remaining are B and D
6 Options remaining are B and C
7 Options remaining are A and C
8 Options remaining are B and C
9 Options remaining are A and B
10 Options remaining are A and B
11 Options remaining are A and D
12 Options remaining are B and C
13 Options remaining are A and D
14 Options remaining are A and B
15 Options remaining are A and D
16 Options remaining are A and D
17 Options remaining are A and D
18 Options remaining are A and D
19 Options remaining are A and C
20 Options remaining are C and D
21 Options remaining are A and D
22 Options remaining are B and D
23 Options remaining are A and B
24 Options remaining are C and D
25 Options remaining are A and C
26 Options remaining are A and C
27 Options remaining are A and B
28 Options remaining are C and D
29 Options remaining are B and C
30 Options remaining are A and B
31 Options remaining are A and C
32 Options remaining are A and C
33 Options remaining are C and D
34 Options remaining are A and C
35 Options remaining are B and D
36 Options remaining are A and D

50:50

37 Options remaining are A and B
38 Options remaining are A and D
39 Options remaining are A and B
40 Options remaining are B and D
41 Options remaining are A and B
42 Options remaining are B and D
43 Options remaining are A and C
44 Options remaining are C and D
45 Options remaining are A and D
46 Options remaining are C and D
47 Options remaining are A and D
48 Options remaining are A and B
49 Options remaining are A and C
50 Options remaining are B and D
51 Options remaining are B and D
52 Options remaining are A and C
53 Options remaining are A and D
54 Options remaining are C and D
55 Options remaining are A and B
56 Options remaining are A and B
57 Options remaining are B and C
58 Options remaining are A and D
59 Options remaining are A and C
60 Options remaining are A and C
61 Options remaining are A and D
62 Options remaining are A and B
63 Options remaining are B and C
64 Options remaining are B and C
65 Options remaining are C and D
66 Options remaining are B and C
67 Options remaining are A and D
68 Options remaining are A and C
69 Options remaining are B and C
70 Options remaining are B and D
71 Options remaining are C and D
72 Options remaining are A and C
73 Options remaining are B and C
74 Options remaining are A and C
75 Options remaining are A and B
76 Options remaining are C and D

£1,000,000

1 Options remaining are B and C
2 Options remaining are C and D
3 Options remaining are B and D
4 Options remaining are B and D
5 Options remaining are B and C
6 Options remaining are C and D
7 Options remaining are B and C
8 Options remaining are B and D
9 Options remaining are C and D
10 Options remaining are A and D
11 Options remaining are A and D
12 Options remaining are B and D
13 Options remaining are A and D
14 Options remaining are B and D
15 Options remaining are A and C
16 Options remaining are C and D
17 Options remaining are A and D
18 Options remaining are A and B
19 Options remaining are B and C
20 Options remaining are C and D
21 Options remaining are B and D
22 Options remaining are A and B
23 Options remaining are B and D
24 Options remaining are B and C
25 Options remaining are B and D
26 Options remaining are B and C
27 Options remaining are A and C
28 Options remaining are A and B
29 Options remaining are A and B
30 Options remaining are B and D
31 Options remaining are A and B
32 Options remaining are A and C
33 Options remaining are A and B
34 Options remaining are C and D
35 Options remaining are B and D
36 Options remaining are A and C

37 Options remaining are A and D
38 Options remaining are B and C
39 Options remaining are B and D
40 Options remaining are A and C
41 Options remaining are B and D
42 Options remaining are A and D
43 Options remaining are B and C
44 Options remaining are B and C
45 Options remaining are B and D
46 Options remaining are B and D
47 Options remaining are A and B
48 Options remaining are A and C
49 Options remaining are B and C
50 Options remaining are C and D
51 Options remaining are A and D
52 Options remaining are B and C
53 Options remaining are A and B
54 Options remaining are B and C
55 Options remaining are A and D
56 Options remaining are A and B
57 Options remaining are C and D
58 Options remaining are A and B
59 Options remaining are C and D
60 Options remaining are C and D
61 Options remaining are A and B
62 Options remaining are B and D
63 Options remaining are A and C
64 Options remaining are B and C
65 Options remaining are B and D
66 Options remaining are A and B
67 Options remaining are C and D
68 Options remaining are B and D

Ask The Audience

£100

	A	B	C	D
1	A:82%	B:0%	C:0%	D:18%
2	A:0%	B:100%	C:0%	D:0%
3	A:100%	B:0%	C:0%	D:0%
4	A:0%	B:100%	C:0%	D:0%
5	A:100%	B:0%	C:0%	D:0%
6	A:11%	B:6%	C:70%	D:13%
7	A:100%	B:0%	C:0%	D:0%
8	A:100%	B:0%	C:0%	D:0%
9	A:0%	B:100%	C:0%	D:0%
10	A:100%	B:0%	C:0%	D:0%
11	A:0%	B:0%	C:100%	D:0%
12	A:100%	B:0%	C:0%	D:0%
13	A:0%	B:0%	C:100%	D:0%
14	A:100%	B:0%	C:0%	D:0%
15	A:0%	B:100%	C:0%	D:0%
16	A:100%	B:0%	C:0%	D:0%
17	A:100%	B:0%	C:0%	D:0%
18	A:100%	B:0%	C:0%	D:0%
19	A:0%	B:100%	C:0%	D:0%
20	A:0%	B:100%	C:0%	D:0%
21	A:0%	B:100%	C:0%	D:0%
22	A:100%	B:0%	C:0%	D:0%
23	A:97%	B:0%	C:3%	D:0%
24	A:100%	B:0%	C:0%	D:0%
25	A:100%	B:0%	C:0%	D:0%
26	A:0%	B:0%	C:100%	D:0%
27	A:0%	B:0%	C:100%	D:0%
28	A:0%	B:100%	C:0%	D:0%
29	A:0%	B:100%	C:0%	D:0%
30	A:0%	B:0%	C:100%	D:0%
31	A:100%	B:0%	C:0%	D:0%
32	A:100%	B:0%	C:0%	D:0%
33	A:0%	B:0%	C:100%	D:0%
34	A:100%	B:0%	C:0%	D:0%
35	A:100%	B:0%	C:0%	D:0%
36	A:100%	B:0%	C:0%	D:0%
37	A:0%	B:100%	C:0%	D:0%
38	A:100%	B:0%	C:0%	D:0%
39	A:100%	B:0%	C:0%	D:0%
40	A:0%	B:100%	C:0%	D:0%
41	A:100%	B:0%	C:0%	D:0%
42	A:0%	B:0%	C:0%	D:100%
43	A:100%	B:0%	C:0%	D:0%
44	A:0%	B:0%	C:0%	D:100%
45	A:0%	B:0%	C:100%	D:0%
46	A:100%	B:0%	C:0%	D:0%
47	A:0%	B:100%	C:0%	D:0%
48	A:100%	B:0%	C:0%	D:0%
49	A:0%	B:100%	C:0%	D:0%
50	A:100%	B:0%	C:0%	D:0%
51	A:0%	B:0%	C:0%	D:100%
52	A:0%	B:100%	C:0%	D:0%
53	A:0%	B:0%	C:100%	D:0%
54	A:0%	B:0%	C:100%	D:0%
55	A:100%	B:0%	C:0%	D:0%
56	A:0%	B:0%	C:0%	D:100%
57	A:0%	B:100%	C:0%	D:0%
58	A:100%	B:0%	C:0%	D:0%
59	A:2%	B:98%	C:0%	D:0%
60	A:0%	B:0%	C:94%	D:6%
61	A:21%	B:0%	C:0%	D:79%
62	A:0%	B:0%	C:100%	D:0%
63	A:0%	B:97%	C:3%	D:0%
64	A:0%	B:0%	C:100%	D:0%
65	A:0%	B:0%	C:0%	D:100%
66	A:100%	B:0%	C:0%	D:0%
67	A:98%	B:2%	C:0%	D:0%
68	A:0%	B:0%	C:0%	D:100%
69	A:100%	B:0%	C:0%	D:0%
70	A:0%	B:0%	C:0%	D:100%
71	A:4%	B:94%	C:0%	D:2%
72	A:9%	B:0%	C:0%	D:91%
73	A:100%	B:0%	C:0%	D:0%
74	A:0%	B:100%	C:0%	D:0%

ASK THE AUDIENCE

75	A:0%	B:0%	C:7%	D:93%
76	A:2%	B:0%	C:98%	D:0%
77	A:0%	B:3%	C:64%	D:33%
78	A:0%	B:0%	C:0%	D:100%
79	A:100%	B:0%	C:0%	D:0%
80	A:0%	B:100%	C:0%	D:0%
81	A:0%	B:0%	C:100%	D:0%
82	A:0%	B:0%	C:100%	D:0%
83	A:100%	B:0%	C:0%	D:0%
84	A:0%	B:0%	C:100%	D:0%
85	A:0%	B:0%	C:100%	D:0%
86	A:0%	B:100%	C:0%	D:0%
87	A:0%	B:0%	C:100%	D:0%
88	A:0%	B:100%	C:0%	D:0%
89	A:0%	B:2%	C:0%	D:98%
90	A:0%	B:0%	C:100%	D:0%
91	A:0%	B:0%	C:0%	D:100%
92	A:0%	B:100%	C:0%	D:0%
93	A:0%	B:100%	C:0%	D:0%
94	A:0%	B:100%	C:0%	D:0%
95	A:0%	B:0%	C:100%	D:0%
96	A:0%	B:100%	C:0%	D:0%
97	A:0%	B:100%	C:0%	D:0%
98	A:0%	B:0%	C:100%	D:0%
99	A:100%	B:0%	C:0%	D:0%
100	A:0%	B:0%	C:100%	D:0%
101	A:7%	B:93%	C:0%	D:0%
102	A:0%	B:0%	C:100%	D:0%
103	A:0%	B:100%	C:0%	D:0%
104	A:0%	B:0%	C:100%	D:0%
105	A:0%	B:0%	C:100%	D:0%
106	A:0%	B:0%	C:100%	D:0%
107	A:0%	B:100%	C:0%	D:0%
108	A:0%	B:100%	C:0%	D:0%
109	A:0%	B:100%	C:0%	D:0%
110	A:88%	B:0%	C:12%	D:0%
111	A:0%	B:100%	C:0%	D:0%
112	A:0%	B:0%	C:100%	D:0%
113	A:14%	B:85%	C:1%	D:0%
114	A:0%	B:0%	C:100%	D:0%
115	A:0%	B:100%	C:0%	D:0%
116	A:0%	B:8%	C:92%	D:0%
117	A:0%	B:100%	C:0%	D:0%
118	A:0%	B:100%	C:0%	D:0%
119	A:100%	B:0%	C:0%	D:0%
120	A:100%	B:0%	C:0%	D:0%
121	A:0%	B:100%	C:0%	D:0%
122	A:0%	B:0%	C:0%	D:100%
123	A:0%	B:0%	C:100%	D:0%
124	A:100%	B:0%	C:0%	D:0%
125	A:100%	B:0%	C:0%	D:0%
126	A:0%	B:100%	C:0%	D:0%
127	A:100%	B:0%	C:0%	D:0%
128	A:0%	B:100%	C:0%	D:0%
129	A:0%	B:100%	C:0%	D:0%
130	A:95%	B:5%	C:0%	D:0%
131	A:0%	B:0%	C:100%	D:0%
132	A:0%	B:100%	C:0%	D:0%
133	A:0%	B:100%	C:0%	D:0%
134	A:100%	B:0%	C:0%	D:0%
135	A:0%	B:0%	C:100%	D:0%
136	A:100%	B:0%	C:0%	D:0%
137	A:100%	B:0%	C:0%	D:0%
138	A:100%	B:0%	C:0%	D:0%
139	A:0%	B:0%	C:100%	D:0%
140	A:0%	B:100%	C:0%	D:0%
141	A:100%	B:0%	C:0%	D:0%
142	A:100%	B:0%	C:0%	D:0%
143	A:0%	B:100%	C:0%	D:0%
144	A:100%	B:0%	C:0%	D:0%
145	A:100%	B:0%	C:0%	D:0%
146	A:0%	B:0%	C:100%	D:0%
147	A:100%	B:0%	C:0%	D:0%
148	A:0%	B:100%	C:0%	D:0%
149	A:0%	B:0%	C:100%	D:0%
150	A:36%	B:64%	C:0%	D:0%
151	A:100%	B:0%	C:0%	D:0%
152	A:89%	B:11%	C:0%	D:0%
153	A:0%	B:0%	C:100%	D:0%
154	A:0%	B:100%	C:0%	D:0%
155	A:100%	B:0%	C:0%	D:0%
156	A:0%	B:100%	C:0%	D:0%
157	A:100%	B:0%	C:0%	D:0%
158	A:100%	B:0%	C:0%	D:0%
159	A:0%	B:100%	C:0%	D:0%
160	A:100%	B:0%	C:0%	D:0%

161	A:95%	B:0%	C:0%	D:5%
162	A:0%	B:100%	C:0%	D:0%
163	A:0%	B:0%	C:100%	D:0%
164	A:100%	B:0%	C:0%	D:0%
165	A:0%	B:0%	C:100%	D:0%
166	A:96%	B:4%	C:0%	D:0%
167	A:100%	B:0%	C:0%	D:0%
168	A:100%	B:0%	C:0%	D:0%
169	A:0%	B:100%	C:0%	D:0%
170	A:100%	B:0%	C:0%	D:0%
171	A:0%	B:100%	C:0%	D:0%
172	A:100%	B:0%	C:0%	D:0%
173	A:97%	B:0%	C:0%	D:3%
174	A:95%	B:0%	C:5%	D:0%
175	A:0%	B:0%	C:100%	D:0%
176	A:97%	B:0%	C:3%	D:0%
177	A:94%	B:2%	C:3%	D:1%
178	A:96%	B:0%	C:1%	D:3%
179	A:100%	B:0%	C:0%	D:0%
180	A:97%	B:3%	C:0%	D:0%

£200

1	A:0%	B:100%	C:0%	D:0%
2	A:0%	B:11%	C:2%	D:87%
3	A:0%	B:0%	C:100%	D:0%
4	A:100%	B:0%	C:0%	D:0%
5	A:0%	B:0%	C:100%	D:0%
6	A:0%	B:0%	C:100%	D:0%
7	A:0%	B:0%	C:0%	D:100%
8	A:0%	B:0%	C:100%	D:0%
9	A:0%	B:0%	C:100%	D:0%
10	A:100%	B:0%	C:0%	D:0%
11	A:96%	B:4%	C:0%	D:0%
12	A:100%	B:0%	C:0%	D:0%
13	A:0%	B:0%	C:100%	D:0%
14	A:0%	B:2%	C:97%	D:1%
15	A:0%	B:100%	C:0%	D:0%
16	A:0%	B:0%	C:100%	D:0%
17	A:0%	B:0%	C:0%	D:100%
18	A:0%	B:100%	C:0%	D:0%
19	A:0%	B:0%	C:100%	D:0%
20	A:100%	B:0%	C:0%	D:0%
21	A:0%	B:100%	C:0%	D:0%
22	A:0%	B:100%	C:0%	D:0%
23	A:100%	B:0%	C:0%	D:0%
24	A:0%	B:0%	C:0%	D:100%
25	A:0%	B:0%	C:100%	D:0%
26	A:0%	B:0%	C:100%	D:0%
27	A:0%	B:100%	C:0%	D:0%
28	A:0%	B:0%	C:0%	D:100%
29	A:100%	B:0%	C:0%	D:0%
30	A:0%	B:93%	C:7%	D:0%
31	A:0%	B:5%	C:95%	D:0%
32	A:0%	B:100%	C:0%	D:0%
33	A:100%	B:0%	C:0%	D:0%
34	A:0%	B:0%	C:100%	D:0%
35	A:0%	B:100%	C:0%	D:0%
36	A:6%	B:0%	C:94%	D:0%
37	A:100%	B:0%	C:0%	D:0%
38	A:0%	B:0%	C:0%	D:100%
39	A:100%	B:0%	C:0%	D:0%
40	A:0%	B:0%	C:100%	D:0%
41	A:0%	B:0%	C:0%	D:100%
42	A:0%	B:100%	C:0%	D:0%
43	A:0%	B:0%	C:100%	D:0%
44	A:0%	B:100%	C:0%	D:0%
45	A:0%	B:100%	C:0%	D:0%
46	A:0%	B:100%	C:0%	D:0%
47	A:100%	B:0%	C:0%	D:0%
48	A:0%	B:0%	C:0%	D:100%
49	A:0%	B:100%	C:0%	D:0%
50	A:0%	B:0%	C:100%	D:0%
51	A:0%	B:0%	C:0%	D:100%
52	A:100%	B:0%	C:0%	D:0%
53	A:0%	B:0%	C:4%	D:96%
54	A:0%	B:100%	C:0%	D:0%
55	A:0%	B:0%	C:0%	D:100%
56	A:0%	B:100%	C:0%	D.0%
57	A:0%	B:0%	C:10%	D:90%
58	A:0%	B:100%	C:0%	D:0%

ASK THE AUDIENCE

	A	B	C	D
59	A:0%	B:0%	C:3%	D:97%
60	A:0%	B:0%	C:100%	D:0%
61	A:0%	B:0%	C:100%	D:0%
62	A:100%	B:0%	C:0%	D:0%
63	A:0%	B:0%	C:100%	D:0%
64	A:0%	B:100%	C:0%	D:0%
65	A:0%	B:7%	C:93%	D:0%
66	A:0%	B:4%	C:0%	D:96%
67	A:100%	B:0%	C:0%	D:0%
68	A:0%	B:0%	C:0%	D:100%
69	A:0%	B:100%	C:0%	D:0%
70	A:0%	B:0%	C:100%	D:0%
71	A:0%	B:0%	C:5%	D:95%
72	A:0%	B:0%	C:100%	D:0%
73	A:0%	B:0%	C:0%	D:100%
74	A:85%	B:10%	C:0%	D:5%
75	A:0%	B:100%	C:0%	D:0%
76	A:0%	B:0%	C:100%	D:0%
77	A:0%	B:0%	C:0%	D:100%
78	A:0%	B:0%	C:93%	D:7%
79	A:0%	B:100%	C:0%	D:0%
80	A:92%	B:5%	C:0%	D:3%
81	A:0%	B:0%	C:0%	D:100%
82	A:0%	B:3%	C:97%	D:0%
83	A:0%	B:100%	C:0%	D:0%
84	A:0%	B:0%	C:100%	D:0%
85	A:92%	B:4%	C:4%	D:0%
86	A:0%	B:0%	C:0%	D:100%
87	A:0%	B:0%	C:100%	D:0%
88	A:0%	B:100%	C:0%	D:0%
89	A:0%	B:13%	C:87%	D:0%
90	A:0%	B:0%	C:0%	D:100%
91	A:100%	B:0%	C:0%	D:0%
92	A:95%	B:0%	C:0%	D:5%
93	A:0%	B:0%	C:0%	D:100%
94	A:0%	B:0%	C:100%	D:0%
95	A:100%	B:0%	C:0%	D:0%
96	A:8%	B:87%	C:0%	D:5%
97	A:0%	B:0%	C:100%	D:0%
98	A:0%	B:0%	C:0%	D:100%
99	A:0%	B:0%	C:100%	D:0%
100	A:98%	B:0%	C:0%	D:2%
101	A:20%	B:0%	C:0%	D:80%
102	A:0%	B:100%	C:0%	D:0%
103	A:100%	B:0%	C:0%	D:0%
104	A:0%	B:0%	C:0%	D:100%
105	A:0%	B:0%	C:100%	D:0%
106	A:9%	B:0%	C:0%	D:91%
107	A:0%	B:0%	C:100%	D:0%
108	A:100%	B:0%	C:0%	D:0%
109	A:0%	B:0%	C:100%	D:0%
110	A:0%	B:100%	C:0%	D:0%
111	A:9%	B:0%	C:91%	D:0%
112	A:0%	B:100%	C:0%	D:0%
113	A:100%	B:0%	C:0%	D:0%
114	A:0%	B:0%	C:0%	D:100%
115	A:0%	B:100%	C:0%	D:0%
116	A:100%	B:0%	C:0%	D:0%
117	A:0%	B:100%	C:0%	D:0%
118	A:100%	B:0%	C:0%	D:0%
119	A:0%	B:0%	C:0%	D:100%
120	A:0%	B:0%	C:100%	D:0%
121	A:0%	B:100%	C:0%	D:0%
122	A:0%	B:0%	C:100%	D:0%
123	A:100%	B:0%	C:0%	D:0%
124	A:0%	B:100%	C:0%	D:0%
125	A:100%	B:0%	C:0%	D:0%
126	A:0%	B:100%	C:0%	D:0%
127	A:0%	B:4%	C:96%	D:0%
128	A:0%	B:100%	C:0%	D:0%
129	A:100%	B:0%	C:0%	D:0%
130	A:0%	B:0%	C:0%	D:100%
131	A:100%	B:0%	C:0%	D:0%
132	A:0%	B:100%	C:0%	D:0%
133	A:100%	B:0%	C:0%	D:0%
134	A:0%	B:0%	C:100%	D:0%
135	A:0%	B:0%	C:0%	D:100%
136	A:100%	B:0%	C:0%	D:0%
137	A:0%	B:0%	C:100%	D:0%
138	A:0%	B:0%	C:0%	D:100%
139	A:0%	B:100%	C:0%	D:0%
140	A:0%	B:0%	C:0%	D:100%
141	A:0%	B:100%	C:0%	D:0%
142	A:0%	B:100%	C:0%	D:0%
143	A:0%	B:0%	C:100%	D:0%
144	A:0%	B:0%	C:0%	D:100%

145 A:0% B:0% C:100% D:0%
146 A:100% B:0% C:0% D:0%
147 A:92% B:0% C:8% D:0%
148 A:0% B:0% C:0% D:100%
149 A:100% B:0% C:0% D:0%
150 A:0% B:0% C:0% D:100%
151 A:100% B:0% C:0% D:0%
152 A:0% B:0% C:100% D:0%
153 A:0% B:3% C:97% D:0%
154 A:0% B:100% C:0% D:0%
155 A:0% B:0% C:100% D:0%
156 A:100% B:0% C:0% D:0%
157 A:36% B:64% C:0% D:0%
158 A:100% B:0% C:0% D:0%
159 A:0% B:100% C:0% D:0%
160 A:0% B:0% C:100% D:0%
161 A:0% B:100% C:0% D:0%
162 A:5% B:0% C:95% D:0%
163 A:0% B:100% C:0% D:0%
164 A:100% B:0% C:0% D:0%
165 A:0% B:100% C:0% D:0%
166 A:0% B:0% C:100% D:0%
167 A:0% B:0% C:0% D:100%
168 A:100% B:0% C:0% D:0%
169 A:0% B:0% C:0% D:100%
170 A:100% B:0% C:0% D:0%
171 A:0% B:0% C:100% D:0%
172 A:0% B:100% C:0% D:0%

£300

1 A:0% B:0% C:100% D:0%
2 A:0% B:0% C:0% D:100%
3 A:0% B:100% C:0% D:0%
4 A:0% B:0% C:0% D:100%
5 A:0% B:0% C:100% D:0%
6 A:0% B:0% C:0% D:100%
7 A:0% B:100% C:0% D:0%
8 A:0% B:100% C:0% D:0%
9 A:0% B:0% C:100% D:0%
10 A:8% B:0% C:92% D:0%
11 A:7% B:12% C:81% D:0%
12 A:0% B:0% C:100% D:0%
13 A:100% B:0% C:0% D:0%
14 A:0% B:0% C:0% D:100%
15 A:82% B:6% C:6% D:6%
16 A:0% B:100% C:0% D:0%
17 A:18% B:0% C:12% D:70%
18 A:0% B:17% C:83% D:0%
19 A:0% B:100% C:0% D:0%
20 A:0% B:100% C:0% D:0%
21 A:0% B:0% C:6% D:94%
22 A:100% B:0% C:0% D:0%
23 A:5% B:95% C:0% D:0%
24 A:0% B:0% C:0% D:100%
25 A:100% B:0% C:0% D:0%
26 A:0% B:100% C:0% D:0%
27 A:0% B:0% C:0% D:100%
28 A:0% B:0% C:91% D:9%
29 A:100% B:0% C:0% D:0%
30 A:100% B:0% C:0% D:0%
31 A:7% B:0% C:93% D:0%
32 A:0% B:100% C:0% D:0%
33 A:100% B:0% C:0% D:0%
34 A:0% B:0% C:0% D:100%
35 A:12% B:76% C:12% D:0%
36 A:0% B:0% C:0% D:100%
37 A:0% B:100% C:0% D:0%
38 A:7% B:0% C:5% D:88%
39 A:100% B:0% C:0% D:0%
40 A:100% B:0% C:0% D:0%
41 A:0% B:0% C:100% D:0%
42 A:42% B:0% C:18% D:40%
43 A:0% B:0% C:5% D:95%
44 A:0% B:100% C:0% D:0%
45 A:0% B:0% C:0% D:100%
46 A:0% B:0% C:100% D:0%
47 A:5% B:0% C:95% D:0%
48 A:0% B:13% C:0% D:87%
49 A:0% B:24% C:64% D:12%
50 A:0% B:0% C:0% D:100%

ASK THE AUDIENCE

51	A:0%	B:42%	C:53%	D:5%
52	A:0%	B:0%	C:0%	D:100%
53	A:0%	B:83%	C:4%	D:13%
54	A:0%	B:0%	C:100%	D:0%
55	A:11%	B:84%	C:5%	D:0%
56	A:0%	B:0%	C:0%	D.100%
57	A:0%	B:97%	C:3%	D:0%
58	A:17%	B:0%	C:83%	D:0%
59	A:100%	B:0%	C:0%	D:0%
60	A:25%	B:0%	C:63%	D:12%
61	A:0%	B:90%	C:10%	D:0%
62	A:0%	B:0%	C:100%	D:0%
63	A:0%	B:100%	C:0%	D:0%
64	A:0%	B:0%	C:19%	D:81%
65	A:0%	B:0%	C:100%	D:0%
66	A:0%	B:0%	C:5%	D:95%
67	A:15%	B:85%	C:0%	D:0%
68	A:19%	B:0%	C:76%	D:5%
69	A:0%	B:100%	C:0%	D:0%
70	A:0%	B:10%	C:90%	D:0%
71	A:0%	B:0%	C:100%	D:0%
72	A:0%	B:0%	C:0%	D:100%
73	A:0%	B:0%	C:100%	D:0%
74	A:5%	B:0%	C:19%	D:76%
75	A:0%	B:0%	C:100%	D:0%
76	A:100%	B:0%	C:0%	D:0%
77	A:0%	B:100%	C:0%	D:0%
78	A:7%	B:0%	C:7%	D:86%
79	A:0%	B:100%	C:0%	D:0%
80	A:0%	B:0%	C:0%	D:100%
81	A:0%	B:0%	C:100%	D:0%
82	A:0%	B:83%	C:0%	D:17%
83	A:13%	B:0%	C:87%	D:0%
84	A:100%	B:0%	C:0%	D:0%
85	A:69%	B:13%	C:6%	D:12%
86	A:40%	B:7%	C:48%	D:5%
87	A:0%	B:5%	C:95%	D:0%
88	A:9%	B:88%	C:0%	D:3%
89	A:0%	B:100%	C:0%	D:0%
90	A:19%	B:0%	C:5%	D:76%
91	A:95%	B:0%	C:0%	D:5%
92	A:0%	B:0%	C:100%	D:0%
93	A:10%	B:3%	C:0%	D:87%
94	A:5%	B:83%	C:0%	D:12%
95	A:7%	B:93%	C:0%	D:0%
96	A:100%	B:0%	C:0%	D:0%
97	A:5%	B:0%	C:0%	D:95%
98	A:89%	B:5%	C:0%	D:6%
99	A:18%	B:82%	C:0%	D:0%
100	A:95%	B:0%	C:0%	D:5%
101	A:0%	B:0%	C:0%	D:100%
102	A:0%	B:0%	C:100%	D:0%
103	A:94%	B:0%	C:0%	D:6%
104	A:0%	B:0%	C:0%	D:100%
105	A:0%	B:0%	C:100%	D:0%
106	A:0%	B:0%	C:0%	D:100%
107	A:0%	B:0%	C:100%	D:0%
108	A:0%	B:100%	C:0%	D:0%
109	A:0%	B:0%	C:0%	D:100%
110	A:100%	B:0%	C:0%	D:0%
111	A:0%	B:0%	C:100%	D:0%
112	A:0%	B:0%	C:0%	D:100%
113	A:100%	B:0%	C:0%	D:0%
114	A:100%	B:0%	C:0%	D:0%
115	A:0%	B:100%	C:0%	D:0%
116	A:0%	B:8%	C:92%	D:0%
117	A:0%	B:0%	C:0%	D:100%
118	A:9%	B:91%	C:0%	D:0%
119	A:0%	B:0%	C:0%	D:100%
120	A:100%	B:0%	C:0%	D:0%
121	A:0%	B:100%	C:0%	D:0%
122	A:12%	B:0%	C:88%	D:0%
123	A:5%	B:0%	C:6%	D:89%
124	A:100%	B:0%	C:0%	D:0%
125	A:0%	B:0%	C:100%	D:0%
126	A:100%	B:0%	C:0%	D:0%
127	A:0%	B:0%	C:100%	D:0%
128	A:100%	B:0%	C:0%	D:0%
129	A:7%	B:0%	C:0%	D:93%
130	A:0%	B:0%	C:100%	D:0%
131	A:58%	B:42%	C:0%	D:0%
132	A:0%	B:100%	C:0%	D:0%
133	A:0%	B:0%	C:100%	D:0%
134	A:100%	B:0%	C:0%	D:0%
135	A:8%	B:92%	C:0%	D:0%
136	A:17%	B:0%	C:5%	D:78%

	A	B	C	D
137	A:0%	B:100%	C:0%	D:0%
138	A:85%	B:0%	C:0%	D:15%
139	A:11%	B:76%	C:13%	D:0%
140	A:0%	B:0%	C:100%	D:0%
141	A:0%	B:0%	C:5%	D:95%
142	A:0%	B:94%	C:0%	D:6%
143	A:100%	B:0%	C:0%	D:0%
144	A:0%	B:95%	C:4%	D:1%
145	A:0%	B:0%	C:100%	D:0%
146	A:0%	B:100%	C:0%	D:0%
147	A:0%	B:100%	C:0%	D:0%
148	A:0%	B:93%	C:0%	D:7%
149	A:100%	B:0%	C:0%	D:0%
150	A:5%	B:5%	C:0%	D:90%
151	A:0%	B:0%	C:100%	D:0%
152	A:100%	B:0%	C:0%	D:0%
153	A:0%	B:0%	C:0%	D:100%
154	A:100%	B:0%	C:0%	D:0%
155	A:0%	B:100%	C:0%	D:0%
156	A:87%	B:0%	C:5%	D:8%
157	A:0%	B:100%	C:0%	D:0%
158	A:0%	B:0%	C:0%	D:100%
159	A:100%	B:0%	C:0%	D:0%
160	A:0%	B:0%	C:100%	D:0%
161	A:0%	B:100%	C:0%	D:0%
162	A:0%	B:0%	C:5%	D:95%
163	A:0%	B:100%	C:0%	D:0%
164	A:8%	B:0%	C:0%	D:92%

£500

	A	B	C	D
1	A:0%	B:0%	C:0%	D:100%
2	A:0%	B:0%	C:100%	D:0%
3	A:0%	B:100%	C:0%	D:0%
4	A:100%	B:0%	C:0%	D:0%
5	A:14%	B:86%	C:0%	D:0%
6	A:0%	B:0%	C:100%	D:0%
7	A:100%	B:0%	C:0%	D:0%
8	A:10%	B: 79%	C:11%	D:0%
9	A:0%	B:10%	C:90%	D:0%
10	A:100%	B:0%	C:0%	D:0%
11	A:0%	B:100%	C:0%	D:0%
12	A:0%	B:0%	C:0%	D:100%
13	A:0%	B:0%	C:100%	D:0%
14	A:0%	B:0%	C:0%	D:100%
15	A:0%	B:100%	C:0%	D:0%
16	A:0%	B:0%	C:0%	D:100%
17	A:0%	B:100%	C:0%	D:0%
18	A:0%	B:0%	C:100%	D:0%
19	A:100%	B:0%	C:0%	D:0%
20	A:0%	B:100%	C:0%	D:0%
21	A:100%	B:0%	C:0%	D:0%
22	A:0%	B:0%	C:100%	D:0%
23	A:100%	B:0%	C:0%	D:0%
24	A:0%	B:0%	C:0%	D:100%
25	A:0%	B:100%	C:0%	D:0%
26	A:0%	B:0%	C:100%	D:0%
27	A:0%	B:0%	C:0%	D:100%
28	A:0%	B:0%	C:100%	D:0%
29	A:0%	B:0%	C:100%	D:0%
30	A:0%	B:0%	C:100%	D:0%
31	A:0%	B:100%	C:0%	D:0%
32	A:0%	B:35%	C:65%	D:0%
33	A:0%	B:100%	C:0%	D:0%
34	A:12%	B:88%	C:0%	D:0%
35	A:100%	B:0%	C:0%	D:0%
36	A:23%	B:0%	C:0%	D:77%
37	A:0%	B:0%	C:0%	D:100%
38	A:0%	B:0%	C:0%	D:100%
39	A:10%	B:0%	C:11%	D:79%
40	A:0%	B:0%	C:100%	D:0%
41	A: 90%	B:0%	C:0%	D:10%
42	A:0%	B:0%	C:0%	D:100%
43	A:0%	B:100%	C:0%	D:0%
44	A:0%	B:0%	C:0%	D:100%
45	A:10%	B:90%	C:0%	D:0%
46	A:22%	B:0%	C:0%	D:78%
47	A:0%	B:0%	C:0%	D:100%
48	A:0%	B:0%	C:0%	D:100%
49	A:0%	B:0%	C:0%	D:100%
50	A:0%	B:0%	C:0%	D:100%

ASK THE AUDIENCE

51	A:22%	B:78%	C:0%	D:0%
52	A:0%	B:0%	C:100%	D:0%
53	A:34%	B:0%	C:0%	D:66%
54	A:0%	B:0%	C:0%	D:100%
55	A:0%	B:100%	C:0%	D:0%
56	A:0%	B:0%	C:0%	D:100%
57	A:0%	B:100%	C:0%	D:0%
58	A:0%	B:100%	C:0%	D:0%
59	A:0%	B:0%	C:0%	D:100%
60	A:45%	B:0%	C:55%	D:0%
61	A:0%	B:0%	C:23%	D:77%
62	A:89%	B:0%	C:11%	D:0%
63	A:0%	B:100%	C:0%	D:0%
64	A:0%	B:0%	C:100%	D:0%
65	A:0%	B:0%	C:0%	D:100%
66	A:100%	B:0%	C:0%	D:0%
67	A:0%	B:100%	C:0%	D:0%
68	A:100%	B:0%	C:0%	D:0%
69	A:0%	B:0%	C:100%	D:0%
70	A:0%	B:100%	C:0%	D:0%
71	A:100%	B:0%	C:0%	D:0%
72	A:0%	B:100%	C:0%	D:0%
73	A:0%	B:12%	C:56%	D:32%
74	A:100%	B:0%	C:0%	D:0%
75	A:0%	B:0%	C:0%	D:100%
76	A:0%	B:0%	C:67%	D:33%
77	A:0%	B:10%	C:90%	D:0%
78	A:100%	B:0%	C:0%	D:0%
79	A:0%	B:14%	C:86%	D:0%
80	A:0%	B:100%	C:0%	D:0%
81	A:0%	B:34%	C:0%	D:66%
82	A:0%	B:0%	C:100%	D:0%
83	A:100%	B:0%	C:0%	D:0%
84	A:0%	B:100%	C:0%	D:0%
85	A:79%	B:11%	C:10%	D:0%
86	A:0%	B:0%	C:0%	D:100%
87	A:0%	B:0%	C:100%	D:0%
88	A:100%	B:0%	C:0%	D:0%
89	A:0%	B:100%	C:0%	D:0%
90	A:0%	B:2%	C:86%	D:12%
91	A:0%	B:100%	C:0%	D:0%
92	A:0%	B:0%	C:100%	D:0%
93	A:0%	B:100%	C:0%	D:0%
94	A:0%	B:0%	C:100%	D:0%
95	A:0%	B:100%	C:0%	D:0%
96	A:0%	B:0%	C:0%	D:100%
97	A:100%	B:0%	C:0%	D:0%
98	A:17%	B:83%	C:0%	D:0%
99	A:0%	B:0%	C:0%	D:100%
100	A:0%	B:0%	C:100%	D:0%
101	A:10%	B:0%	C:0%	D:90%
102	A:77%	B:0%	C:23%	D:0%
103	A:0%	B:0%	C:100%	D:0%
104	A:0%	B:100%	C:0%	D:0%
105	A:90%	B:0%	C:0%	D:10%
106	A:9%	B:91%	C:0%	D:0%
107	A:0%	B:0%	C:100%	D:0%
108	A:0%	B:100%	C:0%	D:0%
109	A:0%	B:0%	C:0%	D:100%
110	A:0%	B:0%	C:100%	D:0%
111	A:100%	B:0%	C:0%	D:0%
112	A:0%	B:15%	C:0%	D:85%
113	A:0%	B:100%	C:0%	D:0%
114	A:0%	B:100%	C:0%	D:0%
115	A:0%	B:0%	C:0%	D:100%
116	A:0%	B:100%	C:0%	D:0%
117	A:0%	B:0%	C:0%	D:100%
118	A:100%	B:0%	C:0%	D:0%
119	A:0%	B:100%	C:0%	D:0%
120	A:0%	B:0%	C:0%	D:100%
121	A:100%	B:0%	C:0%	D:0%
122	A:0%	B:100%	C:0%	D:0%
123	A:0%	B:0%	C:100%	D:0%
124	A:0%	B:0%	C:0%	D:100%
125	A:11%	B:78%	C:0%	D:11%
126	A:0%	B:12%	C:0%	D:88%
127	A:0%	B:100%	C:0%	D:0%
128	A:0%	B:0%	C:0%	D:100%
129	A:0%	B:0%	C:91%	D:9%
130	A:0%	B:100%	C:0%	D:0%
131	A:0%	B:0%	C:100%	D:0%
132	A:0%	B:0%	C:0%	D:100%
133	A:0%	B:0%	C:100%	D:0%
134	A:0%	B:86%	C:11%	D:3%
135	A:0%	B:0%	C:100%	D:0%
136	A:0%	B:0%	C:0%	D:100%

137	A:0%	B:0%	C:100%	D:0%	147	A:0%	B:0%	C:54%	D:46%
138	A:0%	B:100%	C:0%	D:0%	148	A:0%	B:100%	C:0%	D:0%
139	A:0%	B:0%	C:100%	D:0%	149	A:91%	B:0%	C:9%	D:0%
140	A:0%	B:100%	C:0%	D:0%	150	A:11%	B:67%	C:14%	D:8%
141	A:0%	B:0%	C:100%	D:0%	151	A:0%	B:0%	C:0%	D:100%
142	A:32%	B:0%	C:68%	D:0%	152	A:0%	B:100%	C:0%	D:0%
143	A:0%	B:100%	C:0%	D:0%	153	A:100%	B:0%	C:0%	D:0%
144	A:86%	B:14%	C:0%	D:0%	154	A:0%	B:100%	C:0%	D:0%
145	A:0%	B:0%	C:100%	D:0%	155	A:0%	B:0%	C:0%	D:100%
146	A:0%	B:100%	C:0%	D:0%	156	A:0%	B:100%	C:0%	D:0%

£1,000

1	A:0%	B:99%	C:1%	D:0%	30	A:4%	B:0%	C:0%	D:96%
2	A:0%	B:0%	C:100%	D:0%	31	A:97%	B:3%	C:0%	D:0%
3	A:0%	B:100%	C:0%	D:0%	32	A:0%	B:0%	C:100%	D:0%
4	A:0%	B:5%	C:0%	D:95%	33	A:5%	B:95%	C:0%	D:0%
5	A:0%	B:0%	C:100%	D:0%	34	A:0%	B:0%	C:9%	D:91%
6	A:0%	B:9%	C:91%	D:0%	35	A:0%	B:0%	C:91%	D:9%
7	A:7%	B:0%	C:0%	D:93%	36	A:36%	B:64%	C:0%	D:0%
8	A:8%	B:92%	C:0%	D:0%	37	A:9%	B:0%	C:18%	D:73%
9	A:68%	B:14%	C:13%	D:5%	38	A:0%	B:98%	C:2%	D:0%
10	A:27%	B:4%	C:9%	D:60%	39	A:0%	B:5%	C:1%	D:94%
11	A:95%	B:5%	C:0%	D:0%	40	A:94%	B:2%	C:4%	D:0%
12	A:27%	B:6%	C:67%	D:0%	41	A:0%	B:5%	C:0%	D:95%
13	A:5%	B:13%	C:0%	D:82%	42	A:9%	B:67%	C:5%	D:19%
14	A:86%	B:9%	C:5%	D:0%	43	A:27%	B:0%	C:64%	D:9%
15	A:0%	B:0%	C:100%	D:0%	44	A:74%	B:9%	C:17%	D:0%
16	A:100%	B:0%	C:0%	D:0%	45	A:5%	B:0%	C:95%	D:0%
17	A:4%	B:0%	C:96%	D:0%	46	A:81%	B:0%	C:0%	D:19%
18	A:78%	B:18%	C:4%	D:0%	47	A:4%	B:23%	C:68%	D:5%
19	A:14%	B:77%	C:4%	D:5%	48	A:4%	B:96%	C:0%	D:0%
20	A:0%	B:3%	C:5%	D:92%	49	A:0%	B:41%	C:59%	D:0%
21	A:5%	B:58%	C:37%	D:0%	50	A:0%	B:63%	C:33 %	D:4%
22	A:4%	B:90%	C:5%	D:1%	51	A:5%	B:0%	C:95%	D:0%
23	A:0%	B:0%	C:0%	D:100%	52	A:14%	B:83%	C:3%	D:0%
24	A:0%	B:95%	C:5%	D:0%	53	A:86%	B:0%	C:5%	D:9%
25	A:0%	B:0%	C:100%	D:0%	54	A:0%	B:0%	C:100%	D:0%
26	A:9%	B:0%	C:0%	D:91%	55	A:0%	B:0%	C:4%	D:96%
27	A:100%	B:0%	C:0%	D:0%	56	A:0%	B:73%	C:0%	D:27%
28	A:3%	B:19%	C:23%	D:55%	57	A:0%	B:0%	C:95%	D:5%
29	A:5%	B:0%	C:95%	D:0%	58	A:8%	B:88%	C:4%	D:0%

ASK THE AUDIENCE

No.	A	B	C	D
59	A:0%	B:0%	C:100%	D:0%
60	A:0%	B:5%	C:0%	D:95%
61	A:59%	B:19%	C:9%	D:13%
62	A:0%	B:0%	C:100%	D:0%
63	A:0%	B:96%	C:4%	D:0%
64	A:82%	B:9%	C:0%	D:9%
65	A:5%	B:0%	C:95%	D:0%
66	A:0%	B:64%	C:17%	D:19%
67	A:36%	B:5%	C:50%	D:9%
68	A:96%	B:0%	C:4%	D:0%
69	A:9%	B:29%	C:13%	D:49%
70	A:50%	B:5%	C:45%	D:0%
71	A:66%	B:9%	C:25%	D:0%
72	A:5%	B:0%	C:91%	D:4%
73	A:95%	B:5%	C:0%	D:0%
74	A:14%	B:0%	C:86%	D:0%
75	A:91%	B:9%	C:0%	D:0%
76	A:0%	B:4%	C:0%	D:96%
77	A:100%	B:0%	C:0%	D:0%
78	A:5%	B:90%	C:0%	D:5%
79	A:19%	B:9%	C:0%	D:72%
80	A:36%	B:9%	C:4%	D:51%
81	A:0%	B:0%	C:100%	D:0%
82	A:0%	B:0%	C:100%	D:0%
83	A:0%	B:95%	C:0%	D:5%
84	A:0%	B:0%	C:100%	D:0%
85	A:90%	B:0%	C:0%	D:10%
86	A:0%	B:13%	C:87%	D:0%
87	A:81%	B:0%	C:5%	D:14%
88	A:0%	B:10%	C:13%	D:77%
89	A:98%	B:0%	C:2%	D:0%
90	A:100%	B:0%	C:0%	D:0%
91	A:95%	B:5%	C:0%	D:0%
92	A:0%	B:7%	C:0%	D:93%
93	A:96%	B:0%	C:4%	D:0%
94	A:0%	B:0%	C:0%	D:100%
95	A:83%	B:0%	C:4%	D:13%
96	A:86%	B:5%	C:9%	D:0%
97	A:0%	B:95%	C:0%	D:5%
98	A:0%	B:9%	C:0%	D:91%
99	A:9%	B:87%	C:4%	D:0%
100	A:100%	B:0%	C:0%	D:0%
101	A:5%	B:0%	C:95%	D:0%
102	A:9%	B:59%	C:0%	D:32%
103	A:3%	B:0%	C:97%	D:0%
104	A:0%	B:100%	C:0%	D:0%
105	A:0%	B:4%	C:5%	D:91%
106	A:90%	B:0%	C:0%	D:10%
107	A:4%	B:73%	C:10%	D:13%
108	A:77%	B:0%	C:5%	D:18%
109	A:13%	B:0%	C:0%	D:87%
110	A:68%	B:0%	C:23%	D:9%
111	A:0%	B:0%	C:100%	D:0%
112	A:0%	B:69%	C:13%	D:18%
113	A:0%	B:23%	C:77%	D:0%
114	A:9%	B:5%	C:0%	D:86%
115	A:95%	B:0%	C:5%	D:0%
116	A:10%	B:0%	C:0%	D:90%
117	A:5%	B:0%	C:86%	D:9%
118	A:0%	B:0%	C:0%	D:100%
119	A:18%	B:5%	C:77	D:0%
120	A:5%	B:90%	C:0%	D:5%
121	A:0%	B:9%	C:0%	D:91%
122	A:96%	B:4%	C:0%	D:0%
123	A:19%	B:10%	C:7%	D:64%
124	A:4%	B:96%	C:0%	D:0%
125	A:0%	B:10%	C:90%	D:0%
126	A:0%	B:100%	C:0%	D:0%
127	A:0%	B:0%	C:97%	D:3%
128	A:9%	B:0%	C:0%	D:91%
129	A:4%	B:96%	C:0%	D:0%
130	A:5%	B:0%	C:95%	D:0%
131	A:0%	B:91%	C:4%	D:5%
132	A:0%	B:5%	C:16%	D:79%
133	A:0%	B:0%	C:0%	D:100%
134	A:5%	B:4%	C:90%	D:1%
135	A:8%	B:51%	C:0%	D:41%
136	A:0%	B:0%	C:87%	D:13%
137	A:37%	B:11%	C:27%	D:25%
138	A:0%	B:91%	C:9%	D:0%
139	A:0%	B:95%	C:4%	D:1%
140	A:0%	B:5%	C:86%	D:9%
141	A:0%	B:90%	C:9%	D:1%
142	A:2%	B:0%	C:98%	D:0%
143	A:5%	B:1%	C:11%	D:83%
144	A:20%	B:13%	C:67%	D:0%

145	A:14%	B:54%	C:27%	D:5%
146	A:14%	B:0%	C:82%	D:4%
147	A:100%	B:0%	C:0%	D:0%
148	A:4%	B:5%	C:91%	D:0%

£2,000

1	A:0%	B:2%	C:0%	D:98%
2	A:4%	B:96%	C:0%	D:0%
3	A:66%	B:0%	C:23%	D:11%
4	A:0%	B:95%	C:4%	D:1%
5	A:0%	B:2%	C:0%	D:98%
6	A:1%	B:0%	C:98%	D:1%
7	A:12%	B:33%	C:0%	D:55%
8	A:2%	B:98%	C:0%	D:0%
9	A:99%	B:0%	C:1%	D:0%
10	A:13%	B:0%	C:63%	D:24%
11	A:87%	B:12%	C:0%	D:1%
12	A:1%	B:2%	C:97%	D:0%
13	A:0%	B:1%	C:3%	D:96%
14	A:11%	B:22%	C:67%	D:0%
15	A:12%	B:0%	C:0%	D:88%
16	A:0%	B:98%	C:2%	D:0%
17	A:43%	B:0%	C:34%	D:23%
18	A:0%	B:0%	C:10%	D:90%
19	A:11%	B:67%	C:11%	D:11%
20	A:0%	B:4%	C:96%	D:0%
21	A:0%	B:91%	C:0%	D:9%
22	A:0%	B:14%	C:85%	D:1%
23	A:84%	B:2%	C:14%	D:0%
24	A:0%	B:97%	C:0%	D:3%
25	A:11%	B:10%	C:79%	D:0%
26	A:9%	B:0%	C:2%	D:89%
27	A:12%	B:87%	C:0%	D:1%
28	A:0%	B:2%	C:98%	D:0%
29	A:0%	B:90%	C:9%	D:1%
30	A:0%	B:0%	C:11%	D:89%
31	A:68%	B:10%	C:22%	D:0%
32	A:0%	B:3%	C:0%	D:97%
33	A:0%	B:89%	C:0%	D:11%
34	A:0%	B:3%	C:96%	D:1%
35	A:10%	B:88%	C:0%	D:2%
36	A:95%	B:0%	C:2%	D:3%
37	A:1%	B:4%	C:0%	D:95%
38	A:25%	B:12%	C:63%	D:0%
39	A:2%	B:0%	C:1%	D:97%
40	A:86%	B:4%	C:10%	D:0%
41	A:34%	B:53%	C:13%	D:0%
42	A:0%	B:1%	C:98%	D:1%
43	A:0%	B:0%	C:13%	D:87%
44	A:57%	B:12%	C:9%	D:22%
45	A:10%	B:0%	C:12%	D:76%
46	A:9%	B:22%	C:58%	D:11%
47	A:0%	B:33%	C:23%	D:44%
48	A:22%	B:0%	C:35%	D:43%
49	A:97%	B:0%	C:0%	D:3%
50	A:10%	B:68%	C:0%	D:22%
51	A:0%	B:0%	C:99%	D:1%
52	A:2%	B:95%	C:3%	D:0%
53	A:0%	B:2%	C:0%	D:98%
54	A:5%	B:1%	C:94%	D:0%
55	A:92%	B:0%	C:0%	D:8%
56	A:50%	B:29%	C:8%	D:13%
57	A:0%	B:98%	C:2%	D:0%
58	A:97%	B:0%	C:2%	D:1%
59	A:8%	B:67%	C:17%	D:8%
60	A:83%	B:0%	C:1%	D:16%
61	A:1%	B:0%	C:99%	D:0%
62	A:0%	B:2%	C:1%	D:97%
63	A:13%	B:0%	C:87%	D:0%
64	A:99%	B:0%	C:0%	D:1%
65	A:14%	B:7%	C:70%	D:9%
66	A:0%	B:91%	C:4%	D:5%
67	A:91%	B:9%	C:0%	D:0%
68	A:4%	B:87%	C:4%	D:5%
69	A:0%	B:0%	C:9%	D:91%
70	A:0%	B:8%	C:92%	D:0%
71	A:95%	B:0%	C:0%	D:5%
72	A:4%	B:1%	C:0%	D:95%
73	A:97%	B:0%	C:3%	D:0%
74	A:22%	B:78%	C:0%	D:0%

75	A:94%	B:0%	C:3%	D:3%
76	A:0%	B:97%	C:1%	D:2%
77	A:26%	B:9%	C:65%	D:0%
78	A:4%	B:9%	C:25%	D:62%
79	A:2%	B:13%	C:85%	D:0%
80	A:6%	B:2%	C:92%	D:0%
81	A:96%	B:0%	C:2%	D:2%
82	A:0%	B:8%	C:92%	D:0%
83	A:88%	B:12%	C:0%	D:0%
84	A:9%	B:5%	C:0%	D:86%
85	A:8%	B:92%	C:0%	D:0%
86	A:82%	B:4%	C:9%	D:5%
87	A:0%	B:0%	C:92%	D:8%
88	A:0%	B:96%	C:4%	D:0%
89	A:7%	B:0%	C:93%	D:0%
90	A:91%	B:4%	C:5%	D:0%
91	A:17%	B:0%	C:42%	D:41%
92	A:5%	B:91%	C:4%	D:0%
93	A:16%	B:0%	C:84%	D:0%
94	A:4%	B:0%	C:4%	D:92%
95	A:5%	B:0%	C:94%	D:1%
96	A:4%	B:5%	C:0%	D:91%
97	A:74%	B:4%	C:13%	D:9%
98	A:17%	B:62%	C:0%	D:21%
99	A:4%	B:12%	C:9%	D:75%
100	A:90%	B:6%	C:0%	D:4%
101	A:4%	B:42%	C:25%	D:29%
102	A:97%	B:0%	C:0%	D:3%
103	A:0%	B:0%	C:92%	D:8%
104	A:0%	B:6%	C:4%	D:90%
105	A:78%	B:4%	C:5%	D:13%
106	A:0%	B:0%	C:4%	D:96%
107	A:58%	B:29%	C:13%	D:0%
108	A:4%	B:84%	C:12%	D:0%
109	A:4%	B:13%	C:83%	D:0%
110	A:82%	B:5%	C:9%	D:4%
111	A:4%	B:1%	C:0%	D:95%
112	A:8%	B:84%	C:0%	D:8%
113	A:73%	B:8%	C:19%	D:0%
114	A:0%	B:4%	C:5%	D:91%
115	A:96%	B:4%	C:0%	D:0%
116	A:0%	B:5%	C:0%	D:95%
117	A:97%	B:0%	C:0%	D:3%
118	A:0%	B:4%	C:91%	D:5%
119	A:4%	B:95%	C:0%	D:1%
120	A:17%	B:0%	C:42%	D:41%
121	A:61%	B:18%	C:12%	D:9%
122	A:0%	B:4%	C:96%	D:0%
123	A:22%	B:0%	C:9%	D:69%
124	A:92%	B:4%	C:3%	D:1%
125	A:2%	B:94%	C:3%	D:1%
126	A:21%	B:30%	C:37%	D:12%
127	A:0%	B:95%	C:5%	D:0%
128	A:100%	B:0%	C:0%	D:0%
129	A:79%	B:8%	C:4%	D:9%
130	A:12%	B:58%	C:13%	D:17%
131	A:80%	B:12%	C:0%	D:8%
132	A:9%	B:0%	C:83%	D:8%
133	A:0%	B:92%	C:8%	D:0%
134	A:92%	B:4%	C:4%	D:0%
135	A:0%	B:25%	C:41%	D:34%
136	A:9%	B:0%	C:6%	D:85%
137	A:0%	B:87%	C:8%	D:5%
138	A:96%	B:0%	C:0%	D:4%
139	A:1%	B:96%	C:2%	D:1%
140	A:4%	B:83%	C:13%	D:0%

£4,000

1	A:0%	B:5%	C:4%	D:91%
2	A:94%	B:0%	C:6%	D:0%
3	A:1%	B:1%	C:92%	D:6%
4	A:7%	B:93%	C:0%	D:0%
5	A:91%	B:6%	C:3%	D:0%
6	A:12%	B:0%	C:88%	D:0%
7	A:0%	B:5%	C:1%	D:94%
8	A:3%	B:95%	C:2%	D:0%
9	A:70%	B:0%	C:25%	D:5%
10	A:38%	B:12%	C:43%	D:7%
11	A:31%	B:63%	C:0%	D:6%
12	A:7%	B:0%	C:1%	D:92%

ASK THE AUDIENCE

	A	B	C	D
13	A:90%	B:0%	C:9%	D:1%
14	A:0%	B:95%	C:4%	D:1%
15	A:0%	B:40%	C:60%	D:0%
16	A:75%	B:12%	C:6%	D:7%
17	A:19%	B:42%	C:0%	D:39%
18	A:6%	B:0%	C:88%	D:6%
19	A:93%	B:0%	C:7%	D:0%
20	A:0%	B:5%	C:95%	D:0%
21	A:6%	B:92%	C:2%	D:0%
22	A:93%	B:7%	C:0%	D:0%
23	A:0%	B:7%	C:67%	D:26%
24	A:93%	B:6%	C:1%	D:0%
25	A:0%	B:63%	C:31%	D:6%
26	A:19%	B:0%	C:30%	D:51%
27	A:7%	B:18%	C:75%	D:0%
28	A:6%	B:13%	C:81%	D:0%
29	A:7%	B:80%	C:6%	D:7%
30	A:6%	B:1%	C:87%	D:6%
31	A:0%	B:2%	C:98%	D:0%
32	A:7%	B:5%	C:12%	D:76%
33	A:6%	B:87%	C:1%	D:6%
34	A:0%	B:1%	C:61%	D:38%
35	A:0%	B:56%	C:25%	D:19%
36	A:0%	B:2%	C:96%	D:2%
37	A:6%	B:5%	C:20%	D:69%
38	A:0%	B:63%	C:19%	D:18%
39	A:21%	B:16%	C:63%	D:0%
40	A:6%	B:81%	C:8%	D:5%
41	A:0%	B:7%	C:68%	D:25%
42	A:0%	B:94%	C:3%	D:3%
43	A:25%	B:25%	C:31%	D:19%
44	A:0%	B:98%	C:1%	D:1%
45	A:26%	B:0%	C:0%	D:74%
46	A:0%	B:38%	C:37%	D:25%
47	A:4%	B:0%	C:14%	D:82%
48	A:1%	B:2%	C:97%	D:0%
49	A:7%	B:93%	C:0%	D:0%
50	A:12%	B:0%	C:75%	D:13%
51	A:25%	B:31%	C:12%	D:32%
52	A:56%	B:0%	C:6%	D:38%
53	A:0%	B:2%	C:98%	D:0%
54	A:44%	B:37%	C:19%	D:0%
55	A:6%	B:50%	C:19%	D:25%
56	A:0%	B:0%	C:7%	D:93%
57	A:56%	B:25%	C:19%	D:0%
58	A:18%	B:82%	C:0%	D:0%
59	A:19%	B:16%	C:63%	D:2%
60	A:9%	B:0%	C:16%	D:75%
61	A:0%	B:44%	C:56%	D:0%
62	A:13%	B:15%	C:41%	D:31%
63	A:7%	B:75%	C:0%	D:18%
64	A:6%	B:0%	C:6%	D:88%
65	A:0%	B:2%	C:94%	D:4%
66	A:13%	B:0%	C:87%	D:0%
67	A:12%	B:0%	C:38%	D:50%
68	A:0%	B:94%	C:4%	D:2%
69	A:0%	B:6%	C:69%	D:25%
70	A:92%	B:0%	C:6%	D:2%
71	A:7%	B:0%	C:6%	D:87%
72	A:6%	B:2%	C:88%	D:4%
73	A:27%	B:69%	C:0%	D:4%
74	A:85%	B:0%	C:8%	D:7%
75	A:3%	B:5%	C:92%	D:0%
76	A:62%	B:12%	C:7%	D:19%
77	A:6%	B:38%	C:0%	D:56%
78	A:7%	B:12%	C:6%	D:75%
79	A:0%	B:97%	C:2%	D:1%
80	A:0%	B:6%	C:0%	D:94%
81	A:3%	B:96%	C:1%	D:0%
82	A:50%	B:12%	C:7	D:31%
83	A:0%	B:2%	C:1%	D:97%
84	A:49%	B:19%	C:25%	D:7%
85	A:4%	B:1%	C:0%	D:95%
86	A:18%	B:69%	C:5%	D:8%
87	A:0%	B:13%	C:0%	D:87%
88	A:0%	B:3%	C:1%	D:96%
89	A:93%	B:0%	C:7%	D:0%
90	A:7%	B:32%	C:5%	D:56%
91	A:6%	B:7%	C:6%	D:81%
92	A:0%	B:0%	C:94%	D:6%
93	A:7%	B:5%	C:7%	D:81%
94	A:0%	B:0%	C:99%	D:1%
95	A:0%	B:86%	C:8%	D:6%
96	A:12%	B:0%	C:75%	D:13%
97	A:0%	B:94%	C:0%	D:6%
98	A:30%	B:38%	C:25%	D:7%

	A	B	C	D
99	A:8%	B:13%	C:24%	D:55%
100	A:4%	B:87%	C:9%	D:0%
101	A:0%	B:7%	C:0%	D:93%
102	A:13%	B:0%	C:80%	D:7%
103	A:3%	B:97%	C:0%	D:0%
104	A:25%	B:24%	C:51%	D:0%
105	A:19%	B:50%	C:18%	D:13%
106	A:67%	B:26%	C:7%	D:0%
107	A:0%	B:55%	C:45%	D:0%
108	A:0%	B:12%	C:0%	D:88%
109	A:13%	B:87%	C:0%	D:0%
110	A:44%	B:12%	C:43%	D:1%
111	A:0%	B:0%	C:88%	D:12%
112	A:0%	B:0%	C:6%	D:94%
113	A:7%	B:93%	C:0%	D:0%
114	A:63%	B:0%	C:0%	D:37%
115	A:13%	B:0%	C:75%	D:12%
116	A:19%	B:74%	C:7%	D:0%
117	A:0%	B:24%	C:76%	D:0%
118	A:69%	B:8%	C:0%	D:23%
119	A:19%	B:18%	C:14%	D:49%
120	A:0%	B:7%	C:81%	D:12%
121	A:11%	B:63%	C:12%	D:14%
122	A:7%	B:21%	C:61%	D:11%
123	A:25%	B:69%	C:0%	D:6%
124	A:0%	B:7%	C:49%	D:44%
125	A:6%	B:5%	C:2%	D:87%
126	A:20%	B:67%	C:0%	D:13%
127	A:81%	B:0%	C:19%	D:0%
128	A:26%	B:37%	C:12%	D:25%
129	A:0%	B:76%	C:0%	D:24%
130	A:0%	B:32%	C:68%	D:0%
131	A:95%	B:2%	C:3%	D:0%
132	A:0%	B:12%	C:81%	D:7%

£8,000

	A	B	C	D
1	A:50%	B:44%	C:6%	D:0%
2	A:5%	B:75%	C:20%	D:0%
3	A:18%	B:0%	C:68%	D:14%
4	A:79%	B:0%	C:21%	D:0%
5	A:12%	B:24%	C:38%	D:26%
6	A:50%	B:13%	C:0%	D:37%
7	A:7%	B:13%	C:69%	D:11%
8	A:19%	B:63%	C:6%	D:12%
9	A:0%	B:2%	C:1%	D:97%
10	A:19%	B:0%	C:81%	D:0%
11	A:0%	B:0%	C:7%	D:93%
12	A:0%	B:50%	C:13%	D:37%
13	A:2%	B:1%	C:97%	D:0%
14	A:12%	B:82%	C:6%	D:0%
15	A:50%	B:6%	C:25%	D:19%
16	A:93%	B:0%	C:0%	D:7%
17	A:0%	B:3%	C:95%	D:2%
18	A:7%	B:93%	C:0%	D:0%
19	A:44%	B:12%	C:43%	D:1%
20	A:79%	B:21%	C:0%	D:0%
21	A:0%	B:93%	C:7%	D:0%
22	A:0%	B:6%	C:94%	D:0%
23	A:43%	B:7%	C:49%	D:1%
24	A:7%	B:5%	C:75%	D:13%
25	A:18%	B:73%	C:9%	D:0%
26	A:43%	B:8%	C:31%	D:18%
27	A:0%	B:0%	C:97%	D:3%
28	A:81%	B:0%	C:12%	D:7%
29	A:0%	B:48%	C:14%	D:38%
30	A:0%	B:1%	C:99%	D:0%
31	A:0%	B:4%	C:0%	D:96%
32	A:1%	B:97%	C:1%	D:1%
33	A:45%	B:0%	C:22%	D:33%
34	A:1%	B:0%	C:0%	D:99%
35	A:93%	B:0%	C:0%	D:7%
36	A:5%	B:7%	C:1%	D:87%
37	A:7%	B:0%	C:0%	D:93%
38	A:94%	B:0%	C:0%	D:6%
39	A:1%	B:7%	C:0%	D:92%
40	A:39%	B:26%	C:6%	D:29%
41	A:19%	B:0%	C:17%	D:64%
42	A:75%	B:18%	C:7%	D:0%
43	A:0%	B:93%	C:7%	D:0%
44	A:13%	B:0%	C:0%	D:87%

ASK THE AUDIENCE

45	A:0%	B:91%	C:8%	D:1%
46	A:84%	B:15%	C:0%	D:1%
47	A:0%	B:37%	C:19%	D:44%
48	A:0%	B:25%	C:62%	D:13%
49	A:75%	B:19%	C:0%	D:6%
50	A:6%	B:5%	C:8%	D:81%
51	A:75%	B:6%	C:4%	D:15%
52	A:0%	B:88%	C:0%	D:12%
53	A:81%	B:6%	C:7%	D:6%
54	A:0%	B:2%	C:1%	D:97%
55	A:7%	B:44%	C:6%	D:43%
56	A:94%	B:0%	C:6%	D:0%
57	A:93%	B:0%	C:0%	D:7%
58	A:0%	B:92%	C:1%	D:7%
59	A:0%	B:0%	C:7%	D:93%
60	A:73%	B:7%	C:14%	D:6%
61	A:36%	B:45%	C:6%	D:13%
62	A:12%	B:10%	C:38%	D:40%
63	A:0%	B:0%	C:3%	D:97%
64	A:11%	B:76%	C:13%	D:0%
65	A:31%	B:20%	C:0%	D:49%
66	A:6%	B:0%	C:0%	D:94%
67	A:96%	B:0%	C:2%	D:2%
68	A:0%	B:8%	C:13%	D:79%
69	A:6%	B:57%	C:12%	D:25%
70	A:87%	B:0%	C:7%	D:6%
71	A:19%	B:68%	C:13%	D:0%
72	A:82%	B:5%	C:1%	D:12%
73	A:44%	B:18%	C:13%	D:25%
74	A:30%	B:43%	C:1%	D:26%
75	A:98%	B:0%	C:0%	D:2%
76	A:7%	B:16%	C:27%	D:50%
77	A:8%	B:0%	C:69%	D:23%
78	A:17%	B:38%	C:7%	D:38%
79	A:0%	B:56%	C:12%	D:32%
80	A:93%	B:0%	C:0%	D:7%
81	A:5%	B:94%	C:1%	D:0%
82	A:12%	B:6%	C:63%	D:19%
83	A:81%	B:0%	C:19%	D:0%
84	A:7%	B:0%	C:93%	D:0%
85	A:25%	B:69%	C:0%	D:6%
86	A:7%	B:0%	C:31%	D:62%
87	A:6%	B:19%	C:48%	D:27%
88	A:12%	B:43%	C:38%	D:7%
89	A:28%	B:9%	C:25%	D:38%
90	A:5%	B:1%	C:75%	D:19%
91	A:0%	B:74%	C:12%	D:14%
92	A:87%	B:7%	C:6%	D:0%
93	A:25%	B:23%	C:24%	D:28%
94	A:0%	B:2%	C:98%	D:0%
95	A:18%	B:50%	C:14%	D:18%
96	A:12%	B:0%	C:7%	D:81%
97	A:6%	B:62%	C:7%	D:25%
98	A:7%	B:44%	C:41%	D:8%
99	A:25%	B:6%	C:64%	D:5%
100	A:60%	B:0%	C:40%	D:0%
101	A:31%	B:57%	C:12%	D:0%
102	A:0%	B:2%	C:98%	D:0%
103	A:50%	B:13%	C:25%	D:12%
104	A:22%	B:13%	C:15%	D:50%
105	A:6%	B:7%	C:68%	D:19%
106	A:35%	B:0%	C:5%	D:60%
107	A:5%	B:12%	C:75%	D:8%
108	A:93%	B:0%	C:7%	D:0%
109	A:0%	B:0%	C:18%	D:82%
110	A:62%	B:38%	C:0%	D:0%
111	A:18%	B:1%	C:81%	D:0%
112	A:31%	B:44%	C:25%	D:0%
113	A:23%	B:47%	C:6%	D:24%
114	A:0%	B:92%	C:8%	D:0%
115	A:50%	B:0%	C:50%	D:0%
116	A:30%	B:26%	C:13%	D:31%
117	A:30%	B:38%	C:20%	D:12%
118	A:13%	B:50%	C:25%	D:12%
119	A:0%	B:77%	C:17%	D:6%
120	A:6%	B:20%	C:5%	D:69%
121	A:25%	B:24%	C:42%	D:9%
122	A:51%	B:0%	C:0%	D:49%
123	A:18%	B:75%	C:7%	D:0%
124	A:5%	B:0%	C:7%	D:88%

ASK THE AUDIENCE

£16,000

	A	B	C	D
1	A:15%	B:31%	C:46%	D:8%
2	A: 14%	B:4%	C:35%	D:47%
3	A:28%	B:48%	C:24%	D:0%
4	A:92%	B:8%	C:0%	D:0%
5	A:4%	B:87%	C:0%	D:9%
6	A:8%	B:0%	C:17%	D:75%
7	A:67%	B:0%	C:33%	D:0%
8	A:1%	B:66%	C:8%	D:25%
9	A:33%	B:12%	C:16%	D:39%
10	A:8%	B:21%	C:58%	D:13%
11	A:17%	B:67%	C:5%	D:11%
12	A:68%	B:0%	C:15%	D:17%
13	A:46%	B:44%	C:8%	D:2%
14	A:96%	B:4%	C:0%	D:0%
15	A:54%	B:45%	C:1%	D:0%
16	A:25%	B:4%	C:0%	D:71%
17	A:58%	B:10%	C:10%	D:22%
18	A:16%	B:51%	C:25%	D:8%
19	A:0%	B:21%	C:62%	D:17%
20	A:21%	B:6%	C:10%	D:63%
21	A:4%	B:95%	C:1%	D:0%
22	A:16%	B:5%	C:15%	D:64%
23	A:67%	B:0%	C:0%	D:33%
24	A:4%	B:17%	C:79%	D:0%
25	A:80%	B:12%	C:5%	D:3%
26	A:21%	B:8%	C:16%	D:55%
27	A:0%	B:71%	C:25%	D:4%
28	A:79%	B:4%	C:0%	D:17%
29	A:4%	B:9%	C:74%	D:13%
30	A:3%	B:12%	C:34%	D:51%
31	A:5%	B:50%	C:8%	D:37%
32	A:21%	B:12%	C:17%	D:50%
33	A:26%	B:46%	C:4%	D:24%
34	A:5%	B:24%	C:71%	D:0%
35	A:4%	B:96%	C:0%	D:0%
36	A:95%	B:0%	C:0%	D:5%
37	A:12%	B:29%	C:28%	D:31%
38	A:8%	B:4%	C:13%	D:75%
39	A:5%	B:0%	C:8%	D:87%
40	A:0%	B:11%	C:84%	D:5%
41	A:0%	B:71%	C:12%	D:17%
42	A:8%	B:1%	C:8%	D:83%
43	A:91%	B:4%	C:5%	D:0%
44	A:38%	B:4%	C:0%	D:58%
45	A:5%	B:52%	C:23%	D:20%
46	A:29%	B:9%	C:21%	D:41%
47	A:4%	B:12%	C:63%	D:21%
48	A:4%	B:65%	C:25%	D:6%
49	A:42%	B:33%	C:8%	D:17%
50	A:0%	B:47%	C:29%	D:24%
51	A:50%	B:12%	C:25%	D:13%
52	A:12%	B:0%	C:88%	D:0%
53	A:83%	B:4%	C:0%	D:13%
54	A:24%	B:46%	C:26%	D:4%
55	A:16%	B:25%	C:8%	D:51%
56	A:28%	B:24%	C:43%	D:5%
57	A:4%	B:16%	C:68%	D:12%
58	A:0%	B:13%	C:4%	D:83%
59	A:63%	B:21%	C:9%	D:7%
60	A:4%	B:9%	C:0%	D:87%
61	A:65%	B:22%	C:5%	D:8%
62	A:17%	B:30%	C:28%	D:25%
63	A:0%	B:84%	C:12%	D:4%
64	A:62%	B:29%	C:0%	D:9%
65	A:79%	B:13%	C:8%	D:0%
66	A:21%	B:8%	C:50%	D:21%
67	A:9%	B:79%	C:12%	D:0%
68	A:63%	B:13%	C:16%	D:8%
69	A:15%	B:33%	C:46%	D:6%
70	A:13%	B:78%	C:0%	D:9%
71	A:17%	B:8%	C:4%	D:71%
72	A:66%	B:7%	C:22%	D:5%
73	A:4%	B:5%	C:87%	D:4%
74	A:58%	B:10%	C:24%	D:8%
75	A:5%	B:4%	C:79%	D:12%
76	A:4%	B:63%	C:16%	D:17%
77	A:16%	B:67%	C:12%	D:5%
78	A:54%	B:8%	C:21%	D:17%
79	A:33%	B:12%	C:12%	D:43%
80	A:75%	B:5%	C:4%	D:16%
81	A:13%	B:29%	C:54%	D:4%
82	A:38%	B:33%	C:21%	D:8%
83	A:97%	B:2%	C:0%	D:1%
84	A:21%	B:30%	C:33%	D:16%

85	A:34%	B:1%	C:65%	D:0%
86	A:66%	B:0%	C:26%	D:8%
87	A:17%	B:55%	C:23%	D:5%
88	A:39%	B:21%	C:16%	D:24%
89	A:63%	B:9%	C:13%	D:15%
90	A:12%	B:7%	C:16%	D:65%
91	A:8%	B:84%	C:3%	D:5%
92	A:0%	B:22%	C:17%	D:61%
93	A:8%	B:29%	C:58%	D:5%
94	A:54%	B:29%	C:5%	D:12%
95	A:16%	B:54%	C:9%	D:21%
96	A:50%	B:29%	C:8%	D:13%
97	A:46%	B:21%	C:9%	D:24%
98	A:67%	B:12%	C:4%	D:17%
99	A:35%	B:4%	C:37%	D:22%
100	A:50%	B:36%	C:9%	D:5%
101	A:37%	B:33%	C:21%	D:9%
102	A:12%	B:71%	C:5%	D:12%
103	A:5%	B:45%	C:46%	D:4%
104	A:0%	B:84%	C:4%	D:12%
105	A:12%	B:46%	C:38%	D:4%
106	A:3%	B:67%	C:17%	D:13%
107	A:8%	B:21%	C:8%	D:63%
108	A:5%	B:12%	C:83%	D:0%
109	A:4%	B:91%	C:5%	D:0%
110	A:17%	B:9%	C:36%	D:38%
111	A:35%	B:24%	C:16%	D:25%
112	A:29%	B:9%	C:16%	D:46%
113	A:63%	B:12%	C:21%	D:4%
114	A:21%	B:9%	C:70%	D:0%
115	A:8%	B:0%	C:5%	D:87%
116	A:63%	B:16%	C:17%	D:4%

£32,000

1	A:54%	B:18%	C:16%	D:12%
2	A:46%	B:16%	C:9%	D:29%
3	A:74%	B:17%	C:4%	D:5%
4	A:4%	B:37%	C:29%	D:30%
5	A:12%	B:4%	C:84%	D:0%
6	A:37%	B:18%	C:21%	D:24%
7	A:10%	B:13%	C:71%	D:6%
8	A:46%	B:17%	C:28%	D:9%
9	A:29%	B:66%	C:0%	D:5%
10	A:20%	B:12%	C:43%	D:25%
11	A:37%	B:20%	C:13%	D:30%
12	A:58%	B:24%	C:4%	D:14%
13	A:0%	B:38%	C:37%	D:25%
14	A:58%	B:23%	C:19%	D:0%
15	A:9%	B:21%	C:0%	D:70%
16	A:0%	B:8%	C:88%	D:4%
17	A:16%	B:9%	C:17%	D:58%
18	A:38%	B:25%	C:4%	D:33%
19	A:40%	B:42%	C:3%	D:15%
20	A:24%	B:10%	C:31%	D:35%
21	A:71%	B:4%	C:25%	D:0%
22	A:21%	B:29%	C:37%	D:13%
23	A:16%	B:24%	C:51%	D:9%
24	A:28%	B:55%	C:5%	D:12%
25	A:26%	B:57%	C:17%	D:0%
26	A:60%	B:7%	C:29%	D:4%
27	A:11%	B:58%	C:8%	D:23%
28	A:15%	B:34%	C:7%	D:44%
29	A:3%	B:13%	C:25%	D:59%
30	A:12%	B:37%	C:42%	D:9%
31	A:9%	B:24%	C:21%	D:46%
32	A:51%	B:22%	C:23%	D:4%
33	A:46%	B:12%	C:13%	D:29%
34	A:3%	B:25%	C:35%	D:37%
35	A:62%	B:21%	C:17%	D:0%
36	A:11%	B:64%	C:12%	D:13%
37	A:0%	B:17%	C:83%	D:0%
38	A:9%	B:21%	C:21%	D:49%
39	A:33%	B:49%	C:1%	D:17%
40	A:81%	B:5%	C:3%	D:11%
41	A:9%	B:4%	C:12%	D:75%
42	A:11%	B:15%	C:53%	D:21%
43	A:0%	B:25%	C:54%	D:21%
44	A:21%	B:63%	C:4%	D:12%
45	A:23%	B:15%	C:52%	D:10%
46	A:20%	B:73%	C:7%	D:0%

ASK THE AUDIENCE

47	A:22%	B:24%	C:29%	D:25%
48	A:42%	B:13%	C:16%	D:29%
49	A:4%	B:0%	C:28%	D:68%
50	A:21%	B:16%	C:63%	D:0%
51	A:12%	B:31%	C:11%	D:46%
52	A:29%	B:33%	C:25%	D:13%
53	A:30%	B:37%	C:17%	D:16%
54	A:9%	B:36%	C:47%	D:8%
55	A:36%	B:16%	C:25%	D:23%
56	A:21%	B:12%	C:25%	D:42%
57	A:27%	B:7%	C:62%	D:4%
58	A:42%	B:15%	C:31%	D:12%
59	A:8%	B:59%	C:23%	D:10%
60	A:16%	B:47%	C:29%	D:8%
61	A:6%	B:13%	C:60%	D:21%
62	A:5%	B:42%	C:29%	D:24%
63	A:21%	B:0%	C:12%	D:67%
64	A:19%	B:9%	C:72%	D:0%
65	A:20%	B:25%	C:12%	D:43%
66	A:80%	B:5%	C:4%	D:11%
67	A:28%	B:30%	C:34%	D:8%
68	A:55%	B:12%	C:24%	D:9%
69	A:13%	B:29%	C:21%	D:37%
70	A:12%	B:23%	C:23%	D:42%
71	A:8%	B:74%	C:13%	D:5%
72	A:21%	B:30%	C:37%	D:12%
73	A:7%	B:72%	C:16%	D:5%
74	A:4%	B:8%	C:23%	D:65%
75	A:2%	B:28%	C:65%	D:5%
76	A:34%	B:42%	C:11%	D:13%
77	A:4%	B:21%	C:38%	D:37%
78	A:17%	B:58%	C:9%	D:16%
79	A:24%	B:59%	C:5%	D:12%
80	A:34%	B:7%	C:13%	D:46%
81	A:33%	B:37%	C:21%	D:9%
82	A:12%	B:26%	C:20%	D:42%
83	A:19%	B:50%	C:24%	D:7%
84	A:9%	B:50%	C:20%	D:21%
85	A:37%	B:20%	C:19%	D:24%
86	A:13%	B:54%	C:21%	D:12%
87	A:31%	B:13%	C:45%	D:12%
88	A:42%	B:9%	C:36%	D:13%
89	A:7%	B:69%	C:12%	D:12%
90	A:25%	B:16%	C:13%	D:46%
91	A:18%	B:40%	C:9%	D:33%
92	A:12%	B:13%	C:25%	D:50%
93	A:42%	B:8%	C:50%	D:0%
94	A:74%	B:13%	C:4%	D:9%
95	A:23%	B:15%	C:8%	D:54%
96	A:37%	B:8%	C:46%	D:9%
97	A:26%	B:29%	C:32%	D:13%
98	A:14%	B:25%	C:45%	D:16%
99	A:63%	B:12%	C:9%	D:16%
100	A:16%	B:63%	C:13%	D:8%
101	A:9%	B:24%	C:61%	D:6%
102	A:13%	B:12%	C:8%	D:67%
103	A:56%	B:24%	C:12%	D:8%
104	A:9%	B:25%	C:16%	D:50%
105	A:13%	B:55%	C:15%	D:17%
106	A:29%	B:27%	C:30%	D:14%
107	A:5%	B:64%	C:8%	D:23%
108	A:0%	B:16%	C:75%	D:9%

£64,000

1	A:13%	B:35%	C:32%	D:20%
2	A:60%	B:38%	C:0%	D:2%
3	A:32%	B:16%	C:8%	D:44%
4	A:80%	B:14%	C:4%	D:2%
5	A:11%	B:64%	C:12%	D:13%
6	A:24%	B:4%	C:40%	D:32%
7	A:52%	B:12%	C:20%	D:16%
8	A:40%	B:24%	C:29%	D:7%
9	A:25%	B:23%	C:32%	D:20%
10	A:18%	B:28%	C:38%	D:16%
11	A:36%	B:45%	C:11%	D:8%
12	A:15%	B:53%	C:32%	D:0%
13	A:73%	B:16%	C:0%	D:11%
14	A:38%	B:2%	C:12%	D:48%
15	A:4%	B:57%	C:31%	D:8%
16	A:23%	B:17%	C:51%	D:9%

ASK THE AUDIENCE

No.	A	B	C	D
17	A:11%	B:29%	C:56%	D:4%
18	A:12%	B:37%	C:40%	D:11%
19	A:9%	B:3%	C:20%	D:68%
20	A:15%	B:44%	C:24%	D:17%
21	A:52%	B:2%	C:7%	D:39%
22	A:16%	B:15%	C:44%	D:25%
23	A:11%	B:2%	C:84%	D:3%
24	A:34%	B:28%	C:36%	D:2%
25	A:40%	B:13%	C:31%	D:16%
26	A:34%	B:63%	C:2%	D:1%
27	A:61%	B:11%	C:24%	D:4%
28	A:28%	B:36%	C:8%	D:28%
29	A:12%	B:17%	C:43%	D:28%
30	A:3%	B:29%	C:24%	D:44%
31	A:2%	B:36%	C:48%	D:14%
32	A:28%	B:56%	C:12%	D:4%
33	A:44%	B:41%	C:4%	D:11%
34	A:16%	B:78%	C:3%	D:3%
35	A:83%	B:7%	C:8%	D:2%
36	A:15%	B:72%	C:11%	D:2%
37	A:7%	B:2%	C:1%	D:90%
38	A:20%	B:12%	C:61%	D:7%
39	A:28%	B:20%	C:44%	D:8%
40	A:3%	B:37%	C:28%	D:32%
41	A:12%	B:44%	C:40%	D:4%
42	A:8%	B:24%	C:60%	D:8%
43	A:8%	B:15%	C:13%	D:64%
44	A:7%	B:24%	C:13%	D:56%
45	A:20%	B:32%	C:36%	D:12%
46	A:32%	B:8%	C:6%	D:54%
47	A:7%	B:49%	C:32%	D:12%
48	A:47%	B:51%	C:1%	D:1%
49	A:7%	B:53%	C:0%	D:40%
50	A:48%	B:4%	C:32%	D:16%
51	A:15%	B:61%	C:20%	D:4%
52	A:2%	B:60%	C:7%	D:31%
53	A:60%	B:3%	C:12%	D:25%
54	A:64%	B:7%	C:20%	D:9%
55	A:7%	B:17%	C:60%	D:16%
56	A:8%	B:9%	C:36%	D:47%
57	A:28%	B:4%	C:44%	D:24%
58	A:72%	B:2%	C:8%	D:18%
59	A:12%	B:11%	C:61%	D:16%
60	A:32%	B:56%	C:8%	D:4%
61	A:10%	B:16%	C:68%	D:6%
62	A:8%	B:89%	C:1%	D:2%
63	A:56%	B:20%	C:0%	D:24%
64	A:7%	B:82%	C:9%	D:2%
65	A:16%	B:4%	C:12%	D:68%
66	A:3%	B:38%	C:46%	D:13%
67	A:20%	B:40%	C:24%	D:16%
68	A:56%	B:24%	C:11%	D:9%
69	A:41%	B:23%	C:12%	D:24%
70	A:32%	B:48%	C:17%	D:3%
71	A:8%	B:76%	C:9%	D:7%
72	A:53%	B:16%	C:8%	D:23%
73	A:52%	B:9%	C:11%	D:28%
74	A:8%	B:48%	C:40%	D:4%
75	A:20%	B:4%	C:64%	D:12%
76	A:64%	B:9%	C:23%	D:4%
77	A:16%	B:80%	C:4%	D:0%
78	A:44%	B:9%	C:43%	D:4%
79	A:20%	B:28%	C:36%	D:16%
80	A:15%	B:32%	C:20%	D:33%
81	A:17%	B:11%	C:56%	D:16%
82	A:8%	B:60%	C:7%	D:25%
83	A:56%	B:3%	C:33%	D:8%
84	A:12%	B:11%	C:51%	D:26%
85	A:28%	B:56%	C:6%	D:10%
86	A:76%	B:20%	C:3%	D:1%
87	A:36%	B:8%	C:32%	D:24%
88	A:32%	B:20%	C:40%	D:8%
89	A:52%	B:32%	C:16%	D:0%
90	A:25%	B:47%	C:15%	D:13%
91	A:60%	B:12%	C:4%	D:24%
92	A:40%	B:35%	C:17%	D:8%
93	A:3%	B:53%	C:12%	D:32%
94	A:68%	B:20%	C:7%	D:5%
95	A:0%	B:72%	C:16%	D:12%
96	A:29%	B:47%	C:15%	D:9%
97	A:28%	B:16%	C:15%	D:41%
98	A:20%	B:16%	C:60%	D:4%
99	A:44%	B:9%	C:19%	D:28%
100	A:52%	B:28%	C:16%	D:4%

ASK THE AUDIENCE

£125,000

1	A:12%	B:84%	C:1%	D:3%	43	A:9%	B:55%	C:19%	D:17%
2	A:6%	B:10%	C:66%	D:18%	44	A:4%	B:30%	C:48%	D:18%
3	A:7%	B:28%	C:58%	D:7%	45	A:24%	B:2%	C:3%	D:71%
4	A:78%	B:11%	C:9%	D:2%	46	A:10%	B:42%	C:46%	D:2%
5	A:12%	B:1%	C:84%	D:3%	47	A:71%	B:4%	C:23%	D:2%
6	A:11%	B:30%	C:18%	D:41%	48	A:72%	B:3%	C:13%	D:12%
7	A:66%	B:18%	C:6%	D:10%	49	A:5%	B:18%	C:11%	D:66%
8	A:4%	B:84%	C:0%	D:12%	50	A:33%	B:62%	C:2%	D:3%
9	A:10%	B:24%	C:19%	D:47%	51	A:0%	B:0%	C:95%	D:5%
10	A:24%	B:10%	C:30%	D:36%	52	A:27%	B:4%	C:3%	D:66%
11	A:9%	B:36%	C:24%	D:31%	53	A:90%	B:5%	C:2%	D:3%
12	A:30%	B:31%	C:23%	D:16%	54	A:66%	B:11%	C:20%	D:3%
13	A:36%	B:19%	C:8%	D: 37%	55	A:21%	B:54%	C:23%	D:2%
14	A:72%	B:18%	C:3%	D:7%	56	A:82%	B:14%	C:3%	D:1%
15	A:40%	B:2%	C:54%	D:4%	57	A:29%	B:6%	C:61%	D:4%
16	A:8%	B:2%	C:12%	D:78%	58	A:60%	B:10%	C:6%	D:24%
17	A:29%	B:6%	C:10%	D:55%	59	A:72%	B:5%	C:4%	D:19%
18	A:42%	B:53%	C:5%	D:0%	60	A:18%	B:12%	C:11%	D:59%
19	A:10%	B:43%	C:36%	D:11%	61	A:0%	B:17%	C:78%	D:5%
20	A:2%	B:6%	C:1%	D:91%	62	A:17%	B:30%	C:5%	D:48%
21	A:24%	B:48%	C:24%	D:4%	63	A:24%	B:4%	C:60%	D:12%
22	A:49%	B:40%	C:6%	D:5%	64	A:53%	B:25%	C:17%	D:5%
23	A:17%	B:30%	C:36%	D:17%	65	A:72%	B:18%	C:2%	D:8%
24	A:18%	B:10%	C:24%	D:48%	66	A:11%	B:8%	C:48%	D:33%
25	A:55%	B:23%	C:22%	D:0%	67	A:31%	B:49%	C:10%	D:10%
26	A:37%	B:23%	C:10%	D:30%	68	A:41%	B:24%	C:18%	D:17%
27	A:36%	B:18%	C:16%	D:30%	69	A:4%	B:30%	C:36%	D:30%
28	A:24%	B:17%	C:49%	D:10%	70	A:17%	B:16%	C:63%	D:4%
29	A:9%	B:18%	C:43%	D:30%	71	A:5%	B:42%	C:30%	D:23%
30	A:8%	B:30%	C:6%	D:56%	72	A:5%	B:67%	C:11%	D:17%
31	A:18%	B:17%	C:47%	D:18%	73	A:38%	B:57%	C:2%	D:3%
32	A:24%	B:43%	C:30%	D:3%	74	A:82%	B:2%	C:5%	D:11%
33	A:54%	B:10%	C:17%	D:19%	75	A:6%	B:9%	C:13%	D:72%
34	A:37%	B:25%	C:23%	D:15%	76	A:10%	B:24%	C:60%	D:6%
35	A:2%	B:18%	C:8%	D:72%	77	A:5%	B:35%	C:4%	D:56%
36	A:37%	B:30%	C:15%	D:18%	78	A:10%	B:6%	C:54%	D:30%
37	A:24%	B:29%	C:10%	D:37%	79	A:36%	B:2%	C:58%	D:4%
38	A:5%	B:84%	C:2%	D:9%	80	A:30%	B:11%	C:36%	D:23%
39	A:22%	B:35%	C:43%	D:0%	81	A:6%	B:48%	C:42%	D:4%
40	A:72%	B:5%	C:5%	D:18%	82	A:23%	B:49%	C:23%	D:5%
41	A:12%	B:71%	C:4%	D:13%	83	A:24%	B:36%	C:24%	D:16%
42	A:88%	B:6%	C:1%	D:5%	84	A:10%	B:49%	C:23%	D:18%

85	A:66%	B:18%	C:7%	D:9%
86	A:5%	B:78%	C:6%	D:11%
87	A:42%	B:13%	C:42%	D:3%
88	A:16%	B:36%	C:21%	D:27%
89	A:23%	B:20%	C:30%	D:27%
90	A:3%	B:78%	C:8%	D:11%
91	A:17%	B:16%	C:42%	D:25%
92	A:79%	B:16%	C:5%	D:0%

£250,000

1	A:24%	B:33%	C:33%	D:10%
2	A:4%	B:56%	C:2%	D:38%
3	A:32%	B:21%	C:4%	D:43%
4	A:97%	B:0%	C:2%	D:1%
5	A:2%	B:12%	C:66%	D:20%
6	A:11%	B:20%	C:26%	D:43%
7	A:44%	B:46%	C:2%	D:8%
8	A:34%	B:32%	C:0%	D:34%
9	A:45%	B:0%	C:47%	D:8%
10	A:2%	B:10%	C:87%	D:1%
11	A:36%	B:21%	C:34%	D:9%
12	A:22%	B:46%	C:2%	D:30%
13	A:45%	B:19%	C:34%	D:2%
14	A:83%	B:3%	C:5%	D:9%
15	A:7%	B:41%	C:46%	D:6%
16	A:23%	B:67%	C:8%	D:2%
17	A:82%	B:9%	C:6%	D:3%
18	A:4%	B:49%	C:47%	D:0%
19	A:2%	B:10%	C:3%	D:85%
20	A:4%	B:1%	C:40%	D:55%
21	A:2%	B:3%	C:95%	D:0%
22	A:68%	B:26%	C:5%	D:1%
23	A:34%	B:33%	C:24%	D:9%
24	A:54%	B:43%	C:0%	D:3%
25	A:18%	B:1%	C:70%	D:11%
26	A:32%	B:56%	C:10%	D:2%
27	A:9%	B:36%	C:47%	D:8%
28	A:22%	B:45%	C:11%	D:22%
29	A:2%	B:61%	C:32%	D:5%
30	A:69%	B:11%	C:18%	D:2%
31	A:32%	B:56%	C:11%	D:1%
32	A:3%	B:10%	C:50%	D:37%
33	A:54%	B:43%	C:2%	D:1%
34	A:43%	B:21%	C:32%	D:4%
35	A:8%	B:35%	C:22%	D:35%
36	A:32%	B:33%	C:10%	D:25%
37	A:35%	B:4%	C:28%	D:33%
38	A:53%	B:24%	C:22%	D:1%
39	A:2%	B:5%	C:21%	D:72%
40	A:49%	B:40%	C:5%	D:6%
41	A:25%	B:34%	C:21%	D:20%
42	A:23%	B:44%	C:30%	D:3%
43	A:59%	B:7%	C:2%	D:32%
44	A:2%	B:69%	C:21%	D:8%
45	A:50%	B:2%	C:43%	D:5%
46	A:24%	B:44%	C:30%	D:2%
47	A:15%	B:4%	C:21%	D:60%
48	A:21%	B:45%	C:31%	D:3%
49	A:48%	B:21%	C:23%	D:8%
50	A:7%	B:8%	C:61%	D:24%
51	A:59%	B:30%	C:2%	D:9%
52	A:33%	B:55%	C:1%	D:11%
53	A:32%	B:32%	C:26%	D:10%
54	A:20%	B:8%	C:71%	D:1%
55	A:5%	B:2%	C:85%	D:8%
56	A:1%	B:89%	C:1%	D:9%
57	A:19%	B:2%	C:18%	D:61%
58	A:14%	B:68%	C:10%	D:8%
59	A:10%	B:30%	C:48%	D:12%
60	A:12%	B:42%	C:13%	D:33%
61	A:8%	B:2%	C:44%	D:46%
62	A:33%	B:59%	C:2%	D:6%
63	A:9%	B:5%	C:51%	D:35%
64	A:21%	B:33%	C:9%	D:37%
65	A:10%	B:55%	C:33%	D:2%
66	A:46%	B:32%	C:20%	D:2%
67	A:23%	B:31%	C:24%	D:22%
68	A:0%	B:22%	C:24%	D:54%
69	A:8%	B:86%	C:0%	D:6%
70	A:34%	B:43%	C:23%	D:0%

	A	B	C	D
71	A:22%	B:3%	C:72%	D:3%
72	A:20%	B:8%	C:27%	D:45%
73	A:3%	B:49%	C:44%	D:4%
74	A:12%	B:3%	C:41%	D:44%
75	A:0%	B:59%	C:9%	D:32%
76	A:23%	B:2%	C:19%	D:56%
77	A:45%	B:4%	C:6%	D:45%
78	A:37%	B:11%	C:34%	D:18%
79	A:5%	B:83%	C:3%	D:9%
80	A:9%	B:34%	C:36%	D:21%
81	A:31%	B:21%	C:42%	D:6%
82	A:20%	B:46%	C:1%	D:33%
83	A:27%	B:3%	C:24%	D:46%
84	A:21%	B:58%	C:0%	D:21%

£500,000

	A	B	C	D
1	A:28%	B:33%	C:28%	D:11%
2	A:4%	B:10%	C:43%	D:43%
3	A:36%	B:25%	C:0%	D:39%
4	A:34%	B:27%	C:18%	D:21%
5	A:7%	B:68%	C:21%	D:4%
6	A:18%	B:43%	C:25%	D:14%
7	A:32%	B:0%	C:64%	D:4%
8	A:21%	B:35%	C:39%	D:5%
9	A:32%	B:21%	C:11%	D:36%
10	A:43%	B:21%	C:25%	D:11%
11	A:43%	B:7%	C:32%	D:18%
12	A:46%	B:7%	C:32%	D:15%
13	A:5%	B:14%	C:16%	D:65%
14	A:10%	B:11%	C:61%	D:18%
15	A:21%	B:25%	C:50%	D:4%
16	A:22%	B:11%	C:29%	D:38%
17	A:32%	B:27%	C:31%	D:10%
18	A:18%	B:21%	C:2%	D:59%
19	A:32%	B:21%	C:22%	D:25%
20	A:33%	B:10%	C:54%	D:3%
21	A:14%	B:36%	C:32%	D:18%
22	A:6%	B:14%	C:16%	D:64%
23	A:61%	B:14%	C:3%	D:22%
24	A:39%	B:7%	C:50%	D:4%
25	A:14%	B:25%	C:54%	D:7%
26	A:9%	B:5%	C:69%	D:17%
27	A:39%	B:18%	C:5%	D:38%
28	A:29%	B:36%	C:31%	D:4%
29	A:32%	B:50%	C:4%	D:14%
30	A:31%	B:11%	C:27%	D:31%
31	A:54%	B:36%	C:0%	D:10%
32	A:40%	B:46%	C:5%	D:9%
33	A:14%	B:29%	C:50%	D:7%
34	A:64%	B:4%	C:3%	D:29%
35	A:7%	B:75%	C:0%	D:18%
36	A:4%	B:5%	C:39%	D:52%
37	A:50%	B:25%	C:21%	D:4%
38	A:36%	B:16%	C:20%	D:28%
39	A:25%	B:21%	C:39%	D:15%
40	A:23%	B:11%	C:31%	D:35%
41	A:50%	B:11%	C:18%	D:21%
42	A:18%	B:32%	C:14%	D:36%
43	A:24%	B:22%	C:51%	D:3%
44	A:35%	B:25%	C:29%	D:11%
45	A:50%	B:10%	C:15%	D:25%
46	A:26%	B:20%	C:21%	D:33%
47	A:12%	B:43%	C:29%	D:16%
48	A:11%	B:36%	C:35%	D:18%
49	A:43%	B:25%	C:4%	D:28%
50	A:36%	B:14%	C:32%	D:18%
51	A:25%	B:33%	C:24%	D:19%
52	A:18%	B:14%	C:61%	D:7%
53	A:25%	B:9%	C:27%	D:39%
54	A:43%	B:11%	C:25%	D:21%
55	A:4%	B:46%	C:18%	D:32%
56	A:18%	B:39%	C:36%	D:7%
57	A:25%	B:16%	C:34%	D:25%
58	A:21%	B:4%	C:57%	D:18%
59	A:25%	B:14%	C:36%	D:25%
60	A:17%	B:43%	C:29%	D:11%
61	A:32%	B:25%	C:43%	D:0%
62	A:54%	B:0%	C:43%	D:3%
63	A:36%	B:11%	C:29%	D:24%
64	A:21%	B:25%	C:29%	D:25%
65	A:32%	B:21%	C:11%	D:36%
66	A:9%	B:46%	C:34%	D:11%

67	A:43%	B:17%	C:21%	D:19%
68	A:52%	B:21%	C:16%	D:11%
69	A:27%	B:31%	C:38%	D:4%
70	A:8%	B:39%	C:12%	D:41%
71	A:0%	B:20%	C:69%	D:11%
72	A:29%	B:21%	C:18%	D:32%
73	A:2%	B:67%	C:18%	D:13%
74	A:36%	B:11%	C:10%	D:43%
75	A:29%	B:39%	C:18%	D:14%
76	A:7%	B:29%	C:25%	D:39%

£1,000,000

1	A:2%	B:5%	C:3%	D:90%
2	A:13%	B:12%	C:13%	D:62%
3	A:5%	B:27%	C:59%	D:9%
4	A:36%	B:18%	C:32%	D:14%
5	A:45%	B:13%	C:33%	D:9%
6	A:17%	B:24%	C:36%	D:23%
7	A:13%	B:42%	C:45%	D:0%
8	A:14%	B:36%	C:36%	D:14%
9	A:13%	B:27%	C:23%	D:37%
10	A:4%	B:9%	C:59%	D:28%
11	A:36%	B:4%	C:55%	D:5%
12	A:23%	B:64%	C:0%	D:13%
13	A:9%	B:23%	C:18%	D:50%
14	A:45%	B:5%	C:20%	D:30%
15	A:44%	B:9%	C:47%	D:0%
16	A:5%	B:50%	C:27%	D:18%
17	A:27%	B:13%	C:41%	D:19%
18	A:18%	B:36%	C:42%	D:4%
19	A:9%	B:23%	C:64%	D:4%
20	A:43%	B:11%	C:36%	D:10%
21	A:41%	B:13%	C:27%	D:19%
22	A:0%	B:9%	C:50%	D:41%
23	A:11%	B:59%	C:15%	D:15%
24	A:9%	B:25%	C:29%	D:37%
25	A:23%	B:18%	C:36%	D:23%
26	A:50%	B:41%	C:4%	D:5%
27	A:27%	B:18%	C:45%	D:10%
28	A:41%	B:44%	C:1%	D:14%
29	A:32%	B:0%	C:23%	D:45%
30	A:4%	B:68%	C:13%	D:15%
31	A:59%	B:32%	C:8%	D:1%
32	A:23%	B:27%	C:36%	D:14%
33	A:10%	B:36%	C:9%	D:45%
34	A:27%	B:19%	C:25%	D:29%
35	A:48%	B:30%	C:0%	D:22%
36	A:4%	B:42%	C:18%	D:36%
37	A:2%	B:38%	C:48%	D:12%
38	A:5%	B:72%	C:11%	D:12%
39	A:48%	B:16%	C:0%	D:36%
40	A:10%	B:35%	C:31%	D:24%
41	A:4%	B:48%	C:23%	D:25%
42	A:33%	B:10%	C:18%	D:39%
43	A:11%	B:42%	C:43%	D:4%
44	A:23%	B:17%	C:43%	D:17%
45	A:2%	B:28%	C:42%	D:28%
46	A:10%	B:24%	C:48%	D:18%
47	A:25%	B:37%	C:23%	D:15%
48	A:24%	B:31%	C:23%	D:22%
49	A:25%	B:9%	C:55%	D:11%
50	A:72%	B:0%	C:10%	D:18%
51	A:18%	B:23%	C:10%	D:49%
52	A:2%	B:60%	C:24%	D:14%
53	A:24%	B:30%	C:36%	D:10%
54	A:19%	B:30%	C:47%	D:4%
55	A:32%	B:24%	C:16%	D:28%
56	A:11%	B:42%	C:42%	D:5%
57	A:19%	B:17%	C:54%	D:10%
58	A:4%	B:43%	C:35%	D:18%
59	A:42%	B:30%	C:8%	D:20%
60	A:24%	B:60%	C:2%	D:14%
61	A:15%	B:19%	C:43%	D:23%
62	A:9%	B:19%	C:48%	D:24%
63	A:49%	B:36%	C:4%	D:11%
64	A:24%	B:10%	C:41%	D:25%
65	A:9%	B:55%	C:13%	D:23%
66	A:42%	B:22%	C:26%	D:10%
67	A:29%	B:37%	C:25%	D:9%
68	A:5%	B:47%	C:12%	D:36%

Answers

Fastest Finger First

1	BCDA	2	CADB	3	ACDB	4	CBDA	5	DCBA
6	CBDA	7	BDCA	8	CDBA	9	CABD	10	BDAC
11	BCDA	12	CADB	13	BCAD	14	DACB	15	BCAD
16	CBAD	17	ABCD	18	BDAC	19	ADCB	20	DBAC
21	CDAB	22	ABCD	23	DCBA	24	ADCB	25	DABC
26	DBCA	27	DACB	28	BADC	29	CADB	30	BCDA
31	ADBC	32	BDCA	33	BACD	34	CDBA	35	ADCB
36	BDCA	37	ADBC	38	CBDA	39	BDAC	40	BCAD
41	DBAC	42	CBDA	43	ACDB	44	BDCA	45	ACBD
46	CDAB	47	BDCA	48	BADC	49	CABD	50	ABCD
51	BADC	52	ABDC	53	CBDA	54	DABC	55	DCAB
56	BCDA	57	CBAD	58	ACBD	59	CDAB	60	ADCB
61	CADB	62	BDCA	63	CBAD	64	DBCA	65	ACBD
66	BCAD	67	CDAB	68	BACD	69	CBDA	70	CABD
71	ABCD	72	CADB	73	CADB	74	DBAC	75	BDCA
76	ADBC	77	BCDA	78	CBAD	79	DBAC	80	BCDA
81	ADCB	82	DCAB	83	BCDA	84	ACDB	85	BACD
86	CBAD	87	BDCA	88	CADB	89	DBAC	90	ADBC
91	CBAD	92	BDCA	93	DBCA	94	CDAB	95	DBAC
96	BDCA	97	CBDA	98	ADBC	99	ACDB	100	ACDB
101	BADC	102	DBAC	103	ADCB	104	BCAD	105	ADBC
106	DBAC	107	CADB	108	ADCB	109	BADC	110	DBAC
111	ADBC	112	BDAC	113	CBDA	114	ACDB	115	DACB
116	ADBC	117	CBAD	118	DBCA	119	BDAC	120	ACBD
121	DCBA	122	ABDC	123	DBAC	124	ACDB	125	CADB
126	DACB	127	BACD	128	BDAC	129	DBAC	130	CDBA
131	BACD	132	ACBD	133	BCAD	134	ACBD	135	DBCA
136	CBDA	137	CBAD	138	BACD	139	DCAB	140	BDCA
141	DCAB	142	CABD	143	BDAC	144	CBAD	145	BDCA
146	DCBA	147	BACD	148	DBCA	149	CBAD	150	BCDA

If you answered correctly, well done! Turn to page 41 to play for £100!

ANSWERS

£100

1	A	2	B	3	A	4	B	5	A	6	C	7	A
8	A	9	B	10	A	11	C	12	A	13	C	14	A
15	B	16	A	17	A	18	A	19	B	20	B	21	B
22	A	23	B	24	A	25	A	26	C	27	C	28	B
29	B	30	C	31	A	32	A	33	C	34	A	35	A
36	A	37	B	38	A	39	A	40	B	41	A	42	D
43	A	44	D	45	C	46	A	47	B	48	A	49	B
50	A	51	D	52	B	53	C	54	C	55	A	56	D
57	B	58	A	59	B	60	C	61	D	62	C	63	B
64	C	65	D	66	A	67	A	68	D	69	A	70	D
71	B	72	D	73	A	74	B	75	D	76	C	77	C
78	D	79	A	80	B	81	C	82	C	83	A	84	C
85	C	86	B	87	C	88	B	89	D	90	C	91	D
92	B	93	B	94	B	95	C	96	B	97	B	98	C
99	A	100	C	101	B	102	C	103	B	104	C	105	C
106	C	107	B	108	B	109	B	110	A	111	B	112	C
113	B	114	C	115	B	116	C	117	B	118	B	119	A
120	A	121	B	122	D	123	C	124	A	125	A	126	B
127	A	128	B	129	B	130	A	131	C	132	B	133	B
134	A	135	C	136	A	137	A	138	A	139	C	140	B
141	A	142	A	143	B	144	A	145	A	146	C	147	A
148	B	149	C	150	B	151	A	152	A	153	C	154	B
155	A	156	B	157	A	158	A	159	B	160	A	161	A
162	B	163	C	164	A	165	C	166	A	167	A	168	A
169	B	170	A	171	B	172	A	173	A	174	A	175	C
176	A	177	A	178	A	179	A	180	A				

If you have won £100, well done! Turn to page 79 to play for £200!

£200

1	B	2	D	3	C	4	A	5	C	6	C	7	D
8	C	9	C	10	A	11	A	12	A	13	C	14	C
15	B	16	C	17	D	18	B	19	C	20	A	21	B
22	B	23	A	24	D	25	C	26	C	27	B	28	D
29	A	30	B	31	C	32	B	33	A	34	C	35	B
36	C	37	A	38	D	39	A	40	C	41	D	42	B
43	C	44	B	45	B	46	B	47	A	48	D	49	B
50	C	51	D	52	A	53	D	54	B	55	D	56	B
57	D	58	B	59	D	60	C	61	C	62	A	63	C
64	B	65	C	66	D	67	A	68	D	69	B	70	C
71	D	72	C	73	D	74	A	75	B	76	C	77	D
78	C	79	B	80	A	81	D	82	C	83	B	84	C

85 A	86 D	87 C	88 B	89 C	90 D	91 A
92 A	93 D	94 C	95 A	96 B	97 C	98 D
99 C	100 A	101 D	102 B	103 A	104 D	105 C
106 D	107 C	108 A	109 C	110 B	111 C	112 B
113 A	114 D	115 B	116 A	117 B	118 A	119 D
120 C	121 B	122 C	123 A	124 B	125 A	126 B
127 C	128 B	129 A	130 D	131 A	132 B	133 A
134 C	135 D	136 A	137 C	138 D	139 B	140 D
141 B	142 B	143 C	144 D	145 C	146 A	147 A
148 D	149 A	150 D	151 A	152 C	153 C	154 B
155 C	156 A	157 B	158 A	159 B	160 C	161 B
162 C	163 B	164 A	165 B	166 C	167 D	168 A
169 D	170 A	171 C	172 B			

If you have won £200, well done! Turn to page 115 to play for £300!

£300

1 C	2 D	3 B	4 D	5 C	6 D	7 B
8 B	9 C	10 D	11 C	12 C	13 A	14 D
15 A	16 B	17 D	18 C	19 B	20 B	21 D
22 A	23 B	24 D	25 A	26 B	27 D	28 C
29 A	30 A	31 C	32 B	33 A	34 D	35 B
36 D	37 B	38 D	39 A	40 A	41 C	42 D
43 D	44 B	45 D	46 C	47 B	48 D	49 C
50 D	51 C	52 D	53 B	54 C	55 B	56 D
57 B	58 C	59 A	60 C	61 B	62 C	63 B
64 D	65 C	66 D	67 B	68 C	69 B	70 C
71 C	72 D	73 C	74 D	75 C	76 A	77 B
78 D	79 B	80 D	81 C	82 B	83 C	84 A
85 A	86 C	87 C	88 B	89 B	90 D	91 A
92 C	93 D	94 B	95 B	96 A	97 D	98 A
99 B	100 A	101 D	102 C	103 A	104 D	105 C
106 D	107 C	108 B	109 D	110 A	111 C	112 D
113 A	114 A	115 B	116 C	117 D	118 B	119 D
120 A	121 B	122 C	123 D	124 A	125 C	126 A
127 C	128 A	129 D	130 C	131 A	132 B	133 C
134 A	135 B	136 D	137 B	138 A	139 B	140 C
141 D	142 B	143 A	144 B	145 C	146 D	147 B
148 B	149 A	150 D	151 C	152 A	153 D	154 A
155 B	156 A	157 B	158 D	159 A	160 C	161 B
162 D	163 B	164 D				

If you have won £300, well done! Turn to page 149 to play for £500!

ANSWERS

£500

1 D	2 C	3 B	4 A	5 B	6 C	7 A
8 B	9 C	10 A	11 B	12 D	13 C	14 D
15 B	16 D	17 B	18 C	19 A	20 B	21 A
22 C	23 A	24 D	25 B	26 C	27 D	28 C
29 C	30 C	31 B	32 C	33 B	34 B	35 A
36 D	37 D	38 D	39 D	40 C	41 A	42 D
43 B	44 D	45 B	46 D	47 D	48 D	49 D
50 D	51 B	52 C	53 D	54 D	55 B	56 D
57 B	58 B	59 D	60 C	61 D	62 A	63 B
64 C	65 D	66 A	67 B	68 A	69 C	70 B
71 A	72 B	73 C	74 A	75 D	76 C	77 C
78 A	79 C	80 B	81 D	82 C	83 A	84 B
85 A	86 D	87 C	88 A	89 B	90 C	91 B
92 C	93 B	94 C	95 B	96 D	97 A	98 B
99 D	100 C	101 D	102 A	103 C	104 B	105 A
106 B	107 C	108 B	109 D	110 C	111 A	112 D
113 B	114 B	115 D	116 B	117 D	118 A	119 B
120 D	121 A	122 B	123 C	124 D	125 B	126 D
127 B	128 D	129 C	130 B	131 C	132 D	133 C
134 B	135 C	136 D	137 C	138 B	139 C	140 B
141 C	142 A	143 B	144 A	145 C	146 B	147 D
148 B	149 A	150 B	151 D	152 B	153 A	154 B
155 D	156 B					

If you have won £500, well done! Turn to page 183 to play for £1,000!

£1,000

1 B	2 C	3 B	4 D	5 C	6 C	7 D
8 B	9 A	10 D	11 A	12 C	13 D	14 A
15 C	16 A	17 C	18 A	19 B	20 D	21 C
22 B	23 D	24 B	25 C	26 D	27 A	28 D
29 C	30 D	31 A	32 C	33 B	34 D	35 C
36 B	37 D	38 B	39 D	40 A	41 D	42 B
43 C	44 A	45 C	46 A	47 C	48 B	49 C
50 B	51 C	52 B	53 A	54 C	55 D	56 B
57 C	58 B	59 C	60 D	61 A	62 C	63 B
64 A	65 C	66 B	67 C	68 A	69 B	70 C
71 A	72 C	73 A	74 C	75 A	76 D	77 A
78 B	79 D	80 C	81 D	82 C	83 B	84 C
85 A	86 C	87 A	88 D	89 A	90 A	91 A
92 D	93 A	94 D	95 A	96 A	97 B	98 D
99 B	100 A	101 C	102 B	103 C	104 B	105 D

106 A 107 B 108 A 109 D 110 A 111 C 112 B
113 C 114 D 115 A 116 D 117 C 118 D 119 C
120 B 121 D 122 A 123 D 124 B 125 C 126 B
127 C 128 D 129 B 130 C 131 B 132 D 133 D
134 C 135 B 136 C 137 A 138 B 139 B 140 C
141 B 142 C 143 D 144 C 145 B 146 C 147 A
148 C

If you have won £1,000, well done! Turn to page 215 to play for £2,000!

£2,000

1 D 2 B 3 A 4 B 5 D 6 C 7 D
8 B 9 A 10 C 11 A 12 C 13 D 14 B
15 D 16 B 17 C 18 D 19 B 20 C 21 B
22 C 23 A 24 B 25 C 26 D 27 B 28 C
29 B 30 D 31 A 32 D 33 B 34 C 35 B
36 A 37 D 38 C 39 D 40 A 41 B 42 C
43 D 44 A 45 D 46 C 47 B 48 D 49 A
50 D 51 C 52 B 53 D 54 C 55 A 56 C
57 B 58 A 59 B 60 A 61 C 62 D 63 C
64 A 65 C 66 B 67 A 68 B 69 D 70 C
71 A 72 D 73 A 74 B 75 A 76 B 77 C
78 D 79 C 80 C 81 A 82 C 83 A 84 D
85 B 86 A 87 C 88 B 89 C 90 A 91 C
92 B 93 C 94 D 95 C 96 D 97 A 98 B
99 D 100 A 101 D 102 A 103 C 104 D 105 A
106 D 107 A 108 B 109 C 110 A 111 D 112 B
113 A 114 D 115 A 116 D 117 A 118 C 119 B
120 D 121 A 122 C 123 D 124 A 125 B 126 C
127 B 128 A 129 A 130 B 131 A 132 C 133 B
134 A 135 B 136 D 137 B 138 A 139 B 140 B

If you have won £2,000, well done! Turn to page 245 to play for £4,000!

£4,000

1 D 2 A 3 C 4 B 5 A 6 C 7 D
8 B 9 A 10 C 11 B 12 D 13 A 14 B
15 C 16 A 17 B 18 C 19 A 20 C 21 B
22 A 23 C 24 A 25 B 26 D 27 C 28 D
29 B 30 C 31 C 32 D 33 B 34 D 35 B
36 C 37 D 38 B 39 C 40 B 41 C 42 B
43 C 44 B 45 D 46 B 47 D 48 C 49 B
50 C 51 B 52 D 53 C 54 A 55 B 56 D

57 A	58 B	59 C	60 D	61 B	62 C	63 B
64 D	65 C	66 C	67 D	68 B	69 C	70 A
71 D	72 C	73 B	74 A	75 C	76 B	77 D
78 D	79 B	80 D	81 B	82 A	83 D	84 B
85 D	86 B	87 D	88 D	89 A	90 D	91 D
92 C	93 D	94 C	95 B	96 C	97 B	98 C
99 D	100 B	101 D	102 C	103 B	104 C	105 B
106 A	107 C	108 D	109 B	110 C	111 C	112 D
113 B	114 A	115 C	116 B	117 C	118 A	119 D
120 C	121 B	122 C	123 B	124 C	125 D	126 B
127 A	128 D	129 B	130 C	131 A	132 C	

If you have won £4,000, well done! Turn to page 273 to play for £8,000!

£8,000

1 A	2 B	3 C	4 A	5 C	6 D	7 C
8 B	9 D	10 C	11 D	12 B	13 C	14 B
15 A	16 A	17 C	18 B	19 C	20 A	21 B
22 C	23 A	24 C	25 B	26 A	27 C	28 A
29 D	30 C	31 D	32 B	33 A	34 D	35 A
36 D	37 D	38 A	39 D	40 A	41 D	42 A
43 B	44 D	45 B	46 A	47 D	48 C	49 A
50 D	51 A	52 B	53 A	54 D	55 B	56 A
57 A	58 B	59 D	60 A	61 B	62 C	63 D
64 B	65 A	66 D	67 A	68 D	69 B	70 A
71 B	72 A	73 D	74 B	75 A	76 B	77 C
78 D	79 B	80 A	81 B	82 C	83 A	84 C
85 B	86 D	87 C	88 B	89 D	90 C	91 B
92 A	93 D	94 C	95 B	96 D	97 B	98 B
99 C	100 A	101 B	102 C	103 B	104 A	105 C
106 D	107 C	108 A	109 D	110 A	111 C	112 A
113 B	114 B	115 C	116 D	117 A	118 C	119 B
120 D	121 C	122 D	123 B	124 D		

If you have won £8,000, well done! Turn to page 299 to play for £16,000!

£16,000

1 A	2 C	3 B	4 A	5 B	6 D	7 A
8 B	9 D	10 C	11 B	12 A	13 B	14 A
15 B	16 D	17 A	18 B	19 C	20 D	21 B
22 D	23 A	24 C	25 A	26 D	27 B	28 A
29 C	30 D	31 B	32 D	33 B	34 C	35 B
36 A	37 B	38 D	39 D	40 C	41 B	42 D

43 A	44 D	45 B	46 D	47 C	48 B	49 A
50 B	51 A	52 C	53 A	54 B	55 D	56 A
57 C	58 D	59 A	60 D	61 A	62 B	63 C
64 B	65 A	66 C	67 B	68 A	69 C	70 B
71 D	72 A	73 C	74 A	75 C	76 B	77 B
78 A	79 D	80 A	81 C	82 C	83 A	84 B
85 C	86 A	87 B	88 D	89 A	90 D	91 B
92 D	93 C	94 A	95 B	96 A	97 A	98 C
99 D	100 B	101 A	102 B	103 C	104 B	105 A
106 B	107 D	108 C	109 B	110 C	111 A	112 D
113 A	114 C	115 D	116 A			

If you have won £16,000, well done! Turn to page 325 to play for £32,000!

£32,000

1 A	2 D	3 A	4 B	5 C	6 A	7 C
8 A	9 B	10 D	11 A	12 A	13 C	14 A
15 D	16 C	17 A	18 D	19 B	20 D	21 A
22 B	23 A	24 B	25 C	26 A	27 B	28 D
29 A	30 B	31 D	32 B	33 A	34 D	35 A
36 B	37 C	38 D	39 B	40 A	41 D	42 B
43 C	44 B	45 A	46 A	47 B	48 A	49 D
50 C	51 D	52 B	53 D	54 C	55 A	56 D
57 C	58 A	59 B	60 C	61 C	62 B	63 D
64 C	65 D	66 A	67 B	68 A	69 D	70 D
71 B	72 D	73 B	74 D	75 C	76 B	77 D
78 B	79 B	80 B	81 B	82 D	83 B	84 B
85 A	86 C	87 D	88 A	89 B	90 D	91 B
92 D	93 C	94 A	95 D	96 C	97 A	98 C
99 D	100 B	101 C	102 D	103 A	104 D	105 C
106 A	107 D	108 C				

If you have won £32,000, well done! Turn to page 349 to play for £64,000!

£64,000

1 B	2 A	3 D	4 A	5 B	6 D	7 B
8 C	9 B	10 B	11 A	12 B	13 A	14 C
15 B	16 A	17 B	18 C	19 D	20 B	21 D
22 D	23 C	24 B	25 A	26 B	27 A	28 B
29 C	30 D	31 C	32 B	33 A	34 B	35 A
36 B	37 C	38 B	39 A	40 C	41 B	42 C
43 D	44 B	45 A	46 D	47 A	48 B	49 D
50 A	51 B	52 D	53 B	54 A	55 C	56 B

57 C	58 A	59 C	60 B	61 C	62 B	63 A
64 B	65 D	66 B	67 B	68 D	69 B	70 A
71 B	72 A	73 D	74 B	75 C	76 A	77 B
78 A	79 B	80 D	81 C	82 B	83 C	84 B
85 B	86 A	87 B	88 C	89 A	90 B	91 B
92 B	93 B	94 A	95 B	96 B	97 D	98 C
99 B	100 C					

If you have won £64,000, well done! Turn to page 371 to play for £125,000!

£125,000

1 B	2 D	3 C	4 A	5 C	6 D	7 A
8 B	9 C	10 D	11 B	12 C	13 D	14 A
15 C	16 D	17 A	18 B	19 A	20 D	21 C
22 A	23 B	24 D	25 B	26 D	27 C	28 D
29 C	30 B	31 C	32 B	33 A	34 D	35 D
36 A	37 D	38 B	39 C	40 D	41 B	42 A
43 B	44 C	45 A	46 B	47 C	48 A	49 D
50 A	51 C	52 D	53 A	54 C	55 B	56 A
57 C	58 B	59 A	60 D	61 C	62 A	63 C
64 B	65 A	66 C	67 D	68 A	69 D	70 C
71 A	72 D	73 B	74 A	75 D	76 C	77 D
78 A	79 C	80 A	81 C	82 B	83 A	84 B
85 A	86 D	87 A	88 D	89 A	90 B	91 C
92 A						

If you have won £125,000, well done! Turn to page 391 to play for £250,000!

£250,000

1 A	2 B	3 D	4 A	5 D	6 C	7 A
8 B	9 D	10 C	11 B	12 A	13 C	14 B
15 D	16 B	17 A	18 C	19 B	20 D	21 C
22 A	23 B	24 A	25 C	26 D	27 C	28 B
29 C	30 B	31 A	32 D	33 A	34 C	35 B
36 C	37 B	38 A	39 D	40 C	41 B	42 D
43 C	44 B	45 A	46 B	47 D	48 C	49 B
50 C	51 D	52 B	53 C	54 B	55 C	56 B
57 A	58 B	59 A	60 D	61 C	62 A	63 C
64 A	65 C	66 A	67 B	68 D	69 B	70 A
71 B	72 D	73 B	74 C	75 D	76 A	77 D
78 A	79 B	80 C	81 D	82 B	83 A	84 B

If you have won £250,000, well done! Turn to page 409 to play for £500,000!

ANSWERS

£500,000

1	A	2	D	3	D	4	B	5	D	6	C	7	C
8	C	9	B	10	A	11	D	12	C	13	D	14	A
15	A	16	D	17	A	18	D	19	A	20	C	21	D
22	D	23	A	24	C	25	C	26	C	27	B	28	D
29	C	30	A	31	C	32	A	33	C	34	A	35	B
36	D	37	A	38	D	39	A	40	D	41	A	42	D
43	C	44	C	45	D	46	D	47	A	48	B	49	A
50	B	51	D	52	C	53	D	54	C	55	A	56	B
57	C	58	D	59	C	60	C	61	D	62	A	63	C
64	C	65	D	66	B	67	D	68	C	69	C	70	D
71	C	72	A	73	B	74	A	75	A	76	D		

If you have won £500,000, well done! Turn to page 427 to play for £1,000,000!

£1,000,000

1	B	2	D	3	B	4	B	5	C	6	D	7	C
8	B	9	C	10	D	11	A	12	B	13	D	14	B
15	C	16	C	17	A	18	B	19	B	20	D	21	B
22	A	23	B	24	B	25	D	26	B	27	C	28	B
29	A	30	B	31	B	32	A	33	B	34	C	35	B
36	C	37	A	38	B	39	D	40	C	41	B	42	D
43	B	44	C	45	D	46	D	47	B	48	C	49	B
50	D	51	D	52	C	53	A	54	B	55	D	56	A
57	C	58	A	59	C	60	D	61	B	62	D	63	A
64	C	65	D	66	A	67	C	68	D				

If you have won £1,000,000, well done! You're a millionaire!

Score sheets

Write your name and the names of any other contestants in the space provided. Shade in each of the boxes lightly with a pencil once you or one of your fellow contestants has won the amount in that box. If you or any of the other contestants answer a question incorrectly and are out of the game, use a soft eraser to rub out the relevant boxes so that the final score is showing.

SCORE SHEET

contestant's name	contestant's name
....	....
50:50 ☐ ☐ ☐	50:50 ☐ ☐ ☐

15	£1 MILLION	15	£1 MILLION
14	£500,000	14	£500,000
13	£250,000	13	£250,000
12	£125,000	12	£125,000
11	£64,000	11	£64,000
10	£32,000	**10**	£32,000
9	£16,000	9	£16,000
8	£8,000	8	£8,000
7	£4,000	7	£4,000
6	£2,000	6	£2,000
5	£1,000	**5**	£1,000
4	£500	4	£500
3	£300	3	£300
2	£200	2	£200
1	£100	1	£100

SCORE SHEET

contestant's name	contestant's name
....	....
50:50 ☐ ☐ ☐	50:50 ☐ ☐ ☐

15	£1 MILLION		15	£1 MILLION
14	£500,000		14	£500,000
13	£250,000		13	£250,000
12	£125,000		12	£125,000
11	£64,000		11	£64,000
10	£32,000		10	£32,000
9	£16,000		9	£16,000
8	£8,000		8	£8,000
7	£4,000		7	£4,000
6	£2,000		6	£2,000
5	£1,000		5	£1,000
4	£500		4	£500
3	£300		3	£300
2	£200		2	£200
1	£100		1	£100

SCORE SHEET

contestant's name		contestant's name	
50:50 / phone / audience		50:50 / phone / audience	
15	£1 MILLION	15	£1 MILLION
14	£500,000	14	£500,000
13	£250,000	13	£250,000
12	£125,000	12	£125,000
11	£64,000	11	£64,000
10	£32,000	10	£32,000
9	£16,000	9	£16,000
8	£8,000	8	£8,000
7	£4,000	7	£4,000
6	£2,000	6	£2,000
5	£1,000	5	£1,000
4	£500	4	£500
3	£300	3	£300
2	£200	2	£200
1	£100	1	£100

SCORE SHEET

contestant's name	contestant's name ....
50:50 ☐ ☐ ☐	50:50 ☐ ☐ ☐

15	£1 MILLION	15	£1 MILLION
14	£500,000	14	£500,000
13	£250,000	13	£250,000
12	£125,000	12	£125,000
11	£64,000	11	£64,000
10	£32,000	10	£32,000
9	£16,000	9	£16,000
8	£8,000	8	£8,000
7	£4,000	7	£4,000
6	£2,000	6	£2,000
5	£1,000	5	£1,000
4	£500	4	£500
3	£300	3	£300
2	£200	2	£200
1	£100	1	£100

SCORE SHEET

contestant's name

....

50:50

15	£1 MILLION
14	£500,000
13	£250,000
12	£125,000
11	£64,000
10	£32,000
9	£16,000
8	£8,000
7	£4,000
6	£2,000
5	£1,000
4	£500
3	£300
2	£200
1	£100

contestant's name

....

50:50

15	£1 MILLION
14	£500,000
13	£250,000
12	£125,000
11	£64,000
10	£32,000
9	£16,000
8	£8,000
7	£4,000
6	£2,000
5	£1,000
4	£500
3	£300
2	£200
1	£100

SCORE SHEET

contestant's name

....

50:50

15	£1 MILLION
14	£500,000
13	£250,000
12	£125,000
11	£64,000
10	£32,000
9	£16,000
8	£8,000
7	£4,000
6	£2,000
5	£1,000
4	£500
3	£300
2	£200
1	£100

contestant's name

....

50:50

15	£1 MILLION
14	£500,000
13	£250,000
12	£125,000
11	£64,000
10	£32,000
9	£16,000
8	£8,000
7	£4,000
6	£2,000
5	£1,000
4	£500
3	£300
2	£200
1	£100

SCORE SHEET

contestant's name

....

50:50

15	£1 MILLION
14	£500,000
13	£250,000
12	£125,000
11	£64,000
10	£32,000
9	£16,000
8	£8,000
7	£4,000
6	£2,000
5	£1,000
4	£500
3	£300
2	£200
1	£100

contestant's name

....

50:50

15	£1 MILLION
14	£500,000
13	£250,000
12	£125,000
11	£64,000
10	£32,000
9	£16,000
8	£8,000
7	£4,000
6	£2,000
5	£1,000
4	£500
3	£300
2	£200
1	£100

SCORE SHEET

contestant's name	contestant's name ....
50:50 ☐ ☐ ☐	50:50 ☐ ☐ ☐

15	£1 MILLION	15	£1 MILLION
14	£500,000	14	£500,000
13	£250,000	13	£250,000
12	£125,000	12	£125,000
11	£64,000	11	£64,000
10	£32,000	10	£32,000
9	£16,000	9	£16,000
8	£8,000	8	£8,000
7	£4,000	7	£4,000
6	£2,000	6	£2,000
5	£1,000	5	£1,000
4	£500	4	£500
3	£300	3	£300
2	£200	2	£200
1	£100	1	£100

SCORE SHEET

contestant's name		contestant's name	
50:50		50:50	
15	£1 MILLION	15	£1 MILLION
14	£500,000	14	£500,000
13	£250,000	13	£250,000
12	£125,000	12	£125,000
11	£64,000	11	£64,000
10	£32,000	10	£32,000
9	£16,000	9	£16,000
8	£8,000	8	£8,000
7	£4,000	7	£4,000
6	£2,000	6	£2,000
5	£1,000	5	£1,000
4	£500	4	£500
3	£300	3	£300
2	£200	2	£200
1	£100	1	£100

SCORE SHEET

contestant's name		contestant's name	
________________		________________	
50:50		50:50	
15	£1 MILLION	15	£1 MILLION
14	£500,000	14	£500,000
13	£250,000	13	£250,000
12	£125,000	12	£125,000
11	£64,000	11	£64,000
10	£32,000	10	£32,000
9	£16,000	9	£16,000
8	£8,000	8	£8,000
7	£4,000	7	£4,000
6	£2,000	6	£2,000
5	£1,000	5	£1,000
4	£500	4	£500
3	£300	3	£300
2	£200	2	£200
1	£100	1	£100

SCORE SHEET

contestant's name

....

50:50

15	£1 MILLION
14	£500,000
13	£250,000
12	£125,000
11	£64,000
10	£32,000
9	£16,000
8	£8,000
7	£4,000
6	£2,000
5	£1,000
4	£500
3	£300
2	£200
1	£100

contestant's name

....

50:50

15	£1 MILLION
14	£500,000
13	£250,000
12	£125,000
11	£64,000
10	£32,000
9	£16,000
8	£8,000
7	£4,000
6	£2,000
5	£1,000
4	£500
3	£300
2	£200
1	£100

SCORE SHEET

contestant's name

....

50:50

15	£1 MILLION
14	£500,000
13	£250,000
12	£125,000
11	£64,000
10	£32,000
9	£16,000
8	£8,000
7	£4,000
6	£2,000
5	£1,000
4	£500
3	£300
2	£200
1	£100

contestant's name

....

50:50

15	£1 MILLION
14	£500,000
13	£250,000
12	£125,000
11	£64,000
10	£32,000
9	£16,000
8	£8,000
7	£4,000
6	£2,000
5	£1,000
4	£500
3	£300
2	£200
1	£100

SCORE SHEET

contestant's name	contestant's name
....	....
50:50 / Phone / Audience	50:50 / Phone / Audience

15	£1 MILLION	15	£1 MILLION
14	£500,000	14	£500,000
13	£250,000	13	£250,000
12	£125,000	12	£125,000
11	£64,000	11	£64,000
10	£32,000	10	£32,000
9	£16,000	9	£16,000
8	£8,000	8	£8,000
7	£4,000	7	£4,000
6	£2,000	6	£2,000
5	£1,000	5	£1,000
4	£500	4	£500
3	£300	3	£300
2	£200	2	£200
1	£100	1	£100

SCORE SHEET

contestant's name	contestant's name ....
50:50 ☐ Phone ☐ Audience ☐	50:50 ☐ Phone ☐ Audience ☐

15	£1 MILLION	15	£1 MILLION
14	£500,000	14	£500,000
13	£250,000	13	£250,000
12	£125,000	12	£125,000
11	£64,000	11	£64,000
10	£32,000	**10**	£32,000
9	£16,000	9	£16,000
8	£8,000	8	£8,000
7	£4,000	7	£4,000
6	£2,000	6	£2,000
5	£1,000	**5**	£1,000
4	£500	4	£500
3	£300	3	£300
2	£200	2	£200
1	£100	1	£100

SCORE SHEET

contestant's name

....

50:50

15	£1 MILLION
14	£500,000
13	£250,000
12	£125,000
11	£64,000
10	£32,000
9	£16,000
8	£8,000
7	£4,000
6	£2,000
5	£1,000
4	£500
3	£300
2	£200
1	£100

contestant's name

....

50:50

15	£1 MILLION
14	£500,000
13	£250,000
12	£125,000
11	£64,000
10	£32,000
9	£16,000
8	£8,000
7	£4,000
6	£2,000
5	£1,000
4	£500
3	£300
2	£200
1	£100

SCORE SHEET

contestant's name	contestant's name ....
50:50 ☐ ☐ ☐	50:50 ☐ ☐ ☐

15	£1 MILLION	15	£1 MILLION
14	£500,000	14	£500,000
13	£250,000	13	£250,000
12	£125,000	12	£125,000
11	£64,000	11	£64,000
10	£32,000	10	£32,000
9	£16,000	9	£16,000
8	£8,000	8	£8,000
7	£4,000	7	£4,000
6	£2,000	6	£2,000
5	£1,000	5	£1,000
4	£500	4	£500
3	£300	3	£300
2	£200	2	£200
1	£100	1	£100

SCORE SHEET

contestant's name

....

50:50

15	£1 MILLION
14	£500,000
13	£250,000
12	£125,000
11	£64,000
10	£32,000
9	£16,000
8	£8,000
7	£4,000
6	£2,000
5	£1,000
4	£500
3	£300
2	£200
1	£100

contestant's name

....

50:50

15	£1 MILLION
14	£500,000
13	£250,000
12	£125,000
11	£64,000
10	£32,000
9	£16,000
8	£8,000
7	£4,000
6	£2,000
5	£1,000
4	£500
3	£300
2	£200
1	£100

SCORE SHEET

contestant's name	contestant's name
....	....
50:50 ☐	50:50 ☐
☐	☐
☐	☐

15	£1 MILLION	15	£1 MILLION
14	£500,000	14	£500,000
13	£250,000	13	£250,000
12	£125,000	12	£125,000
11	£64,000	11	£64,000
10	£32,000	**10**	£32,000
9	£16,000	9	£16,000
8	£8,000	8	£8,000
7	£4,000	7	£4,000
6	£2,000	6	£2,000
5	£1,000	**5**	£1,000
4	£500	4	£500
3	£300	3	£300
2	£200	2	£200
1	£100	1	£100

SCORE SHEET

contestant's name	contestant's name
....	....
50:50	50:50

15	£1 MILLION	15	£1 MILLION
14	£500,000	14	£500,000
13	£250,000	13	£250,000
12	£125,000	12	£125,000
11	£64,000	11	£64,000
10	£32,000	10	£32,000
9	£16,000	9	£16,000
8	£8,000	8	£8,000
7	£4,000	7	£4,000
6	£2,000	6	£2,000
5	£1,000	5	£1,000
4	£500	4	£500
3	£300	3	£300
2	£200	2	£200
1	£100	1	£100

SCORE SHEET

contestant's name		contestant's name	
50:50	☐ ☐ ☐	50:50	☐ ☐ ☐
15	£1 MILLION	15	£1 MILLION
14	£500,000	14	£500,000
13	£250,000	13	£250,000
12	£125,000	12	£125,000
11	£64,000	11	£64,000
10	£32,000	**10**	£32,000
9	£16,000	9	£16,000
8	£8,000	8	£8,000
7	£4,000	7	£4,000
6	£2,000	6	£2,000
5	£1,000	**5**	£1,000
4	£500	4	£500
3	£300	3	£300
2	£200	2	£200
1	£100	1	£100

SCORE SHEET

contestant's name

....

50:50

15	£1 MILLION
14	£500,000
13	£250,000
12	£125,000
11	£64,000
10	£32,000
9	£16,000
8	£8,000
7	£4,000
6	£2,000
5	£1,000
4	£500
3	£300
2	£200
1	£100

contestant's name

....

50:50

15	£1 MILLION
14	£500,000
13	£250,000
12	£125,000
11	£64,000
10	£32,000
9	£16,000
8	£8,000
7	£4,000
6	£2,000
5	£1,000
4	£500
3	£300
2	£200
1	£100

SCORE SHEET

contestant's name		contestant's name	
50:50 ☐ ☐ ☐		50:50 ☐ ☐ ☐	
15	£1 MILLION	15	£1 MILLION
14	£500,000	14	£500,000
13	£250,000	13	£250,000
12	£125,000	12	£125,000
11	£64,000	11	£64,000
10	£32,000	**10**	£32,000
9	£16,000	9	£16,000
8	£8,000	8	£8,000
7	£4,000	7	£4,000
6	£2,000	6	£2,000
5	£1,000	**5**	£1,000
4	£500	4	£500
3	£300	3	£300
2	£200	2	£200
1	£100	1	£100

SCORE SHEET

contestant's name

....

50:50

15	£1 MILLION
14	£500,000
13	£250,000
12	£125,000
11	£64,000
10	£32,000
9	£16,000
8	£8,000
7	£4,000
6	£2,000
5	£1,000
4	£500
3	£300
2	£200
1	£100

contestant's name

....

50:50

15	£1 MILLION
14	£500,000
13	£250,000
12	£125,000
11	£64,000
10	£32,000
9	£16,000
8	£8,000
7	£4,000
6	£2,000
5	£1,000
4	£500
3	£300
2	£200
1	£100

SCORE SHEET

contestant's name	contestant's name
....	....
50:50 ☐ Phone ☐ Audience ☐	50:50 ☐ Phone ☐ Audience ☐

15	£1 MILLION	15	£1 MILLION
14	£500,000	14	£500,000
13	£250,000	13	£250,000
12	£125,000	12	£125,000
11	£64,000	11	£64,000
10	£32,000	10	£32,000
9	£16,000	9	£16,000
8	£8,000	8	£8,000
7	£4,000	7	£4,000
6	£2,000	6	£2,000
5	£1,000	5	£1,000
4	£500	4	£500
3	£300	3	£300
2	£200	2	£200
1	£100	1	£100

SCORE SHEET

contestant's name

....

50:50 ☐ ☐ ☐

15	£1 MILLION
14	£500,000
13	£250,000
12	£125,000
11	£64,000
10	£32,000
9	£16,000
8	£8,000
7	£4,000
6	£2,000
5	£1,000
4	£500
3	£300
2	£200
1	£100

contestant's name

....

50:50 ☐ ☐ ☐

15	£1 MILLION
14	£500,000
13	£250,000
12	£125,000
11	£64,000
10	£32,000
9	£16,000
8	£8,000
7	£4,000
6	£2,000
5	£1,000
4	£500
3	£300
2	£200
1	£100

SCORE SHEET

contestant's name		contestant's name	
50:50 ☐ ☐ ☐		50:50 ☐ ☐ ☐	
15	£1 MILLION	15	£1 MILLION
14	£500,000	14	£500,000
13	£250,000	13	£250,000
12	£125,000	12	£125,000
11	£64,000	11	£64,000
10	£32,000	**10**	£32,000
9	£16,000	9	£16,000
8	£8,000	8	£8,000
7	£4,000	7	£4,000
6	£2,000	6	£2,000
5	£1,000	**5**	£1,000
4	£500	4	£500
3	£300	3	£300
2	£200	2	£200
1	£100	1	£100